Global Lockdown

Global Lockdown

Race, Gender, and the Prison-Industrial Complex

EDITED BY

JULIA SUDBURY

Routledge
New York • London

Published in 2005 by
Routledge
270 Madison Avenue
New York, NY 10006
www.routledge-ny.com

Published in Great Britain by
Routledge
2 Park Square
Mlton Park, Abingdon
Oxon OX14 4RN U.K.
www.routledge.co.uk

Library of Congress Cataloging-in-Publication Data

Global lockdown : race, gender, and the prison-industrial complex / edited by Julia Sudbury.
  p. cm.
Includes bibliographical references and index.
ISBN 0-415-95056-2 (hb)—ISBN 0-415-95057-0 (pbk.)
1. Female offenders. 2. Women prisoners. I. Sudbury, Julia.
HV6046.H586 2004
365'.6'082—dc22

2004013889

Table of Contents

Acknowledgments

This book is inspired by the many women in prison who have shared their stories with me over the years. I dedicate it to each of them knowing that I can never pay back the generosity and trust they have shown me. The book has been a labor of love (and sometimes tears) for many people. I am indebted to the many contributors who stayed committed to our vision for the book throughout the lengthy process. I am grateful in particular for the dedication and support of Asale Angel Ajani, who worked on early stages of the project. I thank the many activist-intellectuals who have shaped the analysis gathered in these pages, in particular Angela Y. Davis, who first encouraged me to adopt a research agenda dedicated to creating a world without prisons. I would like to thank everyone at Critical Resistance, the Prison Activist Resource Center, the Arizona Prison Moratorium Coalition, Incite! Women of Color Against Violence, and Social Justice journal for their insights and commitment to struggle. I thank Faith Nolan for the laughter and music and for sharing her uncompromising commitment to women inside. Margo Okazawa-Rey's friendship and support have been invaluable during the birthing of the book. I am grateful to the Mills College Department of Ethnic Studies and the Mills community for providing a home and financial support for the project. I am grateful for assistance provided by the Institute for Women's Studies and Gender Studies and Faculty of Social Work at the University of Toronto; the Sex, Race and Globalization Project at the University of Arizona; and the Association of American University Women. I appreciate Dereka Rushbrook's invaluable administrative and translation work. Finally, I would like to honor all of my friends and family members, from Winchester, London, Longbeach, Enugu, and elsewhere. Their guidance and unconditional love sustain me in staying the course.

Introduction

Feminist Critiques, Transnational Landscapes, Abolitionist Visions

JULIA SUDBURY

This book is the outcome of feminist scholarly engagements with grassroots struggles for social and economic justice. It is a book about the criminalization and punishment of women of color and third-world women, but it is also about colonization, global capitalism, neoliberalism, and militarism. The contributors to the book are intellectuals, both organic and academic, former prisoners, political prisoners, activists, survivors, women in recovery, former sex workers, immigrants, and indigenous women. In these pages, they share antiracist, anticapitalist, anticolonial, and feminist critiques that have been shaped by interactions over several decades with diverse communities of resistance. Thus, the ideas gathered here are part of a collective body of knowledge rather than the individual property of the authors. In particular, these writings have been shaped by conversations with numerous women who remain behind bars, some of whom appear in these chapters under pseudonyms. While guaranteeing confidentiality, this practice also renders many of the imprisoned thinkers who have contributed to this volume anonymously. Despite these limitations, the chapters represent many hours of labor from dedicated individuals committed to bringing a radical analysis of women's imprisonment to a wide audience. Rather than a destination, I prefer to view the completion of this volume as one step on a scholarly and activist journey. I hope that the reader will embrace any gaps or limitations as an incentive to take further steps in that journey.

Thinking Through Globalization and Imprisonment

The title of this book seeks to suggest a dialogue between two social movements that have to date remained separate. "Lockdown" is a term commonly used by prison movement activists to refer to the repressive confinement of human beings as punishment for deviating from normative behaviors.[1] Although prisons and jails are the most visible locations for lockdown, the term encourages us to think about connections with other spaces of confinement, such as immigration detention centers, psychiatric hospitals, juvenile halls, refugee camps, or Indian boarding schools. Lockdown evokes activist slogans, distancing the scholarship in this book from the discourse of the state. Although official language is often adopted by criminologists, who use the terms "inmates," "offenders," and "correctional institutions" as if these were natural and uncontested, I prefer to deploy the insurgent discourse used by those committed to the abolition of prisons.[2]

By describing the lockdown as "global," I do not intend to suggest the existence of a universal and undifferentiated global carceral regime. Instead, I use the term to evoke the antiglobalization movement's critique of global capital and U.S. corporate dominance.[3] Scholarship on globalization has generated a new language to talk about the transformations wrought by economic restructuring, from global cities to the global village. Like Saskia Sassen's global city, the global prison is a local manifestation of transnational flows of people, products, capital, and ideas.[4] The chapters in this volume argue that both the fabric of the prison and the people caged within it are shaped by global factors, from free trade agreements and neoliberal restructuring to multinational corporate expansion. The prison is thus simultaneously local and global, or, to use a neologism coined by Nawal El Saadawi, it is "glocal," a product of local, national, and global political, economic, and cultural phenomena.[5]

By framing the prison as intimately connected to global capitalism, neoliberal politics, and U.S. economic and military dominance, this book provides the intellectual rationale for a radical rethinking of both prison and antiglobalization activism and research. It suggests that antiglobalization activists and scholars should pay attention to the spaces of confinement that warehouse those who are surplus or resistant to the new world order. This focus would help to make the antiglobalization movement more reflective of the immediate survival concerns of communities of color and indigenous people in the global North.[6] This analysis also suggests that prison activists and researchers should reframe their work as part of a wider anti-imperialist, anticapitalist endeavor. In so doing, prison activists would need to establish international coalitions and prison scholars would need to develop research agendas that generate cross-border, transnational knowledge. In particular, prison activists and scholars in the United States would need to develop strategies to challenge the global spread of the U.S. model of mass incarceration and U.S. corporate penal expansion.

It is no coincidence that the work of feminists of color leads to this call for the integration of antiglobalization and antiprison praxis. Feminists of color have been at the forefront in developing transnational feminist practices as a framework for understanding the gendered impacts of global economic and political restructuring.[7] Transnational feminist practices parallel antiracist feminism in theorizing the intersections of gender with race, class, and sexuality. However, they differ from many feminisms of color because of a central concern with how these processes articulate with the cross-border flows of goods, people, capital, and cultures associated with globalization. Unlike global feminism, transnational feminist practices do not depict "women's oppression" as unitary and universal. Nor do they subscribe to the vision of women's experience as a fragmented mosaic of cultural and national difference. Rather, this approach focuses on the linkages that emerge out of transnational networks of economic and social relations. The operations of multinational corporations, International Monetary Fund (IMF)–led structural adjustment policies, free trade agreements, export processing zones, and outsourcing practices are therefore redefined as "women's issues," dramatically expanding the scope of feminist concerns. Attention is also paid to the rise of fundamentalist, nationalist, and communalist scripts written on women's bodies in response to the economic insecurity and loss of political and cultural sovereignty generated by the global marketplace. Transnational feminist practices assist us in unpacking the global prison by drawing our attention to the ways in which punishment regimes are shaped by global capitalism, dominant and subordinate patriarchies, and neocolonial racialized ideologies. In so doing, they place the experiences of women of color and third-world women at the center of our analysis of prisons and the global economy. Women's testimonies of survival under neoliberal cutbacks, border crossing, exploitation in the sex and drug industries, and life under occupation and colonial regimes provide a map of the local and global factors that generate prison as a solution to the conflicts and social problems generated by the new world order. This introduction provides a brief overview of women's imprisonment at the beginning of the twenty-first century. I then offer a new theoretical framework and methodology for social research on women's imprisonment. I end by mapping the concerns and contributions of this volume.

The Explosion in Women's Imprisonment

In 1999, the Nigerian federal government released almost one fifth of the prison population, including hundreds of women, as an emergency measure to tackle the problem of rampant overcrowding.[8] The following year, President

Clinton granted clemency to Kemba Smith and Dorothy Gains, African American women who were serving terms of over twenty years under harsh mandatory minimum drug laws. Just over a year later, the Russian Duma released all women who were pregnant, disabled, over fifty, or single mothers from a bloated prison system holding approximately one million prisoners.[9] These moments offer a snapshot of the global crisis in women's imprisonment. Spiraling incarceration rates, rampant overcrowding, and systemic human rights violations are common features of women's prisons from Lagos to Los Angeles. Beginning in 1973, an explosion in the number of women in prisons and jails in the United States has contributed to one of the largest prison building booms in world history. Whereas in 1970 there were 5,600 incarcerated women, by June 2001, 161,200 women were held in U.S. prisons and jails, representing a staggering 2,800 percent increase.[10] The women's prison population is not alone in witnessing phenomenal growth. Men's imprisonment in the United States has also grown exponentially, and as we entered the new millennium, the total population of prisons and jails surpassed two million. But although women make up only 9 percent of those incarcerated nationally, the rate of population growth for incarcerated women outstrips that of men.

Although the United States is the world's most avid incarcerator, this pattern of growth is mirrored in most nations of the global North. In Britain, in the decade to 2002, the annual average number of women in prison increased by 173 percent, leading to periodic calls to tackle the crisis in women's prisons.[11] Despite such calls, the population continued to grow to an all-time high of 4,299 in 2002.[12] In Australia, where the total number of prisoners doubled between 1982 and 1998,[13] activists have decried the explosion in the women's prison population and called for investigations into the deaths of women in custody associated with the increase.[14] Prison growth in the global South has been less visible but no less dramatic. From Mexico to South Africa, exploding prison populations have resulted in the construction of private, U.S.-style megaprisons. Statistics that look at gender but not race and class underrepresent the impact of the prison explosion on women of color and indigenous women. In all the countries just mentioned, oppressed racialized groups are disproportionately targeted by the criminal justice system. The crisis of women's prisons can therefore be read as a crisis for working class women of color and indigenous women worldwide.

What has caused this unprecedented explosion in women's prison populations worldwide? There are two challenges facing researchers who seek to ask this question. First, we need to unravel the intersections of race, class, gender, and nation that structure women's experiences of the criminal justice system.

Rather than viewing women's bodies solely as gendered, we need to recognize that gender is always racialized and classed. We cannot therefore seek to provide answers to the explosion in women's incarceration through the lens of gender and patriarchy alone. Instead we must investigate the impact of the restructuring of capital and class relations heralded by the emerging globalization of capital, as well as the challenges to racial hegemony that have taken place in Western industrialized nations in the past three decades. We are assisted in this endeavor by the work undertaken by feminists of color and by antiracist feminists. These texts locate women prisoners of color in the context of specific historical and contemporary patterns of racialized punishment and begin to map out an intersectional analysis of criminalization and punishment.

A second challenge is to seek answers that are not predetermined by the common-sense belief that there is causal relationship between the numbers of women offenders and women in prison. If more (or fewer) women are being arrested, prosecuted, and punished, it is often assumed that more (or fewer) women are committing serious crimes. But, despite media-inflated panics about rising crime, the thirty-year prison boom has not been matched by an exponential increase in crime rates. In fact, during the 1990s when reported crime rates in the United States underwent a sustained downturn, the prison population doubled. And while the mass media have flirted periodically with the idea that the West is beset by a violent crime wave of liberated women—a notion only strengthened by a rash of journalistic books on "women who kill"—women continue to be incarcerated in the large part for nonviolent survival crimes. Even where these survival strategies—whether sex work, drug couriering, or welfare fraud—are recognized, they are stigmatized and homogenized by the label "offending behavior." Women's personal histories are then mined as rich sources for understanding this aberrant behavior, and childhood abuse, domestic violence, or familial disfunction presented as the root cause. Presenting women's experiences of abuse as the cause of incarceration individualizes and personalizes their treatment at the hands of the criminal justice system. It obscures the broader social disorder signified by mass incarceration, and it sidesteps the question of why the state responds to abused women with punishment.

Underlying both of these approaches is the assumption that imprisonment is a logical, just, and timeless response to women in conflict with the law. But, as the contributors to this volume demonstrate, criminal justice systems are far from static and seldom dispense real justice. In the past two decades, criminal justice systems throughout the world have expanded to include more activities in their net, to punish previously criminalized activities more harshly, and to treat women who have already served their time more punitively. Such data suggest that the quest to understand contemporary patterns of women's incarceration is doomed to failure if it looks to women's behavior to provide the solutions. Clearly a new approach is needed.

Shifting the Discourse on Women's Imprisonment

This book aims to shift the current discourse on women's imprisonment in four significant ways. First, we resist the tendency in some criminological texts and the popular media to depict women in conflict with the law in psychological and individualized terms.[15] Ironically, feminist preferences for qualitative and hands-on research methods and interests in the personal and psychological realms tend to contribute toward this problem. Interviews with incarcerated women run the risk of simply replicating the discourse of individual responsibility and the language of correction that prisoners learn (and sometimes internalize) as they are processed by the system. Unless researchers step back from the ideas that circulate within the domain of dominant prison discourse, we will become distracted by discussions of familial disfunction, childhood abuse, drug addiction, and alcoholism. While the spotlight is turned on the personal failings of poor women and women of color, the political and economic interests that drive prison expansion remain in the shadows. The authors in this book do not aim to remove individual women prisoners from the field of analysis either as theorists or as respondents. On the contrary, many of the contributors use interview data with formerly and currently incarcerated women. However, we do aim to connect the individual and personal with macroeconomic and geopolitical analyses.

In order to move beyond microlevel analyses of women's imprisonment, we need to engage with the literature on the political economy of prisons. In recent years, scholars and activists have documented the emergence of a range of players in both the public and private sectors who participate in and benefit from the shift to a "tough-on-crime" culture. Although they differ in the emphasis given to political or economic forces, these researchers have a common commitment to revealing the diverse interests involved in promoting the "new penology," a shift from rehabilitation and reform to incapacitation and mass warehousing of surplus populations.[16] Examinations of politicians eager to present their opponents as "soft on crime," media outlets seeking headline-grabbing stories in the war of the ratings, and private corporations that build and operate prisons and detention centers for profit have shown that the global prison boom is the outcome of public policy and private greed.[17] An important intervention in this regard was made by one of the contributors to this volume, Linda Evans, while serving a federal sentence. Noting that prisons have been touted as a "recession-proof" economic base, Evans and Goldberg argued that prisons serve a dual function of warehousing those surplus to the global economy and creating profits for private prison operators and companies servicing prisons. This interweaving of state and corporate interests, the authors argued, has led to the emergence of a prison-industrial complex. Fear of communism justified huge military expenditures during the Cold War, generating what Dwight Eisenhower labeled a "military-industrial complex," and this was replaced after the disintegration of the Soviet bloc by a media-inspired fear of crime. The prison boom therefore became a leading economic motor during the downsizing, layoffs, and corporate relocations of the 1980s and 1990s.[18] Scholarship on the political economy of prisons has been critically important in revealing the role of the state in labeling, policing, and punishing poor and racialized communities. However, this work has all too often pursued a gender-blind approach. This volume seeks to establish a new body of research that combines insights into the political economy of prisons with a rigorous feminist analysis of gender, race, class, and nation.

Our second aim is to lay to rest unidimensional analyses that provide *either* a race-based *or* a gendered *or* a class-based analysis. In so doing, we are greatly influenced by feminists of color who have argued that the locations of women of color at the intersection of overlapping and mutually constitutive systems of oppression provide a unique and important viewpoint.[19] If the quintessential prisoner is a man of color,[20] what happens to our common-sense notions of crime and punishment when we shift the center to focus on a group that has been more readily understood as victims of crime? Our position does not rely on essentialist notions of gender and race. The term "women of colo(u)r" refers to particular projects of building political subjectivity through naming.[21] As such, it is a strategic invention, used to point to commonalities that might be used as a basis for shared political agendas. The essays gathered in this book do not posit the existence of a unitary and global woman prisoner. Instead, they seek to provide localized and specific instances of criminalization, punishment, and resistance, centered on the experiences of women of color and third-world women. These localized descriptions do not produce a fragmented mosaic of unconnected stories, nor do they produce a master narrative of global women's oppression; rather they are deeply and intricately connected through the globalizing ideologies and structures that this book seeks to unravel.

Although this volume builds on recent theorizing about the political and economic causes and consequences of the prison boom, we seek to transcend the tendency in such literature to remain bounded by the borders of the nation-state. Such work fails to explore the transnational interconnections between different countries and overlooks the unique practices of repression and opposition emerging from the borderlands between nation-states. It also tends to ignore the impact of neoliberal globalization as a driving force behind domestic economic policies that have contributed toward the impoverishment of communities of color and working class communities. Whereas scholars within the United States tend toward a narrow U.S.-centrism, those outside the United States have been more interested in international comparisons and have edited important volumes on women's imprisonment in diverse national locations.[22] This work has drawn parallels between the trends toward a "law-and-order" agenda in Britain, Australia, New Zealand, the United States, and Canada, but it has fallen short of theorizing about the ways in which such synergies occur. International comparisons of this type tend to reify rather than problematize rigid boundaries between nation-states. However, such boundaries are simultaneously solid and porous, allowing the free flow of goods, capital, and culture while criminalizing human traffic. The study of imprisonment in an era of globalization must therefore pay attention to the political and cultural synergies and economic shifts that occur at a supranational level. Angela Y. Davis's work is of critical importance in this regard because of her insistence on tracing the complicated relationship between the expansion of gendered and racialized punishment and the transformations signaled by the globalization of capital.[23] Expanding beyond the U.S. focus of Davis's work, our third aim is to infuse the study of women in prison with the theoretical insights of transnational feminist scholarship on the gendered impacts of globalization.[24]

Neoliberal globalization has been a major driving force in instigating the mass migration of poor women and men from the global South. As the North American Free Trade Agreement (NAFTA) and the European Union eliminated tariffs for importation of foreign products, domestic markets in the global South collapsed, throwing workers into destitution and desperation. For example, in Mexico, agricultural produce is now imported from U.S. farmers, leading to mass unemployment and migration from agricultural areas such as Chiapas and Oaxaca.[25] As migrants pursue ever more dangerous routes to enter the United Kingdom, Canada, the United States, or Australia, they are met with anti-immigrant sentiment and racial profiling leading to arrest and incarceration pending deportation. The criminalization of immigrants is therefore an important factor in both filling jails and prisons and generating new prison construction.[26] However, scholars have yet to locate the intersection of race, citizenship, and national status at the center of theorizing about the incarceration boom. Studies of immigration and studies of imprisonment have thus been artificially kept in separate spheres. And immigrant rights and prison activists seldom share the same platform. Our fourth aim is therefore to center border crossing and the criminalization of migration in our analysis of women's prisons.

Contents of This Volume

Readers involved in the academic study of women in prison may be surprised to find that this volume is not a collection of writings by the usual suspects.

Instead, this volume seeks to liberate women prisoners from the criminologists and learn what other academic disciplines as well as activists and former prisoners have to tell us about the prison boom and its impact on women of color. What would prison studies look like if they were conducted by a philosopher, a sociologist, an anthropologist, a political scientist, or a geographer? The essays gathered here create a multidisciplinary dialogue that generates new insights into women's imprisonment. My work within the antiprison movement has taught me that prisoners and former prisoners who have had firsthand experience of the penal system often have unique insights into its workings. In particular, political prisoners have been at the forefront in both providing the intellectual fuel for prison activism on the outside and providing political education on the inside. Rather than positioning women prisoners as the objects of investigation, this volume incorporates the insights of prison intellectuals and activists, including Lisa Neve, Robbie Kina, Debbie Kilroy, Kemba Smith, Stormy Ogden, and Linda Evans.

This book is organized in three sections. Although readers may pick and choose to read chapters that appeal most, reading the sections in the order in which they appear will provide a coherent exposition of the concerns, methodologies, and findings of the new field of transnational feminist prison studies.

Globalization and Criminalization

The first section explores the ways in which the survival strategies adopted by women of color under the constraints of colonization, gendered racism, and neoliberal globalization have been criminalized and policed, thus producing the "criminals" necessary to fuel the transnational prison-industrial complex. The transformations wrought by neoliberalism have specific effects in particular locations. In the global South, colonial legacies and a heavy debt burden have opened the doors to the economic "solutions" offered by the IMF and World Bank. In Africa, women have faced dramatic challenges related to the introduction of free trade and structural adjustment programs. Women respond to the worsening of conditions at home by engaging in a range of survival strategies. For those who are able to do so, traveling to Europe for work is viewed as a means not only for personal survival but also to gain access to food and basic necessities for an extended family. However, on arrival, they must contend with racialized and xenophobic popular and official discourses that equate immigrant status with criminality. Asale Angel-Ajani's essay explores the construction of a moral panic over immigrant criminality in Italy and demonstrates that it is intricately intertwined with ideas about gender, sexuality, and nation. Although more Eastern Europeans are involved in the sex industry than African women, the latter have been deployed by the right to symbolize Italy's moral decline into lawlessness. Angel-Ajani argues that a combination of economic restructuring, racialization, gendered discrimination, and heightened policing of immigrants is fueling a growth in prison populations that parallels the economic growth enjoyed by elites in the global economy.

In the global North, the ascendance of neoliberal politics has led to cuts in welfare, health provision, and social services and economic insecurity and vulnerability for communities of color. As the essay by Kim Pate and Lisa Neve demonstrates, economic restructuring in Canada articulates with long-standing colonial and patriarchal regimes to generate the context for the criminalization of Aboriginal women and girls. The position of women with mental disabilities has been particularly affected by a combination of deinstitutionalization and cutbacks, leading, Pate and Neve argue, to homelessness, substance abuse, violence, and ultimately reinstitutionalization in the penal system. Although the criminal justice system is both ineffective and expensive, it has become the state's primary response to racialized and poor women with disabilities. The story of how Lisa came to be labeled a "dangerous offender" and given an indefinite sentence is a cautionary tale about the globalized destruction of social safety nets and the criminalization of women's and girls' attempts to survive multigenerational impacts of colonization, poverty, abuse, neglect, and disability.

Globalization and free trade have generated borders that are (selectively) porous. In this context, anxieties about nonsanctioned border crossings have led wealthy nations to expand the reach of their policing and surveillance operations. As Kamala Kempadoo's chapter on the new crusade against trafficking in women demonstrates, it has also led to the heightened policing and control of the mobility, bodies, and sexuality of migrant women. Kempadoo pushes us to question hegemonic depictions of migrant women workers. Whereas contemporary antitrafficking discourses paint the image of a heroic United States leading international efforts to save victimized women from exploitative and abusive nonwestern men, Kempadoo argues that antitrafficking measures are better understood as part of a broader set of government practices that govern and control transnational flows of labor. Although legislation is ostensibly created to protect vulnerable women, it in fact results in criminalizing women in the global sex trade and adding to existing immigration controls.

The next four chapters in this section draw our attention to the ways in which gendered interpersonal and state violence, racism, colonization, and economic inequality intersect in the lives of women of color and third-world women. These interlocking systems of oppression, the contributors demonstrate, create situations that threaten women's safety and economic security. At the same time, women's survival strategies lead them into conflict with the law. Stormy Ogden received a five-year sentence for welfare fraud at a time when she was suicidal, addicted, and severely abused. Ogden's writing embodies her desire to create meaning of her own experiences through the process of documentation and reflection. Poverty, childhood abuse, domestic violence, alcoholism, rape, and suicide are central to those experiences. But as she shows us, this suffering cannot be understood outside the particular histories of the Yokuts and Pomo nations. It is this intersection of sexual and colonial violence, Ogden suggests, that both generates and naturalizes the criminalization of Native women. Despite the dramatic overrepresentation of indigenous women and men in prisons and jails in the United States, relatively little attention has been paid to this group. Ogden's chapter seeks to remedy this invisibility.

When faced with life-threatening violence, Robbie Kina, an Aboriginal woman from Australia, "chose" to take her abusive partner's life. With brutal simplicity, Kina gives an account of her life as a sex worker and victim of domestic rape and assault and her subsequent trial and conviction. Determined not to become "just another black death in custody," Kina successfully fought her conviction on the basis of the many years of extreme violence that she had been subjected to. The colonial legacy of state and interpersonal violence against women in indigenous communities is the backdrop to this story.[27] Aboriginal women in Australia make up 2 percent of the general population but 30 percent of the women's prison population. In the past decade, this population has skyrocketed as a result of tough-on-crime policies and the war on drugs. At the same time, neoliberal policies have impoverished Aboriginal communities, driving women like Kina into the streets to seek a living in the violent criminalized economies of the sex and drug trades.

Beth Richie adds an important counterpoint to the narrative of women incarcerated as an outcome of oppressive heterosexual relationships. In order to make visible the workings of gender and sexuality in processes of criminalization, we need to "queer" our analysis. Richie explores the entrapment of young black lesbians by a convergence of harsh penal policy, aggressive law enforcement, gendered violence, and heteronormative imperatives. Her chapter breaks new ground by placing questions of power, deviance, and nonnormative sexuality at the center of analyses of mass incarceration. The final chapter in this section also reflects on the regulation of women's sexuality and gender roles. Shahnaz Khan interviewed women incarcerated in Pakistan under the Zina Ordinance. Established by General Zia's military regime as part of the Islamist Hadood Ordinances, the Zina Ordinance outlaws illicit sex as a means for promotion of a new moral order. However, as Khan documents, its application is restricted to poor women, who are most often charged by their families or husband for going against their families' wishes. Rather than viewing Zina as an expression of tradition, Khan argues that structural and historical factors are at the root of the rise of the religious right in Pakistan. She draws our attention to another impact of globalization, the bolstering of fundamentalisms that use and police women's bodies and sexuality as symbols of purity and tradition.

Women Inside the Global Prison

The second section of this book maps the impact on women of color and third-world women of the unprecedented law-and-order buildup of the past three decades and documents the transformations in carceral regimes that have occurred as a result. In the first essay, Kemba Smith, writing from her prison cell, provides a personal account of the consequences of the U.S. experiment with mass incarceration. Her trenchant and deeply personal critique of prison expansion posits an economic motive behind her own incarceration and resists individualizing discourses of women's criminality. The "war on drugs" has become the primary social control mechanism legitimating the surveillance and punishment of African American communities. Smith received a 23.5-year sentence for conspiracy because of her involvement with an abusive partner who was involved in the drug industry. Since receiving clemency, Smith has established a foundation dedicated to ending the war on drugs.

In the second chapter, Rebecca Bohrman and Naomi Murakawa provide a broader context for Kemba Smith's story by analyzing the shifting role of the state in an era of neoliberal globalization. Political scientists, pointing to the transformations wrought by free trade, open markets, and privatization, frequently embrace former president Clinton's formulation that the era of big government is dead. Bohrman and Murakawa reject this formulation, arguing instead that the shift is not from big to small government but rather from a goal of social provision to social control. Detailing this shift in the United States, they demonstrate that it has had particularly damaging effects on women of color, who have been affected both by the weakening of the welfare net and by the growth of the carceral state.

The next four chapters explore the transformation of penal regimes that has taken place as a result of the globalization of the war on drugs and examine the intersections of gender, class, race, and nation in these processes. The war on drugs has been mobilized by the United States as the basis for a globalized buildup of surveillance, policing, and border control mechanisms. As the United States's southern neighbor and a primary route for deliveries to the world's leading drug-using nation, Mexico has been under particular pressure to adopt punitive drug laws. Cristina Jose Kampfner introduces us to the "mano dura" (hard hand) of Mexican drug policy, which has led to the targeting of poor women "burros" and addicts and has contributed to a doubling of the women's prison population. Kampfner finds that prisons "produce, deepen, and concentrate" unequal gender roles and other social inequalities, exacerbating rather than resolving the causes of Mexican women's involvement in criminalized activities. In Mexico, Bolivia, and Colombia, as Juanita Díaz-Cotto demonstrates, U.S. military assistance to drug enforcement agencies has led to a weakening of civil society and an increase in human rights violations as well as an alarming increase in prison populations. As Díaz-Cotto shows, women participate in the lower levels of the drug trade as a result of economic insecurity or addiction. Their labor in this criminalized arena is subjected to harsh penalties, both in the United States and Europe, where women importing drugs from Latin America face long mandatory minimums, and in their home countries, where they bear the brunt of governmental crackdowns on the drug trade. Díaz-Cotto reframes Latina/o imprisonment in the United States, by locating it within a transnational framework. In so doing, she provides important insights as well as providing a new methodology for prison research in the Americas.

Decentering the Americas in the study of the war on drugs, Manuela da Cunha takes us to Portugal, which for much of the past decade was the European Union's number one incarcerator. Da Cunha argues that the war on drugs has led to a reorganization of the Portuguese prison population. Increasingly, clusters of kin, friends, and neighbors are imprisoned together as a result of the massive repressive targeting by police of poor urban neighborhoods populated with poor whites and lusophone African immigrants. As a result, the prison has become an everyday and normalized part of daily life for the residents of these neighborhoods, suggesting that, like the United States, Portugal is becoming a carceral state. The new divide, da Cunha suggests, is not between the imprisoned and the free but between those whose lives include prison in the horizon and those whose lives do not. In the final chapter in this cluster, I explore the creation of a moral panic surrounding an influx of Jamaican women carrying criminalized drugs into Britain and explore the New Labour government's response. The crackdown on Jamaican "mules" has generated a rise in cross-border imprisonment and fueled the growth of a symbiotic relationship between the state and multinational prison corporations. In failing to address the structural causes of women's participation in the drug industry, I argue, the government provides a steady flow of imprisonable bodies as fuel for the transnational prison-industrial complex.

The next two chapters focus on the intersections of colonization and imprisonment. In the Nigerian context, argues Biko Agozino, the birth of the prison can be traced to the African slave holocaust and colonial repression. Policy proposals such as the New Economic Plan for African Development, Agozino argues, are likely to exacerbate Nigerian women's dependence and poverty, thus deepening their vulnerability to victimization by the criminal justice system. Nigerian women are therefore "hostages" of neocolonialism, manifested both in the overcrowded penal system (itself a remnant of British rule) and in socioeconomic policies embraced by the state. Both arenas are manifestations of the unequal relation between global South and North. Elham Bayour's chapter turns to imprisoned women in another region marked by a history of colonization and resistance. The emergence of Palestinian women "suicide bombers" in response to heightened repression in the wake of September 11, 2001 has generated much debate about the role of women in the Arab-Israeli conflict. Viewed as little more than passive vessels of a male dispute by some western feminists,[28] Palestinian women have seldom been called on to discuss their own motivations for political involvement. Elham Bayour seeks to challenge the stereotyped and homogenized image of the silent veiled Arab woman by documenting the experiences of former political prisoners. Her interviews with women formerly incarcerated in Israeli prisons were carried out in three Palestinian refugee camps. The sexual abuse of women political prisoners, as symbolic markers of Palestinian national and cultural identity, Bayour argues, demonstrates the complex relationship between colonization, militarism, and patriarchy. The atrocities carried out by U.S. military police at Abu Ghraib prison in Iraq demonstrate that Bayour's observations on gender, detention, and torture are in no way unique to this location but, instead, are one manifestation of racialized and militarized state punishment.

A recurrent theme in the chapters by Díaz-Cotto, Agozino, and Bayour is the link between prisons and militarism. In the final chapter in this section, Linda Evans develops a framework for thinking through the connections between domestic and external wars. She examines the ways in which increased surveillance, policing, and mass incarceration are militarizing U.S. society while at the same time U.S. military interventions worldwide are used as a form of global social control. Using her experience as a federal prisoner in the United States as a starting point, Evans argues that penal institutions are the embodiment of a militarized society. Evans closes her chapter with a call for antiracist feminists and prison activists to base our activism on an understanding of the complex international connections between economic globalization and domestic and external wars against terrorism. In response to this call, the next section turns to women's resistance to criminalization and imprisonment.

From Criminalization to Resistance

How can working-class women of color shift their designation as raw materials for the prison industry, or objects of scholarly study and state rehabilitation, and instead engage in acts of resistance? If, as Gilmore argues in this volume, the state individualizes social disorder through the process of arrest, the first step is to challenge "the 'naturalness' of crime, of poverty, of the power of the state." In her analysis of Mothers Reclaiming Our Children (Mothers ROC), Gilmore demonstrates how this multiracial group of women in Los Angeles build on historical and international models of self-help to resist the fragmentation brought about by the arrest and incarceration of their loved ones. The African American women's club movement provides a model of "social mothering" that enables the diverse group of women to create a community of resistance that embraces both reformist and radical ends. The prison explosion in California, Gilmore demonstrates, is a result of macroeconomic structural adjustments. However, through their activism, the Mothers ROC resist the inevitability and hegemonic power of such global structures. Indeed, the intimate relationship between the women's family lives and their political activism points to the role of the prison as a key site of organic local opposition to the global economy.

Many of the chapters in this book have pointed to the revictimization by the state of women who are survivors of domestic violence and sexual assault. The majority of women in prison have been the victims of male violence, and as Lisa Vetten and Kailash Bhana argue in this section, the authoritarian, controlling prison environment has much in common with the structure of abusive relationships. Vetten and Bhana describe their involvement in a multiracial South African campaign that challenges the punishment of women who have survived violence at the hands of an intimate partner. The Justice for Women Campaign seeks to reform sentencing practices and win early release in cases in which women kill their abusive partners. Using a combination of tactics, from demonstrations and media coverage to research and lobbying, activists have been successful in changing popular opinions about women who kill and gaining the promise of pardons for some of the women.

Although several of the authors in this volume have argued for transnational activist networks against women's imprisonment, there are few models of successful cross-border organizing. The chapter by Melissa Upreti describes a successful transnational collaboration between the New York–based Center for Reproductive Rights and the Forum for Women, Law and Development in Nepal. The campaign was inspired by the criminalization and incarceration of young, predominantly poor rural Nepali women for having abortions. The campaign overturned the abortion ban; however, some of the women remain behind bars, charged with infanticide. Although popular representations of third-world men as hyperpatriarchal might encourage the reader to view the Nepali abortion ban as evidence of a retrogressive patriarchal tradition, the authors demonstrate that it exists on a spectrum of human rights abuses against women seeking to practice reproductive freedom. Indeed, the criminalization of women for allegedly "abusing" their fetuses is an increasingly common practice in the United States.[29] Nepali women's access to abortion is restricted not only by the Nepali state but also by the United States, which polices women's clinics in the global South through the global gag rule.[30]

If the prison cements its power and undermines resistance by "disappearing" potential social actors, one powerful mechanism for disabling the potency of the prison is to make prisoner activism visible to the "free world." For the members of Sisters Inside in Queensland, the involvement of women prisoners in developing an agenda for social change is the key to successful prison activism. A member of the group and former prisoner, Debbie Kilroy describes the organizing principles and practices of this unique multiracial organization, which is managed jointly by women in prison and women on the outside. By speaking out about state sexual abuse and demanding their human rights, women prisoners use their experiences as the basis for a radical agenda for change. Rather than calling for the release of specific groups of women who "do not belong in prison," Sisters Inside view imprisonment as a form of state terror and advocate the abolition of prisons. This abolitionist vision does not reject legal reform and service delivery but rather views them as stepping stones on the path to a broader, more radical vision of social change.

Inevitably, in any edited collection there are gaps. This volume is only a beginning. I hope that many other articles and books using a transnational feminist approach to examine the global prison will be forthcoming in the coming years, providing fuel for a transnational movement to abolish the prison-industrial complex. Even as this book proposes transnational feminist prison studies as a critically important new field of scholarship, we should pause to consider the dangers of institutionalization and cooptation. Just as prison abolitionists refuse to engage in any activity that might extend the life or reach of the prison-industrial complex, scholars engaging in prison studies need to be careful not to create structures that reify and reproduce carceral regimes. This book is therefore not a call for the establishment of transnational feminist prison studies programs at universities or colleges. Instead, the authors in this volume recognize the contingent and temporary nature of the work we are undertaking. Ultimately, I hope for this work to become obsolete as the prison walls crumble and we are called on to play our role in building a world without prisons.

References

1. I refer here to the prison movement in North America, a diverse movement that encompasses the following activities: (i) campaigns for political prisoners; (ii) religious freedom and rights of indigenous prisoners; (iii) human rights abuses in women's prisons and child custody cases; (iv) reform of the war on drugs and tough-on-crime sentencing; (v) opposition to prison privatization and financing; (vi) resistance to detentions and deportations as a result of the war on terror; and (vii) a moratorium on prison construction and ultimate abolition of prisons.

2. For a cogent argument for penal abolition see Angela Y. Davis, *Are Prisons Obsolete?* (New York: Seven Stories Press, 2003). For a discussion of abolitionist strategies see Julia Sudbury, "Women of Color, Globalization and the Politics of Incarceration," in *The Criminal Justice System and Women*, ed. B. R. Price and N. Sokoloff (New York: McGraw Hill, 2003).

3. I am referring here to the broad-based social movement against global capitalism, neoliberalism, and free trade exemplified by the demonstrations against the World Bank and World Trade Organization in Seattle, Genoa, Prague, and Cancun. The massive attendance at the World Social Forum, a popular alternative to the World Economic Forum that has taken place in Porto Alegre, Brazil, and Mumbai, India since 2001, demonstrates that diverse antiglobalization forces have cohered as a movement. See also Naomi Klein, *Fences and Windows: Dispatches from the Front Lines of the Globalization Debate* (New York: Picador USA, 2002).

4. Saskia Sassen, *The Global City: New York, London, Tokyo* (Princeton: Princeton University Press, 1991).

5. Nawal El Saadawi, speech given at the World Social Forum, Mumbai, India, January 2004.

6. Elizabeth "Betita" Martinez, "Where Was the Color in Seattle?: Looking for Reasons Why the Great Battle Was So White," *Colorlines* 3, No. 1 (2000).

7. Chandra Talpade Mohanty, *Feminism without Borders: Decolonizing Theory, Practicing Solidarity* (Durham: Duke University Press, 2003). Jacqui Alexander and Chandra Talpade Mohanty, *Feminist Genealogies, Colonial Legacies, Democratic Futures* (New York: Routledge, 1997). Inderpal Grewal and Caren Kaplan, *Scattered Hegemonies, Postmodernity and Transnational Feminist Practices* (Minneapolis: University of Minnesota Press, 1994).

8. Saib Feyisetan, "Obasanjo Approves Taskforce's Recommendation—Released 1043 Prisoners," *PRAWA News* (Lagos: Penal Reform and Welfare Association, 1999).

9. Reuters, "All Jailed Mothers to Be Pardoned," February 25, 2002, Moscow: Reuters.

10. U.S. Department of Justice Bureau of Statistics, "Federal Prison Population Increases a Record Amount, State and Local Inmate Growth Moderates" (2001). http://www.ojp.usdoj .gov/bjs/pub/press/pjim01pr.htm (accessed October 28, 2002).

11. Home Office, *Statistics on Women and the Criminal Justice System* (London: The Home Office, 2003: 41)

12. Ibid, 41.

13. Carlos Carcach and Anna Grant, *Imprisonment in Australia: Trends in Prison Populations and Imprisonment Rates* (The Australian Institute of Criminology, 1999).

14. Sisters Inside, "Substance Abuse in Australian Communities," submission to the House of Representatives Parliamentary Standing Committee on Family and Community Affairs, Queensland (Queensland: Sisters Inside, 2001).

15. For a critique of this trend see Shoshana Pollock, "Moving Inside: The Role of Lawbreaking in Black Women's Attempt to Gain Economic Independence," paper presented at American Society of Criminology, November 1999.

16. Malcolm Feeley and Jonathon Simon, "The New Penology: Notes on the Emerging Strategy of Corrections and Its Implications," *Criminology* 30, No. 4. (1992).

17. Joel Dyer, The Perpetual Prisoner Machine: How America Profits from Crime (Boulder: Westview Press, 2000), Elliott Currie, Crime and Punishment in America (New York: Henry Holt and Co., 1998), Katherine Beckett, Making Crime Pay: Law and Order in Contemporary American Politics (New York: Oxford University Press, 1997), Christie 1993.

18. Eve Goldberg and Linda Evans, *The Prison Industrial Complex and the Global Economy* (Berkeley, CA: Agit Press, 1998). The term "prison-industrial complex" was coined by Mike Davis with reference to the prison building boom in California. See Mike Davis, "Hell Factories in the Field: A Prison Industrial Complex," *The Nation* 260, 7 (February 20, 1995). See also Critical Resistance Publications Collective, "Critical Resistance to the Prison-Industrial Complex," Special Edition, *Social Justice* 27, 3 (2000), Angela Y. Davis, "Masked Racism: Reflections on the Prison Industrial Complex," *Colorlines* 1, 2 (Fall 1998): 12–17. The renewed military buildup after September 11, 2001, has demonstrated that the post-Cold War slowdown was a temporary lull rather than a permanent redirection of resources. Post-September 11 synergies between the military- and prison-industrial complexes are discussed by Evans in this volume.

19. Patricia Hill Collins, *Black Feminist Thought: Knowledge, Consciousness and the Politics of Empowerment* (Boston: Unwin Hyman, 1990), Chandra Talpade Mohanty, Ann Russo, and Lourdes Torres, *Third World Women and the Politics of Feminism* (Bloomington: Indiana University Press, 1991), Enakshi Dua and Angela Robertson, *Scratching the Surface: Canadian Anti-Racist Feminist Thought* (Toronto: Women's Press, 1999), Heidi Mirza, *Black British Feminism: A Reader* (London: Routledge, 1997), Julia Sudbury, *Other Kinds of Dreams: Black Women's Organisations and the Politics of Transformation* (London: Routledge, 1998).

20. For important contributions to the study of race and punishment in the United States that render black women's imprisonment invisible, see Michael Tonry, *Malign Neglect: Race, Crime and Punishment in America* (New York: Oxford University Press, 1995) and Jerome Miller, *Search and Destroy: African-American Males in the Criminal Justice System* (Cambridge: Cambridge University Press, 1996).

21. Angela Y. Davis, "Reflections on Race, Class, and Gender in the USA," in *The Angela Y. Davis Reader*, ed. J. James (Malden: Blackwell Publishers, 1998).

22. Sandy Cooke and Susanne Davies, *Harsh Punishment: International Experiences of Women's Imprisonment* (Boston: Northeastern University Press, 1999), Nicole Rafter and Frances Heidensohn ed., *International Feminist Perspectives in Criminology* (Buckingham: Open University Press, 1995).

23. Angela Y. Davis, "Race and Criminalization: Black Americans and the Punishment Industry," in *The Angela Y. Davis Reader*, ed. J. James (Malden: Blackwell Publishers, 1998), Angela Y. Davis and Cassandra Shaylor, "Race, Gender and the Prison Industrial Complex: California and Beyond," *Meridians* 2, 1 (2001): 1–25.

24. Kamala Kempadoo ed., *Sun, Sex and Gold: Tourism and Sex Work in the Caribbean* (Lanham: Rowman and Littlefield, 1999), Miriam Ching Yoon Louie, *Sweatshop Warriors: Immigrant Women Workers Take on the Global Economy* (Cambridge: South End Press, 2001).

25. Diego Cevallos, "NAFTA Equals Death, Say Peasant Farmers," Inter Press Service, http://www.commondreams.org (accessed December 3, 2002).

26. Michael Welch, "The Role of the Immigration and Naturalization Service in the Prison-Industrial Complex," *Social Justice* 27, No. 3 (2000).

27. Because of the complex interactions of socioeconomic marginalization, loss of land rights, and the ongoing legacy of genocidal assimilation policies including the removal of children from their families, Aboriginal women are twenty-eight times more likely to be admitted to hospital for assault injuries than other Australian women. Neena Bhandari, "Aboriginal Violence Against Women," *Contemporary Review* 283, No. 1655 (2003): 353–6.

28. Andrea Dworkin, "The Women Suicide Bombers," *Feminista* 5, No. 1 (2002). http://www.feminista.com/v5n1/dworkin.html (accessed March 17, 2004).

29. Dorothy Roberts, *Killing the Black Body: Race, Reproduction, and the Meaning of Liberty* (New York: Pantheon Books, 1997), 150–201.

30. Under the Mexico City Policy, commonly known as the "global gag rule," reinstituted by President George W. Bush in January 2001, non-U.S. nongovernmental organizations that receive U.S. family planning funds are restricted from using their own funds to provide legal abortion services, lobby their governments for abortion law reform, or provide referrals and counseling regarding abortion. See Center for Reproductive Rights, *Breaking the Silence: The Global Gag Rule's Impact on Unsafe Abortions* (New York: Center for Reproductive Rights), http://www.reproductiverights.org (accessed April 2, 2004).

Part I
Criminalizing Survival

CHAPTER 1

Domestic Enemies and Carceral Circles

African Women and Criminalization in Italy

ASALE ANGEL-AJANI

The story of her departure—a story I repeat over and over—is something of a mystery to me. I do not know how she arrived in Italy or the circumstances of her life. She had been an inmate at Rebibbia Femminile in Rome for three years, this much I know. I also know that she had requested to be deported back to Nigeria at the end of her sentence and that she was very ill during her last year in prison. On the day she was to leave Italy she was confined to a wheelchair, in which she could only sit slumped over, too weak to hold her head up and too weak to utter a sound. During her exit medical examination the prison physicians determined that she had AIDS. The physicians wrote a letter to the prison officials disclosing their findings and making recommendations, saying they were uncertain whether she would survive her long journey home. Rather than deliver this letter themselves, however, the doctors placed the letter in the woman's lap and called a guard to take her back to the prison ward.

It is possible that the physicians' letter went unnoticed, or perhaps the prison officials felt no responsibility for this woman who was going to be deported. Even as they struggled to fit her and her wheelchair into the taxi that was called to take her to the airport, not a single administrator mentioned her condition or verbally expressed any concern about her health. They tucked her documents—plane ticket, passport, and letters confirming her release—into her breast pocket and paid the taxi driver enough to drop her off at the airport's front entrance. A witness said that she could not even lift her head when the prison administrators and a few inmates waved their good-byes.

When she arrived at the airport, unescorted, maybe she was unable to speak, or perhaps the ticket agent refused to listen to her as she tried to explain the computer error. But the result was still the same: once the ticket agent typed in the woman's name and saw that she was wanted for a crime that she had committed three years ago, the same crime for which she had been serving time, the ticket agent called the Carabinieri to come and arrest her. The Carabinieri didn't think it unreasonable that a visibly ill woman in a wheelchair would be making a dash for the frontier to escape the law. In fact, they were so convinced that she was a fugitive that even after they found her letters from the courts and the prison administration, they held her in custody at the police station for more than five hours, then placed her in the back of their car and drove her back to Rebibbia Femminile, Rome's only penal institution for women. When she arrived at the prison, it was late evening and most of the officials were gone for the day. The head of the prison police and an *educatora* (social worker) refused to accept the woman, telling the Carabinieri who brought her that because she had been released, she couldn't stay at the prison because she could claim that the institution was holding her hostage.

The woman seemed not to have friends or family members in Rome. She was in critical need of medical attention, but she was now technically an "undocumented immigrant" in Italy and at that time it was illegal for her to seek medical care at a hospital. As Carabinieri, prison police, the social worker, and a prison clergyman stood over the woman, arguing about what to do with her, a nun, one of the first women to tell me this story, asked if she could take the woman back to her convent, where the sick woman could receive some food and basic care. The arguing officials thought it was a bad idea because this woman was, after all, a convicted criminal. In the end, they allowed the sister to take the woman to the convent, where she stayed for a week before she booked another flight from Rome to Nigeria. Although she safely boarded the plane, no one is certain if she survived the trip.

This essay is in part a questioning of this mysterious although true tale of a woman who cannot leave a country because of her assumed status as a criminal and dangerous individual. Her story not only signals a crisis, but also for the growing number of African women traveling through or migrating to Italy, it highlights an often silent reality in contemporary literature on globalization and transnationalism. We do not live in a world of unbounded borders. For many of us with suspicious and foreign-sounding names, dark skin, and lives that are led in other languages, we live with policed borders and demarcated territories. I explore the discourse of criminality that surrounds the lives of documented and undocumented immigrants in Italy. Academics, and sociologists and criminologists in particular, have long debated the problem of "immigrant criminality." As I demonstrate in this chapter, there is an increasing culture of suspicion, hostility, and criminalization of immigrants, and particularly African women, in Italy.

Over the past several years, Europe has moved toward more repressive immigration laws and strict enforcement measures. The intensifying policing of national borders has created state-sanctioned practices of targeting particular immigrant groups, especially women from South America, sub-Saharan African countries, and nonimmigrant groups such as the Roma (gypsies), as potential "criminals." In addition, in Italy and the rest of Europe (much like the United States), discourses on immigration are joined together with the rhetoric of crime and prevention in such a way that migrant populations are popularly viewed as being clandestine or "illegal" and therefore more prone to criminal behavior.

Not surprisingly, then, discourses on crime and on who commits it are saturated with the language of national citizenship, social class, gender, and race. Issues of immigration, like those of crime and criminals, are viewed as public policy dilemmas in which themes of immigrant criminality are so prevalent that, as Michael Keith notes, "The broad contours of the historical processes of criminalization of migrant minorities are now relatively uncontroversial."[1] Likewise, Biko Agozino argues that the societal imagination already regards immigrants as criminals because "spatial mobility is expected to imply anomie."[2] The climate of anti-immigrant rhetoric relies on the dual discourses of criminalization and cultural difference. In Italy, immigrants of color are very visible and their numbers are few (roughly 2.2 percent of the population), thus making them easy targets of the practical realities of criminalization. Furthermore, notions of racial and cultural difference can negatively affect public knowledge about immigrants and policing practices additionally fuel the public's imagination and misperceptions.

The Criminalization of Immigrants

There are 1.5 million documented immigrants and an estimated 20 percent undocumented immigrants in Italy.[3] With its population of 57.8 million, it is surprising that Italy has among the highest rates of immigrant imprisonment in southern Europe, following Greece and Spain.[4] Emilio Reyneri suggests that both the hypervisibility of immigrants and the inexperience of the courts may lead to discriminatory arrests and imprisonment.[5] In any case, as Alessandro dal Lago writes, "we know that often the over-representation of migrants in judicial statistics and crime rates is the product of their social weakness and, moreover, of the process of labeling."[6] It is within this context that the courts and the public broadly define what is "deviant behavior" when performed by an immigrant or other disagreeable character, such as Roma, and disregard the same behavior as an eccentricity when performed by a "citizen."[7] For example, while conducting fieldwork in Rebibbia Maschile Nuovo Complesso, I interviewed a Senegalese man who was serving a two-month sentence for driving without an Italian license (he was driving with a license from Senegal). Even the director of the Educatori, who was present during the interview, was astonished by both his arrest and the sentence and insisted to the Senegalese man that he was detained for another reason. As the director said, "It is impossible, you cannot be serving two months for this! You must have committed a crime." Indeed, as prison matriculation documents and court transcripts confirmed, the Senegalese man was arrested for driving without an Italian license.

Labeling immigrants as criminal is prevalent in Italy, as Salvatore Palidda demonstrates in his research on the social construction of deviance and immigrant criminality.[8] Palidda examines the arrest rates of Nigerians, Senegalese, Moroccans, Algerians, Tunisians, Albanians, Poles, and migrants from the former Yugoslavia in comparison with documented complaints brought against them by people in the community (presumably Italian citizens). On the whole, Palidda shows that although immigrants represented 23 percent of the total arrest population they represented 57 percent of the total population who had complaints brought against them.[9] Moroccans, who are generally viewed as being the most criminally inclined immigrant group, had approximately 6,000 arrests for 1994 and slightly over 13,000 complaints brought against them. The Senegalese had 463 arrests in 1994 and over 4,126 complaints brought against them, whereas Algerians had 2,580 arrests and 2,757 complaints.[10] Palidda's research would seem to support evidence that indicates an increasing "culture of panic and emergency" with regard to immigration that has created social panic among the public, fed by the mass media and driven by anti-immigrant policies. In short, the non–European Union (EU) immigrant in Italy is "a cultural type built through interactions occurring no[t] only between social actors but also between cultural representations."[11]

Immigrants in Africa, particularly those from Latin America, and Eastern Europe, and nonimmigrants in communities such as the Roma, must grapple with public perceptions of their communities as criminal. It has been reported that 24 percent of the prison population is foreign.[12] It should be pointed out that this percentage reflects all foreigners detained in Italian prisons, including citizens from the United States, Canada, and the United Kingdom, and other foreigners (not necessarily immigrants) who pass through Italy en route to other destinations. In 1998 almost 50 percent of those admitted to prison were foreigners and 90 percent were undocumented.[13]

The discourse of immigrant criminality and the overrepresentation of foreigners in penal institutions have led to the establishment of citizen committees in several large cities, particularly in the North. These committees, among other things, mobilize against street crime and have targeted migrants from

Morocco and street venders from Senegal.[14] In conjunction with increasingly high arrest rates, Roma, Eastern Europeans, and immigrants of color in Italy struggle with a coalition of left and right wing activists forming citizen committees. In cities that have experienced economic restructuring (such as urban renewal projects), citizen committees have organized against street crime and in some cases the very presence of immigrants.[15] As sociologist Dario Melossi informs us,

> The attention of these "communitarian groups" focuses in particular on crime and deviance amongst recent immigrant groups and their visibility in the everyday life of their neighborhood. At the core of the problem there no longer seems to be simply a threat to one's property or personal safety, but rather a generalized risk for the whole society, for an idea of order—of democratic order . . . .[16]

To be sure, it is not only the right wing factions who are involved in community initiatives that target immigrants. A report in the Italian newspaper *Corriere della sera* captures the sentiment of a PDS (Democratic Party of the Left—formerly the Communist Party) leader in Turin and adds the newspaper's own somewhat sardonic commentary,

> "I believe that citizens are right when they protest against their letter box being filled with used condoms, or if they are surrounded by pushers when they are coming back home, or if they are forced to watch people having sex with whores, or because the mountain bikes of their sons are stolen and their wives are afraid to walk alone in the streets." These are the words by Sergio Chiamparino, 46 years old, leader of the Turin PDS, father of a 16-year-old boy (now fearing for his new mountain bike), living in the well-known and dangerous Murazzi area, close to the center of the city. Some days ago Italian people living in the Murazzi [area] protested against Senegalese and Moroccan immigrants.[17]

As with many societies, Italian discourses about dangerous zones usually represent them as the areas where the highest number of disenfranchised people reside (including immigrants and the poor). The most "dangerous zones" in Rome and other Italian cities are usually the train stations and the area surrounding them and the outskirts of the city where immigrant and Roma communities are often forced to live in makeshift dwellings.

Women, Nationality, and Criminal Representations

In Italy, the discourse on immigrant criminality resides mainly in the areas of drugs and prostitution.[18] Today these "deviant behaviors" are characterized as being almost "un-Italian" in nature. Especially among the police, but also in the general public, it is not uncommon that Tunisian and Moroccan men and Colombian and Nigerian women are considered drug traffickers or dealers, and women from West African nations, including, especially, Nigeria, and Eastern European women are seen as being solely responsible for prostitution. Although prostitution is not illegal in Italy, its practice criminalizes the practitioner in people's minds. This perceived link between criminal behaviors and nationalities is so widespread that it has become a part of popular discourse. For example, it is not uncommon to hear "Nigerian" substitute for "prostitute," and popular representations of prostitution are exhibited through (black) African female bodies.[19]

Sadly, this inclination to name all African sex workers "Nigerians" and all African women Nigerian and therefore sex workers grows out of the fact that the small number of sub-Saharan African women who traffic in prostitution tend to be largely Nigerian or at least African women entering Italy with Nigerian passports. As Agence France-Presse reporter Ljbomir Milasin documented with reference to street prostitution on July 28, 2000:

> Earlier this month, Italy deported nearly 100 Nigerian immigrants, all believed to be prostitutes . . . . Among the immigrants, Nigerians make up the bulk but many also come from Albania, Moldova, Russia and Ukraine.

All immigrant women are subjected to negative representations, but it is striking to note that in most representations, the sex worker is depicted as specifically Nigerian or at least African in the media and in popular discourse. Yet, in sheer numbers prostitution by Eastern European women is more common.[20] It is estimated that two thirds of the nearly twenty thousand documented Albanian women work in the sex industry. Albanian, ex-Yugoslavian, and Polish women have the highest official rates of prostitution, either on the streets, which is more common among Albanian sex workers, or in massage or tanning parlors.[21] Eighty percent of foreign prostitution occurs on the street and is dominated by Nigerian and Albanian women, 75 percent of whom are forcibly trafficked into the trade.[22] It would seem that Nigerian sex workers are, at least in the most obvious ways, more "noticeable" than Albanian or other Eastern European women. The media reinforce the apparent difference and otherness of African women when they publish pictures of scantily clad African women in the streets. In part, these images play into long-standing debates about the hypersexuality of black Africans.[23] As Donald Carter notes, the existing "Italian gender asymmetry would relegate African women . . . to the lowest possible rankings, and so the image of the black woman is shown as body, primarily as an object of erotic and uncontained potentialities, one that could never be empowered: an image that stands so far outside the world of Italian power that within it, it would have to receive an 'exotic status.'"[24]

There is a link that has thus been forged between sexuality and nation (Nigeria) as opposed to sexuality and region of the world (Eastern Europe). This connection should not be overlooked as it has great significance for the lives of African women. For instance, what might this specificity mean for women carrying Nigerian passports or who determines who looks Nigerian? These representations are far reaching and affect African women greatly (though, to be sure, these negative representations affect Eastern European women and Latin American women as well). For example, African women have suffered vicious attacks by both the police and Italian men on the street. These attacks, which go unreported, caused several African women to protest representations of them as prostitutes in Naples and other cities in 1994.[25] Although few authors have written about the representation of African and other foreign women as sexual objects in Italy, Vanessa Maher reports that a study in Turin found that approximately a thousand Nigerian and Eastern European prostitutes work under threatening and brutal conditions. She suggests that Italians believe "that Africans are childlike and unthreatening because [they are] subordinate, and that African women, unlike southern Italian, Moroccan, or Roma women, are sexually available.[26] The traffic in Nigerian prostitution confirms this prejudice."[27]

The estimated figure for foreign women who engage in street prostitution in all of Italy is between nineteen thousand and twenty-five thousand and it is estimated that one in every ten women who are involved in the trade are victims of forced trafficking.[28] A study of foreign prostitution in Italy found that African women were by and large brought into prostitution through organized trafficking rings.[29] These operations are similar to those of other criminal organizations that traffic in migrants. As reported by Celestine Bohlen for the *New York Times* on July 9, 1997, "One of the ten Nigerians interviewed . . . described her ordeal as beginning at a disco in Lagos where someone suggested she could go to Europe to work and study. 'I paid a lot of money to an agency, which organizes trips to Italy. . . . The money was not enough, and so I signed a contract where I promised to work as a maid for a family in Naples and I soon understood that my job was another one. I was threatened, and they said that I had to pay, otherwise my family would have been threatened too.'"[30] Although trafficking in women for the sex trade is, unfortunately, a common practice throughout the world, the policing of women working in this sector as the perpetrators of a crime (although, as I have already indicated, street prostitution is not illegal), rather than subjects and victims of a larger criminal circuit, has garnered more support from the general public than policing the people behind the trade. This is partially related to the discursive ways immigration and criminality are viewed through the lens of the cultural politics of race and nation. So, for example, Nigeria becomes the site of the criminal African subject, and the national location provides the "proof" of cultural difference and criminal behavior.

At the heart of the increased attention to immigrants and crime in Italy is the notion that the law is a national institution that "symbolizes the imagined community of the nation and expresses fundamental unity and equality of its citizens."[31] Historically, law and order have often not been synonymous in Italy, despite serious attempts to make them so. During the last few years, and starting especially with the fall of government corruption and the electoral victory of the Olive Tree Alliance in 1996, the importance of law and legality has come to represent a new national solidarity and subsequently a stronger national identity. This commitment to law and order, especially with regard to immigration, has captured the public imagination in such a way that the flow of "illegal" immigrants is understood as a sign of Italy's national decline. Because Italy was viewed as having a lax border by Italian citizens and other Europeans, the EU insisted that Italy comply with the immigration, border, and policing standards formalized by the EU in 1993. Currently, the reelection of Silvio Berlusconi, according to Jorge Pina, has undocumented immigrants and their advocates worried about waves of mass deportations. Pina writes that "For this right-wing alliance, an immigrant is equivalent of delinquent, which is why the results of the elections are so disheartening. . . . During the electoral campaign, the Northern League, one of the parties in the Berlusconi bloc, launched an intense crusade in favor of expelling foreigners." Further, Pina quotes immigrant rights activist Mario Sow on the subject of deportation: "They say it is only meant for those who are here illegally, but underneath it refers to everyone."[32]

In the face of public concern about immigration and law and order, discussions of immigrant criminality have become more prominent. In 1999, the statistical data gathering institute DOXA reported that 54 percent of Italians saw immigration "in terms of the risk of an increase in both petty delinquency and organized crime." Further, DOXA found that replies to questions about immigrants in general connected immigrants with "non-specific references to delinquency and crime: a further 20 percent of replies make specific mention of drug consumption and sale, and 10 percent define immigrants as 'dishonest and ill-bred.'"[33] In 2000, another statistical reporting agency, CENIS, found that 75 percent of Italians believed that immigrants were responsible for the (perceived) increase in crime.[34] It is in this climate that the rate of the expulsion of foreigners increased from four thousand to five thousand in the 1970s and 1980s to fifty-four thousand in 1998 and sixty-five thousand in 1999.[35]

Race and notions of otherness do matter in the fields of policing practices and policy making. Of course, for American audiences, this comes as no surprise given the extraordinary amount of evidence of police misconduct based on race and nationality that has long plagued the United States.[36] But for Italy, this signifies a shifting perception of crime and criminality and raises the specter of racial targeting in policing tactics. Consider the comments made to me during an interview with a Carabinieri officer:

> With the extracomunitari we must stop them. We must ask for their documents. We must see if they are irregular. . . . Some people understand why we stop them. But there are always some people who pretend that they cannot speak Italian. They don't want to get into trouble, or they already are in trouble and want to avoid arrest. We stop the extracomunitari first to see their documents. But we are not stopping them only for that. We can't because there is nothing we can do if people don't have documents. For example, I cannot detain any man for not having his documents. But I can detain him if I see that he has an order of expulsion or that he is a suspect in a crime. Many of the extracomunitari are from Africa and most have been in prison here in Italy. They come from Algeria, Morocco, and those places—also, many girls from Nigeria and South America. Those girls have spent time in our prisons in Italy. Most of these people are bringing drugs into our country. The Africans sell drugs on the street, they steal and the girls are prostitutes. Not all of them, but listen, most of the Africans that I stop, over 75 percent, I believe are guilty. I don't know why, but it just is. Look at their countries, they are always killing each other or starving and then they want to come to Europe to escape their problems and they bring the problems with them. I see this every day in my job, so I know this is the truth.

Amnesty International documented that victims of police abuse have reportedly sustained kicks, slaps, punches, beatings with truncheons, racial slurs, sexual assault, and threats with guns.[37] Much of the alleged abuse by law enforcement has occurred while police stopped individuals on suspicion of having committed a criminal offense or during identity checks. An overwhelming majority of the victims of police violence are immigrants and Roma. As Amnesty International reports with alarm, "a high portion of the allegations of ill-treatment by law enforcement officers concern immigrants from outside West-Europe (the majority of them are from Africa) and an increasing number of allegations concern Roma (Gypsies)."[38] The brunt of increased police violence has been borne by immigrants and Roma but especially by people who are detained in conjunction with drug-related offenses and those who intervene on behalf of others being mistreated by the police, and particularly since 1994, participants in street demonstrations have also been victims of police violence.[39]

In a study conducted in Emilia-Romagna, Dario Melossi found that one in seven male immigrants on foot were stopped by police, compared with one in ninety Italian men.[40] Although neither study indicates a connection between the high rate of immigrant foot stops and police abuse, a majority of the abuses occurred on the street according to Amnesty International, "at the moment of arrest and during the first 24 hours in custody, before the detainee has seen a lawyer or been brought before a judicial authority."[41]

Incarcerating Immigrants

At university law faculties throughout Italy, criminal law has been taught as the "Magna Carta of the criminal" rather than that of the "honest citizen."[42] This perspective grows out of a general skepticism that many Italians had about discourses on crime. Italy has experienced a number of changes in its penal system, but prison reform in the early 1970s significantly changed Italy's practice of imprisonment and its perspective on criminality. In the 1970s there were several rebellions and protests in prisons.[43] These rebellions were largely connected to the broader countercultural movement of the late 1960s and 1970s. The prison rebellions brought attention to the squalid living conditions of the inmates and the brutality that they endured.

The prison legislation between 1971 and 1975 reflected the embattled times of the early 1970s. There was continual oscillation between innovative and conservative proposals, which in the end contradicted one another. For example, while the Law on Prison 354 of July 26, 1975 provided some benefits to offenders, including improved prison conditions and alternatives to incarceration, it also enacted punitive measures, lengthening prison sentences for those charged with crimes against the state and restricting inmate access to the outside world. Although many policy makers characterized 354 as progressive prison reform, Massimo Pavarini argues that the Italian criminal justice system reflects the authoritarian legal system of the thirties, which deployed arbitrary judicial and administrative strategies.

Many scholars argued that the Law on Prison 354 was only a partial adjustment to prison reform, particularly because the law emphasized detention and exclusion and did not regard the inmates as anything more than prisoners. The law transformed the perception of the criminal for the government. Prior to 1973 most inmates—both male and female—were considered "hardened criminals," serving time in prison for murder or repeated theft. Many of these "hardened criminals" were older and from the working classes.[44]

For nearly twenty years, Italy has had one of the lowest prison populations in Western Europe. However, during the 1990s, the prison population dramatically increased, and with it emerged new attitudes about criminality. From 1990 to 1993, the prison population grew from thirty-four thousand to over fifty thousand in just five years. Pavarini warns, "if this trend continues, with an increase of roughly fifteen hundred prisoners a month, Italy will reach the current imprisonment rates of the United Kingdom in little over a year."[45] In a two-year period the prison population had increased by 50 percent.[46]

The prison population of the 1990s, according to Stefano Anastasia, consisted of drug addicts, immigrants, and unemployed youth who come from the most disenfranchised sectors of Italian society.[47] Massimo Pavarini suggests that the shift in inmate demographics is a "result of a new selection procedure in the imprisonment population." He finds that "in two short years, the number of drug abusers rose from under 20% to over 60% of the entire prison population. In the same period the percentage of prisoners originating from outside of the European Economic Community rose from 5% to over 20%. The repressive selectivity basically directed at these two ostracized groups highlights a significant change in what society takes to be a new danger."[48]

Although it is uncertain exactly why there has been a sharp increase in the incarceration of immigrants and drug addicts, Pavarini argues that the anticorruption or "clean hands" campaign may provide an answer. He suggests that through the campaign the state, primarily the police, the judiciary, and the prisons, has achieved legitimacy that is "unequaled in the history of the Italian Republic."[49] Since Operation Clean Hands, judges have increasingly assigned preventative detention to a majority of the accused, thus creating a system of overcrowding. The crisis of overcrowded prisons caused former Italian President Oscar Luigi Scalfaro in 1998 to criticize the excessive use of this sentence.[50]

The increase in the prison population of drug-addicted and foreign inmates that started in the 1990s cannot be linked only to the legitimizing effects of certain state apparatuses since the clean hands campaign. The wider discourse of law and order, particularly in the early 1990s, appears connected to broader EU policy concerns, which include the anticorruption and anti–organized crime campaigns; the Martelli law of 1991, which sought to control the entry of immigrants into Italy; and the 1990 law, Iervolino–Vassalli, which heightened the criminal penalties for drug use. The clean hands campaign and the Martelli and Iervolino–Vassalli laws were implemented in roughly the same period and one to two years before Italians became citizens of the EU under the Maastricht Treaty, on November 1, 1993.[51] Regardless of what may have inspired the changing public perception of crime and the criminal justice system, the new legitimacy of the state and the high approval rating of the police will surely add to the criminalization of immigrants.

In her study of prisons around the world, Vivien Stern notes that the figures for incarcerated racial minorities and foreigners are disproportionately high. In Western Europe, she writes, "The proportions of foreigners in prison are at least double and often treble or more times the proportions in the country as a whole . . . . For Western Europe as a whole the average percentage of foreigners in prison is 19% whilst foreigners make up an average of 7% of the population."[52] Stern reports that the majority of the foreigners detained in Western Europe are asylum seekers or poor immigrants, and, as Massimo Pavarini once wrote about Italy, "for every corrupt politician lawfully detained, a hundred black immigrants are interned."[53]

Speaking on the subject of racism and imprisonment in Italy, a Ghanaian woman detained in Rebibbia Femminile once said to me during an interview in 1997,

> [E]verything is difficult for we foreigners. We are the last consideration. . . . We learn the rules, the language, and how we are to survive through our own mistakes. We are not home. They [the prison administration] put all the Italians in one room and all the strangers [foreigners] in different rooms. They think that we [foreign women] need to be together. Is this racism? But we cannot help each other—we know nothing of the laws and the system. We are both dogs and children here.

Harsh negative representations and the practical realities of being a criminalized population make it such that policy and policing tactics are based on the "evidence" of that image. As we see with the case in Italy, where a mere thirty years ago crime and criminals were thought of as being revolutionary actors against the state, now immigrant populations, particularly migrants coming from North and sub-Saharan Africa, Latin America, and Eastern Europe, and the Roma, are not only targets but victims of the state. It is no accident that anywhere there is migration, there is an accompanying discourse of criminalization, suspicion, and mistrust.

On the overall increase in the imprisonment of foreign and second-generation immigrants throughout Europe, Loïc Wacquant suggests that the overrepresentation of people of color and African Americans in particular in U.S. prisons and jails may not be, as many have argued, "American exceptionalism."[54] In fact, he shows that manner in which the U.S. prison system has manifested itself as a force that regulates and contains the poor disfranchised has become a similar comportment of the European penal system. Wacquant writes, "There is every chance that the societies of Western Europe will generate analogous, albeit less pronounced, situations to the extent that they, too, embark on the path of the penal management of poverty and inequality, and ask their prison system not only to curb crime, but also to regulate the lower segments of the labor market and to hold at bay populations judged to be disreputable, derelict, and unwanted. From this point of view, foreigners and quasi-foreigners would be 'the blacks' of Europe."[55]

At a time of unprecedented globalization and a booming market for some, there has also been unprecedented incarceration and victimization of immigrants, women and people of color, and the poor. The parallel growth of economies and prisons is too strong for us to ignore. These parallels force us to ponder the broader problems of criminalization, which are connected to racialization, gender discrimination, and the rapid social and economic restructuring that is forcing some to cross borders and turn to alternative (or illegal) economies. The significance of these parallels points to a greater awareness that immigrant women and women of color are precariously positioned in this world of increasing transnationalism and are facing fewer economic options while suffering the violent cycle of criminalization because of their race, gender, national origin, and legal status.

References

1. Michael Keith, "From Punishment to Discipline? Racism, Racialization and the Policing of Social Control," in *Racism, the City and the State*, ed. M. Cross and M. Keith (New York: Routledge, 1993), 193–209: 198.
2. Biko Agozino, "Changes in the Social Construction of Criminality among Immigrants in the United Kingdom," in *Immigrant Delinquency: Social Sciences*, ed. European Commission (Luxembourg: European Commission, 1996), 103–132: 103.
3. It is estimated that 181,000 immigrants entered Italy in 2000, causing Italy's population to increase to 57.8 million (Migration News, August 2001).
4. Niccolo d-Aquino, "Immigrant Supplanting Emigration," *Europe* (April 2000): 47; Melossi, Dario. 2003. "'In a Peaceful Life': Migration and the Crime of Modernity in Europe/Italy." *Punishment and Society*. Vol. 5 No. 4: 371–397.
5. Emilio Reyneri, "Migrant Insertion in the Formal Economy, Deviant Behaviour and the Impact on Receiving Societies: Some Hypotheses for a Cross-National Research," in *Immigrant Delinquency: Social Sciences*, ed. European Commission (Luxembourg: European Commission, 1996), 31–42: 41.
6. Alessandro dal Lago, "The Impact of Migration on Receiving Societies: Some Ethnographic Remarks," in *Immigrant Delinquency: Social Sciences*, ed. European Commission (Luxembourg: European Commission, 1996), 43–50: 43.
7. Reyneri 1996.
8. Palidda, Salvatore. "La construction sociale de la d'viance et de la criminalit parmi les immigré: Les cas Italien." In *Immigrant Delinquency: Social Sciences*, edited by European Commission. Luxembourg: European Commission, 1996.
9. Palidda 252. I cite these numbers with caution, as one could argue that in fact these numbers do reflect the propensity of immigrants to commit crimes because they make up a small percentage of the population. However, it should also be remembered that the representation of the immigrant as criminal affects their rates and reports of arrest.
10. Palidda 252.
11. dal Lago 44.
12. Mary Wisley, "Doing Time behind Foreign Bars," *Wanted in Rome* 12, 15 (1996): 3–5; Dario Melossi, "'In A Peaceful Life': Migration and the Crime of Modernity in Italy, E.U." *Punishment and Society* (forthcoming).
13. Melossi 2003.
14. dal Lago 1996.
15. For an excellent example of neighborhood residents of Crocetta (Modena) who gained a stronger sense of identity and community through their demonstrations against non-EU drug dealers and, in essence, non-EU immigrants, see Chiodi, Milena Chiodi, "Immigrazione, Devianza e Percezione d'Insicrezza: Analisi del Quatiere Crocetta a Modena," in *Dei*

Delitti e Delle Pene [special issue]: Immigrazione e insicrezza, ed. Dario Melossi (Naopli: Edizioni Scientifiche Italiane, 1999), 115–140.

16. Melossi 2003.

17. dal Lago 45.

18. Dario Melossi, *Multiculturalismo e Sicurezza in Emilia-Romagna: Prima Parte. Quaderni di Città Sicure*, 15 Gennaio/Febbraio (Bologna: Periodico Bimestrale della Regione Emilia-Romagna, 1999), forthcoming; Chiodi 1999.

19. This practice of linking black women to prostitution was commonplace in the eighteenth and nineteenth centuries as well, when both African men and women became the representative icons for deviant sexuality. See Sander Gilman, *Difference and Pathology: Stereotypes of Sexuality, Race, and Madness* (Ithaca, NY: Cornell University Press, 1985).

20. Coalition Against the Trafficking in Women, "Fact Book on Global Sexual Exploitation: Italy," 1999, http://www.uri.edu/artsci/wms/hughes/catw/italy.html (accessed May 15, 2001).

21. Figures for the year ending 1994 indicate that the numbers of persons charged with encouraging and/or exploiting prostitution are the highest among foreigners from Albania, ex-Yugoslavia, Nigeria, and Tunisia. Men and women of the same nationality as the trafficked women conduct most of the traffic of their own nationals.

22. Coalition Against the Trafficking in Women, 1999.

23. The notion of the hypersexuality of Africans is just one discursive product of colonization. In Italy's own colonial history Facetta Nera was a popular song by Italian soldiers during the invasion of Ethiopia in 1935. The song, "Little Black Face," serves as an example of a popular representation that cast black women in particular in the role of sexual object. See Donald Martin Carter, *States of Grace: Senegalese in Italy and the New European Immigration* (Minneapolis: University of Minnesota Press, 1997): 179.

24. Carter 186.

25. Personal communication, Azzi, July 30, 1994.

26. Vanessa Maher, "Immigration and Social Identities," in *Italian Cultural Studies: An Introduction*, ed. D. Forgacs and R. Lumley (Oxford: Oxford University Press, 1999), 160–177: 166.

27. There is a propensity for other European countries to screen closely all Nigerians who pass through their borders because it is assumed that Nigerians are more inclined to traffic in drugs. For example, Biko Agozino (1996) reports on widespread discrimination against Nigerians by the Home Office (UK).

28. International Organization for Migration, *Trafficking in Women to Italy for Sexual Exploitation* (Washington, D.C.: International Organization for Migration, 1996); Coalition Against the Trafficking in Women, 1999.

29. International Organization for Migration, 1996.

30. Celestine Bohlen, "Exotic Imports Have Captured Italy's Sex Market," *New York Times*, July 9, 1997.

31. Paul Gilroy, *Ain't No Black in the Union Jack: The Cultural Politics of Race and Nation* (Chicago: Chicago University Press, 1991): 74.

32. Jorge Pina, "Berlusconi Win Worries Immigrants, Activists," www.oneworld.org/ips2/may01/00_29_001.html (accessed August 8, 2001).

33. DOXA, "Immigrants in Italy," 1999, http://www.doxa.it/inchieste/delinq/intro.html (accessed August 7, 2001).

34. Migration News, Electronic News Letter, University of California at Davis, August 2000.

35. U.S. Refugee Committee, "Country Report: Italy," http://www.refugees.org/world/countryrpt/europe/italy.html (accessed August 12, 2001).

36. Human Rights Watch, *Police Brutality in the United States* (New York: Human Rights Watch, 1991).

37. Amnesty International, 1995.

38. ibid 1995: 2

39. Since the police shooting of antiglobalization protester Carlo Giuliani in Genoa during the G-8 summit, the media has scrutinized police tactics for the excessive force displayed by security forces.

40. Dario Melossi, "Immigrazione, Pluralismo Cultural e Sicurezza: una Ricerca in Emilia-Romagna," in *Dei Delitti e Delle Pene [special issue]: Immigrazione e insicrezza,* ed. D. Melossi (Napoli: Edizioni Scientifiche Italiane, 1996), 36–75: 39–40.
41. Amnesty International, 2.
42. Massimo Pavarini, "The New Penology and Politics in Crisis: The Italian Case," in *Prisons in Context,* ed. R. D. King and M. Maguire (Oxford: Clarendon Press, 1994), 49–61: 51.
43. Franca Faccioli, "Il carcere in Italia: appunti su un dibattito," in *Donne in Carcere: Ricerca sulla detenzione femminile in Italia,* ed. E. Campelli et al. (Milano: Feltrinelli, 1992), 11–21.
44. Pavarini 1994.
45. Pavarini, 49.
46. Loïc Wacquant, "'Suitable Enemies': Foreigners and Immigrants in the Prisons of Europe," in *Punishment and Society, The International Journal of Penology,* Volume 1, number 2 (London: Sage Publications, 1999), 215–222.
47. Stefano Anastasia, "Il vaso di Pandora. Carcere e pena dopo le riforme," in *Il Vaso di pandora: Carcere e pena dopo le riforme,* ed. Mauro Palma (Roma: Istituto della Enciclopedia Italiana, 1997), 5–16.
48. Pavarini 1994, 55.
49. Pavarini 1994, 59.
50. International Helsinki Federation for Human Rights, 1999.
51. Guild 1996.
52. Vivian Stern, *A Sin Against the Future: Imprisonment in the World* (Boston: Northeastern University Press, 1998), 121.
53. Pavarini 1994, 59.
54. Wacquant 1999.
55. Wacquant 1999, 216.

CHAPTER 2

Challenging the Criminalization
of Women Who Resist

LISA NEVE AND KIM PATE

I never did feel like Canada's most dangerous woman. I felt like Lisa. As much as they were pushing me to accept the fact that I was a lifer, in my heart I knew that I was just Lisa.

On June 29, 1999, the Alberta Court of Appeal released its decision to overturn the designation of Lisa Neve as a dangerous offender. Lisa, a young Aboriginal woman from Saskatchewan, was 21 years of age when she was labeled the most dangerous woman in Canada and sentenced to an indeterminate prison sentence. Poor, young, racialized women and girls are among the fastest growing prison populations in Canada and worldwide. The "war on drugs"; evisceration of education, health, and other social support services; and "gender-neutral" zero tolerance policies have contributed significantly to this phenomenon.

An important aspect of the prison explosion that has largely been overlooked is the high proportion of women behind bars who suffer from mental disabilities. Women and girls who have cognitive and/or mental disabilities are more likely to be criminalized and jailed. Once imprisoned, they are then classified as maximum security prisoners despite the negligible risk that they pose to the public. Many of these women were previously institutionalized in psychiatric hospitals and/or involved in other mental health services. Many are criminalized as a result of their disability-induced behavior in institutions and/or the community. Prison is thus a continuation of the institutional and coercive control exercised by the state in the lives of these highly vulnerable women.

19

Through the lens of Lisa's experience, this chapter explores the factors contributing to the increasing criminalization and incarceration of racialized women and girls in Canada. In the first section, Lisa shares her story of living with mental illness and her struggle with harmful criminal justice interventions in her own words. In the second part, we dissect Lisa's construction as a dangerous offender and discuss the court ruling that ultimately overruled this designation. The authors then explore the stereotypes about young women and violence that inform the treatment of poor, racialized, and disabled women. We conclude with an analysis of the impact of economic restructuring and the dismantling of social safety nets on the criminalization of women and girls. As we write, we want to honor and thank the women in and from prison, our sisters, our friends, our allies. Your courage, strength, and brilliance inspire and encourage us. Your lived experience makes you our finest leaders, mentors, guides, and conscience.

Lisa's First Experience with Prison

I went to jail. I remember the first time I went there, I was so scared. I walked on the unit and I didn't know anybody. I didn't know the game, so I had to learn really quick how to get things that you want. I learned that acting out meant people didn't try to shrink me, I just got attention. So I would freak out and get restrained and sent to segregation. I was always in segregation for something or other, because I was so bitter and angry. I felt robbed of my childhood, so I misbehaved. I think that I was ill back then, I remember having so many issues in my mind, voices, but I didn't want to tell anybody because I thought they would send me over to the hospital. They had sex offenders there and I didn't want to go, so I just acted out, cut myself, banged my head, and scratched myself. I don't know what I was doing.

Then when I was eighteen, I got charged with assault and I went to a remand center for the first time. I freaked out and I swallowed these screws from a crib board. The guards jumped me and they dragged me upstairs and put me in a straitjacket and a helmet because I wouldn't stop banging my head, and I was kicking and screaming. It was a really traumatic experience for me. It was just a never-ending story. I would go in and do something stupid and go back into the psychiatric hospital.

I think it goes back to when I was twelve and got apprehended by social services. I went to school with four of my friends and we all brought a bottle from home. We mixed it in an ice cream container, and we drank it all and got really drunk. So they called the principal and I had to go down to the office. The cops came and they said, "What happened?" I said, "Well, I don't want to go home," because I thought I would be grounded, I was really scared, so the cops handcuffed me and took me to the children's service center. So we went there and I was supposed to be with the twelve- to fifteen-year-olds. I was never stripped searched before. They said, "Take off your clothes," and I said, "No way, I'm not taking off my clothes," and so they took my clothes off me and I was fighting back, so they put me with the fifteen- to eighteen-year-olds because they thought that I was violent and unruly. The girls didn't like me because I had a family, and then when I got my period they said I was dying and I sat in the bathtub and cried and they were just really mean to me.

So I started running away, and that's how I got involved in prostitution and drugs and I wanted so bad to go home, but it was too late, I was already acting out a lot, and they put me in secure treatment all the time. I used to get locked up and restrained because I was bitter and angry. I used to bang my head. I think I was very ill back then, because things in my mind didn't make sense. I always had this awful feeling that something bad was going to happen. My behavior was just seen as out of control, so they decided to send me on this ninety-day program, where I spent thirty days in Calgary at the Calgary Young Offender Centre, thirty days in Edmonton at the Young Offender Centre, and thirty days at Alberta Hospital, in a locked forensic unit. I also spent a lot of time in segregation because I was hurting myself and then I was holding hostages. When I held the hostage I just asked to be shot because my friend got killed and I felt responsible because I introduced her to the person who killed her. So I thought that I deserved to die. Looking back now, I just think that I was just trying to deal with stuff but I couldn't grieve and I felt guilty but I couldn't deal with it in jail. Maybe things would have been so much different if I was on the medication that I am on now.

When I turned eighteen, I got an assault charge and went to a remand center. That's when I freaked out and they put me in a straightjacket. I got ninety days and the Fort Saskatchewan provincial jail wouldn't take me so I had to spend it in the remand center. When I got out, I met this guy Richard. And I thought he was really a nice guy, he was just beautiful looking and I wanted to try another boyfriend and be a "normal cool person" so we started going out. He started hitting me almost immediately, but not bad at first, just like a slap or name-calling. Later in our relationship, he started hurting me so bad, like he would just beat me so I couldn't even see; my eyes were just swollen shut. And then he moved me to Edmonton, and he said I wasn't allowed to talk to anybody but my lawyer, so I started spending a lot of time at my lawyer's office just to get away and finally he convinced me to charge Richard and I did. Two other girls charged him too, because he was pimping, and so Richard went to jail.

It came time for the trial, and I testified, and Richard's lawyer was really awful to me, saying to me, "Aren't you in fact a prostitute?" And "You're a suspect in a murder." He was just awful to me and the Crown never objected once, so I was really mad. So finally he was found guilty, and then it came time for the sentencing and he got eighteen months and I felt so betrayed. I went against everything I believed in, I testified, I violated my own code, to stop the circle of violence, and this is what happens? He gets eighteen months? I was so upset, and so I called my doctor and said I was going to kill myself and he said, "Well come to the hospital." So I turned myself in and went to the psych ward and this doctor is talking to me and says "Well, why are you here?" and I'm like "I'd like to kill this guy who kills kids" and he said "Who's that?" I said Richard's lawyer's name.

The next day I signed myself out. Two days later I was at a restaurant with some friends and we got a call from another friend who said, "The cops were here looking for Lisa." So I said, "Well tell them I will turn myself in before midnight," so I called this really good lawyer I knew, to help me turn myself in. I was sent to jail. The next day I went to court and they revoked my bail. I was out on bail for aggravated assault and they charged me with uttering death threats, two counts, and so I went to jail, and I just waited awhile to see what's happening. Then I was charged with aggravated assaults and a robbery charge for this time we went after a girl who beat up our friend and made her miscarry —we just saw her after we came from seeing our friend in hospital. The girl who beat her, and my friend and I, were all working. We decided to teach her a lesson for doing that to our friend. We cut off her clothes and chucked them, so that was the robbery I had from before.

I went to court for uttering threats and I got two and a half years, and then I also had to go up for robbery. I assumed that I'd get a couple of years. So I was at the remand center and I was still waiting for my robbery trial and I heard these rumors that they were going to make me a dangerous offender and my lawyer said there was no way. They offered me a four-year plea bargain and I said, "No," because I thought I could beat that.

I got four and half years for the "threats." Then I was at the remand center and they called me downstairs and this cop handed me this piece of paper, and I asked, "What, am I being subpoenaed or something?" He said, "No you have been served," and I didn't understand what this paper was, so I called my lawyer and he came down and he said they are applying to have you declared a dangerous offender, and I was so scared, I thought, "Oh my God, you know my whole life will only be in jail," but everyone kept telling me it's never going to happen they won't do it, judge won't go for it. So I went to court for thirty days and everyone testified. There were cops saying that I said I killed people and then, they brought in people I fought with on the street, hookers and people like that.

I testified. I took the stand, although my lawyer said not to. I said, "Look all I have left is the truth, like I can't do anything else so I want to fight for my life." So I took the stand and I explained things the best I could. I know I was really sarcastic and it looked bad for the judge, but I didn't care because I thought, "I have to say my side." My parents testified and it was heartbreaking to put my family through that. Then finally they came through the verdict. So that

November 1994 I got sentenced to an indeterminate sentence, and at first I was in shock.

I went back to the remand center. The guard who had got to know me brought me doughnuts and said, "Lisa you have to go to segregation. People who get life are on suicide watch for forty-eight hours." The other girls on the unit were kind of freaking out saying, "No don't make her go," and so the goon squad came and took me to the digger . . . and I was on a camera and in nothing but a security gown, we called them baby dolls. I just couldn't believe it at first. I was in so much shock and I didn't think how serious it was, and then I went to RPC [Regional Psychiatric Centre—dually designated prison and psychiatric hospital] and it was there that it got to me that I thought that I am never getting out of prison.

All I could think was, "This is my life, this is going to be it forever," and they said the earliest a dangerous offender has ever got out was eleven years, so I got really depressed and then I hung myself. Then I was sent back to the hospital and then I came back to the jail. I was in segregation and I thought, "You have to decide, are you going to live or are you going to die?" And I chose to live, so I filed an appeal against my uttering death threat sentence and I got it knocked down eighteen months. So I was serving three and a half years plus the indeterminate sentence. So I went to Edmonton for a while and there was a murder and a riot there and I went back to RPC, and then to [the segregated maximum security unit in the men's prison in the] Sask[atchewan] Pen[itentiary].

That's when I really reconnected with Kim [Pate]—I knew her when I was first in. She was getting the women out of seg[regation] in P4W [Prison for Women]. She wanted to intervene in my case but the court didn't let her . . . she still hung in there though.

When I finally got a grip on everything I thought I'm going to get some help for my mental health issues and I'm going to be honest with these people. It changed my life forever. Then we fought my max classification and got me to the Healing Lodge.[1] In prison, it was the best thing that ever happened to me. I still felt like a little ray of hope that this appeal will be successful and they said well nobody has ever won their appeal, and I thought well nobody has ever been declared a dangerous offender and gotten an indeterminate sentence, so, I mean how do they know? But it took a long time, and two years later, I was down at my unit and they called me and said you got a call from your lawyer. I was so scared I was crying and I went down to the Elders Lodge and they put the phone through and it was my mom and my lawyer and he said, "Lisa it's over. You are free!" So, on July 1, 1999, I was released. It was amazing.

I think that the most earth-shattering thing in my life was being called a dangerous offender—the most dangerous woman in Canada! Me? I think that the whole court thing and six and a half years in prison made me a stronger person. I learned how to cope. And I decided I didn't want to get by getting beat up or being violent to protect myself anymore. I took proper medication and got my life back, went to the Healing Lodge, and started working on getting where I am now. Now I feel I'm successful.

For thirty days during the dangerous offender hearing I heard everyone say all these horrible things about me, and then I got a life sentence. So it was earth shattering. It did change me you know. For the first three years I was real rowdy. I know that I caused a lot of trouble. But for the last few years I was getting it together and working with other women inside. I started using the grievance system and legal ways to fight back.

I mean I had demons in my room before and voices in my head. I had delusions; like I told the cops I killed people I didn't. It's been almost three years now and I'm doing so well and I don't feel like I have all these things going on in my mind and I don't feel like I'm fighting myself. I'm not slashing because someone's telling me to in my head. I'm not scared of the T.V.; I used to be scared of the T.V. because I thought it was sending me messages. And I think if I were to do this ten years ago I would have spared myself a lot of trouble, and that breaks my heart to think that I could've had a good life, that so much was wasted from when I was twelve until I was twenty-eight. All those years that I could have been doing things better.

Writing and helping other kids not to go where I have is way more important to me than anything else. Because it's my chance to speak out and it's my chance to tell kids like I was that they're not alone. Stopping someone else from going through what I had to experience would be one of my biggest accomplishments. I want my life to mean something. I don't want it all to have been for nothing. I want to speak out about what happened and I don't want to ever forget for one minute, any of it, not one ounce of pain, not one ounce of happiness. I want them to see that I'm not a monster, that other kids and women aren't either. They made me feel like a monster. It's over four years since I got out and I've never reoffended. I just got my own apartment, I volunteer with kids and other women and parents and advise Canadian Association of Elizabeth Fry Societies and other women's and justice groups about changes to the law and policies.

My hopes for the future are that I want to work with girls in the young offender center. I remember my beginning, my first day when they went to strip search me and I freaked out and then they put me in with the older girls and they used to beat me up and be mean to me and then I learned how to fight back. They thought they were helping by taking me away, they thought my parents were bad. I was just being a kid. They made me that way, I wasn't born bad, but I was expected to be bad, so I was. I mean people can only push you around so much and then you can't take it anymore. And I was the youngest, so people always picked on me, and I learned quick and fast that if you're going to get to the top you have to learn how to fight, and I did. I fought my way to the top, not that I'm proud that I was in that group with the heavies, but that's what happened. But it was because I was sick of being picked on and I thought that I could only deal with it if I got to be the one picking on people rather than being picked on. Not that it makes it right either way.

I also want to get rid of the dangerous offender act. I don't think that we live in a country where you can send people to jail based on what they may do. The dangerous offender label, well, I'm not the only one who'll think, "It'll never happen to me." I don't think that I ever felt so scared in my whole entire life. I thought that I would be in prison until I died. For the rest of my life, I will speak out whenever I can. I'm not going to let this experience just be something that I forget, or that will one day be okay for me. It will never be okay. I think that it's the craziest thing in a country that is supposed to be so liberated, that they can send a woman to jail for life and let a wife-beater and a child molester get four or five years. A man can kill a woman and get off with five years, you know? It's an experience that I'll never forget but I know it's not me, I know that I'm not Canada's most dangerous woman. I know that I'm a person, I'm a sister, I'm a friend, I'm a partner. I never was and I am not a dangerous offender. I know that now. And nobody could ever tell me now that I am Canada's most dangerous woman, because I succeeded against all odds.

Deconstructing the Designation of a Dangerous Offender

When Lisa was 12 years old, she was dragged into secure "treatment," followed fairly quickly by secure custody. The system was not impressed by her assertive and confident manner. Unlike so many other young women her age, she was clearly a respected and undisputed leader. These qualities are not ones that are generally accepted, much less encouraged or nurtured, in our social control systems—be they child welfare or criminal justice in orientation. They are seen as particularly unacceptable when embodied by a young woman. Sexism, racism, heterosexism, and class biases intersect to provide a discriminatory lens through which women like Lisa are viewed and judged.

As a result, it did not take long for the adults in authority to label Lisa as a "problem" in need of "correction." Once the labels were applied, they not only stuck, but they also attracted other labels, which built upon and expanded the previous ones. Consequently, Lisa was initially described as "mischievous" and "a brat"; then she was called "an instigator," "negative," and, eventually, "aggressive," "sociopathic," and a dangerous offender. Lisa's characterization as the most dangerous woman in Canada by Justice Murray in 1994 was largely based upon accounts of her institutional behavior in young offender centers, as well as her "unfeminine" renegade behavior while working the street. This then led to her designation as a maximum security prisoner by the Correctional Service of Canada for more than four years.

Including her pretrial detention, Lisa spent approximately six years in jail for an offence that the Court of Appeal eventually determined warranted a three-year sentence, rather than the indeterminate one imposed by Justice Murray. To make matters worse, she also spent most of her time living in some of the most severe and limiting prison conditions in Canada.

In overturning the previous ruling, the Court of Appeal of Alberta concluded that attempts to predict future behavior are problematic, especially where such predictions are based upon labels and psychiatric analyses that are unreliable and invalid. As the judges pointed out in their decision, "predicting future behaviour based on past conduct is an inexact science. It is precisely because this finding must rest at least in part on predictions of human behaviour —and often conflicting ones at that—that . . . the difficulties and dangers inherent in a determination of future danger have been well recognized for years."[2] Quoting the Law Reform Commission of Canada, the Court of Appeal noted that " . . . in the last few years legal and medical journals have been inundated with reports of studies considering various aspects of the reliability and predictive accuracy of psychiatric assessments of dangerousness. More remarkable than the bulk of this literature is its unanimity—it concludes that *clinical predictions of dangerousness are at best suspect, and at worst, totally unreliable* [emphasis added by the Court]."[3]

The Court also identified that Lisa's experiences on the street, selling her body and performing sex acts, contributed to the context of her criminalization by limiting and determining her options. Stereotypes about those experiences as well as her acts of resistance were central features identified by the Court as contributing to the labeling of Lisa as dangerous. Madam Justices Fraser, Conrad, and Picard further noted that "[E]very offence which Neve committed was entangled in some way with her life as a prostitute."[4] The Court took into account the realities of life on the street, particularly for young sex trade workers. For instance, they highlighted the fact that many young prostitutes are assaulted and murdered and that the majority of those murdered were female. They went on to assert that "No one should be surprised, therefore, to learn that many prostitutes arm themselves for defensive purposes. . . . While those living life at the margins of society cannot argue that their actions, whatever the motivation, should not attract criminal culpability, it does not follow that the circumstances in which the events occurred are irrelevant for sentencing purposes. . . . It is not possible to evaluate moral blameworthiness without having an understanding of the context in which the criminal act occurred."[5]

It is hoped that the decision of the Alberta Court of Appeal in Lisa's case will result in broader systemic changes to the administration of justice for women in Alberta and across Canada. In overturning Lisa's designation as a dangerous offender, the Court cast significant doubt on the entire assessment and classification process, particularly when that process does not place the individual in the context of her life experiences. As the justices pointed out, labeling Lisa a dangerous offender "effectively implies . . . that a woman's thoughts about murder can somehow be equated with a man's commission of a murder."[6] The successful appeal against this label was an important step in challenging the stigmatization and criminalization of poor, racialized women.

Neoliberalism and the Politics of Crime

Lisa's case illustrates that current attempts to "correct" individuals and/or groups of women are fundamentally flawed. Indeed, it is clear that it is the law that is increasingly coming into conflict with people, especially poor, racialized, and disabled women, rather than women who are coming into conflict with the law.

Women are the fastest-growing prison population worldwide. In order to understand this trend, we must examine shifts in social policy that have occurred in the context of globalization. In 1996, the Canadian federal government decided to follow the U.S. lead by eliminating the Canada Assistance Plan (CAP) and with it Canadian standards of social, medical, and educational resourcing. The elimination of the CAP was followed by a swathe of cuts as conservative provincial governments utilized their newfound freedom to reduce public spending on welfare and social programs. By creating criminally low welfare rates and bans on receipt of state resources, provincial governments relegated many poor people to the criminalized underclass. The neoliberal destruction of social safety nets—from social and health services to economic and education standards and availability—is resulting in the increased criminalization of the most marginalized and vulnerable members of our communities. The result is the virtual inevitability of criminalization. There is a direct relationship between neoliberal economic and social policies and the increased criminalization of the most marginalized, especially young, racialized, and poor women and those with mental and cognitive disabilities.

The Prairie Provinces have witnessed some of the worst examples of the criminalization of women and girls. Aboriginal women continue to suffer the devastating impact of colonization. From residential school and child welfare seizure to juvenile and adult detention, Aboriginal women and girls are vastly overrepresented in institutions under state control. Indeed, even as activists work to deinstitutionalize and decarcerate, we are fearful that "treatment" will be the next colonial control of choice. This is already occurring, as is exemplified by the case of G, a pregnant young Aboriginal woman who was institutionalized for forced treatment of her drug use.[7] The focus on FAS/FAE (fetal alcohol syndrome and fetal alcohol effect) is gendered, classed, and racist in approach and has a disproportionate impact on poor, racialized women.

In the prairie region most of the women in prison are Aboriginal. The increasing number of women in prison is clearly linked to the evisceration of health, education, and social services. The cycle of inadequate social services, criminalization, and incarceration intensifies in times of economic downturn. It is very clear where current policies are sending the people who are experiencing the brunt of the downturn in the economy. Jails are our most comprehensive homelessness initiative.

Cutbacks in public spending have affected young women with mental and cognitive disabilities particularly harshly. In the past decade, efforts to deinstitutionalize those with cognitive and mental disabilities have been subverted by lack of resources, driven by the push to cut government spending and reduce the deficit. Progressive trends of the past to deinstitutionalize those with cognitive and mental disabilities have been subverted by resource depletion, attitudes, and policies occasioned by the deficit dementia of the last decade. The result is that more and more people who used to fill psychiatric and mental health facilities are literally being dumped into the streets and, ultimately, into the wider, deeper, and stickier social control net of our criminal justice system.

They attempt to survive, they attempt to self-medicate, and they attempt to cope with their situations as well as the behavior that evolves from being in a situation where they are increasingly disenfranchised, criminalized, and imprisoned. Once in prison, they tend to attract a number of psychiatric labels and to be characterized by the Correctional Service of Canada as among the most difficult prisoners. Most of these women and girls pose the greatest risk to themselves and their own well-being. They are, however, incredibly difficult to "manage" in prison settings, especially if they resist restraint, lock-up, and medications; slash and carve their bodies; burn themselves; swallow items; or try to kill themselves. As a result, they spend a disproportionate amount of their time classified as maximum-security prisoners. This means that in addition to serving most of their sentences in the segregated maximum-security units in the men's as well as the women's prisons, they are most likely to be placed in segregation. Mental health concerns that are disabling undoubtedly create very real needs for those who have them and for those who try to control prisons. But equating mental and cognitive disabilities with risks only serves to perpetuate a social construction of persons with mental disabilities as dangerous. This is precisely the kind of stereotyping that is prohibited by the equality provisions of the section 15 *Canadian Charter of Rights and Freedoms.*

The reaction of Correctional Services Canada (CSC) to the growing number of prisoners with mental disabilities has been to develop mental health services in prisons. However, this practice serves only to exacerbate the trend to increasingly criminalize women with mental and cognitive disabilities. Developing such services in prisons at a time when they are increasingly nonexistent in the community is resulting in more women receiving federal sentences because there will be a presumption that there is an ability to gain access to services in prison that are not available in community settings. Prisons are not and cannot be treatment or healing centers. Despite laudable attempts to develop rehabilitative and treatment programs in prisons, they remain what they were originally designed to be, places designed to punish and segregate those whom we decide are scapegoats for society's ills. In 1990, CSC published Creating Choices, a document that promised to change the face of incarceration for federally sentenced women. Subsequently, five new prisons were built. These new prisons aimed to be women centered and to promote regimens that would empower women. Despite these ambitious goals, women prisoners considered violent or dangerous continue to experience inhuman and brutal treatment. CSC may pretty them up, replace the obvious bars with reinforced concrete and thick glass, and pretend that the new prisons are nice and unlike prisons, but they do not fool those who are locked up there.

Rethinking Women's Violence

Lisa's designation as a dangerous offender contains important lessons about the construction of young women's violence. During the 1990s, media reports in Canada and the United States generated considerable public concern by proclaiming the existence of a "crime wave" of juvenile violence. As Christie Barron points out:

> Violent youths have become "folk devils," to whom are attributed characteristics that feed societal panic but clash with the youths' perceptions of self. Youths are pathologized within professional discourse and portrayed as unremorseful monsters in need of medical treatment.[8]

Central to this media-inflated moral panic has been the claim that girls, especially poor, racialized girls, are participating in violent gang-related activities at greater rates than ever before. Although there have been no empirical changes in the levels and patterns of girls' aggressive behavior, there are marked differences in state responses to violent actions, especially those perpetrated by youth. The development of "zero tolerance" policies has resulted in increased policing and prosecuting of all forms of violence committed by boys and girls. In addition, women and girls have been charged or countercharged under zero tolerance policies in a backlash against women's efforts to hold men accountable for violence. The application of "gender-neutral" zero tolerance policies to girls, especially as a result of their reactions to violence in schools and their own homes, fails to recognize the unique context of women's violence. It also leads to the increased criminalization of young women who are involved in relatively minor altercations in schoolyards or who defend themselves or others from violence perpetrated by abusive men.

In addition, there has been an increased criminalization of young women's survival skills. In the past, it was relatively easy to institutionalize or enforce social controls on young women if they ran away, missed curfew, engaged in sexual activity, or displayed behavior that might be defined as "unfeminine" or, worse yet, unmanageable. Under the old *Juvenile Delinquents Act*, a young woman could be imprisoned in a juvenile home for such activities. The introduction of the *Young Offenders Act (YOA)* in 1982 was supposed to end the arbitrary detention of young women for such activities. However, the way the YOA is being implemented by police and judges belies its legislative intent. Although the articulated aim of the act was to separate the "criminal" actions of youth from child welfare–related issues, the lack of community-based options, coupled with the cuts to social, health, and education services, has resulted in the continued use of the juvenile system to respond to child welfare, mental health, homelessness, poverty, and other noncriminal challenges facing youth.

The new *Youth Criminal Justice Act*, which came into force on April 1, 2003, is a clear attempt to reassert the value of keeping youth in the community rather than criminalizing those who are oppressed and vulnerable. Already, several youth jails have been fully or partially closed as a result, with a striking reduction in the number of young people being sentenced to custodial terms. Notable exceptions are the lack of decrease in the rates of imprisonment of Aboriginal youth. Many fear that the continued failure to develop resources in the community will sabotage any gains made as a result of the legislative changes. The act will fail to rectify this situation if only the law changes but economic policies, policing, and prosecutorial practices do not.

Ann Campbell and others challenge us to consider whether it is morally or ethically appropriate to require women and girls who need to use violence and aggression as a means to survive to relinquish these tools. She argues that:

> Secure in our relationships and relatively protected from physical harm, most women do not need to use aggression as a tool to keep the world at bay. But when the ties that bring women close to others are destroyed what do they have to fear in aggression? . . . the indisputable law on the street is fight or get beaten . . . where ever women face lives of brutal exploitation that destroy their faith in the value of trust and intimacy, they will be driven to it. We cannot demand that women desist from its use when their survival requires it.[9]

In Lisa's case, the brutality of life on the streets, compounded by the aggression she experienced while she was confined in the juvenile justice system and later a violent relationship, taught her that she had only two options: she could be either the perpetrator or the victim of violence. Lisa chose to survive, and survival required her to fight. As she says, "I was sick of being picked on and I thought that I could only deal with it if I got to be the one picking on people, rather than being picked on."

Instead of making it *a priority* to lock up youth, we must begin to try to deal with the factors that compel young women to behave violently. Too many young women experience victimization in their homes and in the community. They are too often victimized by juvenile services and authorities that dismiss them as "bad girls" instead of trying to understand why they are driven to act violently. Attempts to "eliminate" youth violence will need to take into consideration the social contexts of the youth as well as the circumstances in which they resort to the use of violence. Without such contextualization, we cannot hope to understand how these contexts seem to make the use of violence not only legitimate but necessary.

As a young Aboriginal woman living on the streets, supporting herself by selling her body and dealing with a significant mental illness, Lisa needed considerable assistance and support. However, state interventions cast her as an offender rather than a potential recipient of social services from a very early age. As such, the social context for her "crimes"—both those actually committed and those anticipated by the criminal justice system—was overlooked and she was instead expected to change without regard to the lack of resources available to her. In the absence of external support, Lisa's efforts to survive led her inexorably into conflict with the law. Many of the incidents that led to Lisa's incarceration were acts that she carried out in defense of herself, her friends, or her livelihood. Mark Totten confirms that "the literature suggests that women's use of violence is qualitatively different from that of men: whereas male violence tends to be more frequent, serious, and utilitarian, female violence is more often contextualized in significant factors related to self-defence, anticipation of an upcoming physical or sexual assault, and prior victimization by physical and sexual abuse."[10] If we are to learn the lessons from Lisa's mistaken designation as "Canada's most dangerous woman," we need to alter radically our understanding of the roots and nature of women's violence.

Where Do We Go from Here?

As the economic, social, and political climates within Canada continue to produce ever more daunting challenges to the survival of the most marginalized, we must struggle to resist the rush to vilify women and girls. We must challenge the increased criminalization of those with cognitive and mental disabilities. In addition, we must demand the development of community-based mental health services. Where we cannot prevent them from being criminalized in the first place, we need to work to have women and girls taken out on passes and/or released into the community so that they may have access to such services. The criminal justice system is the least effective and most expensive system that could be used to respond to cognitive and mental disabilities. However, because it cannot refuse to "service" anyone who is criminalized, regardless of that person's disability, there is a tendency for the criminal justice system to become the only point of service for vulnerable women. We must resist the tendency for institutionally based mental health services alone to replace care in the community.

Lisa's story demonstrates the fundamental connection between women's survival strategies and their criminalization. It is unrealistic to tell women and girls not to take drugs to dull the pain of abuse, hunger, or other devastation or tell them that they must stop the behavior that allowed them to survive the multigenerational impacts of colonization, poverty, abuse, and disability without providing them with income, housing, and medical, educational, or other supports. We must absolutely reject the current tendency to jail women because of what they "need" and then release them to the street with little more than psychosocial, cognitive skills or drug abstinence programming, along with the implicit judgment that they are in control of and therefore responsible for their situations, including their own criminalization.

As social programs are undermined, the mantra of personal responsibility deflects attention from the structural roots of criminalized behaviors. If we are to challenge the prison buildup, we must create radical social and economic solutions. Instead of accepting band-aid attempts to patch up our increasingly inadequate social safety net with ineffective national or provincial initiatives on "crime prevention" and "homelessness," we must demand fundamentally different approaches. These must not presume that the most dispossessed people are potential criminals or that homelessness is a "choice" selected from a broad menu of options and opportunities. Rather than breakfast programs for poor children, we need to provide adequate income and nutrition for all. Instead of providing only limited shelters for those escaping violence or the street, we should demand adequate housing, healthcare, and social supports as a human right.

Rather than criminalizing and jailing the poor for welfare fraud and other survival crimes, if we were truly interested in encouraging people to be "prosocial" and mindful of others, criminally low welfare rates should result in the criminalization of those who craft, pass, and enforce the laws and policies, *not* those subjected to them. The human and financial costs of incarcerating women are too great. When money is spent on building and operating new prisons, provincial and federal governments have fewer resources for social programs and welfare support. We must demand that the monies currently being spent to watch, chase, catch, charge, prosecute, and jail people be reinvested in rebuilding our social, health, and education services. Only then will we break the cycle of criminalization and imprisonment.

References

1. Only women classified as minimum or medium security prisoners may have access to the thirty-bed Okimaw Ohci Healing Lodge (OOHL) for Aboriginal women prisoners. Aboriginal women represent 3 percent of Canadian women but 30 percent of women serving more than two years of imprisonment and approximately half of the women classified as maximum security prisoners. The Canadian Human Rights Commission, in a special report on federally sentenced women, indicates that the dynamic risk assessment tool used to classify prisoners discriminates against Aboriginal women. Canadian Human Rights Commission, *Protecting Their Rights: A Systemic Review of Human Rights in Correctional Services for Federally Sentenced Women* (Ottawa: CHRC, 2003), 25. As a result of discriminatory assessment and classification tools, coupled with the massive overrepresentation of Aboriginal women in Canadian prisons, only approximately 25 percent of Aboriginal women even have access to the OOHL.
2. *R. v. Neve*, Alberta Court of Appeal, June 29, 1999, 47.
3. Ibid.
4. Ibid. 71.
5. Ibid. 67.
6. Ibid. 56.
7. *Winnipeg Child and Family Services* v. G.(D.F.), [1997] 3 S.C.R. 925.
8. Christie L. Barron, *Giving Youth a Voice: A Basis for Rethinking Adolescent Violence* (Halifax, Nova Scotia: Fernwood Publishing, 2000).
9. Ann Campbell, "Girls' Talk: The Social Representation of Aggression by Female Gang Members," *Criminal Justice and Behavior* 11, no. 2 (1984): 139–156, 140.
10. Mark Totten, *The Special Needs of Females in Canada's Youth Justice System: An Account of Some Young Women's Experiences and Views* (Ottawa: Department of Justice, 2000), 51.

Definitions of Trafficking

"Trafficking" is most commonly attached to international conventions that sought to address the early twentieth century emergence of women as cross-border migrant workers on the world stage, yet since the midnineteenth century feminist definitions have been central to international conceptualizations. Today, two main currents in feminism are important to contemporary debates and the framing of the issue. One traces to Western/Euro-American middle-class antiprostitution feminist lobbies in the late nineteenth century around the "white slave trade," which reemerged in the late 1970s as "female sexual slavery." Lodged in a radical feminist analysis of social relations that prioritizes gender relations, this perspective attaches trafficking exclusively to prostitution, which in turn is viewed as the worst form of patriarchal oppression and the most intense form of victimization of women.[3] The central premise is that prostitution is "sexual harassment, sexual abuse, and sexual violence" and women, collectively, the victims of male violence. In other words, "when we bring our knowledge about violence against women and girls to an analysis of the global sex industry, what we see is . . . an institution of male dominance at its most virulent, a system of power and control that keeps women and girls inside it in conditions of perennial gang rape."[4] The sex industry, which coerces women into prostitution and holds women in sexual slavery, thus violates women's rights and bodily integrity.[5] Women, it is assumed, never freely enter into sexual relations that are not located in their autonomous sexual desire. Rather, they are seen to be always forced into prostitution—in short, trafficked —through the power and control men exercise over their lives and bodies. In this view, patriarchal institutions, such as the family, marriage, and prostitution, are defined for women as violence, rape, and abuse, and women who participate in such institutions are believed to be deceived victims of male power and privilege.[6] Moreover, a universal notion of "women's sexual autonomy and integrity" is posited in this perspective, creating an undifferentiated category of woman and a singular definition of women's sexual desire, leaving little space for varied experiences or specific cultural constructions of female sexuality. Women's liberation, universally, is believed can be obtained only through the abolition of institutions that uphold patriarchy. As Phyllis Chesler and Donna Hughes note about this feminist perspective: "American women launched a liberation movement for freedom and equality. They achieved a revolution in the Western world and created a vision for women and girls everywhere."[7]

The second approach to the subject, which I have elsewhere named a "Third World" or "transnational" feminist perspective, takes up trafficking as both a discourse and practice that emerges from the intersections of state, capitalist, patriarchal, and racialized relations of power with the operation of women's agency and desire to shape their own lives and strategies for survival and livelihood.[8] Patriarchy is viewed as one, but not the only or necessarily the primary, relation of dominance that conditions women's lives. Racism, imperialism, and international inequalities are taken equally to configure women's lives, and gender and sexuality are not assumed a priori to be universally agreed upon or singular constructs. Moreover, whereas patriarchy is taken to mean the degradation of femininities around the globe where women's labor and lives are, in variable ways, constructed in hegemonic discourses as less valuable than those of men and in the service of masculine sexual interests, and where women are often defined by and treated by the state as second-class citizens or as property of men, women are not simply located as victims of terrifying or paralyzing male power or as a homogeneous group. Rather, they are co-located in this perspective as agentic, self-determining, differentially positioned subjects who are capable of negotiating, complying with, as well as consciously opposing and transforming relations of power, whether these are embedded in institutions of slavery, prostitution, marriage, the household, or the labor market. Female agency and activity, in such a perspective, may then present themselves in various ways, sometimes reinscribing, other times contesting, masculine sexualized dominance and control, depending upon specific conditions, histories, and cultural contexts.[9] Furthermore, it is understood that this agency can at times be attached to income-generating or survival strategies that involve sexualized energies and parts of the body, thus is comparable to other types of productive labor, and as such is defined as "sex work," although it is cautioned that any analysis of sexual-economic activities require careful, contextualized, and historicized analysis.[10] Nevertheless, by taking agency and sexualized labor into account, engagement in sex industries and sex work abroad appear as possibilities that women willingly or consciously undertake within specific cultural, national, or international parameters. Thus, rather than conceptualizing prostitution itself as an inherent violence to women, it is the working and living conditions women may find themselves in once in the sex trade and the violence and terror that accompany travel into, and work in, an informal or underground sector that are taken to violate women's rights and are seen to constitute trafficking.

Aside from the media hyperbole that surrounds the issue of trafficking, the transnational feminist perspective is confirmed by empirical research on migration, work, prostitution, and activities in other informal or underground activities. Situations in which women are abducted or kidnapped, chained to beds in brothels, and held as sex or other types of slaves are rarely documented. Rather it is within labor recruitment and migratory processes and/or in work sites at the destination that coercion, extortion, physical violence, rape, deception, and detention take place. Debt bondage and contracted but "bound" or forced labor are also far more common occurrences than slavery, despite the attempts by many researchers to define the issue as slavery.[11] Contemporary forms of forced labor in sex industries, which includes aspects of consent and agency on behalf of the worker, are validated by research that documents active participation in cross-border migrations by the "victims"—that, for example, women and girls consciously and willingly seek to move abroad in order to improve their lives and those of their families. What these actors often do not know, or sometimes tacitly accept, are the dangers of underground routes they have to take to cross a border; the financial costs; the type of activities; the working and living conditions on arrival; the high level of dependence on a particular set of recruiters, agents, or employers; the health risks; the duration of the job; their criminalized status once in an overseas location; the enforcement violence; and/or periods of detention or incarceration they may face. Most "trafficked persons," it has been documented, express some personal desire to migrate, and about half of women in the global sex trade appear to be conscious of the fact that they will be involved in some form of sex work prior to migration.[12] The criminalization of prostitution, however, exacerbates the violence migrant women experience at the hands of recruiters, smugglers, employers, police, immigration officials, or wardens of detention centers, jails, or prisons, among whom the triple stigmas of criminal, whore, and immigrant promote intense disrespect and inhumane treatment. "Trafficking of women," from such a perspective, is defined as "all acts involved in the recruitment and/or transportation of a woman within and across national borders for work or services by means of violence or threat of violence, abuse of authority or dominant position, debt bondage, deception or other forms of coercion."[13]

From such a feminist perspective, the global sex trade is one site where trafficking occurs, yet is not the only one, and in the early twenty-first century is seen to be shaped in various ways by hegemonic and local patriarchies, globalized capitalism, and the widening gaps between the "haves" and the "have nots," as well as reconfigurations of empire in the early twenty-first century that reinscribe international hierarchies around notions of racial, religious, and national difference. The abuse of rights and liberties of women, men, boys, and girls in sectors that require unskilled or semiskilled nonsexual labor, such as domestic service, agricultural and manufacturing work, or sport and entertainment, then also becomes relevant to the analysis and has been taken up in new analyses of slavery and international criminal activities that violate legal systems of governance and citizenship (such as smuggling).[14] This notion of trafficking also becomes relevant to analyses of the regulation of (im)migrants' and women of color's labor and lives in postindustrial nations and to the examination of how governments seek to control and discipline these population within national borders. In sum, this definition rests upon notions of coercions, force, and violence, or threat of violence, that are embedded in processes and conditions in which women and men today move around the world and work, in their search for social and economic security, and that are circumscribed by racist and sexist national laws and practices that govern and control transnational flows of labor.

The Twenty-First Century International Antitrafficking Framework

Since the turn of the century, certain international developments around the issue of trafficking have greatly influenced the ways in which the subject is understood, the type of research taking place—feminist and other, and the kinds of projects and interventions initiated by nongovernmental organizations (NGOs) and government and intergovernmental agencies. In the rest of this chapter, I use the 2000 UN Convention on Transnational Crime as the general framework and specifically the Victims of Trafficking and Violence Protection Act passed by the United States in the same year to examine the new developments in state antitrafficking discourses and implications for migrant sex workers.

The most obvious shift from the previous, international UN approach to trafficking is that since 2000 it has become explicitly linked to efforts to tackle all types of organized criminal activities that cross national borders. Thus, whereas since the early twentieth century the UN convention was primarily focused on the international sex trade, this was replaced in 2000 by a protocol that supplements the Convention on Transnational Crime. The earlier, stand-alone trafficking convention was thus dissolved and trafficking subsumed under the heading of crime. The trafficking of persons, especially women and children, is also located in the new convention as akin to the trafficking of drugs and weapons and defined as of almost equal magnitude, taking place for a range of industries only one of which was the sex industry. Antitrafficking in this framework is synonymous with a war on international criminal activities, defined as the movement of persons, weapons, or drugs that defies or circumvents legal boundaries and borders. Simultaneously, the link to legislation to curb trafficking—through immigration control—is more explicit and visible, where governments in the global North increasingly express concern that the actions of traffickers and migrant smugglers interfere with orderly migration and assist others to circumvent national immigration restrictions.[15] Although this is not necessarily a new dimension and has been recognized as a feature of UN policy prior to 2000, it is one that has gained significance since the turn of the twenty-first century and sits unapologetically at the very heart of the mainstream, contemporary trafficking legislation and international antitrafficking discourse. Nevertheless, the protocol also requires that "states that ratify it take some steps to protect and assist trafficked persons" with full respect for their human rights and criminalizes third-party involvement in prostitution (the "exploitation of the prostitution of others") when this involves cross-border and transnational activities.[16] The UN framework does not criminalize all prostitution, to allow for differences in national legislation on the issue.

The new United Nations International Convention Against Transnational Organized Crime was agreed upon in November 2000, has been signed by some 140 member states, and took effect on September 29, 2003. It is supplemented by three protocols—one on the smuggling of migrants, a second to "Prevent, Suppress and Punish Trafficking in Persons, Especially Women and Children," and a third that addresses illicit manufacturing of and trafficking in firearms. The antitrafficking protocol came into force on December 26, 2003. Simultaneously, many other international polices and national legislative initiatives have been taken around the world. These include new documents, policies, and guidelines by international bodies such as the International Organization for Migration (IOM), the International Labor Organization (ILO), the United Nations Children's Fund (UNICEF), and the UN High Commission on Human Rights, much of which focuses on the management of "irregular" international migration flows. The West African ECOWAS (Economic Community of West African States) Declaration and Action Plan on Human Trafficking, adopted in December 2001; the Law Against Human Trafficking passed by the Colombian Parliament in June 2002; the SAARC (South Asian Association for Regional Cooperation) Convention of January 2002; the ARIAT (Asian Regional Initiative against Trafficking) Regional Action Plan of March 2000; the European Union Council Directive on Short-term Residency Permits for Victims of Trafficking of February 2002; and the Philippines' Anti Trafficking in Persons Act, passed in May 2003, all tie into the umbrella framework of the UN Convention on Transnational Crime and signal a growing concern at the turn of the century by the international political community and national governments with unregulated migration flows and profitable, cross-border underground activities.[17]

Trafficking and Women from the Global South

The global hegemonic paradigm has a number of implications for migrant women from the global South. First, whereas concerns about women's human rights and violence against women were central to feminist agitation on the subject of trafficking, this is now completely overshadowed by state concerns for law enforcement and immigration control. Migrant women, defined as "trafficked victims," are more often than not treated as illegal immigrants under such priorities and arrested, detained, and deported. Research by Anti-Slavery International in ten countries concludes that despite the purported concern to "protect victims," government efforts "often lead to trafficked persons being swiftly returned to their home countries as undocumented migrants."[18] Indeed, the designers of the antitrafficking protocol state that "generally, developed countries to which persons are often trafficked have taken the position that there should not be a right [for the trafficked person] to remain in their countries."[19] Only those who agree to cooperate with the state to prosecute or apprehend their traffickers are allowed to stay. Thus, despite the often stated humanitarian concern with "protecting victims" in antitrafficking legislation and discourse, "trafficked victims" who end up in North America or Western Europe are usually expected to "go back home." Even in countries where some form of residence is granted to persons who have been trafficked, this usually extends for only a limited period or for the duration of the criminal proceedings. Such terms of residency have therefore been described as a "stay of deportation" rather than a form of residency.[20] Because of this tendency, growing numbers of migrant women of color add to the already large number of persons who are processed through criminal justice systems, which in a country such as the United States has reached record highs, with increasing numbers being detained or incarcerated for nonviolent crimes, such as illegal migration, drug use and trafficking, and sex work.[21]

Second, because of its attention to effects rather than causes, the new antitrafficking discourse is expected not to reduce trafficking significantly but to change some migration and work patterns and to push activities even further underground.[22] Migrant women and men who are trafficked are detained and deported for infringing upon national immigration laws (even though they may be "rescued") and are generally forced to return to the same conditions that initially prompted their move. They are once again exposed to the conditions that enable trafficking. Some "victims" thus end up being "retrafficked" or are put back in a situation that propels them to seek new avenues for migration. In some cases, on return home, governments have aided in their harassment, as is the case of the deportation of Nigerian women from Italy in 2000, many of whom were publicly paraded and shamed on their return.[23] In other cases, deported sex workers have been executed, as was the case documented by Human Rights Watch/Asia, where the Burmese military executed twenty-two human immunodeficiency virus (HIV)-positive sex workers after they had been forcibly repatriated from Thailand.[24] Efforts to avoid such abuse at the hands of the state will obviously take place, and undoubtedly migrant women and recruitment and employment agents try to find new avenues and channels in order to circumvent state abuse or efforts to send them back home. Moreover, as Anti-Slavery International observes, many so-called trafficked persons tend to define themselves not as "victims of trafficking" but as "migrant workers who have had some bad luck as a result of a bad decision" and consider "rescue" by state authorities "capture"—of the state not as a savior, but oppressor.[25] Indeed, in an operation in Southern Europe in 2003, 696 "victims of trafficking" were identified, yet only 67—about 10 percent—accepted offers of assistance provided by law enforcement officials.[26] It must then also be questioned whether antitrafficking efforts that require cooperation with state authorities serve as an attractive option for migrants. As one commentator remarks about the contemporary global antitrafficking frenzy, "When are anti-traffickers going to realize people don't want to be rescued, they want to be safe. They don't want to go back; they want to go on. . . ."[27] With strong evidence showing that immigrant women experience high levels of abuse, sexual assault, and brutalization at the hands of the law, such as border and community police, immigration officials, and detention center wardens, "rescue" by the state may not be desired, and confidence or trust in the authorities is weak. A search for avenues for people to obtain economic and social security that circumvents state legal boundaries and law enforcement authorities is therefore likely to continue rather than abate, and U.S. statistics illustrate that this trend is under way. Among the immigration offenders who were charged with unlawfully entering the country between 1996 and 2000, about 50 percent were "repeat offenders," indicating multiple attempts by almost half of the population to return to a country from which they had formerly been ousted.[28] Increasing restrictions on immigration in the contemporary global political-economic context are then also likely to increase the vulnerability of women and girls from the global South to being smuggled across borders, harassed at entry points, forced to work in undocumented status and sectors in "developed" economies, "rescued" by law enforcers, detained under laws as illegal immigrants or criminals, deported with a record as a lawbreaker, and exposed once again to the conditions that sent them out of their homes and communities in the first place. Trafficking, one could conclude, will increase as a result of state so-called antitrafficking efforts, continuing to swell the number of people classified as criminals in countries such as the United States, among whom women of color are the fastest-growing population.

Third, although it is clearly stated in UN policies that it is the pursuit of profit that creates and sustains human trafficking and is generally understood that it is the current global economy that produces particular flows of migrant workers, it is overwhelmingly international criminal gangs who are identified through the UN framework as the profit seekers and the main beneficiaries from trafficking. These gangs—invariably men—are then the "evildoers." International networks that supply undocumented workers into particular labor market sectors are, however, not the only exploiters and profiteers in the trafficking scenario. "Consumers" and the demand side of trafficked labor include men (and women) who purchase sex (clients), those who control and manage industries and businesses that employ undocumented labor, military apparatuses that depend upon "rest and recreation" to sustain the health and morality of the troops, as well as middle-class or professional households in need of child care and domestic service. These actors and institutions, however, are not the primary focus of attention by governments intent on halting trafficking. The narrow lens of the new antitrafficking approach and the skewed representation of migration are particularly evident for the United States. There, although it has been established that most of the trafficking occurs not for underground sex industries run by criminal elements but for sweatshops, farming, service, and domestic work that are attached to formal sectors of the economy, state and public attention is quickly drawn to groups of middle-persons who are held up as the "real" menaces—recruiting agents and those who assist others to move without legal documents or money—who are commonly identified as greedy, immoral men from the global South and postsocialist states. Thus, the first U.S. government report to document trafficking into the country identifies Mexican, African, and Middle Eastern families; Thai and Latin American traffickers; Russian, East European, and Italian organized crime groups and syndicates; Asian, Mexican, and Nigerian smuggling rings; the Canadian "West Coast Players"; Chinese triads; Hmong gangs; and so on as the primary agents who profit and benefit from trafficking.[29] Media and research reports on trafficking worldwide often reproduce this focus. This leaves uninterrogated corporations, businessmen, militaries, or elites who gain pleasure, power, and profit from the exploitation of undocumented labor and creates a new "demon" akin to the black drug dealer or Arab terrorist who not only is depicted as completely disrespectful of women but also is used to justify drastic punitive measures against populations of color.

The U.S. War on Trafficking

The U.S. 2000 Victims of Trafficking and Violence Protection Act replicates the previously described foci of the UN convention, albeit with more gusto. It explicitly recognizes that thousands of people move around the world each year and are forced to work in sweatshops, construction sites, brothels, agriculture, and domestic service. However, although it seems to displace attention from prostitution by identifying the root causes to include a number of factors, such as "greed, moral turpitude, economics, political instability and transition, and social factors," the act is specifically designed to address what it terms "severe forms of trafficking" and emphasizes "sex trafficking" (commercial sex acts that are "induced by force, fraud, or coercion") and child prostitution.[30] The specific attention to the apprehension and prosecution of those who facilitate women moving into the sex trade complements national laws that criminalize all acts of prostitution; thus, most involvement in prostitution within U.S. national borders is defined as a criminal offense. Furthermore, as a part of the act, the U.S. State Department has defined a set of "minimum standards for the elimination of trafficking" and has created a three-tier system to evaluate and rank the rest of the world, the results of which are reported annually in a Department of State TIP (Trafficking in Persons) report. The act also provides protection for those who are violated and abused by trafficking (the victims). Financial assistance is given for various projects and activities at the community, state, federal, and international level that support women and men considered vulnerable to trafficking, and a new, nonimmigrant "T-visa" was introduced in the United States in 2002 designed especially to protect "trafficked victims."[31] The visa allows a person who agrees to act as a witness against the person's traffickers to stay in the United States legally for up to three years, after which she or he may apply for permanent residency. It is, however, intended only for those who would suffer "extreme hardship" or harm if returned to their home countries and is wholly contingent upon whether the persons cooperate with the law.

The U.S. act was brought into existence under the Clinton Administration cloaked in a mantle of humanitarian concerns for the rights of, especially, women and children, who were seen to be in great danger at the hands of organized gangs of smugglers. Nevertheless, with the change of administration and under the conservative, hypermasculinist leadership of Bush Jr., the U.S. State Department has stripped the act of any humanitarian pretense and uses it to pursue an aggressive policy to rid the world of what it sees as internationally organized criminal gangs, to curb irregular immigration into the United States, and to step up its efforts to abolish prostitution. Support for victims is a secondary consideration.[32] This inattention for the victims perhaps also explains why, despite the fact that the U.S. government estimates that around 50,000 persons are trafficked into the United States each year and that in 2000 approximately 7 million undocumented persons resided in the country, by mid-2003 only 200 applications for a T-visa had been filed, 24 granted, and 4 denied.[33]

It is, however, the three-tier system that has raised the most issues and problems. In the first instance, the United States exempts itself from any monitoring, and perhaps just as unsurprisingly, the countries that are placed in Tier 1, which are hailed as complying most fully with the standards, are in most cases destination or "consumer" countries—primarily "developed" nations.[34] Furthermore, the act stipulates that sanctions be placed on other governments if they fail to comply with the U.S. standards, such as "the termination of non-humanitarian, non-trade related assistance" and "opposition from the U.S. to assistance from international institutions" such as the IMF and the World Bank.[35] From October 1, 2003 such sanctions would be in operation.[36]

To compound this problem, the standards set by the United States were constructed in a completely unilateral and uninformed fashion. According to Anne Gallagher, former advisor on trafficking to the United Nations High Commissioner on Human Rights, although the U.S. State Department claimed widespread consultation in constructing the minimum standards, few key persons who were long involved and are widely held as the experts in the field of trafficking were consulted. In addition, she points out, the act made no provision for a country that may be accused of noncompliance to respond to the charge.[37] This problem, although softened in the 2003 U.S. State Department annual trafficking report by the claim that "all or part of the Act's sanctions can be waived," does not erase the premise that economic sanctions can be unilaterally imposed and is exacerbated by the striking fact that evaluations of countries are based on very scattered or ad hoc evidence of trafficking and a lack of analysis.[38] Human Rights Watch concludes, for example, that the annual report fails "to meaningfully evaluate state efforts to combat trafficking in persons" and is "Undercut by Lack of Analysis."[39] This organization goes on to note "the State Department consistently credits countries for their efforts to combating trafficking even when they have not passed legislation criminalizing all forms of forced labor as trafficking or when they have failed to sign or ratify the Protocol. . . ."[40] In other words, only select situations seem to be worthy of scrutiny and consideration under the Bush regime. This is perhaps not so surprising, when one can read in the TIP reports that the purpose of the ranking and reporting by the U.S. State Department is to serve "as a major diplomatic tool for the U.S. Government" and that waivers for the sanctions can be made "upon a determination by the President that the provision of such assistance to a government would promote the purposes of the Act or is otherwise in the national interest of the United States." Although these criteria are not emphasized or foregrounded as important selection criteria, they do reveal the underlying purposes of the act—to support U.S. national and international interests. The claim to be objectively documenting and evaluating abuse and hyperexploitation is, indeed, thinly masked. As Malarek describes, a political jockeying takes place behind the scenes around classifications in the U.S. three-tier system, through which, for example, the United States backed off a plan to crack down on trafficking and reclassified certain countries' efforts to avoid imposing sanctions on Israel, Russia, South Korea, and Greece.[41] Concurrently, George W. Bush Jr. determined to impose sanctions on Burma, Cuba, and North Korea, a move that is also viewed as ideologically and politically motivated rather than rooted in hard facts about trafficking, given the status of these countries in U.S.–foreign relations.[42] Similarly, in the case of Iran, which was placed in the lowest tier in 2002, the U.S. State Department acknowledged that no information was available for that country with respect to some aspects of its law enforcement.[43] The arbitrary use of evidence and the unsystematic collection of data have therefore led analysts to conclude that some nations will be punished "only on the basis of insufficient evidence." The fact that Iran along with many countries with majority Arab and/or Muslim populations, such as Indonesia, the United Arab Emirates, Afghanistan, Bahrain, Lebanon, Sudan, Qatar, Turkey, and Saudi Arabia, were all placed in Tier 3 in 2002, and thus were defined by the U.S. State Department as sanctionable, also strongly suggests a link in the 2002–2003 U.S. state policies on trafficking with its war on terrorism that targets the Muslim and Arab worlds.

Critique has also been voiced about statistics used to support claims of trafficking and upon which the global evaluation and assessment rests. The U.S. State Department begins its 2002 TIP report with the statement, "Over the past years, at least 700,000 and possibly as many as four million men, women and children were bought, sold, transported and held against their will in slave-like conditions," yet the inaccuracy in figures that amounts to millions can hardly be a basis for any precise conclusions, let alone a ranking of "good and bad" nations. The lack of any statistics to support the ranking of countries according to their antitrafficking achievements is compounded by discrepancies in definitions of trafficking, where in some instances all prostitution is equated with trafficking, in others it is not. Figures on trafficking remain extremely inaccurate, and time and again it is heard that "numbers are not available" or that no statistics exist on the matter.[44] Many who have been involved in research and activism around undocumented migration and forced labor situations for a number of years are acutely aware that much more is not known than is actually empirically documented. The "facts," as one expert researcher notes, are based on information from small-scale qualitative research projects and anecdotal evidence. To date, it is argued, it is unknown how estimates are arrived at and how trafficking has been measured. In short, "we simply don't know."[45] Likewise, according to most research on trafficking, cases of kidnapping for the purposes of forced prostitution are rarely documented. The inaccuracies in figures and discrepancies in evidence should be cause for extreme suspicion of the reliability of the research, yet when it comes to the subject of criminalized and underground sectors of the global economy, few eyebrows are raised and figures are adopted without question. However, on the basis of tenuous and often tendentious reports, political favoritism, diplomacy, and U.S. State Department interests, as well as a lot of media sensationalism, the United States has created an "authoritative" instrument, backed by a threat of sanctions, to eradicate "trafficking" from the rest of the world. U.S. imperialism, it would appear, is firmly embedded in the new act, legitimized by the UN framework. Only those victims who agree to cooperate in this imperialist construction are promised any support or protection.

Implications for the Global Sex Trade

The new international government antitrafficking crusade has profound implications for the women in the global sex trade. The contradictions that have been created through the U.S. act, legitimized by the broader UN protocol, in which the "good nations" in Tier 1 are the primary consumers and violators of trafficked labor yet are not scrutinized due to their placement at the apex of the global hierarchy, place sex workers the world over in danger. For example, since the early 1990s its has been well documented that thousands of migrant Filipina and other Asian as well as some European women, many of whom were defined as "trafficked," have worked and still work at U.S. military bases in South Korea that are subject to U.S.–Korean control.[46] A "defacto policy of the U.S. military has resulted in a sort of collusion with local businesses, local government and military bases to support an entertainment/prostitution industry," concludes one reporter.[47] The boost given to the U.S. military as a consumer of such sexual labor remains, however, unquestioned or completely overlooked by the U.S. government, to the extent that in 2002, South Korea was moved into the position of "good nation" category of Tier 1 for what were described as "extraordinary strides" in combating trafficking.[48] In the Caribbean, in countries such as the Dominican Republic, Jamaica, and Cuba, North American citizens—male and female—engage local women and men in sexual relations while on vacation, compensating them for their time and energy with cash, gifts, travel, consumer items, and status. Sex tourism is a booming business contributing to the success of the tourism industry in the Caribbean today that is for the most part owned and controlled by multinational and U.S.-based companies and firms and which sustains the regional economy and the livelihoods of many women and men.[49] However, deceptions in the recruitment process to work at the tourist resorts, physical abuse by hotel and bar owners, managers, and clients, extortions, threats of violence to families, and police harassment condition some of the women's experiences as they enter the tourism sector to make a living.[50] In both places, despite the obvious benefit and pleasure that U.S. industries and its military and citizens derive, the current focus of the hegemonic antitrafficking paradigm combined with the specific exemption of the United States from monitoring its own and allied governments' practices allows a number of injustices to women to continue. In both the South Korean and Caribbean scenarios, Asian and Caribbean women are facing harm and violence engendered by the interests of the wealthy nations, yet this is ignored. It is appropriate to invoke Stiglitz's notion of "hypocrisy" of Western countries, with the United States as "one of the prime culprits" where, through globalization, the West ensures "that it garners a disproportionate share of the benefits at the expense of the developing world,"[51] and through which the new antitrafficking crusade is reproduced.

Whether prostitution is legal, criminalized, or tolerated under national law, the emphasis on transnational criminal activities and immigration controls, and on traffickers as evil, foreign or immigrant men in the UN framework, and more specifically in the U.S. act, places migrant women from the global South who are involved in the sex trade under extra scrutiny and exposes them to the dangers of being apprehended, harassed, detained, deported, and recycled back into underground, criminalized activities.[52] The panic over "trafficking in women" has conveniently helped to eclipse state-sponsored exploitation of migrant people and puts a "benevolent" and "paternalistic" face on border guards who are well known for their systematic abuse of migrants.[53] New attempts to recriminalize prostitution, such as in France, force the trade of sex even further underground, again placing sex workers in positions of criminality.

The framework also sustains a racialization of sex sectors. In the Netherlands the lifting of the ban on brothels in 2000 has allowed European Union citizens and Polish and some Newly Independent States citizens to work as independent entrepreneurs in legal businesses in the sex sector but continues to criminalize participation in the sex sector by women from countries from the South. In September 2000, for example, "at least 3,000" young Nigerian women awaited deportation from Italian prisons for having been involved in prostitution, and deportations of the women have continuously taken place since then. In March 2003, on one weekend alone, eighty-four "suspected prostitutes" were deported to Nigeria from Italy, joining the "several thousands" of other Nigerian women who have been deported from European countries such as Italy, Germany, and Belgium since the late 1990s.[54] In Canada, the legalization of exotic dancing, and the state construction of the "temporary worker" for foreign exotic dancers, has created two distinct classes of workers: one that has rights and is entitled to state protections, the other that is primarily constituted by Latinas and Asian women and is subjected to violence and exploitation from recruiters, employers, police, and immigration authorities. As one report concludes:

> Their condition as Temporary Foreign Workers puts them in a very vulnerable position as workers, where their ability to remain in Canada depends completely on the goodwill of their employer. This exposes them to physical and psychological abuse by club owners, managers and agents. This is further aggravated by the criminalization and social stigmatization that exotic dancers are subjected to by the Latino community and society at large, as well as the continued harassment by law enforcement officials.[55]

The racialization is underscored by the very title of the U.S. act. Trafficked women, who are primarily identified as from Asia, Africa, South and Central America, and the Caribbean, are defined as "victims," a label that invokes notions of helpless, meek, and passive subjects. African, Asian, Latina, and Caribbean women are in the discourse robbed of any agency or self-determination and different from the Western/Anglo-Euro sex worker, who in some contexts is a "legal" subject through citizenship and is generally assumed to be able to act independently. It continues the dichotomy that resides in various debates and approaches to prostitution around the world in which sex workers of the global North are positioned as actors and Third World women, including sex workers, are imagined as innocent, ignorant, and completely powerless and thus in need of rescue, assistance, and guidance by more "educated" or "enlightened" women and men in the North.[56] The image of "victim" that predominantly settles on Asian women and Latinas in the U.S. antitrafficking context, who are to be rescued from their brutal traffickers, also does nothing to challenge racist and orientalist stereotypes of men of developing, non-Western nations. The overrepresentation of Arab and Muslim nations at the bottom of the three-tier system furthermore reinforces the image of criminal, non-Western men who have no regard for the well-being of women and who are incapable of conducting their own affairs in a "civilized" fashion. It justifies global relations in which the United States and Western Europe are seen to hold the moral high ground in matters of gender and sexuality.

The sex trade is also the ready site for governments to catch criminals and thus to demonstrate quickly to the rest of the world, and particularly the U.S. government, that they are engaged in antitrafficking efforts. Raids on a suspected brothel or red-light district in a country where prostitution is criminalized can automatically produce a number of "illegal" undocumented migrant women and can quickly deliver "traffickers." For governments that strive to be classified as a "good nation" by the United States or those that avoid punishment (through military aggression, economic embargos, cuts in development aid, etc.), intervention in the sex sector is a quick and easy fix. In India, with a government anxious to prove that it is "combating terrorism," raids on brothels in Delhi have been justified as an antiterrorist strategy, as the red-light districts are primarily owned and operated by Muslims. Such attacks on sex sectors are convenient ways for a government to score immediate results on multiple fronts. In all instances, it is women, and predominantly poor women of color, and small-time middle-men who are harassed, detained, deported, prosecuted, or incarcerated.

Finally, the conflation of trafficking with prostitution that has occurred in the U.S. act has created space for the mobilization of antiprostitution sentiments and lobbies that seek to punish individuals or groups that do not adhere to the U.S. definitions of prostitution as a criminal act. Governments that permit the existence of sex worker rights organizations or that have decriminalized or legalized the sex trade are liable to be ranked by the United States as aiding and abetting in trafficking and are subject to sanctions and punishment by the U.S. State Department. NGOs and other local groups that support sex worker's rights are similarly subject to the termination of funds and aid through U.S. agencies. On January 15, 2003, U.S. Agency for International Development (USAID) field missions around the world received notice that organizations that advocated prostitution as an employment choice or supported the legalization of prostitution were under suspicion. The provision was part of a communiqué about USAID's new foreign policy under the Bush administration. It announced that funding would be cut to projects perceived as supporting "trafficking of women and girls, legalization of drugs, injecting drug use, and abortion." This stance is reiterated in the U.S. "war" on HIV/AIDS, where the U.S. Global AIDS Bill, signed into law by Bush in May 2003, prohibited funding for organizations that do not have a policy "explicitly opposing prostitution and sex trafficking."[57] Organizations that may work for and with sex workers and that do not condemn them for being in prostitution can no longer receive funding. Poor women, possibly HIV positive, and all women and men whose livelihood may depend upon some trade of sexual services and labor, whether as marriage partners, friends, or sex workers, and who either see or have no viable alternatives are thus branded as undeserving of assistance, compassion, or empowerment. Feminists who agitate against prostitution and who subscribe to the new trafficking framework are complicit with the new attempts to criminalize and punish women in the sex trade.[58] Certain radical feminist U.S.-based organizations, such as the Coalition Against Trafficking in Women (CATW) and the San Francisco–based Prostitution, Research and Education project, lobby the U.S. State Department to maintain the criminalization of prostitution in its antitrafficking efforts, to step up its activities to punish transnational organized criminals, and to oppose initiatives that seek to empower those women and men whose best alternatives or only source of livelihood may be to sell sexual labor.[59] Alliances between the U.S. State Department, the CIA, USAID, antiprostitution feminists, and Christian fundamentalists consolidate the imperial attack upon the world's poor.[60] Arguing for such alliances, Phyllis Chesler and Donna Hughes state, "feminists . . . should stop demonizing the conservative and faith-based groups," as such groups "have become international leaders in the fight against sex trafficking."[61] Some sex workers' rights NGOs are already beginning to feel the heat, and the work they engage in, to fight against the oppressions and injustices women in the sex trade face, is under threat. Nevertheless, despite the abuse and intimidation that many migrant sex workers face from antitrafficking lobbies, they are mounting significant campaigns. As one sex worker's rights activist notes:

Two migrant sex workers incarcerated in Canada following "rescue" raids publicly denounced their treatment in the media. They insisted they were not "sex slaves" and that the "raids" and their result were the worst thing to have happened to them since they arrived in Canada. Nigerian women who have been consistently deported from Italy, have been known to openly challenge policies and laws that seek to control their movement or incarcerate them, recently organized together under SWAN, the Sex Workers Alliance of Nigeria. . . . Others have taken a lesson from the feminist establishment and the Christian Right by creating alliances of their own with labor, migrant and human rights groups. . . . Sex worker groups in Bangladesh, India and Cambodia have agitated, sometimes by the thousands, under the banner of "Workers' Rights Not Sewing Machines". . . .[62]

Marches have taken place in various European cities denouncing antitrafficking legislation and campaigns. Likewise, sex workers' rights activists in Asia have taken action to counter the injustices embedded in the new trafficking paradigm adopted by "first-world feminists and women's NGOs who have now joined the UN workers and other international organizations" and call for a counterdiscourse and international support in fighting off the pressure that is increasingly hampering their efforts to empower and organize sex workers.[63]

Conclusion

Trafficking has a specific discursive history, and although lodged in the violence women experience in migration processes attached to their search for a livelihood and better economic and social conditions, is linked to the ways in which Western states and intergovernmental agencies attempt to control global flows of labor and women's sexuality. Panics around the "white slave trade" were important precursors to the contemporary discourse. By the start of the twenty-first century trafficking was explicitly attached to "wars" against transnational organized crime, terrorism, and HIV/AIDS, grounded in the contemporary round of globalization through which wealthy, powerful nations increasingly command the rest of the world to serve their interests and needs, and women and men from Asia, Africa, the Caribbean and Latin America, and former Soviet Union territories are subjected to increased monitoring, policing, criminalization, and control. The new trafficking discourse, embedded in the 2000 UN convention and taken to new heights by the U.S. State Department, has produced an ideology in which people, particularly women and children, of developing, postcolonial, Arab, and newly independent nations are located as pawns of greedy abusive men of their own cultures. The roles of corporate capital and the state in perpetuating this violence are, by and large, ignored. The main messages are about apprehending and punishing cross-border "criminals" and rescuing, in a chivalrous, paternalistic, or missionary fashion, helpless "fallen" women from violent men of non-Western, "rogue" or disorderly nations. The way in which it is framed by national governments, led "heroically" by the U.S. government, however, serves to deepen the level of violence, criminalization, and economic terror for many people around the world. The continued demand for cheap labor by corporations, state military apparatuses, and leisure and professional classes, which are wholly complicit in sustaining conditions of economic inequality, exploitative conditions, and the criminalization of poor people, goes unfettered and unchallenged in this new crusade. That a large proportion of those subject to this contemporary violence are women of color from the global South, who are ending up in inhumane and criminalized situations in wealthier parts of the world, must be of concern to us if we are intent on living in a century in which social and economic justice will reign. That some sex workers are demanding a critical examination of this discourse requires from those of us committed to social justice also to listen carefully to those whose lives are the material and subject of "trafficking."

References

1. The main ideas in this chapter were first presented at the conference "Practicing Transgression: Radical Women of Color for the 21st Century," University of California-Berkeley, February 7–10, 2002 and since then have been expanded and revised in a number of ways. I am grateful to a variety of people for providing insightful feedback and comments along the way and wish to thank especially the Toronto Transnational Feminist Reading Group, the Women's Studies faculty at Stony Brook University, Julia Sudbury, and Anna Louise Crago. These ideas also inform the framework of my forthcoming edited book, *Shifts in the Debate: New Approaches to Trafficking, Migration, and Sex Work in Asia*, which was inspired by the work of the Global Alliance Against Trafficking in Women (GAATW).

2. See for example, Donna J. Guy, *Sex and Danger in Buenos Aires: Prostitution, Family, and Nation in Argentina* (Lincoln: University of Nebraska Press, 1991); Marjan Wijers and Lin Lap-Chew, *Trafficking in Women, Forced Labor and Slavery-like Practices in Marriage, Domestic Labor and Prostitution* (Utrecht: STV, 1997); Change, *Combatting Trafficking in Persons: A Directory of Organisations* (London: Anti-trafficking Programme, 2003).

3. Kathleen Barry, *Female Sexual Slavery* (New York: New York University Press, 1984).

4. Dorchen A. Leidholdt, *Weakening the International Regime for the Elimination of Trafficking in Women* (New York, 2000).

5. Patricia H. Hynes and Janice Raymond, "Put in Harm's Way: The Neglected Health Consequences of Sex Trafficking in the United States," in *Policing the National Body: Race, Gender and Criminalization*, ed. J. Silliman and A. Bhattacharjee (Cambridge, Mass.: South End Press, 2002).

6. Kathleen Barry, *Female Sexual Slavery* (New York: New York University Press, 1984); Sheila Jeffreys, *The Idea of Prostitution* (Melbourne: Spinifex, 1997).

7. Phyllis Chesler and Donna Hughes, "Feminism in the 21st Century." *The Washington Post* February 27, 2004. Page B07.

8. Kamala Kempadoo, "Globalizing Sex Worker Rights," in *Global Sex Workers: Rights, Resistance and Redefinition*, ed. K. Kempadoo and J. Doezema (New York: Routledge, 1998); Kamala Kempadoo, "Women of Color and the Global Sex Trade: Transnational Feminist Perspectives." *Meridians* 1:28–51 (2001).

9. See also Wendy Chapkis, *Live Sex Acts: Women Performing Erotic Labor* (New York: Routledge, 1997).

10. Thanh Dam Truong, *Sex, Money and Morality: The Political Economy of Prostitution and Tourism in South East Asia* (London: Zed Books, 1990); Marjolein van de Veen, "Rethinking Commodification and Prostitution: An Effort at Peacemaking in the Battles over Prostitution." *Rethinking Marxism* 13:30–51 (2001); Maggie O'Neill, *Prostitution and Feminism: Towards a Politics of Feeling* (Cambridge: Polity Press, 2001).

11. Debt-bondage and indentureship are the most common forms of contemporary forced labor practices, and this is acknowledged by most "experts" in the field. See for example Hynes and Raymond 2002 and Kevin Bales, *Disposable People: New Slavery in the Global Economy* (Berkeley/Los Angeles: University of California Press, 1999).

12. See for example Elaine Pearson, *Human Traffic, Human Rights: Redefining Victim Protection* (London: Anti-Slavery International, 2002).
13. Wijers and Lap-Chew 1997. See also Siriporn Skrobanek, Nattaya Boonpakdi, and Chutima Janthakeero, *The Traffic in Women: Human Realities of the International Sex Trade* (London: Zed Press, 1997).
14. See for example Bales 1999 and David Kyle and Rey Koslowski, "Introduction," in *Global Human Smuggling: Comparative Perspectives*, ed. D. Kyle and R. Koslowski. (Baltimore: John Hopkins University Press, 2001).
15. Anne Gallagher, "Human Rights and the New UN Protocols on Trafficking and Migrant Smuggling: A Preliminary Analysis," *Human Rights Quarterly* 23:975–1004 (2001a).
16. United Nations, "The Protocol to Prevent, Suppress and Punish Trafficking in Persons (Summary)" (2000).
17. See the newsletter of the Global Alliance Against Traffic in Women (GAATW), *Alliance News* 18, July 2002 for the full coverage of these various plans and conventions.
18. Pearson 2002.
19. United Nations, "The Protocol to Prevent, Suppress and Punish Trafficking in Persons (Summary)" (2000).
20. The Anti Slavery 2000 report indicates that this is the case for the Netherlands. Janie Chuang notes that this pertains to the United States. See Janie Chuang, "Trafficking in Women: The United States as Global Sheriff," in *University of Toronto Feminism and Law Workshop Series* (Toronto, 2004).
21. See Anannya Bhattacharjee, "Private Fists and Public Force: Race, Gender and Surveillance," in J. Silliman and A. Bhattacharjee eds. 2002 and Syd Lindsley, "The Gendered Assault on Immigrants," in J. Silliman and A. Bhattacharjee eds. 2002; also John Scalia, "Bureau of Justice Statistics Special Report: Noncitizens in the Federal Criminal Justice System, 1984–94" (U.S. Department of Justice, Office of Justice Programs, 1996), John Scalia and Marika F. X. Litras, "Bureau of Justice Statistics Special Report: Immigration Offenders in the Federal Criminal Justice System, 2000" (U.S. Department of Justice, Office of Justice Programs, 2002).
22. Phil Marshall, "The Trojan Horse and Other Worries," Stop by Stop: Newsletter of the UN Inter-Agency Project on Trafficking in Women and Children in the Mekong Sub-region, Third Quarter (2001): 3.
23. PanAfrican News Agency, "3,000 Nigerian Prostitutes Await Deportation from Italy," September 14, 2000. Stop-traffic News: (http://fpmail.friends-partners.org/pipermail/stop-traffic).
24. UPI April 2, 1992. This matter has been further referred to in the commentary "Burma and the Role of Burmese Women" October 13, 1995. Stop Traffic News: (and by the Network for Sex Work Projects (NWSP), in the Report on the XI International Conference on AIDS July 7–12, 1996 (http://www.walnet.org/csis/groups/nswp/conferences/xiaids/xiaids_sessions3.html).
25. Pearson 2002.
26. David Binder, "Twelve Nations in Southeast Europe Pursue Traffickers in Sex Trade" *New York Times*, October 19, 2003.
27. Http://fpmail.friends-partners.org/stop-traffic/2002/002045.html.
28. Scalia and Litras 2002.
29. Amy Richard O'Neill, "International Trafficking in Women to the United States: A Contemporary Manifestation of Slavery and Organized Crime" (Center for the Study of Intelligence, DCI Exceptional Intelligence Analyst Program, U.S. Government, 1999).
30. U.S. Department of State, "Trafficking in Persons Report" (2002).
31. See the INS information on the T Nonimmigrant Application Process, January 24, 2002 (http://www.ins.gov/graphics/publicaffairs/factsheets/tvisa.htm).
32. See for example the critique by the Director of the Women's Rights, of Human Rights Watch in 2001, 2002, and 2003 (http://www.hrw.org/press/).
33. INS figures in 2003, provided by Ann Jordan of the International Human Rights Law Group, Washington, D.C.
34. Anne Gallagher, "Trafficking in Persons Report (Department of State, United States of America, July 2000)," *Human Rights Quarterly* 23:1135–1141 (2001b); Dimple R. Shah,

"Trafficking in Human Beings: The U.S. Department of State Issues 2002 Trafficking in Persons Report," *Migration Enforcement* 18 (2002).

35. 2001 TIP Report.
36. 2003 TIP Report.
37. See Gallagher 2001a; Gallagher 2001b.
38. For further discussions of the unilateralism and lack of evidence in the Trafficking and Violence Protection Act, see Shah 2002 and Chuang 2004.
39. Human Rights Watch, "U.S. State Department Trafficking Report Undercut by Lack of Analysis" (Human Rights Watch, 2003).
40. Ibid.
41. Victor Malarek, *The Natashas: The New Global Sex Trade* (Toronto: Viking Canada, 2003).
42. Presidential Determination with Respect to Foreign Governments Efforts Regarding Trafficking in Persons. Presidential Determination, No 2003–35. Released by the White House, Washington, D.C., September 9, 2003. For comments upon this determination see, for example, Knight-Ridder Tribune press release by Nancy San Martin under the heading "U.S. Sanctions Cuba for Human Trafficking: Action Called 'symbolic,'" that appeared in U.S. newspapers such as the *Miami Herald* and *Oklahoma Daily*, September 11 and 12, 2003.
43. 2002 TIP Report.
44. See, for example, International Human Rights Law Institute, "In Modern Bondage: Sex Trafficking in the Americas" (DePaul University College of Law, Chicago, 2002).
45. Phil Marshall, "The Trojan Horse and Other Worries," Stop by Stop: Newsletter of the UN Inter-Agency Project on Trafficking in Women and Children in the Mekong Sub-region, Third Quarter (2001): 3.
46. See for example Katherine H. S Moon, *Sex Among Allies: Military Prostitution in U.S.-Korea Relations* (New York: Columbia University Press, 1997).
47. Manila Bulletin, September 25, 2002.
48. U.S. Department of State, "Trafficking in Persons Report" (2002).
49. According to Polly Pattullo, *Last Resorts: The Cost of Tourism in the Caribbean* (Kingston: Ian Randle, 1996), tourism accounts for 30 percent of regional GDP and around 25 percent of employment (formal and informal sectors).
50. Amalia Lucía Cabezas, "Women's Work Is Never Done: Sex Tourism in Sosua, the Dominican Republic," in *Sun, Sex, and Gold: Tourism and Sex Work in the Caribbean*, ed. K. Kempadoo (Lanham: Rowman and Littlefield, 1999); Denise E. Brennan, "Everything Is for Sale Here: Sex Tourism in Sosúa, the Dominican Republic," Ph.D. dissertation thesis (Yale University, 1998).
51. Joseph E. Stiglitz, *Globalization and Its Discontents* (New York: W.W. Norton and Company, 2002).
52. See also Wendy Chapkis, "Trafficking, Migration and the Law: Protecting Innocents, Punishing Immigrants," *Gender and Society* 17, 6 (2003): 923–937.
53. Unpublished paper by Anna Louise Crago presented at the conference Mapping Insurgencies: Sex, Race and Globalization, Committee on Lesbian/Gay/Bisexual Transgender Studies, University of Arizona–Tucson, April 25–26, 2003.
54. Stop-traffic News, "Italy-Nigeria: 3,000 Nigerian Prostitutes Await Deportation from Italy," October 10, 2000 (http://fpmail.friends-partners.org/pipermail/stop-traffic). See also Cheryl Overs, "Unfair Cop," *New Internationalist*, no. 252, February 1994. Further, "Italy Deports 90 Nigerian Prostitutes," Agence France Presse, 9 March 2003.
55. Latin American Coalition to End Violence Against Women and Children, "Coming to Dance, Striving to Survive: A Study on Latin American Migrant Exotic Dancers" (Toronto, 2002).
56. Kempadoo 1998.
57. H.R. 1298, "United States Leadership Against HIV/AIDS, Tuberculosis and Malaria Act" signed into law on May 27, 2003 by President G.W. Bush.
58. See, for example, Ratna Kapur, "The Global War on Trafficking, Terror and Human Rights." *Alliance News*, July (2002): 20–25.
59. A spokeswoman of the CATW, for example, publically calls for "a countering of the pro-prostitution agenda" and vehemently denounces any feminist group or individual that supports sex worker rights (E-mail correspondence November 28, 2002 and April 8, 2003 from Donna Hughes).

60. For example, the U.S. President's cabinet-level Interagency Task Force on Trafficking in Persons is chaired by Secretary of State Colin Powell and includes Dr. Condoleezza Rice, National Security Advisor, Attorney General John Ashcroft, CIA Director George Tenet, Secretary of Health and Human Services Tommy Thompson, Secretary of Labor Elaine Chao, and USAID Administrator Andrew Natsios, and Laura Lederer, known best for her feminist initiative to "take back the night," is Deputy Senior Advisor to the Office to Monitor and Combat Trafficking in Persons, working in close cooperation with the Task Force ("Trafficking in Persons: A Modern-Day Form of Slavery" by Laura J. Lederer. Remarks at White House Conference on Missing, Exploited, and Runaway Children, Washington, D.C., October 2, 2002).

61. Chesler and Hughes 2004.

62. Crago 2003.

63. See public letter circulated by Josephine Ho, director of the Center for the Study of Sexualities, National Central University, Taiwan, on behalf of Zi-Teng sex worker rights organization in Hong Kong.

CHAPTER 4

The Prison-Industrial Complex in Indigenous California

STORMY OGDEN

I write this chapter from the position of a California Indian woman, a tribal woman of Yokuts and Pomo ancestry. I also write as an ex-prisoner and a survivor of colonization. At the beginning of the colonization process two tools of genocide were forced upon Native people: the bottle and the bible. Along with these tools the traditional ways of behavior and conduct of Native people were criminalized. State and federal governments defined Native Americans as deviant and criminal through such procedures as the Dawes Act. With the enforcement of these new laws, Native people were locked up in a spectrum of "punishing institutions," including military forts, missions, reservations, boarding schools, and, more recently, state and federal prisons.[1] Historically, the most brutal methods of social control have been directed at a society's most oppressed groups. In North America, the groups that are most likely to be sent to jail and prison are the poor and people of color. A large proportion of people who end up behind bars are indigenous. On any given day, one in twenty-five Native Americans are under the jurisdiction of the criminal justice system, a rate that is 2.4 times that of whites.[2] Native American women are particularly targeted for punishment. For example, Native American women in South Dakota make up 34 percent of the prison population but only 8.3 percent of the general population.[3]

Angela Y. Davis describes the prison-industrial complex as a complex web of racism, social control, and profit.[4] The experience of racial subordination, repression, and economic exploitation is not new to the Native people of these lands. From the missions to the reservations, California Indians have struggled for survival in the face of an array of brutal mechanisms designed to control and eliminate the region's first peoples. The prison-industrial complex was built on the ancestral lands of the indigenous people of this continent and has contributed to the devastating process of colonization. It is essential for prison scholars and activists to understand the colonial roots of the prison-industrial complex and to make visible the stories of Native prisoners.

My People/Our Lands

Prior to the arrival of Europeans, the area that came to be known as California had the largest indigenous population with the most diverse groups of any area in North America, including Yokuts, Pomo, Hupa, Shumash, and Miwok. Of all the Native cultures, Native California was perhaps the most diverse in ecology, social structure, and history. According to Rupert and Jeanette Costo, California Indians were the most highly skilled explorers of North America and enjoyed a sophisticated knowledge of their environment that they had developed over a period of thousands of years."[5]

The Pomo people occupied approximately seven widely separated localities in the coast ranges north of San Francisco Bay. Our main territory included parts of Mendocino, Lake, and Sonoma counties. The hallmark of our tribal identity existed in the Pomo language, which connected these geographically divided communities. The Yokuts inhabited a three-hundred-mile-wide range that included the San Joaquin Valley and adjoining foothills.[6] The Yokuts were agriculturalists and held the most fertile land in California. We were perhaps the most populous of the many diverse nationalities of indigenous California. Yokuts people who still retain the memory of our history maintain there were at least seventy tribal communities before contact with Europeans. Solidarity between the communities, villages, and tribal family groups was maintained through traditional ceremonies and economic exchange.[7]

Our elders tell us that the natives of California lived in well-ordered societies. Their governing bodies resided in their tribes and the people were guided by relationships that fixed the status and the position of every member. Every part of their tribal society was enriched and maintained through religious and traditional laws. There was no police force and no courts to enforce these laws and obligations because there was a strong belief and support for them from the people. Individuals accepted these laws, knowing that it ensured collective survival. When violations occurred, the rule was restitution instead of retribution. Exile from the tribe was an extreme penalty.

Contact with Europeans in California first occurred through the Spanish missions. Although today these buildings are seen as quaint historic landmarks, for Native people they symbolize terror and death. California Indians were forced off their land, hunted down, and brought to the missions, where they were used as slave labor. Those who resisted were tortured or killed, and the rape of Native women was commonplace. After the founding of the missions, California Indians faced encroachment by Mexican rancheros, who were prepared to use any force necessary to take native land. Native people were hunted down in a genocidal effort to clear the land for Mexican settlement. The Treaty of Guadalupe Hidalgo in 1848, which brought an end to the Mexican–American war, ceded California along with a large swathe of Arizona, Texas, and Nevada to the United States. Although the right of Mexican residents to retain their language and religion was guaranteed in the treaty, no such guarantee was made to Native peoples. Finally, in the 1880s, the Gold Rush, heralded by whites as a lucrative bonanza, drew hundreds of thousands of ruthless settlers to California. These miners and settlers plundered Native lands and raped Native women.[8] California Indians have spent generations fighting against these three waves of invaders. Our struggle has been threefold, for our ancestral land, religious rights, and, simply, the right to live. For Native women, the struggle has also been about the right to freedom from sexual assault. As Andrea Smith demonstrates, colonists depicted Native women as impure and therefore inherently rapeable. Colonization is therefore inextricable from the sexual violation of Native women: "As long as Native people continue to live on the lands rich in energy resources that government or corporate interests want, the sexual colonization of Native people will continue. Native bodies will continue to be depicted as expendable and inherently violable as long as they continue to stand in the way of the theft of Native lands."[9]

The Little Girl Who Grew Up to Be a Convict

The journey began for me at the age of five, when my mother put me into the back seat of our car and drove away from our home and my father. She was driving away from a marriage consumed by alcoholism and domestic violence. Mom thought she was taking us somewhere that would be safe. Little did she know that she was driving me toward a life of sexual abuse and violence at the hands of people who were supposed to love this little girl with the big dark Indian eyes.

The abuse started soon afterward, when the next-door neighbor's son started putting his hands down my panties. I remember telling my grandmother what was going on. She responded, "Now don't tell anyone about this or it will cause problems." But, I did tell and she was right; it did cause problems. It opened the door for my new stepfather and my grandmother's husband to start priming me for sexual abuse. From the ages of seven through ten the abuse began. Both of these men introduced me to adult comic books. What child doesn't like to read comics? My grandfather also started giving me alcohol. My stepfather would bathe me and put me to bed; over time he began to fondle me and "dry hump" me. One night he was caught outside my bedroom window watching me undress for bed. I remember seeing him through the window and his face was all distorted. It was not until recently that I put a name to what he was doing, "jacking off." The abuse from this man did not stop with me. He and my mother were always fighting and the fighting was extremely violent.

At the age of ten, I was well on my way to becoming an alcoholic. This was also the time that another family member began to abuse me, my mother. Her words still ring in my head: "You are just a dirty Indian like your dad, you are a no good half-breed, and you will grow up to be a drunken Indian just like your dad."

Half Breed
a word that has made me
a stranger in my own land

She would frequently throw hot coffee in my face or take her long nails and dig them into my flesh, trying to draw blood.

From the ages of eleven through thirteen, the verbal and sexual abuse elevated. I was given to my grandmother off and on to live, which played into the hands of my grandfather. He told me one time that if I ever wanted to know about sex to just let him know because he would teach me and even take me to get birth control pills. I was never allowed to live with my Dad, even though I cried and begged my mother to allow me to go to him. I was allowed to spend summers with him sometimes, but never the entire summer, just a few weeks at a time. It was always hard on me when I had to return to my mother's house.

All my women's role-models were white
They did not know how to deal with this Indian child
Who grew so dark in the summer
During the school year they would cut and perm that Injun hair
Putting me in pretty dresses and
Then telling me in soft hushed voices,
Your Dad is just a dirty drunk Indian and you will be just like him.

I never told my Dad what was going on at home because things at my Dad's house were not all that great. He was still drinking and abusing his new wife.

It was during this time that I started to abuse drugs and alcohol on my own. My home life was pure hell and it ran over into my school days. I was raped for the first time by four boys who went to my school. My best girlfriend watched as these boys tore off my jeans and menstrual napkin and proceeded to rape me one by one. I remember sitting in the bathtub in the cold water crying. No one was there for me, so I cleaned myself up and went to bed. After this happened I started running away from home and not going to school. I ended up in juvenile hall three times before I left home for good. I thought by running away that all the abuse would stop. But all I did was run to another life that was just as violent, if not more so.

From the ages of fourteen through nineteen I lived with a man who became my first husband. He was thirteen years older than I and was verbally, sexually, and physically abusive to me. I stayed with him because I had no place to go to; I could not return home. I finally did get the courage to run away from him but what I ran to was worse. My days and nights were consumed with alcohol, drugs, bars, and the back seats of cars, rapes, beatings, hospital visits for a broken arm, a gunshot wound, and to have an intrauterine device (IUD) surgically removed because I was raped with a cane. There were too many different men, too many empty bottles, and too many suicide attempts.

In my past I laid upon a strange bed in a hotel
Praying that I would not wake up in the morning.
At these times it was done as a ritual
Long hot showers, purifying my body,
Combing my long dark hair wrapping it into neat braids,
Singing my own death song.
Other times I would be sitting on the side of an empty bed,
Around me would be empty whisky bottles
And a shiny new razor blade in my hand.

At the age of twenty-two I was sentenced to five years in the California Rehabilitation Center at Norco. For me, imprisonment was just a new phase in the abuse.

The Prisonification of Indigenous Women

In the warmth of my fantasy
I awake to the cold gray walls
Of my reality.

"Ms. Ogden you are sentenced to five years which will be served at the California Rehabilitation Center in Norco." The words thundered in my mind as the judge read the sentence. This scenario is becoming more commonplace for women in the United States, especially for Native American women and women of color in general. Women are the fastest growing segment of the prison population.[10] Between 1980 and 1999, the number of women in California's prisons grew by

850 percent.[11] The majority are in prison for economic and drug-related crimes. Women of color are particularly affected. Nationally, African American women are imprisoned at 5.4 times the rate of white women and Latinas at double the rate.[12] As the number of women behind bars grows, the detrimental effects are felt by a whole generation of children because 80 percent of women in prison are the mothers of children under eighteen.[13]

Many of these incarcerated women are in California prisons. Since mandatory minimum sentencing laws went into effect in the mid-1980s, the California prison population has skyrocketed. The vast majority of women sentenced under California mandatory minimum laws are sentenced for nonviolent crimes, namely drug offenses. California now has the distinction of having the most women prisoners in the nation as well as the world's largest prison. The Valley State Prison for Women and the Central California Women's Facility, both located in Chowchilla in California's Central Valley, together house approximately seven thousand women.

Native Americans are more likely to come into conflict with the criminal justice system at an early age. This early involvement in the criminal justice system can be seen as one outcome of colonization. Indigenous tribes had their own systems of criminal justice long before the non-Indian came to these lands. Through storytelling, song, and dance, these rules and laws were passed on from generation to generation. The laws became customs and as customs they were ingrained in the very lifeblood of the people. Everyday behavior had its own rules of conduct, and these were understood and embraced by the people. In contrast, the U.S. criminal justice system in Indian country is complex and highly difficult to understand. Its governing principles are contained in hundreds of statutes and court decisions that have been issued in an incoherent way over a long period of time. Because of federal criminal jurisdiction over Indian lands, Native offenders are mainly incarcerated in federal prisons instead of state or local facilities.

The continuing role of the criminal justice system in colonization is visible in the large numbers of Native Americans, Native Hawaiians, and Alaskan Natives who have been convicted in the white man's courts for hunting, fishing, and subsistence gathering in accordance with their customs, which are intruded upon by the white man's laws. Those laws violate indigenous treaties and rights. Many Native Americans have also been targeted because of their political activism. American Indian Movement activists including Leonard Peltier who were targeted for neutralization by the FBI's (since discredited) COINTELPRO program remain behind bars.[14] More recently, Native youth activists and warriors in the United States and Canada have been imprisoned because of their involvement in defending Native burial grounds and sacred sites, claiming fishing and hunting rights, or opposing corporate exploitation of their lands.[15]

The Colonial Roots of Prison Labor

For five years, I worked as a clerk in the California prison system. Like a slave, I had no choice about the work I did, nor was I paid fully for my labor. The thirty-two dollars a month that I earned had to pay for overpriced feminine products, soap, shampoo, and toothpaste in the prison commissary. Prison labor, rooted in the history of slavery and colonization, plays an important role in the economics of incarceration. The prison-industrial complex has a two-fold purpose: social control and profit. Like the military-industrial complex, the prison-industrial complex interweaves government agencies with business interests that seek to make a profit from imprisoning the poor and people of color. Like any industry, the prison economy needs raw materials and in this case the raw materials are people—prisoners. Prisoners generate profits for the companies that build prisons and house prisoners. They also generate profits by providing a cheap, plentiful, and easily controlled workforce. In the post-emancipation years, prisons in the South recouped their expenses by leasing African American convicts to plantation owners, mine operators, and railroad companies. Imprisonment was designed to deliver a docile labor force and to punish, not to rehabilitate.[16] By the Great Depression, convict leasing was largely phased out and prisons gradually embraced the goal of resocializing prisoners to become productive members of society. In the past two decades, prisons in California have shed the pretense of rehabilitation in favor of large warehouse-style prisons that provide few opportunities for education or training and often keep prisoners in their cells for twenty-three hours a day. Instead, prisoners are exploited as a cheap source of labor, both to maintain the prison itself and to bring in income through prison industries. Prison wardens are clear that they are not here to rehabilitate but only to punish. Clearly, history is repeating itself.

Although commentators have identified the origins of prison labor in the enslavement of African Americans in the Southern states, the history of Indian slavery has largely been overlooked. If we are to map the origins of the prison-industrial complex in California accurately, we must look at the history of forced labor in the Golden State rather than further afield. Economic exploitation and forced labor are not new to Native peoples, especially the indigenous people of early California. For instance, although Indian slavery elsewhere in the United States was rare, California had a state law that codified it. In 1850, the California legislature passed the Government and Protection of the Indians Act, which can only be described as legalized slavery. The act provided for the indenture of "loitering, intoxicated and orphaned Indians" and forced regulation of their employment. It also defined a special class of crimes and punishment for these Indians. Under the act, California Indians of all ages could be "indentured or apprenticed to any white citizen."[17] Justices of the peace took jurisdiction over all cases by, for, or against Indians. Non-Indians could take any California Indian male under the age of eighteen or female under the age of fifteen before a justice of the peace, claim that the child had not been kidnapped, and acquire custody of the child and proprietorship over his or her earnings until he or she reached a certain age. A white man could give bond for the payment of the fine and costs of any California Indian convicted before a justice of the peace of an offense punishable by a fine and require the Indian to work for the white man until the fine was paid.

The law codifying Indian slavery was amended in 1860 to expand the scope of slavery to include adults. This new amendment stated that if a boy, already in servitude, was under the age of fourteen, he could be indentured until the age of twenty-five; and if he were between the ages of fourteen and twenty, he could be held until the age of thirty. This new amendment also included young women, who could be forced to remain in servitude until they were twenty-five years old. In the 1850s and the 1860s, there was such a constant demand for Indians as domestic servants that kidnappings and sales of Native women and children were commonplace.[18] These provisions in the state law resulted in the institution of a slave mart in Los Angeles where captives were auctioned off to the highest bidder for "private service."[19] Although the slave mart has since disappeared, UNICOR, the California prison industry authority, continues to sell captive labor to the highest bidder.

Conclusion

Just as alcoholism has touched the life of every Native person so has the U.S. criminal justice system, in particular the prison system. As Luana Ross points out, most Native people have either been incarcerated themselves or have a relative who is in prison.[20] The outcome of this high rate of imprisonment can only be described as genocidal. The Native world has been devastated by foreign laws that were forced upon us, and the number of jailed Natives is a chilling reminder of this fact. Native people are being locked up at alarming numbers in their own ancestral homeland. For the indigenous women of North America, sexual assault and imprisonment are two interlocking violent colonial mechanisms. The criminalization and imprisonment of Native women can be interpreted as yet another attempt to control indigenous lands and as part of the ongoing effort to deny Native sovereignty.

What was my crime, why 5 years in prison?
Less than $2,000 of welfare fraud
What was my crime?
Being a survivor of molestation and rape
What was my crime?
Being addicted to alcohol and drugs

What was my crime?
Being a survivor of domestic violence
What was my crime?
Being an American Indian woman.

References

1. Luana Ross, *Inventing the Savage: The Social Construction of Native American Criminality* (Austin: University of Texas Press, 1998), 5.
2. Lawrence A. Greenfeld and Steven K. Smith, *American Indians and Crime* (Bureau of Justice Statistics, 1999, NCJ 173386).
3. Government Research Bureau, *Justice in South Dakota: Does Race Make a Difference?* (State of South Dakota, 2002).
4. Angela Y. Davis and Cassandra Shaylor, "Race, Gender and the Prison Industrial Complex: California and Beyond." *Meridiens*, 2, 1 (2001): 1–24.
5. Rupert Costo and H. Jeannette Costo, *Natives of the Golden State: The California Indian* (Riverside: The Indian Historian Press, 1995), 3.
6. F..F. Latta, *Handbook of the Yokuts Indian* (Bakersfield: Bear State Books, 1949), v.
7. Latta 101.
8. Costo xix.
9. Andrea Smith, "Not an Indian Tradition: The Sexual Colonization of Native Peoples." *Hypatia*, 18, 2 (2003): 70–86.
10. Justice Policy Institute, *New Prison Statistics: Nation's Use of Incarceration on the Rise Again*, July 25, 2003. Available from http://www.justicepolicy.org.
11. Center on Juvenile and Criminal Justice, *California Prison Growth*. Available from http://www.cjcj.org.
12. Justice Policy Institute 2003.
13. Joanne Belknap, *The Invisible Woman: Gender, Crime and Justice* (Belmont, CA: Wadsworth Publishing Company, 1996).
14. Ward Churchill and Jim Vander Wall, *The COINTELPRO Papers: Documents from the FBI's Secret Wars Against Dissent in the United States* (Cambridge: Southend Press, 2002). COIN-TELPRO was the FBI's counterintelligence program. Under the leadership of J. Edgar Hoover, the program sought to target and neutralize key leaders of the Black Panthers, American Indian Movement, and other radical movements during the 1960s and 1970s.
15. Little Rock Reed, *The American Indian in the White Man's Prisons: A Story of Genocide* (Taos: Uncompromising Books, 1993), 31.
16. Scott Christianson, *With Liberty for Some: 500 Years of Imprisonment in America* (Boston: Northeastern University Press, 1998), 181–183.
17. Jack Norton, *Genocide in Northwestern California: When Our Worlds Cried* (San Francisco: The Indian Historian Press, 1997), 44.
18. Norton 44.
19. Norton 207.
20. Ross 1.

CHAPTER 5

Through the Eyes of a Strong Black Woman Survivor of Domestic Violence

An Australian Story

ROBBIE KINA

I met Tony while working as a prostitute on Melbourne Street in South Brisbane in 1985. After four or five months we moved in together. This was my first really serious relationship and he was the first man I had lived with. The violence began almost immediately, after we had been together a week. I used to get beaten with a clenched fist or kicked with his steel cap boots all the time, receiving bruising on all parts of my body and face. I'd have a black eye one day and then the next day I'd have the other one bruised and black as well. A few times I tried to defend myself by hitting back but my strength was no match for his and I'd get flogged even worse.

He was always drinking throughout the three-year-long relationship. I had stopped drinking a year before his death, because he gave me a choice to get off the grog or lose him. His drunken rages resulted in him constantly bashing me for the slightest of reasons, many of which had nothing to do with me. I used to worry: "Did I iron his shirt properly," or "did I leave the toothpaste cap off the tube." He was a regular gambler. If he lost on the races he'd bash me. He controlled our finances, taking my money to support his drinking and gambling habits. He threatened to kill me on several occasions. He'd boast how he put women he was living with in the hospital.

My repeated attempts to leave him and escape the violence began early into the relationship. My brother Cliff kept on telling me to leave; sometimes I'd take off to Cliff's place. But a few days later Tony would find me and take me back home where he'd bash me up badly again. He'd threaten to break my arms and legs if I didn't go with him even though I had no intention of going back with him. But I'd go because I was so frightened of him and of what he was capable of doing to me or my family

I came to believe that I couldn't survive on my own. He'd always promised that everything would be alright and that he wouldn't hit me anymore. He was always good to my family, which made my claims of his violence seem like nothing at all.

My biggest regret was when I stopped going to my doctor because of the violence and my shame of what I was being subjected to. I knew that the doctor would know straight away that I was being bashed, raped, and anally raped. There wasn't anything that I didn't tell my doctor. Tony would anal rape me because I was always bleeding heavy with my periods, and I'd have them for three weeks running. My body was so out of whack. But since I've been in my new relationship my body has settled right down and my periods only go for four days.

On a few occasions the police were called by a lady in the same block of flats. Having heard that the police were on their way Tony stopped bashing me and was calm when they walked in. They asked me if I wanted to press charges and I told them no, but what I didn't tell the police was that I was so terrified of Tony and it would have made him even angrier than he already was.

When Tony was working night shifts he would tie me up to the bed so that I couldn't sneak out of the house. This was because one night I went out after he left for work and he got home in the morning before me. This is when my life of hell began. One night he said to me: "I will just have to teach you a lesson." He started to take me to work with him on the construction site that is now known as Toowong village shopping center. Every time I see it or pass by it I shake inside and try hard not to let it show just how much it upsets me, because that is where Tony and his mates repeatedly raped me and did whatever they wanted with me. After that he'd always say to me: "Who would want you now? Slut." This shameful and dirty feeling made me lose confidence in myself and my ability to ever survive on my own.

I remember the morning of the stabbing he was saying: "I bet your fourteen-year-old niece takes it up the arse" and then anal raping me brutally and bashing me. When he finally released me I wanted to leave the house as I couldn't take any more, but I knew that like my other attempts to leave, this one was also doomed. As I left the room I heard the kitten meowing so I decided to feed it. As I was feeding it my eyes caught sight of the kitchen knife. I grabbed it and went back into the room where I stabbed Tony.

The police kept on asking me if I was drinking. I told them that I hadn't been. While I was in the watch-house a doctor from the aboriginal and islander medical center came and took photos of the bruises on my neck and back. Later

I asked my solicitor for her opinion on the photos; she replied that the bruises were not relevant. The evidence produced in court at my committal supports my account of the killing and trial except for the brutal anal rape. When I was interviewed by my barrister about what had actually happened I was unable to tell him about the rape and abuse that Tony had subjected me to and which had driven me to the breaking point. I just couldn't talk about it. So traumatized was I by the memory of my unbearable suffering and by the thought of disclosing my shameful secret that I preferred to face a murder charge knowing that the sentence was life imprisonment.

I had been encouraged by my legal people to plead diminished responsibility in order to reduce the charge from murder to manslaughter. This would have said that I was drunk. I said no I wasn't drinking and I wasn't on any drugs at the time. I didn't believe that the legal people were interested in the history of physical abuse because the present laws of provocation and self-defense do not accommodate situations of domestic violence. I sought counseling from a social worker just before my trial. I was confused as to how to plead. Although a report was submitted to the trial judge, the social worker was not called to give evidence on the dynamics of domestic violence and its relevance to my actions.

I can remember talking to a number of lawyers and I found it difficult to talk to them about the rape.[1] I spent nine months on remand in prison and had little contact with my lawyers. I was told that any application for bail would be refused on the grounds of my previous convictions. Witnesses called by the prosecution were the only evidence presented as to injuries that I had sustained at the hands of Tony previously. They included family members and housemates who could testify that on the morning of the stabbing thumping and crying were heard coming from the bedroom. My fourteen-year-old niece had made a statement to the police, which was handed up at the committal. It included information that Tony had tried to kill me two years before and that he was always bashing me. She said that I had a puffed face and a black eye a few days before the stabbing. However, my niece was not called to give evidence.

At the trial, my defense chose not to call any witnesses. I didn't give evidence regarding the violence. Without the benefit of the courts considering these facts and issues, the defense case for manslaughter based on a defense of provocation proved unsuccessful. The judge did not accept that there was sufficient evidence of provocation to instruct the jury as to that defense. Although the judge remarked that temporary loss of self-control may be occasioned by fear, there was no proper basis on which the jury could consider the question of whether the retaliation was to the provocation offered. After a four-hour trial the jury took fifty-eight minutes before finding me guilty of murder.[2] A local newspaper reported that it was the shortest murder trial in history.

An appeal was lodged nine days later on the grounds that the trial judge had erred in failing to permit the jury to consider the defense of provocation and that I didn't call any witnesses on my behalf and was advised not to give evidence by both my solicitor and barrister. The court of criminal appeal dismissed the appeal on the grounds that there was no evidence to draw the conclusion of the existence of provocation. In those early days the courts didn't want to know about domestic violence and no one would talk about it.

So back in 1988 I was sitting in my prison cell doing a life sentence for the murder of my violent de facto husband. I was silent, ashamed, and feeling dirty about what Tony used to do to me. I kept it all inside, wouldn't say a word about it. Then one day David Goldie from ABC television came in to film a documentary called *Without Consent*. He spoke to me and another lifer about the injustice that was done to us because some of the male prisoners convicted of double murder or repeat violent crimes were doing shorter sentences than us. When people from all over Australia saw my story on television they rallied for my freedom. I received so many letters of support it made me want to fight for justice.

My beautiful family loved and stood by me no matter what, even though I tried to push them away and told them not to come and visit me. But every weekend there they all were waiting for me on our visits. I didn't want them to see how much pain and hurt I was going through, but I didn't stop to think just how much suffering they were going through as well. I guess that I was kind of selfish, but while I was inside that prison I had so much hate, anger, and rage inside me that I didn't think I would ever be capable to love again because of all the bitterness deep down in me.

Then ABC's television show *7.30 Report* did a story on my experience of domestic violence. *Four Corners*, another television show, also did a story on me focusing on the excuse for murder. I think that this was the turning point for me because after it aired lawyers started to take on my case and went for a second appeal in 1993. I spent six years behind prison bars while the appeal was going through and while I waited for a court hearing date. I felt so alone, scared, and frightened. I didn't know how I was going to face that horrible courtroom again and the questions they would be firing at me, knowing that they know about all the things Tony did to me, like rape and anal rape and then letting his mates take turns with me. I'd always have black eyes and a bruised face and Tony would say I was fat and ugly. The strangest thing was that I believed him and I kept on thinking that up until five months after I was a free black woman.

On Friday, November 27, 1993, I went up to Cherbourg for an ex-inmate's funeral. The prison bus didn't get back until 9:30 P.M. and while I was walking up to my cell an officer gave me a fax from my lawyers that said I was required at court the following Monday. All weekend I was a nervous wreck. On Sunday I don't know why but I started packing up my gear and putting aside the things I wouldn't need. I told my niece: "If I don't come back tomorrow, take this box and put it in between the gates and the rest of my stuff, share it out amongst yourselves." All that night I had butterflies in my guts I was so scared of the outcome the next morning.[3] I was so afraid of the appeal that I was thinking of hanging myself. I already had a length of rope hidden, but I didn't want to be just another black death in custody.[4] Also I kept thinking of my loving family and friends and what it would do to them.

Ten years later, I work at Sisters Inside as an Aboriginal support worker for women in prison. Little has improved for black women since I was freed. In fact, there are even more women inside today. The only difference is that there was nothing to support these women before, but now black women have us— Sisters Inside.[5]

References

1. For a discussion of the interactions between white lawyers and aboriginal defendants with particular reference to this case, see Linda Hancock, "Aboriginality and Lawyering," *Violence Against Women* Vol. 2 Issue 4 (1996): 429–447.

2. For an analysis of the trial, see Diana Eades, "Legal Recognition of Cultural Differences in Communication: The Case of Robyn Kina," *Language and Communication* (1996): 215–231.

3. In 1993, on appeal, the Supreme Court of Queensland set aside Robbie's conviction as a miscarriage of justice. Expressing concern about the inadequacies of her defense, the court stated that: "[None] of the lawyers who acted for the appellant received any training or instructions concerning how to communicate or deal with Aborigines or Islanders." Queen v. Robyn Bella Kina. 1993. No. BC9303391. Butterworths Unreported Judgments (Supreme Ct. Queensland Court of Appeal, Australia. November 22, 1993), 17. Cited in the Australian Law Reform Commission, *Equality Before the Law: Justice for Women*, ALRC 69 (Sydney, Australia: Australian Law Reform Commission, 1994). Cited April 1, 2004. Available from http://www.austlii.edu.au. [Editor's note].

4. Between January 1, 1980 and May 31, 1989, ninety-nine Aboriginal and Torres Strait Islander people died in the custody of prison, police, or juvenile detention institutions, including eleven women. Activism by aboriginal communities in response to the deaths led to the establishment of a Royal Commission. Aboriginal and Torres Strait Islander Commission, *The Royal Commission into Aboriginal Deaths in Custody: An Overview of Its Establishment, Findings and Outcomes* (Canberra: ATSIC, 1991). Cited April 1, 2004. Available from http://www.atsic.gov.au. [Editor's note]

5. Sisters Inside Inc. is a community organization that exists to advocate for the human rights of women in the criminal justice system in Queensland and to address gaps in the services available to them. They work alongside women in prison in determining the best way to fulfill these roles. See Debbie Kilroy in this volume.

CHAPTER **6**

Queering Antiprison Work

*African American Lesbians in
the Juvenile Justice System*[1]

BETH RICHIE

Questions of the mass incarceration of women and, more broadly, the gendered dynamics of criminalization become even more politically and intellectually salient when we attempt to integrate issues of violence against women and heteronormative sexuality into the discussion. I do so as an antiprison activist as well as a scholar interested in the new analytic framework that Black feminism and queer theory bring to understanding incarcerated women and girls. At first glance, these appear to be primarily theoretical concerns. However, as I continue to work to influence social policy around the mass incarceration of women, I have come to understand how critical it is to shift public consciousness in Black communities with regard to gender violence and heteronormativity, for ultimately, the larger political project of reducing structural inequality and eliminating the concentration of disadvantage that leads to mass imprisonment requires that the most marginalized group become most central to the struggle against global lockdown.

This chapter will argue for an expansion of antiprison rhetoric and subsequent organizing strategies to include an analysis of how the impact of the prison-industrial complex is, for some, made much more pernicious by gender violence and queer sexuality.[2] It will point to the ways in which the current formulations of the social costs of imprisonment that tend to minimize questions of gender and ignore sexuality altogether render queer prisoners, crimes related to nonnormative sexuality, and violence against incarcerated women invisible to even the most activist-oriented communities of resistance. By considering the case of Black adolescent lesbians who are incarcerated, the limits of even the most progressive race- and class-based paradigms used to study penal policies and practices will become apparent, demanding new methods and new analytical categories. Presented here as more than simply "outliers" or "atypical" cases, the experience of Black young lesbians will be centered in this chapter as an epistemological strategy; as a way to challenge the established paradigm and offer a broader analysis of the impact of mass incarceration. The chapter concludes with a reconsideration of questions of power, deviance, and heteronormativity as a way to develop an expanded social justice framework for antiprison work.

To begin, consider the following stories, which were shared by young women who were participating in a support group conducted in a large urban juvenile detention facility in the United States[3]:

I didn't go to school the morning I was arrested. Just like some friends, I was not feeling the boys that day. We just get sick of them hitting on us. And we are over the teachers too. It happens on a regular basis, in school, around school and in the neighborhood. And don't those security guards care a thing about us. (Linda, age 14)

But staying home didn't help either in some cases. The boys at home are not better. It's bad when you have to watch your back when you bathe, sleep, cook or sit down to watch TV. Being gay, they will run a train on you in a minute. But especially the older ones who can't seem to keep their hands to themselves. (Keisha, age 14)

To me, it was better to just hook up with a younger brother even if you are gay. He won't know as much about how to rein you in. But they get smart really fast, and once you do it, they think they own you. And then they start treating you like you are a punching bag. (Angel, age 16)

And don't try to get into a stable either. Used to be that was a good way to be safe. Now when you hook up with an older man—even one who you might be working for—you are really being set up. It's like you've got to turn tricks all day just to not get beat at night. And still you end up here. (Rehema, age 14).

I got so tired of that life. Way too much sex with men that I didn't want, but I had to do it for money, a place to stay, and even though I got my ass kicked, it was some protection. I went to the neighborhood clinic to get birth control, but don't you know I showed up positive for HIV? Here it is, I live with a pimp who takes advantage of me and I am pregnant again. How can that be true if I am gay? All because of his customer who forced himself on me when I was only supposed to be dancing for him. (Nickki, age 15)

The clinic couldn't really help because what could I tell them? I am hooking? I don't use condoms? I'm gay? I don't even know how it feels to be loved? I picked up some of their papers and tried to read them, but I just stopped. They are not talking to me. (Tiffany, age 16)

Sisters. Get real. Like me, you have to stop thinking the security guards, older men acting as pimps, workers at health clinics will help you. You need to find a way to hook up with one of these brothers who will really stand by you. How? Show them you will stand by them first. Get involved in his con game, spot for him, carry his bundles, put out for his crew even if you are funny. You've got to give up on the straight life and run with those who will really protect you. No girl, no programs can cover for you. (Latara, age 15)

And even if you get caught, find a way to turn the officer out. That's right, if you can't lie or cover for yourself, then turn him out and offer the only sure way to get out of any hard spot you find yourself in; use the p-thing. (Tiffany, age 16)

I know it sounds hard, ladies, but you all have to understand that we don't have a chance in this world. Look around you. Do you see anyone protecting us? Look at your mamas. Who is there for them? Does your teacher care? Does your counselor care? Do your people care? Do the police care? You've got to care for each other . . . raise each other up. And we've got to take care for ourselves before they bang us out of our minds. (Shelia, age 15)

Background

This discussion is typical of those occurring among African American young women in low-income communities who find themselves caught between their intimate desires, their loyalty to people in their community who hurt and betray them, and the tremendous force of conservative laws and public policies. Unlike their privileged counterparts, these young women are negotiating the troubled waters that characterize even so-called normal adolescent development as queer girls in very dangerous urban neighborhoods in the United States during repressive political times. Their accounts describe their attempts to understand the circumstances in which they find themselves and the survival strategies they use to protect themselves that ultimately resulted in their arrest and detention.

At the macro level, they tell a troubling story of a generation of young queer African American women in crisis and the cumulative negative impact of stigmatized racial, class, sexual, and gendered identities. Theirs is also a story of the astonishing extent to which they are exposed to and at risk of various forms of violence and how the combination of their communities' failure to recognize them, social service agencies' failure to support them, and law enforcement's aggressive posture toward them leaves them in very precarious positions. Finally, theirs is a story of the ways that the work against mass incarceration has been unresponsive to their plight. In the end these young queer Black women are left, as Shelia said, "to raise themselves up" without allies, advocates, or analysis.

Our capacity to understand them, build prevention or intervention programs to support them, let alone to organize antiprison struggles around them is limited by the dominant paradigms we use to study incarceration and the ways we understand gender violence among young people. The efforts to respond to their needs are thwarted by our inability to develop a complex analysis that includes systematic and simultaneous attention to both individual agency and structural inequality and to racism as well as gender oppression (including compulsory heterosexuality). Our intellectual and political agenda will not accommodate the challenge that their reality poses; they threaten both the gender-neutral analysis of racism that characterizes much of the antiprison work and the race-neutral analysis of patriarchy and sexuality that many feminist scholars and activists rely upon. Politically, some antiprison activists worry about losing the focus on the issue of mass incarceration to studies of queer sexuality and deviance. Indeed, although these stories pose a serious challenge to the rhetoric of the antiprison project, I hope to show that they also provide an opportunity for a reformulated, more radical antiprison praxis.

Young Black Lesbians in Detention

Although we see a troubling increase in the population of young African American women imprisoned or under state supervision in United States, it is important to note that contrary to popular media images, there is no new crime wave among Black girls.[4] On the contrary. Despite the image that has been constructed of them, girls in jails, prisons, and detention centers and under state supervision are less dangerous to the world around them than the world is to them.

When compared with their white counterparts, Black girls have a much higher rate of arrest, quickly becoming one of the fastest-growing cohorts of incarcerated people in this country.[5] Studies of the pattern of their lawbreaking reveal little evidence that they commit more serious crimes; however, the charges they face are more severe, their cases are less likely to be dropped, and bail is set at such high rates that African American girls are more likely to serve time in pretrial detention than was previously the case.[6] Their lawyers, who are more likely to be public defenders, are less likely to arrange a plea bargain for them, and so they are more likely to serve time as sentenced juvenile offenders in correctional facilities far away from their families.[7] They are more likely to serve their whole sentence today than five years ago, and even when released, they face the long-term consequences associated with having a juvenile conviction that will follow them throughout their lives.

When compared with their Black male counterparts, who, arguably, share many of the cumulative affects of the disadvantaged circumstances and negative consequences mentioned earlier, girls like those whose stories were shared at the beginning of this chapter are much more likely to have been sexually assaulted in both the public and the private sphere and they are less likely to be protected by adults in their lives.[8] On average, they are less likely to receive services or treatment and more likely to run away and attempt to survive through prostitution or establishing relationships with an adult who uses their sexuality to exploit them.

If they are abused or witnesses to domestic violence, girls are more likely to cope with abuse by using drugs or alcohol (and thus are labeled addict not survivor); they face a set of unique reproductive health problems, such as pregnancy, which results in their being studied as threatening unwed mothers rather than rape survivors.[9] Later in their lives, they are more likely to face abuse in their adult relationships and much more likely to face long-term physical and emotional consequences as a result of this abuse.[10] They are also more likely to face social consequences as a result of abuse, such as poverty and involvement in illegal activity.[11] The abuse they experience is more likely to be from multiple perpetrators, including authority figures upon whom they rely for access to services but ultimately face further disenfranchisement.[12]

In order to register fully the challenge that young Black lesbians in detention pose to the antiprison project, a more empirically based review of the literature is warranted. It is worth noting at the outset that most of the research does not explore sexuality as a distinct variable, so in places inferential conclusions must be drawn. Still, as the following data will suggest, young Black lesbians from low-income neighborhoods are profoundly vulnerable and this vulnerability leads some to be involved in illegal activity in very particular ways. Linda's account of sexual harassment is one example. Affecting 84 percent of all young women in this country,[13] the sexual harassment of this population ranges from milder forms such as pornographic graffiti and comments on their body parts to more aggressive physical assaults, reported as early as during elementary school years.[14] Thirty-one percent of girls experience sexual harassment often, and 13 percent report being "Forced to do something sexual at school other than kissing."[15] The rate of sexual harassment of lesbians is between 30 and 50 percent as reported by advocacy groups. This harassment tends to be ignored in formal studies because of the assumptions of heterosexuality that prevail in scientific research.[16] As Linda suggested, even getting to school can pose a physical and emotional risk for young women in neighborhoods where street harassment is part of their journey.[17] The extent to which young women like Linda describe feelings of shame and embarrassment is significant; 25 percent of young women who experience sexual harassment report that they had, indeed, stayed home from school or away from classes because of fear of being harassed or abused.[18] There is some evidence to suggest that these concerns are even more serious and limiting for lesbians,[19] helping to establish the link between sexual harassment, fear, truancy, and juvenile delinquency of young queer girls.[20]

Keisha's account of staying home renders the analysis of gender violence and sexuality even more complicated. For girls like her, home is not a safe place, for, in addition to the possible legal consequences associated with truancy, the risk of physical and sexual abuse of young lesbians in their homes represents a serious problem. According to the national data, unwanted sexual attention affects 54 percent of all girls regardless of sexual identity, which includes 24 percent of all girls who have experienced rape or coercive sex and 17 percent who have experienced incest.[21] National surveillance data indicate that young women experience the highest rate of victimization.[22] As is the case with adult women, roughly one third of all rapes take place during daytime hours, half occurring in or near the victim's home.[23] Of the adolescents who have run away from home, an astonishing 68 percent reported forced intercourse before they left.[24] Lesbians have one of the highest rates of any subgroups of adolescent runaways.

Research on relationship violence—the type that Angel described—suggests that 35 to 50 percent of young women who are dating experience some level of physical abuse.[25] Ethnographic data on Black youth have suggested that the nature and extent of this violence are severe and that even when these young relationships begin and end quickly, they put young women in them at very significant risk.[26] Although partner violence in same-sex relationships is relatively understudied, it has been established as at least as severe as and even more complex than violence between heterosexual partners.[27] Analysis of dating violence among adolescents reported in the *Journal of the American Medical Association* suggests that girls with a history of physical or sexual abuse from dating partners experience the kind of serious consequences (including illegal activity) that the young women described in the support group highlighted. For example, those who are hurt by their dating partners are significantly more likely to engage in substance abuse, including cocaine use, and they are four to six times more likely than their nonabused peers to become pregnant.[28] It is important to note that for some young women who identify as lesbians, the heterosexual imperative leads them to have sexual relationships with boys as a way to avoid shame and stigma.[29] For others, the risk of rape by peers is heightened if their sexual identity becomes known.[30] Even though most research on pregnancy and rape does not disaggregate the data according to sexual identity, between 11 and 20 percent of all girls who become pregnant do so as the direct result of rape, and there is little reason to assume that these studies do not include young women who are lesbians or involved in same-sex relationships.[31]

The extent to which this threat of abuse and forced pregnancy extends to young women, including lesbians, who are in relationships with older men has been established by inferential analysis. There is evidence that in relationships where there is a wider than usual age differential (and by extensions other power imbalances) the risk of abuse is greater. Adult men are responsible for over 59 percent of the babies born to girls fifteen to seventeen years old.[32] Although experiences such as Nicki's of forced intercourse during a sex-for-money transaction are not well studied, it is known that males involved in teen childbearing may not be dating partners but rather adult men who pay adolescents for sex.

Further analysis of the research on prostitution in the United States illustrates the vulnerability of lesbian adolescents in low-income communities of color. National estimates suggest that there are more than 300,000 young women involved in the illegal sex industry in the United States.[33] The arrest rate for juvenile prostitution and other crimes is increasing, the sanctions are becoming more severe, and it could be expected that there would be a disproportionate impact on Black queer youth.[34] In self-reported data, female heterosexual and lesbian survivors of sexual abuse are four times more likely to report exchanging sex for money, often as a way to survive as a runaway. Further, the extent to which early childhood abuse leads to later criminality for adult women has been clearly established by several national studies.[35]

Tiffany's account suggests how complex the issues of sexuality are and how central they are to the pattern of criminalization of Black lesbians. Her story of the consequences of a stigmatized queer identity is supported by the research that suggests that lesbian, gay, bisexual, transgender youth face serious emotional and social consequences, including rejection from family and harassment from peers that is often violent in nature.[36] Where there are few causal studies linking violence toward queer youth and their involvement in illegal activity, it has been established that isolation, abuse, and fear may complicate adolescent antisocial behavior. When combined with the systems' pathologizing of sexual minorities, further negative outcomes can be expected. In fact, the lack of response to these young women as victims *and* as targets of harsh law enforcement strategies has heightened their vulnerability. Left without official institutional protection, activist advocacy, or community support, some young

Black lesbians respond to persistent victimization, threats to their physical and emotional well-being, and the ongoing assault on their psyche by acting in ways that put them in conflict with the law: running away from home, becoming truant, carrying weapons, "buying" protection through associations with male peers or adult men, creating public disturbances, using violence, and selling sex for money or drugs.

The race and class dimensions of the social pattern require explicit discussion. Neither the data on incarceration nor research on gender violence against young women is analyzed by sexuality. However, it is obvious to most social theorists and most activists that there are key differences in the ways that differently situated people experience victimization. As the stories so clearly suggest, cultural factors, institutional racism, and patterns of gendered reactions to subordination have a profound impact on how girls experience aggressive penal practices.

Young Black lesbians not only are more vulnerable to race and class factors that lead to mass imprisonment but also are victimized by similarly situated men and are revictimized by the criminal justice system once they are in it. At best, this population of prisoners is ignored or misunderstood. Worse, they are overtly criminalized because of their stigmatized identities as African Americans, as young people, as young women, and as lesbians. The strategies they use to ensure even minimal safety and small measures of protection are so far outside the dominant understanding of crime and justice that even those who advance a progressive racialized analysis of mass incarceration leave them politically and programmatically unprotected. In the remainder of this chapter, I will show that Black feminist and queer approaches can offer both theoretical and strategic remedies.

A Queer Antiprison Project

What would it be like to "queer" antiprison work? To add theoretical complexity to our understanding of the various forces that lead to social disadvantage and the overimprisonment of certain groups? How can we expand our understanding of the deadly impact of the security state apparatus to include regulation of sexuality (including but not limited to queer sexuality)? What role do communities of resistance play in this equation? What does the term "queer" mean in this context?

A serious exploration into these questions would require that we take as a starting point the need to interrogate the ways that gender, sexuality, race, and class collide with harsh penal policy and aggressive law enforcement to entrap young Black lesbians. To begin this interrogation, I offer a brief review of three prevailing analyses that, in my view, constrain the potentially radical project: dominant feminist understanding of gender violence, the civil rights analysis deployed by lesbian, gay, bisexual, and transgendered (LGBT) activists to frame sexual liberation issues, and the race/class analysis of criminalization. Although each of these approaches provides some theoretical momentum, their impact is limited because they fail to consider the ways in which other variables intersect with sexuality. I offer a different—"queer" paradigm as an alternative.

Feminist researchers and activists who subscribe to mainstream "race-neutral" analysis have firmly established the problems of gender violence as a problem of the abuse of power and patriarchal control of women by men.[37] The advocacy and policy reform that result from this analysis depend heavily on the ability to establish a set of universal vulnerabilities that all women experience similarly. The rigor with which this perspective is argued leaves very little room for the consideration of difference based on race, class, age, sexuality identity, or involvement with illegal activity.[38]

A similar critique could be made of that dimension of the "gay liberation movement" that relied primarily on a mainstream "civil rights" analysis of discrimination based on sexuality.[39] The theoretical work and the subsequent activism on behalf of LGBT people that grew out of this approach focused on civil rights arguments, challenging laws as a way to gain full access to constitutionally guaranteed opportunity and protections. Increasingly, this approach has been a principal organizing strategy, and although many successes have resulted from this approach, the extent to which this political strategy depends on the ability to frame demands for equal rights on respectability is significant.

Those within the LGBT movement who rely on a mainstream civil rights analysis of the problem consider access to mainstream social institutions to be possible and desirable, especially for those who can prove themselves deserving because of their otherwise privileged status. The LGBT people whose primary concerns fall outside the narrow confines of that approach, those whose race, class, appearance, or lack of interest in marriage or other institutional privilege, are seen as threats to the larger civil rights–oriented project of LGBT liberation. Indeed, there is virtually no space in the public discourse that emerges from this analysis for consideration of queer youth who are juvenile delinquents or people who are arrested for nonnormative sexual identity or practices.

The last analytical approach that requires mention in this discussion is the argument that understands imprisonment as fundamentally a question of structural inequality based on race and class and directed toward youth of color. Advanced in a well-crafted set of arguments related to the long-term impact of racial inequality and divestment from low-income communities in the United States, this analysis links issues, such as poverty, concentration of disadvantages, and biased law enforcement, to the criminalization of youth and low-income people of color.[40] It centers racism as the master narrative, not allowing much room for an understanding of the variables of gender and sexuality. As with the dominant approaches to issues of LGBT rights and ending violence against women, my objection is not with the essence of the analysis of structural inequality as a cause of mass incarceration. Rather, the conceptual and political concern with the aforementioned analyses is the extent to which they are static and preclude considerations of other key dimensions of the problem of imprisonment. This critical review presents a necessary backdrop to developing a different analysis, building on (rather than simply rejecting) the premises of the white feminist movement to end violence against women, the civil rights–oriented LGBT liberation work, and antiracist work against mass incarceration.

A queer antiprison politic would call for a dramatically different way of understanding the criminalization and incarceration of young Black lesbians, beyond the three prevailing analyses that might be brought to bear. As the following discussion will show, the stories of Black lesbians in detention demand a queering of antiprison work and the establishment of a more radically oppositional perspective that will broaden the political and intellectual agenda against mass incarceration beyond U.S. borders. Strategically, this would require a reframing of questions of power and deviance embedded in the issue of imprisonment as a way to problematize issues of gender and sexuality within the context of antiprison activism.

Queering the antiprison project requires that we remember that in the most general sense, antiprison work has been a project attempting to look critically at how deviance and, by extension, criminalization have been socially constructed to serve people in power. The contemporary mechanisms of mass incarceration and the associated prison-industrial complex must be understood, at their core, as a project that relies on the production of a criminal class who play a key role in feeding the economic and political interest of the conservative state. Simply put, because prisons require prisoners, criminals must be produced. In the contemporary context, we see a vicious and elaborate web of new laws that require increased sanctions, aggressive policing strategies, and harsh sentencing policies. The system is buttressed by persistent poverty, virulent racism, and the rapidly narrowing of social options for poor people. The targeting of young people from low-income communities of color as "good candidates" for transformation into prisoners, combined with the steady erosion of citizenship rights, keeps the revolving door between correctional facilities and communities spinning. From this point of view, it should be no surprise that those who are the most vulnerable will be the first targets. A truly radical antiprison project would then have to look strategically at how mass incarceration affects the most marginalized groups in order to build an effective praxis of resistance.

That is the promise of queering antiprison work. Such a project would explore the ways in which gender and sexuality factor into the equation where race and class are so solidly placed. Instead of allowing racism and economic inequality to stand conceptually on their own, a Black feminist queer theory of criminalization would enable an analysis of race and class to work alongside heteronormative imperatives.

At the most basic level, this shift would add variables so that antiprison activists would challenge a broader range of processes of criminalization. Child maltreatment charges for substance abuse during pregnancy; involvement in prostitution, which in some states can lead to a felony sex conviction; and the criminalization of consensual sexual relationships between same-sex partners are obvious examples. Currently, these issues fall outside the antiprison work that is based only on an analysis of structural inequality and focuses on issues such as the death penalty and police mistreatment. Although these issues are critically important, it is important to note that there are more people affected by behaviors that have been criminalized because of "sexual deviance" than capital crimes.

This is certainly true for the young women whose stories were told earlier in this chapter. If we relied on Black feminist theories of queer sexuality (where gender is linked directly to power even in poor communities, where nonnormative sexuality is considered adaptive rather than pathological or inconsistent with a race analysis and where variables are understood to intersect), we would be much better prepared to respond to their situation. We could explain how a queer young Black woman can be both a victim of violence and also use violence, how she may identify as queer but also engage in heterosexual activity because of the pressure of heteronormative imperatives, and how even though she and her peers are stigmatized and labeled as outsiders, they still turn to their community because they share a race and class identity with those who isolate them. We might be in a better position to understand their agency as well as their vulnerability to the label of "deviant" and their subsequent criminalization.

Such a lens opens other possibilities. An analysis that positioned gender and sexuality more centrally in the analysis of masculinist tendencies of the law would offer new and productive ways to discuss judicial bias. A Black feminist analysis of Black masculinity would help explain why some men can trace their legal trouble to complicated gender expectations in communities of color and the tenuous relationship with signifiers of patriarchal privilege that are bound by racism.

A Black feminist queer framework would prompt investigations that are both qualitative and quantitative in nature about the process of criminalization and the rate of imprisonment of LGBT people, as well as those who express, demonstrate, or are thought to be involved in transgressive, deviant, or alternative expressions of sexuality. Antiprison activists and scholars would therefore be able to develop a more complicated and sophisticated theoretical understanding, which would lead to a more successful intervention and more radical praxis. The impact of our work would be much further reaching and would include groups who have very little interest or trust in the antiprison work in which we currently engage. And, in the end, young Black lesbians who are living in detention centers because of their multiple identities in dangerous times would have a greater change of being free. That, it seems to me, is the most compelling imperative to queer the antiprison project in the face of increased and concentrated imprisonment.

References

1. I would like to acknowledge Cathy J. Cohen, Lisa P. Jones, and Julia Sudbury for their contributions to this chapter.
2. In this chapter, queer is used to signify lesbian, gay, bisexual, and transgendered people and relationships as well as those who do not conform to hegemonic, normative sexual roles. This notion was advanced by the work of Cathy J. Cohen in her article "Deviance as Resistance: A New Research Agenda for the Study of Black Politics," *Du Bois Review* 1, 1 (2004): 27–45, and other scholars of race and sexuality in the United States.
3. The names used in this chapter have been changed to protect those whose stories are told here.
4. Meda Chesney-Lind, *The Female Offender: Girls, Women and Crime* (Thousand Oaks, CA: Sage Publications, 1997).
5. Howard Snyder and Melissa Sickmard, "Juvenile Offenders and Victims: 1999 National Report," Office of Juvenile Justice and Delinquency Prevention 115 (1999).
6. Samuel Walker, Cassia Spohn, and Miriam DeLone, *The Color of Justice: Race, Ethnicity, and Crime in America* (Belmont, CA: Wadsworth, 2000).
7. Dorothy Roberts, *Shattered Bonds: The Color of Child Welfare* (New York: Basic Books, 2002).
8. Richard Wertheimer et al., "Qualitative Estimates of Vulnerable Youth in Transition to Adulthood: Final Report Submitted to the Annie E. Casey Foundation," *Child Trends* (Washington, D.C., February 2002).
9. Jay G. Silverman et al., "Dating Violence Against Adolescent Girls and Associated Substance Abuse, Unhealthy Weight Control, Sexual Risk Behavior, Pregnancy and Suicidality," *Journal of American Medical Association* 286, 3 (August 1, 2002).
10. Wertheimer 2002.
11. Jody Raphael, "Trapped by Poverty, Trapped by Abuse: New Evidence Documenting the Relationship Between Domestic Violence and Welfare," in *Project for Research on Welfare, Work and Domestic Violence*, edited by the Taylor Institute and the University of Minnesota Research Development Center on Poverty, Risk and Mental Health (April 1997).
12. Beth Richie, *Compelled to Crime: The Gender Entrapment of Battered Black Women* (New York: Routledge, 1996).
13. American Association of University Women, *Hostile Hallways: The AAUW Survey on Sexual Harassment in America's Schools* (Harris/Scholastic Research, 1993); Nan Stein, *Bullying and Sexual Harassment in Elementary Schools: It's Not Just Kids Kissing Kids* (Wellesley, MA: Wellesley College, Center for Research on Women, 1997).
14. Stein 1997.
15. AAUW, 10.
16. Report of the Massachusetts Governor's Commission on Gay and Lesbian Youth, "Making Schools Safe for Gay and Lesbian Youth" (1993).
17. Cynthia G. Bowman, "Street Harassment and the Informal Ghettoization of Women," *Harvard Law Review* 106 (1993): 517.
18. AAUW, 15.
19. Vermont Department of Health, Youth Statistics: The 2003 Vermont Department of Health/Education Youth Risk Behavior Survey. http://www.outrightvt.org/resources/stats.html.
20. New York Gay and Lesbian Anti-Violence Project, *Annual Report* (1996).
21. Susan Russell, with the Canadian Federation of University Women, *Take Action for Equality, Development and Peace: A Canadian Follow-Up Guide to Beijing '95*, ed. Linda Souter and Betty Bayless. Ottawa, ON: CRIAW (Canadian Beijing Facilitating Committee, 1996).
22. Patricia Tjaden and Nancy Thoennes, *National Violence Against Women Survey* (National Institute of Justice and The Centers for Disease Control and Prevention, November 1988).

23. National Criminal Victimization Survey, *Preventing Violence Against Women* (June 1995).
24. Anthony J. Biglan et al., "Does Sexual Coercion Play a Role in the High-Risk Sexual Behavior of Adolescent and Young Adult Women?" *Journal of Behavioral Medicine* 18 (1995): 549.
25. Kirstie K. Danielson et al., "Co-morbidity Between Abuse of an Adult and DSM-III-R Mental Disorders: Evidence from an Epidemiological Study," *American Journal of Psychiatry* 155, 1 (1998): 131–133.
26. Motivational Educational Entertainment Productions, *The MEE Report 2: In Search of Love: Dating Violence Among Urban Youth* (Philadelphia: Center for Human Advancement, 1996).
27. Lisa Waldner-Haugrud and Linda Vaden Gratch, "Sexual Coercion in Gay/Lesbian Relationships: Descriptives and Gender Differences," *Violence and Victims* 12, 1 (1997).
28. Silverman et al., 2002.
29. Margaret Nicholas: "Bisexuality in Women: Myths, Realities and Implications for Therapy. *Women and Sex Therapy, Closing the Circle of Sexual Knowledge*, edited by E. Rothblum (New York: Harrington Park Press, 1988).
30. San Francisco Women Against Rape. http://www.sfwar.org/facts/brochles.htm.
31. Debra Boyer and David Fine, "Sexual Abuse as a Factor in Adolescent Pregnancy and Child Maltreatment," *Family Planning Perspectives* 24 (1992): 4–11, 19.
32. A. Thornton, "The Courtship Process and Adolescent Sexuality," *Journal of Family Issues* 11, 3 (1990): 239–273.
33. Melissa Farley and Howard Barkan, "Prostitution, Violence and Posttraumatic Stress Disorder," *Women and Health* 23, 3 (1998): 37–49.
34. OJJDP Statistical Briefing Book. http://ojjdp.ncjrs.org/ojstatbb/offenders.
35. Angela Browne and Shair Bassuk, "Intimate Violence in the Lives of Homeless and Poor Housed Women: Prevalence and Patterns in an Ethnically Diverse Sample," *American Journal of Orthopsychiatry* 67, 2 (1997): 261–278.
36. Gary Remafedi et al., "The Relationship Between Suicide Risk and Sexual Orientation: Results of a Population-Based Study," *American Journal of Public Health* 88 (1998): 57–60; Safe Schools Coalition of Washington, *Safe Schools Anti-Violence Documentation Project: Third Annual Report* (1996).
37. Rebecca E. Dobash and Russell Dobash, *Rethinking Violence Against Women* (Thousand Oaks, CA: Sage Publications, 1998) and S. Schechter, *Women and Male Violence: Visions and Struggles of The Battered Women's Movement* (Boston: South End Press, 1988).
38. Beth Richie, "Coming Up in the Boogie Down: The Role of Violence in the Lives of Adolescents in the South Bronx," *Health Education and Behavior* 26, 6 (1998): 788–805.
39. It should be noted that in the LGBT movement, there are a number of strategic approaches used to create social change. Here I am referring to one particular set of strategies that encompasses a more conservative or mainstream agenda.
40. Ruth Wilson Gilmore, "Globalization and U.S. Prison Growth," *Race and Class* 40 (1998/99): 171–188.

CHAPTER 7

Imprisoned for *Zina*

Geopolitics and Women's Narratives in Pakistan

SHAHNAZ KHAN

I married my neighbor. My parents were against the marriage although my husband had come with a formal proposal and asked for my hand. My parents said they wanted one *lakh*[1] before they gave him permission to marry me. Then my husband sold his land and was willing to give them the one *lakh* they had asked for. But they still said no. This time they said that he is Punjabi and we are Sindhis[2] and we are of a different *biradari* [community]. So I ran way with him and we got married anyway. My parents found us eventually and charged us with *zina* and both of us are in jail. Now they say give us the one *lakh* we asked for and then we will withdraw the charges. But the money has been spent on hiding from my parents and on lawyers. Now we have no more money. I am afraid that when we are released, that is, my son, my husband, and I, my parents will find us and kill us.

These comments were made by twenty-five year-old Naheed,[3] who has had no formal education. She was charged under the *Zina* Ordinance (also known as *zina* laws) and was an inmate of Kot Lakpat prison in Lahore, Pakistan, where I interviewed her in December 1998.[4]

Zina refers to sex outside marriage—both adultery and fornication. In Pakistan, the *Zina* Ordinance suggests and regulates what constitutes ethical behavior in sex and, more generally, within the family and the social institution of marriage in ways in which women's fundamental rights under the constitution, and some argue in Islam, are violated. Specifically, *zina* laws are part of the *Hadood* Ordinances promulgated in 1979 by General Zia-ul-Haq, the self-proclaimed president of Pakistan, as a first step in his Islamization policies. Drawing upon the sacred texts of Islam, the *zina* laws seek to define and reinforce the notion of a "pure and chaste" Pakistani citizen.

Research documents that thousands of women have been charged and jailed under the *Zina* Ordinance and that the interpretations and repercussions of the laws are class based. Although meant to be applied to all Pakistani citizens, *zina* laws are unevenly exercised. The most vulnerable members of society—impoverished and illiterate women—are the most affected. That is, women who cannot afford lawyers are most likely to be charged and jailed.[5] Furthermore, my data support the view that many of the women incarcerated under *zina*-related charges are not there because of sex crimes but because their families or former husbands used the *zina* laws to have the women jailed when they went against their families' wishes. The *zina* laws were promulgated to help bring about a just and moral society in Pakistan. Critics of the ordinance, however, argue that these laws allow families to draw upon the power of the state to help regulate the morality and sexuality of "their" women and reclaim family honor.[6] This contributes to the growing incidence of state-sanctioned violence against women. I do not wish to analyze the implementation of the *zina* laws as an example of male oppression of women in isolation from broader social and economic forces. However, I do want to identify Naheed as more vulnerable than her husband in this process because of the gender bias in Pakistani law,[7] a bias also present in other countries.[8]

Although 95 percent of the prisoners charged for *zina* are released upon trial, they face years of incarceration before trial. Conditions in the urban jails are under the scrutiny of nongovernmental organizations (NGOs) and charity organizations that work there, and the women who I interviewed for this study stated that jail officials treated them better than their families on the outside. However, rural jails are another matter. There are few NGOs operating in rural areas, and many of the jails have no separate section for women with female staff. Abuse of prisoners could occur in such circumstances.

Moral Regulation

Narratives of the women who I interviewed suggest that their families are the primary agents of their moral regulation. The young women who I interviewed are deemed immoral by virtue of defying parental wishes. The older women charged with *zina* are often constructed as disobedient and therefore immoral wives; at the same time, their accounts frequently suggest that their current or former husbands are attempting to extort money from them. Moreover, the practices associated with *zina* confirm state complicity. This complicity, I argue, is not incidental. As individual bodies become the focus of the regulating gaze, discourse promoting morality in Pakistan remains limited to containing illicit sex. At the same time, attention is deflected away from structural issues, such as increasing indebtedness and rising militarization, practices that might implicate politicians and state officials.

Drawing upon the work of Claude Levi Straus, Gayle Rubin has pointed out in another context that marriages are a form of exchange between kin groups, and women are seen as a precious gift.[9] This gift allows kin groups to build alliances and become related by blood, making families the beneficiaries of the exchanges. Women, on the other hand, are not partners in these exchanges and cannot realize the benefits of their circulation. Comments from women I interviewed suggest that similar transactions have taken place in Pakistan. Members of women's families frequently use the *zina* laws to dictate to women and to intimidate them into marrying and having children with whom they want. Families with little means to cope with increasing inflation and chronic unemployment often find that their daughter's sexuality is a valuable asset, a commodity commanding a high price. Marrying her to the highest bidder in exchange for a "gift" frequently becomes one method of paying off debts. Furthermore, many women are "sold" into marriage to sustain alcohol and drug habits of their male relatives. Indeed, the women whom I spoke to cited increasing poverty and family violence as the main reason for their plight.

My father's relatives were against his marriage to my mother. But he married her anyway. This cut him off from his own relatives. Now father married me to a man who I like and am happy with. He is close in age to me: he is twenty-two years old. Father and mother used to fight. He left the family and the country. I don't know where he is. No one knows where he is. Now mother wants me to divorce my husband. She says that I am only fifteen and a minor and that she has authority over me. She wants me to marry someone who has promised her money. So my mother has charged us with *zina* and my husband with abduction. My marriage has been registered and my husband has the *nikahnama* [marriage certificate].

I am happy with my husband and I do not want to leave him. Twice I have been to court where I was told that I am a minor and should go with my mother and do as she says. But I refused. Finally I came to *Darul Aman* for I am afraid. Next week I will appear before the court again, I will tell them that I want to stay married to my husband.

Gulbano, age 15 years

The constitution of Pakistan grants rights to all citizens, giving Gulbano the liberty to marry whomever she wishes. However, the practices associated with the *Zina* Ordinance override that right and allow her family to intimidate her and have her incarcerated. Furthermore, Gulbano's account challenges the notion put forward by some feminist theorists that it is only men who control women and deny them their rights. Instead, her narrative makes a case for an analysis identifying the complexities of what Deniz Kandiyoti calls the "patriarchal bargain."[10] In this instance, Gulbano's mother does not have a nurturing relationship with her; instead, she attempts to commodify her daughter's body. Several of the women commented that their mothers had sided with their fathers in oppressing them, although a few pointed out that it was out of fear.

Gulbano is Pathan and the money promised to her mother in exchange for her is the bride-price, a common practice among Pathans living in rural areas, where, as Shaheen Sardar Ali points out, "a woman's consent and/or participation in drawing up of her marriage contract is considered of no consequence. She is bartered away at a suitable bride-price."[11] However, both Sardar Ali and Esposito argue that this practice is in contradiction with the Islamic requirement that dower (bride-price) is to be paid to the woman.[12] Through the payment of bride-price to parents, women become property to be bought and sold. Young girls are socialized into this price. Many do not resist, and those who do frequently face accusations of *zina*.

Although *zina* laws have an enormous impact on the lives of the impoverished women who resist familial demands, religion appears to provide them with only a tenuous legitimacy. Historically, religious scholars and jurists have drawn largely upon the *Qur'an* and *Sunnah* to formulate *sharia* (religious law). Religious and customary laws also influence these formulations.[13] For example, under the Hanafi version of *sharia* law commonly used in Pakistan, fathers and grandfathers can contract marriage for minors that cannot be annulled at puberty. John Esposito argues that this power is not supported by any verse in the *Qur'an* or by the *Sunnah*.[14] However, should the minor's marriage have been contracted through fraud or by someone other than the father or grandfather (including the minor's mother), Esposito points out, the minor can repudiate the marriage upon attaining puberty. The Hanafi reading of the sacred texts in Pakistan then allows parents to contract marriages for minor daughters, whose sexuality becomes a commodity that can be purchased through payment of a bride-price. Many women resist this practice. Their resistance brings them into greater contact with the police force and legal system, both institutions commonly understood to be extremely corrupt. Indeed, a recent survey found that out of twelve selected government agencies, the police were deemed the most corrupt followed by the lower courts, the two agencies that women are likely to come into contact with in the process of incarceration.[15]

The use of *zina* laws to intimidate daughters who have married without their parents' permission with the threat of imprisonment suggests that parental rights override men's right/claim to their wives. Often young men are as powerless as young women in deciding their destiny.

> I married against my parents' will and they accused my husband of abducting me. Both of us are now in jail. My husband is my cousin [son of my mother's brother]. I had asked my parents for permission to marry him but they said no. I got married anyway. And my parents registered a case of *zina* against me.
>
> > Nausheen, age 20 years. She has been at Kot Lakpat prison three months and is expecting her first child this month.

Nausheen's situation suggests that having a *nikahnama* is insufficient. She claims that her father as *vali* (guardian) has refused to sanction the marriage. Moreover, her parents have bribed the officials who performed and registered the marriage to say that no marriage exists. They insist that her marriage certificate a well as her marriage is a fraud. Now Nausheen and her husband have to appear in court to argue their case before the judge. This is hampered by the fact that they have little money with which to pay for a lawyer. Court dates are notoriously difficult to obtain in the overburdened system. The couple may have to wait in jail for months before they appear before a magistrate. Had they been charged in a rural court, their situation might have been worse as was the case with Rubina. Although she is fortunate to have a legal aid lawyer, Rubina's case has been registered in Thatta, where there are no jail facilities for female prisoners. I met her in the Karachi jail where she had been transferred and where she was awaiting a court date. Rubina has a certificate to prove that she is indeed divorced from her first husband, who charged her with committing *zina* with her current one. In order to present this evidence in court before a judge, she has to deal with several factors. She has to wait for a female guard to come and escort her to Thatta. Many times these guards do not appear at the appointed time; Rubina has missed two court dates, six months apart. When the guard finally arrived to escort Rubina to the court in Thatta, the judge did not show up due to illness. Sixteen-year-old Gurmat, faced with similar circumstances, commented, "What a nonsense system this is, first we wait for the female guard, then we wait for the judge, all to show them our papers. Who designed this system?" At the same time, fifteen-year-old Saima points out that the only immorality she is guilty of is going against her family wishes; moreover, "My religion allows me to marry who I want." Saima and many of the other women disobey familial demands and express desire for relationships of love and romance. Many turn to the law for protection; however, their lack of resources limits their access to the law.

Religion, custom, and illiteracy interconnect to exacerbate the situation further. In Islam, marriage is a civil contract and the *Qur'an* recommends that contracts be put in writing. "Disdain not to reduce the writing of [your contract] for a future period . . . it is more just in the sight of God, more suitable as evidence, and more convenient to prevent doubts among yourselves."[16] Quranic recommendations are often not followed in Pakistan. Frequently the husband repudiates his wife, as allowed by *sharia*, but does not register the divorce with the district council as required by civil law. Because the divorce is not registered, it is invalid. The woman, however, often believes that she is indeed divorced. Should she remarry, her first husband can and frequently does blackmail her with the threat of *zina*.

> My husband, Ahmad, used to come late at night and sometimes he never came home at all. When I asked him about it, he beat me. He told me that he did not like me and beat me. One day he beat me so badly that I had to have stitches on my forehead and my nose. Then he pronounced *talaq* (divorce by repudiation) three times and said: "You are no longer my wife. I have divorced you. If I see you in my house again I will kill you." So I took my three children and went home to my parents.
>
> My parents are old and they do not have much money. In the house only my brother was working and he has four children. So they all began to pressure [me] to marry again. And eventually I married again to a man they found for me. Amin, my new husband, he was good to me and my children. For a while I was happy. Then my first husband, Ahmad, came back and said that we are not divorced, he has not registered our divorce with the local council and [that] I am committing *zina* with Amin. He went to the police and launched an FIR [First Investigative Report] against us and now we are all in jail, Amin, the children and I too. Ahmad wants money before he withdraws his case. He wants one *lakh*. We are poor people, where will we get that kind of money? I do not understand why we are in jail. I did everything Ahmad wanted. I even left the house when he told me to go. I did everything my parents wanted [from me]. I married the man they found for me when Ahmad divorced me. I do not understand why we are in jail.
>
> Nussrat, age 26 years. She has been in
> Karachi Central Jail for one year.

Husbands find that these laws work in their favor. Paradoxically, they use the threat of *zina* to intimidate their wives as well as compel them to commit *zina* as a source of income. Rashida Bibi, like Naheed, is also from Sindh, where they practice bride-price.

Father owed money to an old man. And he married me to the old man. My new husband not only slept with me but also made me commit *zina* with six other men in exchange for money, which he kept. He also beat me and broke my arm. He has a first wife who was also involved in prostituting me and she also beat me. I registered a case of rape against the old man and his wife with the police. I am in *Darul-Aman*[17] because the old man's son-in-law has threatened me. My father also use to beat me.

> Rashida Bibi, age 18 years. She has been at
> *Darul Aman* for four months.

Impoverished women with few resources provide ideal victims for the police. Jilani (interviewed in 1998) argues that once a case has been initiated and an FIR launched, police are "under pressure to tie up the investigation and send the case for prosecution." Police performance is evaluated annually. Because unresolved cases reflect poor police performance, Jilani points out that they are often looking for a victim who will provide a tidy conclusion for the case. At other times, the police conduct random raids searching for victims to extort money from.

Application of *zina* not only provides docile daughters, mothers, and wives but also promises to provide docile workers who will accept difficult and poorly paid working conditions without organizing for change. These are exactly the kind of workers that multinational corporations are looking for when they invest in a country. The moral regulation of women at the intersection of class, gender, and ethnicity suggests that docile middle-class women are considered moral and agentive, impoverished women are then deemed immoral. These constructions are also influenced by everyday verbal and textual conversations of middle-class women regarding "the loose sexual promiscuous lower class woman" whose sexuality is running wild and needs to be controlled. Feroza Bibi's account suggests that employers draw upon conventional occupational stereotypes of the domestic servant as immoral and unreliable to sanction and persecute those considered undesirable. Feroza is fifty years old and her crime is not that of committing *zina* but of helping to facilitate the immorality of a younger woman.

> I used to work as a sweeper . . . a young girl also worked for the mistress and she ran away.

> When her parents came with the police to question the mistress about girl's disappearance, she told the police that I had helped her run away. They registered a case of *zina* against my husband and I. The police came to our village and brought us to jail. Now my husband and I are both in jail. No one comes to visit us. The mistress and master have also

implicated my older children and they are afraid to come and see their parents. Who will be my *vakil* (lawyer)? Allah is my *vakil.* Maybe Allah will have pity on me; it is *Ramzan* (the Muslim holy month of fasting).

> Feroza Bibi, age 50 years. She had been
> in prison for over a year.

There is another aspect to women's confinement. Najma Parveen, the superintendent, pointed to an informal segregation within the Karachi Central Jail. A barrack has been set aside by the authorities for those known to be sex workers. Such segregation is fueled by the assumption that sex workers ought to be "saved" from their profession. Needless to say, the authorities do not provide substantive alternative life choices for the women who are so saved. Unlike other women charged for *zina*, sex workers frequently have resourceful connections that post their bail and secure their release. Twelve-year-old Sajida was one such sex worker. She was screened out of the barracks reserved for sex workers and put into one reserved for regular prisoners charged under *zina*. Unlike the case of other inmates of her barrack, however, her bail was posted within two months of her incarceration and she left the prison shortly after I met her. Sixteen-year-old Ghazala, another sex worker, who had also been screened into the barracks for "regulars," has no such connections. She has been in prison one and a half years.

> I was in a hotel with a man. I have been to hotels with men before. My mother is sick and my father is dead. I charge twenty-five rupees for *zina*. The first time I was fifteen. When my father died we had a lot of debt and creditors would come to our house and threaten us. Ami [mother] said "don't prostitute yourself." But I don't know where else to get the money so the creditors will not bother us. A friend of mine also does *zina* for money and she showed me how to get clients. The man I was with is in jail as well. We were eating in a hotel and the police caught us. My mother has come to visit me in jail and she is trying to get bail money. But we have no money.

Ghazala's poverty, lack of education, and lack of alternative options to earn a living are some of the reasons why she is in jail. She is not alone. At least 50 percent of the women in prison in Pakistan are there because of the *zina* laws.[18] Most women are illiterate and do not have the financial resources to post bail. Even if they did have the resources, bail has to be posted by a male: their father, their brother, or their husband. Often, these are the people who are responsible for their being in jail in the first place. In a sense, the *zina* laws are used to sweep the streets clean of women, particularly poor, unwanted, and rebellious women.

The laws are supposed to stop women and men from having sex outside marriage, but except for sex workers such as Sajida and Ghazala, there is little conclusive proof that the women in jail had sex in the first place. Many of them were accused of merely aiding and abetting abductions. A report by the Commission of Inquiry on the Status of Women suggests that the police have used the pretext of investigating *zina* to break into homes.[19] Also, they have arrested and locked up married couples for having illicit relations, widows for being suspect, and wives and daughters for not being compliant enough to the men in their families.

The state's treatment of the *zina* victims puts into question the nation's commitment to protect the interests of all its citizens. Women are born into a national symbolic order that treats them as chattels to be bartered. The nation needs morality, and women and lower-class citizens are sacrificed to provide a moral face for the nation. The notion of Pakistan, literally the land of the pure, evokes a desire for a national community of moral citizens with women's role circumscribed to that of a chaste wife, sister, and daughter. Once they are charged with *zina*, their claim to be part of the national narrative becomes difficult to sustain. In articulating themselves as *gharaloo* (domesticated) and believers, they project an image of morality and religiosity in what appears to be an attempt to create a space for themselves within the national narrative. As Pakistan narrates its past and present and tries to imagine its future, there is a struggle over ideology and particularly which interpretations of Islam will help construct the guiding force of the nation. These struggles are indicative of the conflicts within the larger social context. It is to an examination of this that I now turn.

Locating the Context That Sustains *Zina* Law

Pakistan was imagined as a homeland for the Muslims of British India. In the process of the partition of British India (into India and Pakistan), more than ten million people were displaced in 1947 as they moved (both ways) across the newly created national border between the two countries. This border was erected across British India on the basis of a two-nation theory (Hindu/Muslim). Although the founder of Pakistan, Mohammad Ali Jinnah, described the state as secular, he also used religious symbols and imagery when it suited his political purposes. The process of lobbying for and finally securing the state of Pakistan linked nationalism to religion, both of which were important in helping to construct the identity of millions of displaced persons pouring across the border from India. This early linking of nationalism and religion continues to be a significant element of how the nation imagines itself.[20] This connection of religion to nationalism persists, even though in Pakistan's fifty-five-year history of existence, not one politician of national significance has come into power through a religious platform.[21] Invoking Islam has been, however, an important aspect of mobilizing a nationalist consensus, particularly for the frequent wars with India, which in turn have justified military spending. Ayesha Jalal calls this a political economy of defense, which helps sustain the army as a major power broker in Pakistan.[22] The connection was strengthened in 1979 with the promulgation of the *Hadood* Ordinances, of which *zina* laws form a part, and more recently with the endorsement of *sharia* (Islamic religious law) in 1991 by the Nawaz Sharif regime.

General Zia's military regime promulgated the *Hadood* Ordinances as a component of the new moral order in Pakistan in 1979. Critics of the ordinances call them antiwoman (and antiminority[23]) and argue that the regime brought in these laws to bolster its political base through alliances with rightwing religious parties.[24] Subsequent weak regimes have allowed it to continue to wreak havoc in society at the expense of the most vulnerable members of society, lower-class women. All of these regimes have had Western financial and political support. In the West, few questions have been raised concerning the misuse of religion or lack of human rights in Pakistan. The United States in particular has seldom used its influence with Pakistani regimes to press for an end to human rights violations.

Generally, intellectual debate in Pakistan is against the laws, yet they still remain in effect. Why? There is no clear answer to this question; however, I will attempt to approach it in several ways. I will argue that economic and political conditions play a part in sustaining the *Hadood* Ordinances. Moreover, national and international alliances among various power brokers including the military and religious groups to maintain the status quo appear to disregard the rights of the most vulnerable members of society.

The forces of globalization have affected economies worldwide, causing retrenchment of government services such as healthcare, primary education, and state subsidies for essential goods.[25] These structural adjustments are connected to access to international aid. They have helped integrate economies of the south into the north-dominated markets and have also increased poverty and violence in third-world societies.[26] Cultural devaluation of the third world, another significant factor, also stems from the colonial period and is reinforced by the new forms of colonialism linked to globalization. Dislocation due to urbanization generates insecurities among the peoples of the south and exacerbates the situation many people find themselves in. Economic and cultural crises lead even the regimes that define themselves as secular to identify religion as a significant organizing principle of society and to seek greater legitimacy through political alliances with religious forces in their regions. Iraq after the Gulf War is one such example. In a country where much of the infrastructure had been destroyed during the Gulf War, Saddam Hussein fostered alliances with Islamists and passed a series of antiwoman laws, including laws that focused on keeping women "moral." Gema Martin Munoz's comments support my argument, "Whereas at one time the most pressing concern was to achieve modernization, now introducing morality into the political and socioeconomic order has come to the fore as a result of the corruption and the marginalization that the state has generated."[27] She argues that this desire for morality appears connected to a reassertion of Islamic identity.

This is certainly so in Pakistan, where reassertion of Islamic identity has not replaced nationalism but remains connected to nationalism. Indeed, there is an urgency to reassert Islam in a context of recurring political and economic crises. Moreover, as Aijaz Ahmad points out, both India and Bangladesh have larger Muslim populations than Pakistan.[28] The latter's reason for existence has begun to shift from being a homeland for Muslims in the subcontinent to being the home of the pure Muslims of the region. Decontextualized religious laws including the *zina* laws are often used to reinforce symbolically Pakistan's Islamic credentials.

There is another aspect of this process. Pakistan is a heavily indebted country, and it continues to borrow every year. Consequently, the priorities of the Pakistani government include making payments on the national debt and submitting to restructuring directives.[29] In addition, the state is committed to military spending because of its long-standing dispute with India over Kashmir.[30] The Pakistani state also needs to keep multinational corporations happy by providing a docile labor force. This means keeping down the societal violence resulting from the rising price of basic foods and high unemployment related to restructuring. These conditions have recently been exacerbated as Pervez Musharraf, the current president of Pakistan, and another military dictator energetically aligns himself with the United States–led war on terror. Significant aspects of this war are being carried out on Pakistani territory, it is widely believed, against the wishes of large numbers of Pakistanis.

The state juggles these contradictory demands and maintains a delicate balance. The repeal of the *zina* laws threatens this balance. Pakistani nationalism is integrally connected to religion. *Zina* laws are seen as religious laws, and dispensing with them would pose a symbolic challenge to the nation. Their repeal has the potential to ignite a fuse within an unhappy and an increasingly impoverished populace that has not been included in the benefits of globalization; instead, they are the victims of globalization.

Powerful signifiers of nation and religion render ideas about *zina*, or illicit sex, a significant regulator of normative morality. Challenging them means questioning not only religion but also the symbolic force that created and continues to sustain the state of Pakistan. *Zina* laws invoke a desire for moral purity in a context of societal corruption. They examine and identify embodied morality focusing on illicit sexuality. Paradoxically, notions of embodied purity, absence of illicit sex, render invisible the societal impurity of the nation.

This impurity comes out of the economic and political corruption of the state. The moral regulation of impoverished women through *zina* laws, however, rhetorically cleanses the symbolic impurity of the country. Although recent court proceedings have largely ruled in favor of the *zina* victims, these decisions reinforce class and gender relations. Women who are incarcerated in prison or more informally in the *Darul Amans* cannot claim constitutional rights of liberty, equality, and citizenship. They are granted these rights through the judicial process dominated largely by middle- and upper-class males.

Although the state invokes Islam to legitimize *zina* laws, the women's narratives suggest that it is not religion but the state, along with their families, that is responsible for their plight. In rejecting the laws and the system that spawned them, the women also embrace the spirituality associated with religion. Chastity and propriety promoted by religion for the good Muslim woman become important, even for resisting women. They frame their resistance in religious terms, for many invoke the mercy of Allah or resign themselves to the will of Allah as they turn to religion to make sense of their situation. In so doing they often become recruits for the Women Aid Trust (WAT), an organization of the *Jamat-i-Islami* doing rehabilitative work in the jails.

For many women, *zina* is operationalized in ways that connect the process to monetary exchanges, highlighting the material predicaments of their families and suggesting that their economic situation is driving them to take recourse in repressive *zina* laws. Moreover, it leads us to speculate that control of morality and sexuality through *zina* might be used as a façade for material sustenance. What would happen if we did away with the *zina* laws; would the women still suffer? The violence that women face is generated by social and political attitudes. Religion acts as an ideology that pressures women to accept particular norms. These norms are regulated through community pressure. However, communities are not as integrated and under the control of kin groups as they have been in the past. Many of the women fleeing their families, it appears, can be regulated in towns and cities only through *zina* charges. This leads many to speculate that the women who actually commit *zina* are murdered in "honor killings." The ones charged with *zina* are "innocent"[31] women and the families know that they are innocent. The primary purpose of these charges is to bring them into line with family wishes. The women's comments substantiate these commonly held beliefs. Many point out that their families have indicated that if they initiate charges of abduction against their husbands and comply with family wishes, their families would post bail on their behalf and help secure their release. They are in jail, they stated, because they refused, leading me to speculate that there are likely to be thousands who took up these offers of "help." We only know of those who resist and are in prison or have found refuge in the *Darul Amans*. In such places of formal and informal confinement, resisters frequently take advantage of the literacy and skill development programs available to them and negotiate a better bargain with patriarchy. These patriarchal bargains open up new arenas of struggle and negotiations.

Almost since its inception, the *Zina* Ordinance has been challenged. A number of NGOs that provide social and legal assistance to imprisoned women have taken a political stance against the incarceration and criminalization of Pakistani women. These organizations include Shirkat Gah, Lawyers for Human Rights and Legal Aid (LRHLA), and the legal aid cell AGHS connected to the private watchdog organization the Human Rights Commission of Pakistan (HRCP). These agencies have successfully lobbied on the women's behalf and posed legal challenges to the laws, with the result that the government has brought fewer charges than in the past, and the courts have shown greater leniency to those charged with *zina*. Moreover, my conversations with members of the WAT, who do social work in the prisons, suggest that even Islamists are aware of the excess of the *zina* laws.

Support for the *Zina* Ordinance within government circles also appears tenuous at best. Members of the Commission of Inquiry for Women (CIW) called by the government in 1994 noted that the high incarceration rate, along with the low convictions of *zina* victims, suggests widespread misuse of the *Zina* Ordinance. Moreover the commissioners stated that these laws were not in conformity either with Islam or the constitution of Pakistan. They recommended that the *Hadood* Ordinances and the *Zina* Ordinance be repealed. Neither the Benazir Bhutto nor the Nawaz Sharif government (both of which had minority status) was willing to act on these recommendations.

More recently, the current military regime of General Pervez Musharraf has faced calls for the repeal of the *Hadood* Ordinances not only from women's and human rights groups but also from lawyers and other jurists.[32] Former High Court judge Justice Majida Rizvi, chairperson of the National Commission on the Status of Women, speaking on behalf of the commission pointed out that all but two of its seventeen members have once again recommended the repeal of the *Hadood* Ordinances.[33] Calls for its repeal, however, continue to prompt a backlash from religious groups. Sakina Shahid, vice-president of the women's wing of the *Jamat-I-Islam*, called such suggestions "the opinion of a few westernized women" and not of relevance to the bulk of Pakistanis.[34] Her comments are reinforced by members of the *Mutihda Majlis-e-Amal* (MMA), a coalition of religious organizations, which controls the provincial governments of two out of four Pakistani provinces, Northwest Frontier Province (NWFP) and Balochistan. The accusation of being westernized certainly concerns President Musharraf. He too has been faulted as pandering to western interests as he supports the U.S. initiatives against terrorists. Indeed, at the time of writing, he has recently sent the Pakistan army to Taliban hideouts in NWFP. The Taliban are not foreign insurgents but are homegrown young men who were trained and armed by both the Pakistan army and the United Sates to fight the Soviets in Afghanistan. Although Musharraf appears to have support among the educated class of the larger cities, his actions in pursuing these local fighters are extremely unpopular in NWFP and Balochistan. Indeed, he has been the target of three assassination attempts in the last year. Despite continued calls for the *Hadood* Ordinances' repeal, Musharraf does not see this as an opportune time for a change. He recently noted that the *Hadood* Ordinances were a "touchy and thorny issue" and advocated continued debate on the topic. His comments suggest that as a front-line warrior against terrorists, many of whom have sympathizers in Pakistan, Musharraf does not want to help initiate another cause for the religious groups to rally around.

Conclusion

In Pakistan, the state evokes an eternal Islam to justify prosecution for *zina*. Women's stories articulate particular local and national arrangements. Their narratives suggest that the *zina* laws are rooted in economic and political expediency. Women are intimidated into becoming docile bodies and participating in unequal relations with their families, their husbands, and their employers. As the women are biological and cultural reproducers of the nation, their sexuality is a valuable resource that is utilized to service their families and the nation. Should they decide to enter associations of romance and love, they frequently face the wrath of their families. In this refusal to submit to parental pressures and pressures from former husbands, many women find themselves incarcerated in prison or more informally in the *Darul Amans*. Paradoxically, the state both helps families intimidate the women and helps the women escape the grip of their families by providing them shelter in state-run institutions. During the course of their confinement the women learn to be independent of their families and some acquire basic literacy and life-sustaining skills such as embroidery and sewing. They are, however, traumatized by the process. At the same time, regulation of women's sexuality helps build a case for national morality on a base of societal corruption and injustice. The state considers lower-class women expendable, and their liberty is sacrificed for the moral health of the nation. Increasing structural inequality and growing societal violence can then be explained away as a lack of individual morality, rendering the cost of globalization and military spending invisible. Through the *zina* laws the state lays the groundwork for new forms of "traditions" that can be used to control future generations of women both at home and at work. At the same time, the effects of state practices help render women more vulnerable to prostitution and drug trafficking, thus potentially criminalizing impoverished women.

In terms of the current capitalist structure within which Pakistan is embedded, market value determines political priorities. There is no market value in giving women the choice to make decisions about their lives or in the repeal of *zina* laws. In contrast to such determinations of worth, Angela Miles proposes an integrative feminist approach that values life rather than profit.[35] Within this approach the lives of victims of *zina* laws are not considered expendable in the pursuit of globalization and militarization. Moreover, in bringing back the structural issues into a discussion of individual morality, this analysis moves away from a cultural relativist position to identify the effects of the capitalist system that helps create the conditions sustaining *zina* laws.

State and civil interests promote the *Zina* Ordinance as Islamic or allow it as a matter of political expediency. At the same time there are forces that oppose the laws and activists who support women in their struggles. These contradictory forces in society allow women to move out of the helpless victim position and give them room to maneuver. The women whom I interviewed are clear in their desire to control their bodies and opposed to those who lay claim to them. By seeking refuge in *Darul Amans* and by risking incarceration, they are asserting their agency even as these state-sponsored spaces of confinement attempt to neutralize their efforts. Feminist social action can support these women in their struggles by imagining and promoting solidarity through which we identify how the local and global are connected to produce systems of injustice in Pakistan and elsewhere.

References

1. One *lakh* is 100,000 Pakistani rupees, which is the equivalent of 2,500 Canadian dollars.
2. Sindh and Punjab are two different provinces in Pakistan. Naheed's parents are conflating provincial regional groups with ethnicity as is often done in Pakistan.
3. The women's names have been changed.
4. This research was carried out between 1998 and 2002 and funded by the Social Science Humanities Research Council (SSHRC) Canada. During this period I interviewed 150 women in both Karachi and Lahore.
5. Asma Jahangir and Hina Jilani, *The Hadood Ordinances: A Divine Sanction?* (Lahore: Rhotas Books, 1988); Sabiha Sumar and Khalida Nadhvi, "*Zina*: The Hadood Ordinance and its Implications for Women (Pakistan)," *Women Living Under Muslim Laws Dossier #3* (International Solidarity Network, 34980 Combaillaux, Montpellier, 1987).
6. Shahnaz Rouse, "Sovereignty and Citizenship in Pakistan," in *Appropriating Gender*, ed. P. Jeffery and A. Basu (New York: Routledge, 1998); Farida Shaheed, "Woman, State and Power: The Dynamics of Variation and Convergence Across East and West," in *Engendering the Nation-State: Volume I*, ed. N. Hussain, S. Mumtaz, and R. Saigol (Lahore, Pakistan: Simorgh Women's Resource and Publication Centre, 1997); Sadia Toor, "The State, Fundamentalism and Civil Society," in N. Hussain, S. Mumtaz, and R. Saigol, 1997; Rubya Medhi, "The Offence of Rape in the Islamic Law of Pakistan," *Women Living Under Muslim Laws, Dossier 18* B.P. 23, 34790 (Grabels, France, 1991): 98–108; Jahangir and Jilani 1998.
7. Shaheed 1997; Mehdi 1991; Jahangir and Jilani 1988.
8. Elizabeth Comack, "Women and Crime," in *Criminology: A Canadian Perspective*, ed. Rick Linden (Toronto: Harcourt, 2000); Sanjoy Hazarika, "For Women in Indian Prison, a Grim Picture," *The New York Times* (February 29, 1988).
9. Gayle Rubin, "The Traffic in Women," in *Toward an Anthology of Women*, ed. R. Reiter (New York: Monthly Review Press, 1975).
10. Deniz Kandiyoti, "Bargaining with Patriarchy," *Gender and Society* Vol.2 (1988): 274–290.

11. Shaheen Sardar Ali, *Gender and Human Rights in Islam and International Law: Equal Before Allah, Unequal Before Man?* (The Hague: Kluwer Law International, 2000), 176.
12. John Esposito, *Women in Muslim Family Law* (Syracuse, NY: Syracuse University Press, 1982).
13. Shaheed 1997.
14. Esposito 1982.
15. Sabihuddin Ghausi, "Police Top 'Dirty Dozen' Chart," *Dawn* (May 31, 2001).
16. *[The Holy] Qur'an,* trans. AbdullahYusuf Ali (Beirut: Dar al-Arabia, 1968), 11: 282
17. *Darul Amans* are women's shelters sponsored by the state and funded by *Anjuman-i-Himayat-Islam,* a religious organization. Women who seek refuge here find that they are in an informal prison. They cannot leave and, except for their immediate family, other people cannot visit them without permission from the courts. Further, they are also subject to discretionary "judging" by officials in charge. The *Darul Amans* do not have structured procedures and policies that provide any significant protection to the residents. This probably places the residents at greater risk than in prison. See "Locating a Feminist Voice: *Zina* Laws in Pakistan," *Feminist Studies,* 2004 (forthcoming).
18. Human Rights Commission of Pakistan, *State of Human Rights in Pakistan in 1997* (Lahore, Pakistan: Maktaba Jadeed Press, 1997).
19. Commission of Enquiry on the Status of Women, *Report* (Islamabad, Pakistan: Government of Pakistan Publication, August 1997).
20. Ayesha Jalal, "The Convenience of Subservience: Women and the State of Pakistan." in *Women, Islam and the State,* ed. D. Kandiyoti (Philadelphia: Temple University Press, 1991).
21. Many observers point out that the U.S. bombing of Afghanistan and the presence of American troops in Pakistan strengthened anti-Americanism and influenced elections. Religious parties won fifty-one seats in the 2002 election. Where these trends lead us, it appears, depends as much on U.S. foreign policy as it does on local struggles.
22. Ayesha Jalal, "The State and Political Privilege in Pakistan," in *The Politics of Social Transformation in Afghanistan, Iran, and Pakistan,* ed. Myron Weiner and Ali Banuazizi (Syracuse, NY: Syracuse University Press, 1994): 152–184.
23. They are considered antiminority because the Law of Evidence (a part of the *Hadood Ordinances*) renders the legal weight of a non-Muslim's testimony as half that of a Muslim male.
24. Shaheed 1997; Jahangir and Jilani 1988.
25. Walden Bello, "Building an Iron Cage: Bretton Woods Institutions, the WTO and the South," in *Views from the South: The Effects of Globalisation and the WTO on Third World Countries,* ed. S. Anderson (Chicago: First Food Books, 2000); Raghhavan Chakravarthi, *Recolonisation* (Penang: Third World Network 1990).
26. Bello 2000.
27. Gema Martin Munoz, "Islam and the West, an Intentional Duality," in *Islam Modernism and the West,* ed. G.M. Munoz (London: I. B. Tauris, 1999): 3–24, 10
28. Aijaz Ahmad, "Of Dictators and Democrats: Indo-Pakistan Politics in the Year 2000," in *Lineages of the Present: Ideology and Politics in Contemporary South Asia,* ed. A. Ahmad (London: Verso Press, 2000): 301–324.
29. Shahid Javid Burki, "The State and the Political Economy of Redistribution in Pakistan," in *The Politics of Social Transformation in Afghanistan, Iran, and Pakistan,* ed. M. Weiner and A. Banuazizi (Syracuse, NY: Syracuse University Press, 1994).
30. Victoria Schofield, *Kashmir in Conflict: India, Pakistan and the Unfinished War* (New York: I.B. Tauris, 2000).
31. I do not make a distinction between licit and illicit sexuality. Therefore I use the word "innocent" with some caution and point to the ways in which the *Zina* Ordinance helps reinforce a particular version of a chaste moral woman, innocent of the charges of illicit sex, who is then distinguished from the one who is not.
32. Ahmad Raza, "Extra-Marital Sex: A Crime against the State," *OneWorld South Asia* (September 15, 2003).
33. *Daily Times,* "Hadood Ordinance Not a Political Issue" (October 24, 2003).
34. Raza 2003.
35. Angela Miles, *Integrative Feminisms: Building Global Visions 1960s–1990s* (New York: Routledge, 1996).

Part II
Women in the Global Prison

CHAPTER 8

Modern Day Slavery

Inside the Prison-Industrial Complex[1]

KEMBA SMITH

Sitting in an empty classroom in the Education Department at FCI Danbury,[2] while others are participating in Christmas caroling on the yard, I take time to reflect on the holidays that have gone by since I have been in this oppressed state—incarceration. Daydreaming of what it would be like if I were home: the food that I would eat, laying in my grandmother's arms, sitting at the dinner table hours after having eaten, laughing at my Dad and uncles throwing cracks at each other, and most of all seeing my son's excited face Christmas morning.

It is unbelievable that this is my fifth Christmas locked down, not in the sense that the time has been flying, because it has not. On December 12, 1994, still imprisoned, I gave birth to my son. Thirteen days after his birth, I spent Christmas staring at jail cell bars, partially understanding what our ancestors were forced to endure when torn apart from their babies in the Motherland. Longing to be home with my parents, to smell and touch my newborn baby's skin, I wondered what my fate would be.

Today, I still wonder, because I refuse to accept the 24.5 year sentence I have been given. Still I have hope, and strength through God. The government would like for me to be bitter and angry; bound up mentally and emotionally; after all, this is supposed to be my punishment so that I can be an example to deter others from becoming a number within the system. Becoming a voice for thousands of other first-time, nonviolent drug offenders, I am sure it was something they never expected. Thank God for my parents and *Emerge Magazine* for amplifying my voice and believing that I am worth fighting for.[3]

105

Christmas is the worst time of the year for most people incarcerated because of past memories and the ones that we would like to create. Fortunately, I have a soul that runs deep, and my spirit has not been broken, so even in the midst of my situation I still experience joy, however temporary it may be, and my mind is freer than most in society.

I won't focus on self and my present situation, because the season is about giving to others and I want to give you the gift of awareness. Yet still, I represent many brothers and sisters who are casualties in the drug war, and all that I ask for in return is your understanding and action.

Please understand that I am twenty-eight years old and have seen and learned many things while being in the system. Understand that I am not criminally minded, and I am a survivor. Understand that I am spirit-filled and fear God. Understand that I love my people and that knowledge, maturity, and wisdom have shown me just how much. Understand that I have been thrown into an injustice that is bigger than just me. I am seeing other people who are no different from you or me, who are being snatched away from their families for decades or given life sentences for mistakes during their youth.

While laws should be designed to protect our communities from drug kingpins, instead, low-level offenders with little or no involvement in the sale of drugs are being locked up for fifteen, twenty-five, or thirty years. In fact, I know a thirty-year-old black woman, mother of two girls, who was sentenced to thirteen life sentences. My point is you cannot keep assuming that we deserve whatever we get, or that we are heartless criminals.

With the entering of the New Year, I want to give you the gift of vision, to see this system of modern-day slavery for what it is. The government gets paid $25,000 a year by you (taxpayers) to house me (us). The more of us that they incarcerate, the more money they get from you to build more prisons. The building of more prisons creates more jobs. The federal prison system is comprised of 61 percent drug offenders, so basically this war on drugs is the reason why the prison-industrial complex is a skyrocketing enterprise.[4] Many of its employees are getting paid more than the average school-teacher. All of this is to keep me and thousands like me locked down to waste, useless to our community because they want to label us a threat. We are treated as animals and dummies, as if we cannot learn from our mistakes. Take note all of my brothers and sisters, look at how we are being treated, do not allow yourselves to become raw material for the prison-industrial complex.

For too long our community has ignored brothers and sisters who are sentenced under these horrendous drug laws. Even Judge Doumar, the district court judge for my case, stated the following in a recent decision:

When these Guidelines were adopted, I believed them to be unnecessary
. . . . Instead of creating the uniformity in sentencing as intended, the

Guidelines have created a gross disparity in sentencing, influenced by the decisions of individuals. United States Attorneys who have, in essence, the only authority to make the charges or make the substantial assistance motion . . . which would reduce a sentence. Instead in my opinion, Congress has inadvertently created a vast and completely unnecessary bureaucracy, which has not accomplished the goal Congress sought to achieve. Rather the Guidelines have exacerbated the problems that they were designed to eliminate. However, the Guidelines did create a great many new jobs in and out of the sentencing commission.[5]

Several other government officials, including Supreme Court Judges Rehnquist, Breyer, and Kennedy, have publicly acknowledged that there is a problem.

When will our communities come together to demand a just solution? Maybe my brothers and sisters and I on lockdown are expecting too much from our people. After all, there has not been a real movement for decades. Why would Black America want to launch one to help labeled "felons"? Hopefully, once you realize that we are someone's daughter, son, sister, brother, mother, father, and sometimes even grandmother or grandfather, you will begin to organize and recognize the importance of doing so for our future generations. I know women here who are first-time, nonviolent drug offenders who have already served ten years. These harsh drug laws were adopted ten years ago. I wonder how many years I will have to serve before our people demand change. I am already beginning my sixth year. Get involved, get motivated, so that our lives will not be wasted in vain. If not for us, then take action for your child or your child's children or for the future of our people.

References

1. This essay was written by Kemba Smith on December 13, 1999 and posted on the website of the Free Kemba Smith campaign under the title "From the Desk of Kemba Smith." It was also published on January 7, 2000 by the New Journal and Guide (NJG) under the title "Observing the Holidays from Behind Bars: Kemba's Story." As a result of the campaigns on their behalf by Families Against Mandatory Minimums and other organizations, Kemba and Dorothy Gaines, both African American women who had received long sentences under the war on drugs, were granted clemency by President Clinton during the final days of his presidency.
2. A low-security federal women's prison (Federal Correctional Institution) in Danbury, Connecticut.
3. Reginald Stuart, "Kemba's Nightmare," Emerge Magazine, May 1996.
4. In 1985, 34.3 percent of federal prisoners were incarcerated for a drug offense; by 1995 this had increased to 60.8 percent. Stephanie R. Bush-Baskette, The "War on Drugs"" A War on Women?" in Harsh Punishment: International Experiences of Women's Imprisonment, ed. S. Cook and S. Davies (Boston: Northeastern Press, 1999), 219.
5. United States of America v. Kemba Niambi Smith. Criminal Action No. 2:93cr162-11. U.S. District Court of Virginia, Norfolk Division. September 30, 1999.

CHAPTER 9

Remaking Big Government

Immigration and Crime Control in the United States

REBECCA BOHRMAN AND NAOMI MURAKAWA

Politicians and pundits frequently attack big government, calling it bloated, coddling, and inefficient. Former President Bill Clinton declared that "the era of big government is dead" and campaigned on "reinventing government," President George W. Bush suggested that "too much government crowds out initiative," and presidential candidate John Kerry endorsed "smaller and smarter government." We argue that big government is still alive, "reinvented" in the form of expensive and interventionist immigration and crime control. Focusing on U.S. social policy from Lyndon Johnson's Great Society to George W. Bush's Homeland Security, we trace the growth of immigration and crime control in the context of welfare state retrenchment, paying particular attention to how gender, race, and nationality shape policy changes.

We find three distinct trends in immigration and crime control policy, all showing that government has become neither smaller nor smarter. First, political leaders have defunded welfare agencies while bolstering the Immigration and Naturalization Service (INS), the Bureau of Prisons (BOP), and the Drug Enforcement Agency (DEA).[1] Second, immigration and crime control have become more punitive and more interconnected, with agencies sharing personnel, tactics, and agendas. In this pernicious cross-fertilization, INS agents interdict smuggled drugs, DEA agents monitor citizenship status, and both wield the disciplinary tools of deportation and incarceration against immigrants and criminals alike. Third, punitive immigration and crime agendas colonize other agencies, so that even as social welfare agencies lose resources, they nonetheless take on additional burdens of identifying, monitoring, and excluding particular immigrant and criminal categories.

Welfare retrenchment and punishment expansion represent opposite trends in state spending, but they rely on the same ideology. This ideology holds that the liberal welfare state corrodes personal responsibility, divorces work from reward, and lets crime go without punishment; consequently, the lenient welfare regime attracts opportunistic immigrants and cultivates criminal values. Women—particularly women of color, immigrant women, and poor women— are central to these alarmist critiques of the liberal welfare regime: Mexicans migrate to have babies, thereby winning citizenship and its benefits; poor women and women of color wantonly reproduce for welfare benefits, and they produce children only capable of the same. By destroying the welfare state and fortifying the disciplinary state, political leaders are indeed reinventing government. In this remaking of big government, however, holding the budgetary bottom line is less important than preserving racial and gender lines that structure the U.S. state.

Fortifying the Disciplinary State

With the electoral success of the Reagan revolution, many Democrats joined Republicans in a politically profitable competition to shrink government. This competition was exemplified by Clinton's end to "welfare as we know it," in which the Democratic Party dramatically abandoned its faith in government to create New Deals and Great Societies.[2] But politicians have slowed overall government growth only marginally; the major change has been in shifting, not shrinking, budget priorities. This section considers the growth of the disciplinary state, showing that both immigration and crime control have become larger, more punitive, and more racially disproportionate.

Federal spending on the administration of justice—including immigration control, crime control, and drug enforcement—has grown almost every year for the last thirty years, with an average yearly increase of 10 percent. As Figure 9.1 indicates, from 1960 to 2000 the government allocated the federal justice system a growing share of the budget, more than tripling the percentage of resources devoted to justice administration. At the same time, the share of spending on income security, which includes unemployment compensation, housing assistance, and food and nutrition assistance, has decreased steadily since 1975.[3] Even though federal employment is at its lowest level since 1960, law enforcement employment is at its highest level ever. Over the last twenty years the biggest increases in federal employment have been within immigration and crime control agencies. By 2002, the number of federal law enforcement workers surpassed the number of service provision workers.[4]

Both immigration and crime policy have become more punitive and less focused on service and rehabilitation. Most of the INS' growth has been in the

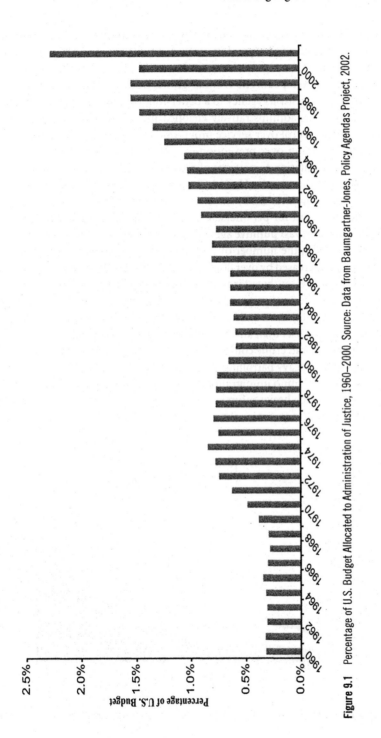

Figure 9.1 Percentage of U.S. Budget Allocated to Administration of Justice, 1960–2000. Source: Data from Baumgartner-Jones, Policy Agendas Project, 2002.

enforcement staff, which has increased by 450 percent since 1975 and now constitutes 75 percent of the total INS staff.[5] Congress has specifically earmarked funds for enforcement, and as a result service and information programs remain underdeveloped.[6] The INS has grown from a vastly underfunded administratively disastrous agency to a better-funded, powerful agency that nevertheless remains administratively chaotic.[7] Just as immigration policy now favors border control over service provision, so too crime control policy now favors incarceration over prevention or rehabilitation. Moving from experiments in rehabilitation to patterns of retribution and simple incapacitation, a penological U-turn in the United States in the last thirty years means that today's prisons are marked by massive overcrowding, less prisoner education, less drug treatment for prisoners, and more prison labor, including the chain gang. Predictably, vast punitive agencies produce vast punished populations. In the last ten years, the number of undocumented immigrants turned back or deported has increased by over 80 percent, and in 2000, there were over 1.6 million arrests at the southwestern border. Similarly, in the last thirty years, the number of incarcerated persons has septupled, and in 2002, with more than 2.1 million persons in prison and jail, the United States incarcerated a greater proportion of its citizens than any nation in the world (Figure 9.2).[8]

Immigration and crime control changes have the harshest consequences for people of color. Heavy patrolling of the southwestern border has a disproportionate effect on Latino immigrants; they compose about 90 percent of all who are deported.[9] Such heavy enforcement of the southwestern border neither deters immigration nor serves stated national security interests. Major patrol

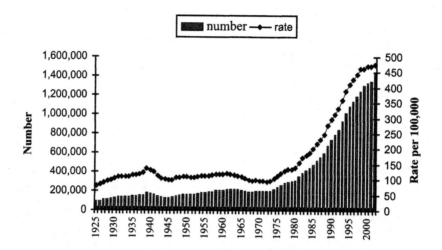

Figure 9.2 Number and Rate of Persons Incarcerated in State and Federal Prisons, 1925–2000.

buildups were placed near urban areas, so border-crossing attempts moved to areas with mountains, deserts, and rivers. Harsh enforcement has relocated rather than reduced border crossings, and with fatal consequences. Between 1997 and 2001, more than one thousand people died while crossing the southwestern border, mostly from extreme heat, cold, or drowning.[10] Unlike the border patrol, internal enforcement is more effective and less racially discriminatory; nonetheless, the ratio of border patrol hours to interior enforcement hours has steadily increased since 1986.[11] The Homeland Security Act of 2002 has only increased the disproportionate targeting of Latino immigrants. The legislation ostensibly responds to fears of terrorism, but most of the new INS hires have been located at the Mexican border, which already has twenty-six times as many agents as the Canadian border. If the administration were primarily concerned with thwarting terrorists, it would more evenly allocate resources to the northern border and interior enforcement.[12]

Just as immigration policy hurts Latino border crossers, crime policy hurts African Americans and Latinos. The racial composition of prisons has reversed in the last half century, with prisons turning from 70 percent white in 1950 to 70 percent black and Latino in 2000. In 2002, African Americans were only 13 percent of the general population but nearly half of the prison population; Latinos were 14 percent of the population but 18 percent of the prison population (see Figure 9.3). In 2000, more African American men were in jail and prison (761,600) than were in higher education (603,000).[13] African American women face similar disparity: African American women have incarceration rates six to seven times those of white women, a ratio roughly equal to the disparity between African American and white men. Moreover, African American women have the fastest-growing incarceration rate. The number of women prisoners has more than doubled in the last decade, jumping from roughly 40,000 women prisoners in 1990 to 85,000 women prisoners in 2000. Despite comparable female populations, the number of women incarcerated in the United States is ten times the total number of women incarcerated in Western European countries. Punitive drug policies have levied a disproportionate toll on women in general and women of color in particular. Among women, drug offenses account for the largest source of total incarceration growth between 1990 and 1999. Of the women convicted of drug felonies in state courts, almost half are convicted solely on "possession" charges. Nationally, black women convicted of drug felonies in state courts are sentenced to prison 41 percent of the time, whereas white women are sentenced to prison only 24 percent of the time. Police officers and DEA agents both acknowledge and defend the use of gendered racial profiling. In sworn testimony, DEA agents have stated that they believe that most drug couriers are black females and that being Hispanic or black was part of the profile they used to identify drug traffickers.[14] Injuries to black and Latino communities extend beyond the imprisoned individual: in

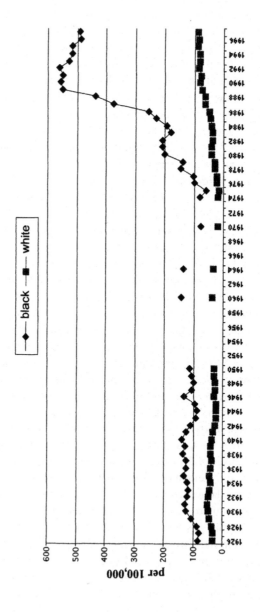

Figure 9.3 Admissions Rate to State and Federal Prisons by Race, 1926–1996.

1999, 767,000 black children and 302,000 Latino children had a parent in prison, with black children nine times and Latino children three times more likely than white children to have an incarcerated parent.[15]

In the midst of welfare state retrenchment, both immigration and crime policy have become more expensive, more punitive, and more racially targeted. Despite calls to make government smaller, cheaper, and decentralized, punitive systems have grown more expansive, more expensive, and more centralized. But there is a unifying logic behind both social welfare *divestment* and border patrol and penal system *investment*. Congressional leaders, complaining that undocumented immigrants cross the border to enjoy welfare benefits, passed the restrictive Illegal Immigration Reform and Immigrant Responsibility Act of 1996 (IIRIRA). In a televised debate the day before the bill's enactment, then Senate Majority Leader Trent Lott said: "In America we have a tremendous problem with illegal immigrants. And they are coming in and they are getting into our welfare systems and our food stamp systems, and they are staying there forever."[16] In the debates over the proposed Personal Responsibility Act in 1995 and 1996, House Republicans cited black criminality as one of the harms of welfare-induced single motherhood. The act states that "the likelihood that a young black man will engage in criminal activities doubles if he is raised without a father and triples if he lives in a neighborhood with a high concentration of single parent families."[17] Congressional leaders justified these two pivotal laws with arguments that social welfare attracts "lazy" immigrants and encourages crime in those who receive assistance. Female welfare seekers and recipients are at the center of this ideological project, which relies on representations of women of color as promiscuous and immoral.

It is ironic, argue many observers, that a conservative Republican president responded to the events of September 11 by constructing an enormous federal bureaucracy, the new Department of Homeland Security. Most of the new spending—hiring air marshals, immigration inspectors, and baggage screeners—is aimed at policing citizens and immigrants. As we have documented, these are the very areas that government was already expanding. Homeland Security–related growth is not, as the *New York Times* and others have suggested, "a sudden shift in the political terrain" but rather an acceleration of the trend toward enlarging the systems of immigrant and criminal control.[18]

Interlocking the Disciplinary State: Convergences Between Immigration and Crime Control

Immigration and crime control have not only grown in parallel fashion, they have also become more interlocking. This section shows that immigration and crime control converge in two notable ways. First, agencies increasingly combine personnel, information, and tactics; that is, Congress cross-deputizes agents, deports for crime control, and imprisons for immigration control. Second, lawmakers approach immigration and crime as inextricably linked problems, placing crime provisions in immigration legislation and immigration provisions in crime legislation.

Combining Personnel, Information, and Tactics

Immigration and crime control agencies increasingly share personnel and information, privileging control over the needs and rights of immigrants and suspects. In 1990, Congress empowered the INS to enforce contraband and narcotics laws, and it required state courts to report information on convicted aliens to the INS. The border patrol has over 9,526 agents that have been cross-designated with Title 21 drug authority by the Drug Enforcement Administration for the purpose of conducting drug search and seizures along the border. In addition, the Office of National Drug Control Policy has teamed up with state and local law enforcement to devise the Comprehensive Interior Enforcement Strategy, which allows federal, state, and local law enforcement agencies complete access to INS information on criminal aliens.[19]

Increasingly, each agency uses the other's punitive tactics. In the IIRIRA, Congress required noncitizens to be deported if they committed a crime with a sentence of one or more years. Compounded by mandatory minimums and the difficulty of applying for asylum, this law vastly expanded the number of potential deportations. Similarly, prisons hold increasing numbers of noncitizens. Between 1984 and 2001, the number of noncitizens in federal prisons jumped from 4,088 to 35,629, and almost 70 percent are Latino. Generally, noncitizens are incarcerated for nonviolent, low-level crimes. Only 1.5 percent of noncitizen federal prisoners are violent offenders, compared with 16 percent of citizen prisoners. Drug offenses and violations of immigration law drive this increase in noncitizen incarceration. In 1984, 1,204 noncitizens in federal prison were charged with a drug offense; by 1999, this figure had increased fifteen-fold to 18,594. Furthermore, noncitizens convicted of a drug offense were more likely than citizens to have played a minor, low-level role in the transaction.[20]

Merging Policy: Immigration Laws as Crime Control and Crime Laws as Immigration Control

In addition to the cross-deputization of personnel and the sharing of tactics, lawmakers increasingly link immigration and crime policy. We see a new trend in which major immigration laws include crime provisions, and major crime laws include immigration provisions. Issues of employment, public spending, and crime have always been linked to the debate over immigration, but Congress has emphasized this linkage more in recent years, as one analyst writes, giving "deportation policy an almost exclusive emphasis on crime."[21] Over the last ten years, almost all major immigration and crime legislation—including the IIRIRA, the Violent Crime Control and Law Enforcement Act of 1994, and the 1996 Anti-Terrorism Law—has justified immigration restrictions in criminological terms and criminal penalties in anti-immigration terms.

The IIRIRA of 1996 focuses both on the speedy deportation of immigrants with any criminal record and on criminalizing more acts. Whereas before 1996, undocumented immigrants who committed crimes were released at the end of their sentence, this legislation requires them to serve their sentences and then remain in prison until they are deported. It also authorized $5 million for a database to track criminal aliens and required that it be used to help local governments in identifying criminals that they could deport. Also, it authorized judges to issue deportation orders as part of a probation or plea agreement, further enmeshing immigration with the criminal justice system. Congress imposed harsher sanctions on undocumented immigrants as well as "streamlining the deportation process," making it much harder to appeal decisions. IIRIRA required noncitizens to be deported if they committed a crime with a sentence of one or more years (rather than the previous benchmark of five or more years); given the severity of mandatory minimums, even the most minor offenses can provoke deportation.

During 1993 and 1994, Congress hotly debated controlling "illegal immigration," but the only immigration provisions it passed were in the Violent Crime Control and Law Enforcement Act of 1994. The tone of the debate is exemplified by Senator Orrin Hatch, who argued for expedited deportation of criminal immigrants "so they do not mess up our country anymore."[22] The legislation contained major immigration provisions, including $1.2 billion to strengthen border control, faster deportation of those denied asylum, and $1.8 billion to help states pay for incarcerating undocumented immigrants convicted of felonies. Some of the Violent Crime Act provisions are laughably tangential to crime, and even the provisions that do relate to crime are based on criminological misperceptions. Immigrants are no more likely to be criminals than native-born citizens once demographic variables are controlled.[23] In the debates over the legislation, members of Congress often cited the statistic that 25 percent of prisoners are undocumented immigrants; although this does hold true for the federal prison system, the percentage of immigrants in the much larger state prison population is far lower (9.6 percent). More significantly, immigrants are one of the fastest-growing groups of prisoners because the 1996 IIRIRA expanded the number of crimes that would incur federal prison time, in particular, the crime of entering the country without proper documents.

The Antiterrorism and Effective Death Penalty Act of 1996 was ostensibly in response to the Oklahoma City bombing, a domestic terrorist attack, but key provisions of the act were aimed at immigrants. Congress rejected measures that might have had some impact on domestic terrorism, such as marking explosives with chemical identifiers; however, Congress passed a ban on "foreign" groups with terrorist connections and a provision allowing the border patrol to more easily turn away immigrants. In particular, they established a procedure of "summary exclusion," making it easier to turn away those without proper documentation, disregarding the possibility that a refugee fleeing persecution might need to rely on false papers. Conservative Republicans pushed a small government response to terrorism, in part because of a Waco- and Ruby Ridge–inspired "fear of our own government."[24] In fact, they sought measures effectively protecting domestic militia groups, but they bolstered federal punishments for immigrants and criminals.

Interlocking immigration with crime control extends the reach of the disciplinary state, jeopardizes privacy, and engenders fear about obtaining basic services. In the convergence of immigration and crime control policy, lawmakers see immigrants as criminals and criminals as subcitizens.

Colonizing the Welfare State: The Long Arm of Immigration and Crime Control

As the disciplinary state has grown larger and more intertwined, it has crept into social welfare agencies. This section shows that recent legislation in the areas of income support, health care, education, and public housing places new exclusions on persons with particular immigrant and criminal status. Even as agencies confront dwindling resources, they bear additional responsibilities of policing, identifying, and excluding categories of immigrants and criminals.

New exclusions reinforce "immigrant" and "criminal" as identities of no return. Lawmakers have cut federal income support and in ways that especially harm immigrant families and people with drug felony convictions. The Personal Responsibility and Work Opportunity Reconciliation Act of 1996 replaced federal income support with a federal block grant program called Temporary Assistance to Needy Families (TANF) that allows states to create their own welfare programs. New provisions in the law single out two groups for permanent exclusion: immigrants (with some exceptions) and people with drug felony convictions.

Cutting benefits for immigrants, both undocumented and legal, was at the heart of welfare reform. In the 1996 IIRIRA, Congress restricted benefits for undocumented immigrants: the law not only made undocumented immigrants ineligible for food stamps, it also imposed a penalty of up to five years in prison for knowingly helping an undocumented immigrant apply for aid. The Personal Responsibility Act excluded legal immigrants from most public assistance, which was expected to save over $25 billion over five years. The new law prevented legal immigrants from obtaining many benefits such as supplemental security income (SSI) and food stamps.[25] Congress also permitted states to bar legal immigrants from receiving benefits from Title XX block grants for child care, assistance for the disabled, and support services for abused children, as well as allowing states to exclude legal immigrants from any state-funded benefit programs. Both legal and undocumented immigrants (with minor exceptions) were barred from receiving Medicaid and all forms of nonemergency medical assistance, requiring hospitals to determine immigration status before treating patients in nonemergency situations.

The Personal Responsibility Act turned aid agencies into investigators. The law required local agencies that administer welfare block grants, SSI, and housing assistance to provide quarterly reports with the names and addresses of people unlawfully in the United States. According to the National Conference of State Legislatures, welfare agencies will pay an additional $700 million to determine clients' immigration status, draining funds from already strapped programs.

There is little evidence that government assistance is actually, as legislators have argued, a "magnet drawing people across the border."[26] Less than 1 percent of surveyed immigrants move to the United States primarily for social services. Legislation that threatens those who use public aid with deportation makes immigrants reluctant to apply for services. Between 1995 and 1999, the receipt of TANF, food stamps, and Medicaid by lawful permanent residents has plummeted. Even though some food stamp cuts were restored in 1998, immigrants as well as state agencies remain confused about eligibility, and some state agencies have mistakenly turned away eligible immigrants.[27] Fear of deportation inhibited parents from applying for food stamps for their eligible children, which produced a dramatic fall in participation rates among eligible immigrant families.[28]

The Personal Responsibility Act also excludes persons convicted of drug felonies from ever receiving TANF or food stamps. The drug felon exclusion, an amendment sponsored by Senator Phil Gramm, passed after two minutes of debate. The only voice of protest came from Senator Edward Kennedy, who underscored criminological inconsistencies, arguing that "under this amendment, if you are a murderer, a rapist, or a robber, you can get Federal funds; but if you are convicted even for possession of marijuana, you cannot."[29]

Given the high rate of drug felony convictions, the Gramm amendment permanently denies eligibility for an enormous population. Of the 347,774 felony drug convictions in state courts in 1996, roughly 40 percent (135,270) were convictions for possession. With recidivism rates for drug conviction at roughly one in three, it is possible that as many as 246,000 people could be denied welfare eligibility every year. Because drug felon exclusion is permanent, the cumulative number of persons denied welfare grows every year. By earmarking drug felons as subject to special punishment, these laws magnify the harm of one of the most racially selective areas of the criminal justice system. Although African

Americans constitute only 13 percent of the U.S. population and 13 percent of all drug users, they account for 35 percent of all drug arrestees, 55 percent of all drug convictions, and 71 percent of all drug sentences.[30]

Immigrant and drug felon provisions disproportionately exclude women. Legal and especially undocumented women workers earn less, are usually found in occupations with few opportunities for upward mobility, and are therefore more likely to require income assistance. Incarcerated women are more likely than incarcerated men to have a drug felony conviction, and roughly 80 percent of incarcerated women are mothers.[31] Legislative debate attacks immigrant women for reproducing in order to obtain citizenship and welfare payments. In a 1993 debate over border patrol spending, Representative Dan Burton complained of "a virtual tidal wave of illegal aliens coming across the Mexican-American border." Citing the high number of births in Los Angeles County, he pressed for more border patrol spending because "each one of those children, when they are born, is eligible for AFDC payments."[32]

Education is another area in which immigrants and criminals are facing possible exclusion. No federal law currently bars immigrants from public schools, although there is growing support for this restriction. The U.S. House of Representatives and the California electorate both passed measures restricting children of undocumented immigrants from public schools. Although the House measure did not become law and Proposition 187 was fought in court, their consideration suggests that many people now see education as a special privilege.

Although immigrant exclusions from public education have failed so far, exclusions based on criminal status have, unfortunately, succeeded. The Higher Education Act was passed in 1965 to establish financial aid programs such as Perkins loans, Pell grants, and work-study programs. In the 1998 reauthorization of the Higher Education Act, Congress expanded federal assistance to college students and reduced interest rates. Against this expansion of opportunity, the 1998 reauthorization included a new provision that denies loan eligibility to persons with drug felony convictions.[33] The exclusion passed by voice vote with little debate.

The drug felon exclusion has a significant impact on students. During the 2000–2001 school year, about 9,000 applicants lost their federal aid after checking "yes" in the drug conviction box on the Federal Application for Financial Aid. During the same year, more than 836,000 applicants left the question blank. Under the Clinton Administration, these nonresponsive applicants were not denied eligibility, partially because of claims of ambiguous question wording. Under the Bush Administration, the magnitude of drug felon exclusions will increase. Rod Paige, the education secretary under Bush, declared that the question phrasing is now clear enough so that failure to answer it will mean denial of aid. As of April 8, 2001, more than 26,000 of 3.9 million applicants have been declared ineligible, 15,000 by admitting to drug convictions and 11,000 by leaving the question blank.[34]

The Department of Housing and Urban Development (HUD) is another component of the welfare state responsible for identifying, and sometimes reporting and excluding, undocumented immigrants and people with drug addictions. HUD is required to report all undocumented tenants, and undocumented immigrants are not eligible for public housing. The Quality Housing and Work Responsibility Act of 1998 requires local housing authorities to screen applicants, and those who were once evicted because of drug-related crimes are prohibited from public housing for three years. This legislation built upon the Anti-Drug Abuse Act of 1988, which provided that public housing tenants could be evicted for engaging in criminal or drug-related criminal activity on or near the premises. The Quality Housing Act also enables local housing authorities to investigate whether the applicant uses illegal drugs or abuses alcohol. Investigation includes questioning the applicant and inquiring at drug treatment centers. The Quality Housing Act punishes people with drug-related crimes and people who are possibly abusing alcohol and drugs, so the potential impact of this provision is enormous.

Without actually reducing immigration or crime, policies subject immigrants and people of color to struggle, suffering, and indignity, entrenching existing racial, national, and gender hierarchies. The policy justification for "drug-felon" exclusions from higher education loans is that drug users cannot recover and will not change. The policy consequence is that these barriers to education make opportunities for legal employment even scarcer. Similarly, the policy justification for health care exclusions is that immigrant women and criminal women are sexually loose and maternally negligent. The policy consequence of inadequate health care is inadequate access to information and services concerning birth control, prenatal care, and child health care. In both cases, the policy's consequences reinforce the policy's justification.

As this section shows, immigrants and criminals face exclusions and restrictions from basic welfare services such as income support, health care, public housing, and education. It is tempting to cast these shifts in governance in sweeping terms of state reconstruction: from doctrines of assimilation to doctrines of exclusion, from doctrines of rehabilitation to doctrines of retribution, from social provision to social lockdown, from welfare state to police state. Thinking specifically about women of color, however, these shifts are not nearly so stark. Historically, notions of assimilation and rehabilitation have set invisible benchmarks of a white middle-class norm; eligibility requirements for social services have had explicit exclusions in national and racial terms and repressive stipulations for women in terms specific to sexuality, reproduction, and motherhood.[35] The remaking of big government is not a shift from beneficent welfare state to nefarious police state; then and now, women of color were subject to exclusions and regulations, with minimal influence in formulating the policies affecting them so profoundly. From our perspective, the police state is far worse than the welfare state, however lacking. The welfare state needs to be made more robust, more inclusive, and more of an actual safety net, not replaced with the disciplinary state.

Conclusion

This chapter describes the remaking of big government for immigration and crime control, accounting for three trends in the punitive escalation and convergence of immigration and crime control. First, there has been a shift in resource allocation between government agencies; the Immigration and Naturalization Service, the Bureau of Prisons, and the Drug Enforcement Agency have absorbed more resources relative to other agencies, particularly agencies of social welfare. Second, the disciplinary state has become more interlocking, with immigration and crime control sharing personnel, tactics, and policy agendas. Third, punitive immigration and crime agendas colonize other agencies, so even as the welfare state loses resources, it takes on additional burdens of identifying, monitoring, and excluding those of particular immigrant and criminal statuses.

The surveillance of suspect categories—"immigrants," "criminals," and now "terrorists"—has deep antecedents in the policies of the last thirty years. As this book is going to press, U.S. suspicion, surveillance, and lockdown are spreading in deeply frightening ways. Policy and conventional wisdom identify more people as threats and potential threats, expanding the categories "immigrant," "criminal," and "terrorist" and blending these categories into each other. With post–September 11 intensified security checks at the Mexico–U.S. border, INS agents are looking for "terrorists," but they are finding drugs and incarcerating more drug carriers. One INS agent, cross-deputized as a DEA agent, described increased drug seizures as "dividends of the war on terrorism." With the forced registration of men from twenty-one countries, national origin alone makes people subject to possible detention, deportation, and brutality, not to mention the humiliation, fear, and inconvenience of registering with an incompetent and backlogged bureaucracy. When asked about interning Arab Americans, the chair of the new Subcommittee on Crime, Terrorism, and Homeland Security responded that Japanese American internment was a legitimate way to contain those who want to harm the United States.[36]

In the new state, both immigration and crime policy impose and patrol borders. National boundaries and prisons define discrete physical spaces, maintain illusions of safety, and wall out and bar in groups of people, usually along lines of identity that are themselves borders with quasi-physical and illusion-maintaining dimensions. The modal tactics of modern immigration and crime control—deportation and incarceration—entail physical removal from the body politic. Deportation and incarceration are tactics that aim to solve the nation's problems by expelling unwanted elements from the body politic, as if evil and violence come from some outside—outside respectable America, from Mexico or prisons or urban ghettos.

What does it mean to have so many convergences between immigration and crime policy? Immigrants' rights activists have commented that immigrants are treated like criminals, and prison abolition activists have commented that the incarcerated are treated like noncitizens. They are both right, but ultimately we should be calling into question whether immigrants should be treated like immigrants and criminals should be treated like criminals. Instead, a broader coalition should be built around the shared concerns of fighting the growing disciplinary state.

References

1. The Homeland Security Act of 2002 abolished the INS, replacing it with the Bureau of Citizenship and Immigration Services and the Bureau of Immigration and Customs Enforcement. The transition to this new immigration administration structure is still under way, so we continue to call it the INS.
2. For an overview of this transformation of the Democratic Party, particularly the relationship between shrinking big government and race, see Paul Frymer, *Uneasy Alliances: Race and Party Competition in America* (Princeton, NJ: Princeton University Press, 1999); Philip A Klinkner and Rogers M. Smith, *The Unsteady March: The Rise and Decline of Racial Equality in America* (Chicago: University of Chicago Press, 1999); Adolph Reed Jr. ed., *Without Justice for All* (Boulder, CO: Westview Press, 1999).
3. The budget data used here were originally collected by Frank R. Baumgartner and Bryan D. Jones, for the *Policy Agendas Project,* with the support of National Science Foundation grant number SBR 9320922 and were distributed through the Center for American Politics and Public Policy at the University of Washington and/or the Department of Political Science at Penn State University. Neither NSF nor the original collectors of the data bear any responsibility for the analysis reported here. We look only at discretionary spending; the only programs that have grown as consistently as immigration and control programs are Medicare and Social Security, programs that are universal entitlements.
4. Professor Donald F. Kettle testimony before the U.S. House Committee on Rules. *Has Government Been 'Reinvented'?* 106th Cong., 2d Sess., May 4, 2000; author analysis of data from U.S. Office of Management and Budget, *Budget of the United States Government, Fiscal Year 2004* (Washington, DC: Government Printing Office, 2003), table 17.3. We combined Justice Department employees with those from the newly created Department of Homeland Security. Service provision agencies include the Education Department, Department of Health and Human Services, and the Social Security Administration
5. Data from Transactional Records Access Clearinghouse (TRAC).
6. U.S. Department of Justice, *FY 2002 Budget Summary* (Washington, DC: U.S. Department of Justice, 2001). Available: http://www.usdoj.gov/jmd/2002summary/. The Illegal Immigration Reform and Immigrant Responsibility Act of 1996 required that "additional border patrol agents shall be deployed among Immigration and Naturalization Service sectors along the border in proportion to the level of illegal crossing of the borders of the United States," from U.S. Public Law 104-208, Sec. 101, 104th Cong., 2nd Sess. September 30, 1996.
7. Milton Morris, *Immigration—The Beleaguered Bureaucracy,* (Washington DC: The Brookings Institution, 1985); Sharon A. Barrios, "Is the Immigration and Naturalization Service Unreformable? Past Experience and Future Prospects," *Administration and Society* 34 (2002): 370–388. For an overview of the INS's long-standing administrative problems,

see U.S. General Accounting Office, *Immigration and Naturalization Service: Overview of Recurring Management Challenges* (Washington, DC: Government Printing Office, October 2001).

8. Immigration data are from Transactional Records Access Clearinghouse (TRAC), *National Profile and Enforcement Trends Over Time* [database online] (Syracuse, NY: Syracuse University, 2002). Available: http://trac.syr.edu/tracins/findings/national/index.html. For more detailed information on INS budget increases, see U.S. Department of Justice, *Budget Trend Data from 1975 Through the President's 2003 Request to the Congress* (Washington, DC: Justice Management Division, 2002). Available: http://www.usdoj.gov/jmd/budgetsummary/btd/1975_2002/2002/pdf/BudgetTrend.pdf.
Incarceration data are from Bureau of Justice Assistance, *Prisoners in 2002* (Washington, DC: U.S. Department of Justice, 2003); Roy Walmsley, *World Prison Population List* (London: Research, Development and Statistics Director, 2003); U.S. Department of Justice, *Sourcebook of Criminal Justice Statistics 2001* (Washington, DC: Bureau of Justice Statistics, 2002), p. 494.

9. Kevin R. Johnson, "The Case Against Race Profiling in Immigration Enforcement," *Washington University Law Quarterly* 78 (2000): 676–736. See also U.S. Office of Immigration Statistics, Department of Homeland Security, *2002 Yearbook of Immigration Statistics* (Washington, DC: Department of Justice, Available: http://uscis.gov/graphics/shared/aboutus/statistics/ENF2002list.htm. INS data show that whereas 92 percent of aliens removed in 2000 were from Mexico, Mexican undocumented immigrants represented 67 percent of the total undocumented immigrant population. However, estimates of the size and composition of the undocumented immigrant population are varying and subject to great uncertainty.

10. U.S. General Accounting Office, *Southwest Border Strategy: Resource and Impact Issues Remain after Seven Years. Report to the Congress* (Washington, DC: Government Printing Office, August 2001); Belinda I. Reyes, Hans P. Johnson, and Richard Van Swearingen, *Holding the Line?: The Effect of The Recent Border Build-Up on Unauthorized Immigration* (San Francisco: Public Policy Institute of California, 2002); Mary Jordan, "Smuggling People Is Now Big Business in Mexico," *Washington Post*, May 17, 2001.

11. Alberto Davila, Jose A. Pagan, and Montserrat Viladrich Grau, "Immigration Reform, the INS, and the Distribution of Interior and Border Enforcement Resources," *Public Choice* 99 (1999): 327–345; Thomas J. Espenshade, "Does the Threat of Border Apprehension Deter Undocumented United-States Immigration?" *Population and Development Review* 20 (1994): 871–892; U.S Government Accounting Office, *Illegal Aliens: Significant Obstacles to Reducing Unauthorized Alien Employment Exist. Report to the Congress* (Washington, DC: Government Printing Office, 1999).

12. Data on allocation of border patrol from the United States Office of Public Management, cited by TRAC Available: http://trac.syr.edu/tracins/findings/aboutINS/newFindings.html.

13. Bureau of Justice Assistance, *Prisoners in 2002*, table 13; Loic Wacquant, "Deadly Symbiosis," *Boston Review* 27, no. 2 (2002): 23–31; Justice Policy Institute, *Cellblocks or Classrooms? The Funding of Higher Education and Corrections and Its Impact on African American Men* (Washington, DC: Justice Policy Institute, 2000).

14. Bureau of Justice Assistance, *Prisoners in 2002*, tables 13 and 14; U.S. Department of Justice, *Sourcebook of Criminal Justice Statistics* (Washington, DC: Bureau of Justice Statistics, 2001), p. 494; Amnesty International, *"Not Part of My Sentence:" Violations of the Human Rights of Women in Custody* (New York: Amnesty International, 1999); Lawrence A. Greenfeld and Tracy L. Snell, *Women Offenders* (Washington, DC: Bureau of Justice Statistics, 1999); Jodi M. Brown and Patrick A. Langan, *State Court Sentencing of Convicted Felons 1994* (Washington, DC: Bureau of Justice Statistics, 1998); National Council of La Raza, *The Mainstreaming of Hate: A Report of Latinos and Harassment, Hate Violence, and Law Enforcement Abuse in the 90's* (Washington, DC: National Council of La Raza, 1999). Gender and racial disparities arise not simply from the discriminatory behavior of law enforcement agents, prosecutors, and judges; they are inscribed into the structure of "gender- and race-neutral" sentencing guidelines. Women often play minor roles in drug dealing and therefore lack information to plea bargain down to more lenient sentences. In addition, sentencing neither accounts for possible coercion from an abusive male partner who deals nor does it consider as mitigating circumstances the role of single mothers in caring for children. See Myrna Raeder, "Gender and Sentencing: Single Mom, Battered Women, and Other Sex-

Based Anomalies in the Gender-Free World of the Federal Sentencing Guidelines," *Pepperdine Law Review* 20, no. 3 (1993).

15. Christopher J. Mumola, *Incarcerated Parents and Their Children* (Washington, DC: Bureau of Justice Statistics, 2000).

16. Federal News Service, *PBS Debate Night with the Congressional Leadership*, Moderated by Jim Lehrer, Williamsburg, VA, September 29, 1996.

17. Personal Responsibility Act, H.R. 4, sec. 100, cited in Dorothy Roberts, *Killing the Black Body: Race, Reproduction, and the Meaning of Liberty* (New York: Pantheon Books 1997), 215.

18. Robin Toner, "The Nation: Now, Government Is the Solution, Not the Problem, " *New York Times*, September 30, 2001.

19. U.S. Public Law 101-649. 101st Cong., 2nd Sess., November 29, 1990; Office of National Drug Control Policy, *Summary: FY 2002 National Drug Control Budget*, September 20, 2001. Available: http://www.whitehousedrugpolicy.gov/publications/policy/budget02/partiv_ins .html; INS, *Interior Enforcement*, July 26, 2001. Available: http://www.ins.usdoj.gov/ graphics/lawenfor/interiorenf/index.htm

20. John Scalia, *Noncitizens in the Federal Criminal Justice System, 1984–94* (Washington, DC: Bureau of Justice Statistics, 1996); Jan Chaiken, *Compendium of Federal Justice Statistics, 1999* (Washington, DC: Bureau of Justice Statistics, 2001); John Scalia and Marika F.X. Litras, *Immigration Offenders in the Federal Criminal Justice System, 2000* (Washington, DC: Bureau of Justice Statistics, 2002).

21. William M. McDonald, "Crime and Illegal Immigration: Emerging Local, State, and Federal Partnerships," *National Institute of Justice Journal* (1997): 232.

22. *Congressional Record*, 103rd Cong., 2nd Sess., 1994, 140: S 12496.

23. Kristen E. Butcher and Anne Morrison Piehl, "Cross-City Evidence on the Relationship Between Immigration and Crime," *Journal of Policy Analysis and Management* 17 (1998): 457–493.

24. Alison Mitchell and Todd S. Purdum, "The Lawmakers: Ashcroft, Seeking Broad Powers, Says Congress Must Act Quickly," *New York Times* October 1, 2001.

25. An exception was made for legal immigrants who have worked in the United States for at least ten years. The Farm Security and Rural Investment Act of 2002 softened food stamp restrictions, restoring benefits to children, the disabled, and immigrants who have lived in the United States for more than five years.

26. U.S. Congress, Congressman David Dreier, 103rd Congress, 1st session. *Congressional Record* (1 July 1993), vol. 139, H 4412.

27. Marc L. Berk, Claudia L. Schur, Leo R. Chavez, and Martin Frankel, "Health Care Use Among Undocumented Latino Immigrants," *Health Affairs* 19 (2000): 51–64; Michael Fix and Ron Haskins, *Welfare Benefits for Non-Citizens* (Washington, DC: The Brookings Institution, February 2002); Rachel L. Swarns, "State Officials Add to U.S. Criticism of New York City's Food Stamp Program," *New York Times* January 21, 1999.

28. U.S. Department of Agriculture, *The Decline in Food Stamp Participation* (Washington, DC: Government Printing Office, July 2001). The same laws that have denied federal assistance to immigrants have also made employment discrimination more likely. The General Accounting Office found a "serious pattern of discrimination," in which surveyed employers began discriminating specifically due to Immigration Reform and Control Act. Of the 4.6 million employers covered by the survey, 10 percent admitted discriminating against people on the basis of national origin, and another 9 percent discriminated against noncitizens. The survey estimates that 227,000 employers instituted a practice of not hiring those with a foreign accent or appearance. See U.S. General Accounting Office, *Immigration Reform: Employer Sanctions and the Question of Discrimination* (Washington, DC: Government Printing Office, March 1990).

29. *Congressional Record*, 104th Cong., 2nd Sess., 142, daily ed. July 23, 1996: S8498. The provision allows states to opt out of the drug felony provision. Only eight states opted out of the provision. Ten states modified the provision, and thirty-two states adopted the provision wholesale. The eight states that opted out completely are Connecticut, Hawaii, New Hampshire, New York, Oklahoma, Oregon, Utah, and Vermont. Of the ten states that modified the provision, five excluded those convicted of drug possession but not drug sales (Arkansas, Florida, Illinois, North Carolina, and Rhode Island). The other five states that modified allowed eligibility for those who are in or have completed drug treatment

(Colorado, Illinois, Iowa, North Carolina, and Washington). In Illinois and North Carolina, recipients have to meet both the drug possession and drug treatment criteria to retain eligibility. See Rukaiyah Adams, David Onek, and Alissa Riker, *Double Jeopardy: An Assessment of the Felony Drug Provision of the Welfare Reform Act* (San Francisco: The Justice Policy Institute, 1998).

30. See Michael Tonry, *Malign Neglect: Race, Crime, and Punishment in America* (New York: Oxford University Press, 1995); Jerome G. Miller, *Search and Destroy: African-American Males in the Criminal Justice System* (Cambridge: Cambridge University Press, 1996).

31. Mary G. Powers, William Seltzer, and Jing Shi, "Gender Differences in the Occupational Status of Undocumented Immigrants in the United States: Experience Before and After Legalization," *International Migration Review* 32 (1998): 1015–1046; Mumola 2000. State policies sometimes compound women's disadvantage by discriminating against parents. For example, California allows childless drug felons to receive state general assistance, whereas drug felons who are parents cannot. See Adams, Onek, and Riker, *Double Jeopardy,* 1998.

32. *Congressional Record,* 103rd Cong., 1st Sess., 139: 4412.

33. A person is ineligible if convicted under federal or state law for possession or sale of a controlled substance. The drug felon amendment provides a "rehabilitation" exemption stating that a student may resume eligibility upon completion of a drug rehabilitation program and successfully clearing two unannounced drug tests.

34. Daniel Golden, "Tougher Bush Stance on Obscure Law Hits Students Seeking Financial Aid," *Wall Street Journal,* April 25, 2001.

35. Historically, maternalist welfare policy is born of privileged women's advocacy during the Progressive Era, when women reformers presented single motherhood as a social problem in need of government intervention. Viewing urban immigrants as a threat, these reformers used welfare as a vehicle for both charity and disciplinary supervision. Using convoluted, "gender- and race-neutral" categorizations, nonwhites have been excluded from SSI benefits through exclusion of domestics and agricultural workers; welfare benefits enforced "man-in-the house" rules race-selectively; and World War II veteran housing benefits were effectively for whites only. See Linda Gordon, *Pitied But Not Entitled: Single Mothers and the History of Welfare 1890–1935* (Cambridge, MA: Harvard University Press, 1994); Robert C. Lieberman, *Shifting the Color Line: Race and the American Welfare State* (Cambridge, MA: Harvard University Press, 1998).

36. Michael Janofsky, "Border Agents Looking for Terrorists Are Finding Drugs" *New York Times,* March 6, 2002; Associated Press, "Coble Says Internment of Japanese-Americans Was Appropriate," February 5, 2003.

CHAPTER 10

Las Mujeres Olvidadas[1]
Women in Mexican Prisons

CRISTINA JOSE KAMPFNER
TRANSLATED BY DEREKA RUSHBROOK

During 1993 to 1994, I was the director of a study undertaken by the Colegio de Mexico's Interdisciplinary Program for the Study of Women in order to determine the situation and living conditions facing women in Mexico's prisons.[2] At the time of the study, women prisoners were a forgotten population, considered too small to merit serious discussion or justify decent facilities. Ten years later, Mexico has become part of the global prison boom, with prison construction being touted as the only solution to spiraling incarcerated populations and entrenched overcrowding. Despite their growing numbers, women in Mexican prisons remain largely invisible to the eye of the policymakers, whether in Mexico City or in Washington, D.C., who help shape the conditions that led to their imprisonment. Making these women visible is the first step in challenging their subordination, both in the penal system and in Mexican society as a whole. Mexican women prisoners share the same demographics as women in U.S. prisons. They are poor, undereducated, and many of them have suffered from physical or sexual abuse. They also share the detrimental impact of drug enforcement policies dictated by the United States. Latinas in Mexico are often doing time for the same crimes as women in the United States, including running and/or selling drugs, theft to support a habit or at the dictates of their husbands or boyfriends, and in some situations killing an abusive partner. Often these women are not drug users but were introduced to small quantities of drugs when visiting their husbands in prison or were "burros" transporting drugs for money to feed their families. As victims of the "war on drugs," imposed on Mexico by the United States, these women face minimum prison sentences of seven years. They leave behind children and families who rely on them for survival.

I begin with a statistical overview of the prison population in order to contextualize the problem. Mexico has a total of 445 penal institutions of all kinds, from detention centers in large cities to jails in the smallest and most remote communities. These institutions include "centers for social readaptation" (CERESO), penitentiaries, municipal and state-level jails, and the modern federal high-security prisons. Of these, approximately 230 contain a corner, a cell, or a small section dedicated to housing the female prison population because there are very few women's prisons in Mexico.[3] This lack of institutions designed exclusively for women is the first source of the disadvantages that women face in the penal system. The lack of women's facilities is justified with the argument that women represent only 4 percent of the national prison population. However, this argument merely serves to obscure the fact that, in the prison as well as in other institutions of society, the needs of women are consistently subordinated to those of men. In this field, the operative rubric of order and security, among others, works to disadvantage women. Because they rarely use force, attempt escape, riot, or pose a risk to security in these facilities, their demands are rarely seen as a priority and satisfying them tends to be postponed indefinitely. If women are forgotten within the prison population, indigenous women tend to be further marginalized within the female prison population. At the time of the study, indigenous women made up 5 percent of the Mexican prison population. Today indigenous women are about 2.5 percent or half the proportion of ten years earlier.[4] This does not represent a real decline in numbers because the overall incarcerated population has increased. However, it is likely that new policies providing for translators and legal council in native languages, other than Spanish, has had a positive impact on the treatment of indigenous women.

In absolute numbers, the number of women imprisoned in Mexico was 3,479 at the time of the study, which, as noted previously, represented 4 percent of the total prison population of 91,788. Ten years later, the women's prison population has more than doubled. As of 2003 there were 7,500 women prisoners in a total prison population of 182,500. In Mexico City alone, there were 22,000 men and 1,100 incarcerated women.[5] This dramatic increase in women's incarceration is largely due to Mexico's adoption of the war on drugs, which, under U.S. pressure, has introduced enhanced policing and lengthy mandatory minimum sentences for possession and sale. It can also be linked to the feminization of poverty brought about by successive peso devaluations as well as Mexico's entrance into the North American Free Trade Agreement. The rising social and economic cost of imprisonment is a hidden face of Mexico's integration into the global marketplace. Because men have also faced spiraling incarceration rates in the past ten years, women continue to represent only 4 percent of the imprisoned population. This percentage is similar to that found in other countries at similar stages of development. In more advanced industrialized countries, where women constitute a larger percentage of those in conflict with the law (just as they do in other activities), the proportion of women in prison almost never exceeds 15 percent of the total population.

It is not difficult to discern that behind these statistics are ideologies, representations, and practices that maintain the unequal positions held by men and women in Mexican society, in other words, the social construction of gender. An array of experts has proposed that women's limited participation in criminal offenses constitutes one of the clearest pieces of evidence that informal mechanisms of control are much more effective and stronger with women.[6] Other authors have suggested that women are the absent subject of punishment discourse.[7] Similarly, Facio and Zaffaroni agree that stereotypical images of men and women and the invisibility of women are key factors that impede the just treatment of criminalized women.[8] Despite these debates about gender and criminality in Mexico, there have not been any studies on Mexican prisons that apply a gendered analysis. The explanations surrounding female criminality that prevail today continue to privilege biological or psychological perspectives. The former are a continuation of a line of thought initiated by Lombroso, for whom the fundamental explanation of criminal behavior was to be found in the natural—animal—biological instincts of men and women. The latter, based in positivist thought, situate female criminality as a disease, either social or individual.[9]

The majority of studies in Mexico therefore approach female criminality with the assumption that traditional gender roles do not need to be questioned and analyzed. These studies thus fail to take a critical stance or to provide a gendered analysis. Even the most recent studies are based on explanations of female criminality that are deeply rooted in essentialist frameworks that present women as naturally weak or as mentally ill. Among other persistent stereotypes in these studies, we still find "the Mexican woman" portrayed as a being with masochistic qualities.[10] This is why, having completed a review of the existing literature, we resolved to undertake a qualitative study that would give voice to women prisoners with the aim of examining, from their perspectives, not only what brought them to prison but also the living conditions they face once incarcerated. This understanding allows us to call into question the fundamental assumptions of the current penitentiary model. Our work was undertaken from a feminist perspective because we consider that this type of analysis offers the most potential to bring about change in the conditions we observed. At the same time, a feminist analysis sheds light on important aspects of the problem that have been overlooked in earlier studies.

A Profile of Incarcerated Women

Our study included 79 percent of the women in the national prison system, a total of 2,424 women. We carried out face-to-face interviews with 159 of these women during visits to penitentiaries in eleven Mexican states to observe the conditions under which the women lived. We also used questionnaires to survey another 1,265 women housed in small centers dispersed throughout the country. This highly representative sample allows us to discuss the general profile of women who find themselves in prison. In terms of age, 70 percent are between eighteen and thirty-five years old, an important fact given that this represents the majority of women's reproductive years. In terms of their marital status, a third are single, another third married, and the remaining third are in common-law marriages, with a very small percentage widowed or divorced. Regardless of their marital status, 86 percent of the imprisoned women are mothers, and they have, on average, 3.5 children each.

In terms of schooling, 70 percent have at most an elementary education, and within this group 20 percent are illiterate. The remaining 30 percent have either completed some secondary or preparatory school or enrolled in some technical training that they had rarely managed to finish. With respect to employment prior to entering prison, half of the women were homemakers, and the other half participated in the workforce as petty traders, domestics, waitresses, secretaries, cashiers, prostitutes, and, less frequently, in agricultural or industrial employment. In terms of their offenses, although the percentages varied greatly from one region to another, on average 36 percent of the women were imprisoned for "offenses against health," including drug offenses, 33 percent for theft or fraud, 14 percent for murder, 4 percent for assault, 3 percent for child kidnapping, and 2 percent each for kidnapping or sexual offenses. The remaining 6 percent were accounted for by a variety of other offenses including property damage and breaking and entry.

Rather than elaborating upon specificities that distinguish one prison from another, my goal is to try to present some of the general circumstances shared by women no matter where they are imprisoned. One significant finding is that the penitentiary system reinforces the social construction of gender. Prisons reproduce the social differences that generate disadvantages for women, whose needs are then neglected in prisons as they are elsewhere in society. Thus, I argue that women become a sort of absent subject, invisible within the institution. The problems that are found in the prisons, including that of overpopulation, are rarely considered to pertain to women. It is also in this sense that we consider that the penitentiary system, like societal institutions, is fundamentally erected as a masculine model in which the norm is dictated by and departs from the needs of men, with women merely added on to this model. To support this conclusion we need only look at the architectural design of our prisons and the distribution of their spaces, as well as the norms, regulations, discourses, and manuals that explain their function in order to see that women are not taken into account. The excuse that is offered for this is always the same: the fact that women make up only 4 percent of the prison population. But small numbers alone cannot justify the neglect of women's specific needs, nor do they explain why women are always relegated to second place.

Another example of this relegation is the work that is given to women to do within the prisons. With little or no reflection, the prison authorities assign and confine women to cleaning and sewing, including embroidery and textiles. This practice reproduces existing gender roles, and at the same time it offers the women few opportunities to improve on their situation. This practice often hides another reality, as it does in the family: the fact that women's domestic labor permits other members of the family to dedicate themselves to better remunerated activities. Other work opportunities are not widely available in prison, but the few that do exist are given to men automatically. Although men's employment needs are prioritized, women are discriminated against, further ignoring the fact that in the majority of cases the welfare of the children depends upon the mother. Thus, existing gender constructions continue to be the basis for the creation of work for women prisoners: there is not a single prison in the country where women's work is not related to cleaning, sewing, cooking, laundry, or manual labor. Moreover, in conjunction with the lack of other employment, women face additional difficulties in selling what they do produce (woven bags, dolls, carpets, and so on) and even in obtaining the materials they need to produce these items. As the poor are disproportionately targeted by the criminal justice system, women prisoners belong to the most economically marginalized sector of Mexican society. The denial of most income-generating opportunities to women prisoners therefore leads to considerable economic insecurity for them and their families.

Since the nineteenth century, imprisoned women in Mexico have fit the following profile: young, poor, illiterate or poorly educated, and, almost always, single mothers with the sole responsibility for the maintenance of their children. The activities that bring them into conflict with the law may vary; the motive will not: where before it was petty robbery, now women smuggle small quantities of drugs as "mules." In both instances, their motivation is poverty. The justice that is practiced is discriminatory and partial for these single women, as in many cases they are sentenced to prison only because they do not have the resources to pay the fines that are disproportionate in relation to their crimes. The prevalence of a positivist philosophy of crime and punishment in Mexico has prevented many commentators from acknowledging injustices in the criminal-legal system. Based on a consensual model of society, the positivist position assumes that everyone shares the same values and the same definitions of what constitutes a crime. Nothing could be further from the truth. Pavarini notes that positivist criminology privileges the etiological natures of the offense while ignoring the fact that an offense is anything that is defined as such by the elite.[11] As we deconstruct the concept of "crime," we must also take apart our traditional understandings of gender and women's roles. Both gender and class provide conceptual frameworks that frequently remain unquestioned when we analyze public policy in these areas.

Pavarini argues that rather than considering crime in isolation as a positive fact, we must also take into account related processes such as criminalization and the politicization of crime. The case of robbery can be used as an example. The production of its "causes" (the etiological approach) is found in the way in which it is defined (as well as in the offense itself), at the same time that its "social causes" (poverty, unemployment, poor socialization, family instability) permit it to be presented as a "problem." This deconstructive work suggests that we must consider the probability of committing a crime to be related to social status. This particular crime—robbery—would have no meaning outside societies with regimes of private property. This type of focus allows us to analyze the criminalized behavior of broad population groups as well as the differential legal treatment of men and women.

The Mano Dura (Hard Hand) of Mexican Drug Policy

Because of the high percentage of women imprisoned for drug-related offenses, it is necessary to reflect upon the problem of criminalized drugs. As we heard in countless interviews, women rarely played a significant role within drug networks. Instead, their role in the drug business is secondary, as is evidenced by the deprivations and difficulties that they face when they are incarcerated. In prison, their primary concern is that of how to send money to their children. In contrast, the economic power of the true drug traffickers is impossible to hide even in prison, evident both in their day-to-day behavior and in the manner in which they are attended to by other prisoners and even the prison staff. The drug trade is an aspect of globalization that involves innumerable transnational networks of organized crime. It is an enterprise that, in its current stage, has taken on many of the characteristics of legitimate multinational corporations. This wealth does not belong, of course, to the women, as they in any case constitute the bottom rung of a ladder in which they participate because of poverty. Because they have no importance or power in the drug hierarchy, they are considered disposable. Knowing that they can easily be replaced, their employers are likely to give them up to the authorities in order to fill arrest quotas. Other than in the largest cities, where significant numbers of women prisoners are addicts, it is rarely the case that women incarcerated for drug-related offenses consume drugs. Female addicts have little access to treatment; instead they are bombarded with the slogan "Say no to drugs." This approach is indicative of a misguided policy that locates the addiction in the individual, as a matter of choice or will, when its true causes are to be found in the political and social arenas.

The "mano dura" or zero tolerance approach to drugs is linked to broader historical trends. Think, for example, of the Cold War years in which the United States undertook a battle against another "malign and strange phenomenon whose forces sought to undermine American society"—communism. As with U.S. efforts to eradicate leftist movements in Latin America from the 1950s onward, the disparity between the resources deployed by drug-consuming and drug-producing countries in this new war is striking. From another perspective, the mano dura that the state has deployed against the weakest link in the chain in order to demonstrate its power is in stark contrast to the position that the state has adopted in the face of the massive sale of tranquilizers. Both inside and outside prison, this class of drugs is readily prescribed to women, ironically, in the case of prisoners, to allow them to endure—or to numb themselves to—their difficult realities. Of course, the defenders of the war against drugs are unlikely to classify tranquilizers in this category, as they are not pleasure-inducing drugs. They ignore the highly addictive qualities of these pharmaceuticals. This ambivalence might be related to the "social benefits" brought about by their consumption: women, the principal consumers of tranquilizers, have less opportunity to reflect on their difficult and painful realities while they consume this medication. It is precisely this approach that we can see leading to the prescription of these substances to women in prison, where it makes them easier to control.[12] In short, women are those who benefit least from the drug trade and those who suffer the most when they are detained.

Interpersonal and Police Violence Against Women

Another serious problem is that of violence against women, a phenomenon that has historically and systematically been ignored, both by Mexican law and by judicial practices. It is not rare to find numerous episodes of abuse and negligence in the history of criminalized women. To understand the phenomenon of violence against women we must start with an analysis that takes into account the distinct ways in which men and women are socialized in Mexican society and recognize that forces outside the family perpetuate this violence. Since the Middle Ages, it has been clear that Mexican society does not condemn violence against women and only takes an occasional stance against excessive violence. It is evident today that there is a large margin of tolerance and complicit silence surrounding these practices, which occur much more frequently than is commonly recognized.[13] Forms of nonphysical violence that are also used to maintain control over women include verbal abuse, threats, and the denial of affection or economic resources.

The possibility of escaping from this abuse is open to only a small number of Mexican women. For the rest, escape is not a viable option because they have no place to go or, worse, because they do not know any other way of life. There are also cases in which a woman is immobilized by fear for her life. This fear is most likely justified when we remember that the majority of murdered women are killed by their intimate partners. In some instances, the women we interviewed had received lengthy sentences for killing an abusive partner. Self-defense was rarely considered as a mitigating circumstance in these cases. It is important to note that, in different ways, violence is also present in the treatment of criminalized women by the police. Countless interviewees told of abuse, ill-treatment, threats, insults, rape, or torture that were inflicted on them during their detention. The descriptions of police aggression that women shared with us are dramatic. Evidently, the police are the least merciful with the most economically marginalized women. Experiences of state and intimate violence produce incalculable physical and moral damage and have severe long-term consequences. It would therefore be desirable for prisons to employ staff who are sufficiently trained and specialized to give adequate attention to women who have been the victims of violence. This is also true for women who consume drugs or for prisoners with mental illnesses, who, in most instances, have no access to specialized treatment programs.

Training programs in Mexican prisons constitute another problem identified in our study. In Mexican families, education is not seen as a priority for girls. This ideology continues into the prison, where women's educational needs are subordinated to those of men. The programs that are provided ignore the fact that women prisoners are adults with a life experience that should be used as a point of departure for learning. The poor conceptualization of prison educational programs denies women the opportunity to prepare for work other than domestic labor later in life and reinforces their position among the most poorly remunerated and least socially valued. The link between higher levels of education and social mobility for women and lower birth rates has already been documented in many countries. We also know that the benefits of increasing women's educational levels invariably multiply and result in a higher standard of living for their children. Within the current social model that the prison system faithfully continues to reproduce, women are fundamentally, and at times exclusively, responsible for children. Despite this, women are given fewer opportunities and less resources to support their offspring. An additional problem that stands out in women's participation in prison education programs is the fact that these activities tend to take place in the men's section of the prison and the majority of participants are men. This presents one more obstacle as it is often impossible to guarantee the safety of women who participate.

Overpopulation has been one of the primary sources of concern surrounding the penal system in recent years. Although this problem is much more severe for men, we also found that it applies to women. It is often thought that there are so few women that overcrowding cannot be a problem, but this fails to take into account that women are housed in the smallest and most marginal spaces within the prison, usually in poor conditions. We must also take into consideration that, although their numbers may be as few as twenty in any one prison, at times they are forced to remain in a single room day and night. Ten years after our study first brought it to national attention, overcrowding in Mexican women's prisons is seldom noticed. Seventy-five women may sleep in a small room without this being considered a cause for concern. The situation is similar in the United States. In Michigan in the 1990s, I observed 125 women sleeping in a small exercise room at the Huron Valley Women's Facility. Despite this egregious example of overcrowding, the institution would not accept that the living arrangements were insufficient.

Conclusion

Our research has demonstrated that when the criminal justice system ignores women's positions of social inequality, the justice that is provided is partial. That is to say, when equal sanctions are imposed on those who do not have equality, the system reproduces a situation of real, deep, complex inequality. Given this finding, we believe that the situation of women inside Mexican prisons cannot improve until women's condition improves on the outside. The solution to the problem of imprisonment is to be found in society at large. The problem does not originate in the prisons. Rather, prisons produce, deepen, and concentrate in a small space society's deepest contradictions. The confinement of women becomes a process of secondary marginalization that is derived from a process of primary marginalization. Specific marginal, impoverished sectors are the most susceptible to entering the circuits of justice, and it is these groups that are overrepresented among the prison population. These populations are subjected to a secondary marginalization, confinement, because they have lived in a context of primary marginalization. Disgracefully, for most women prisoners, leaving the state of secondary marginalization implies a return to primary marginalization.

Ten years after the publication of our findings, little has changed for the better. Women are still given long sentences for drug possession, even of small quantities. The globalization of crime control continues to affect the sentences that are imposed on these women. The adoption of drug policies modeled on the United States' failed war on drugs and the export of mandatory minimum sentences to Mexico have had a particularly harsh impact on women, especially poor women. We must challenge the harsh sentencing of Mexican women and improve the conditions of these women who have been forgotten inside Mexican prisons. It will take the collective efforts of many on both sides of the U.S.-Mexico border to bring about change in prison conditions and to turn the tide of prison expansion in Mexico.

References

1. The Forgotten Women.
2. Readers interested in this topic should consult the complete study: Elena Azaola and Cristina José Yacamán, *Las Mujeres Olvidadas: Un Estudio Acerca de la Situación de las Cárceles Para Mujeres de la República Mexicana* (México: Programa Interdisciplinario de Estudios de la Mujer, El Colegio de México/Comisión Nacional de Derechos Humanos, 1996). This study was completed for the subsecretary of Protección Civil, Prevención y Readaptación Social de la Secretaría de Gobernación.
3. Estadísticas Penitenciarias de la Secretaría de Gobernación, 1994.
4. Estadísticas Penitenciarias de la Secretaría de Gobernación, 1994.
5. Estadísticas Penitenciarias de la Secretaría de Gobernación, 2002, 2003.
6. Pat Carlen, *Women's Imprisonment* (London: Routledge and Kegan Paul, 1983); Carol Smart, *Feminism and the Power of Law* (London: Routledge, 1989); Elena Larrauri, *Mujeres, Derecho Penal y Criminología* (México: Siglo XXI, 1994).
7. Raúl Zaffaroni, "La Mujer y el Poder Punitivo," in *Sobre Patriarcas, Jerarcas, Patrones y Otros Varones*, ed. Alda Facio et al. (Costa Rica: Llanud, 1993).
8. Alda Facio et al., 1993; Zaffaroni, 1993.
9. A critical vision of these views can be found in Alessandro Baratta, *Criminología Crítica y Crítica del Derecho Penal* (México: Siglo XXI, 1986) and "Resocialización o Control Social? Por un Concepto Crítico de Reintegración Social del Condenado," in *El Sistema Penitenciario: Entre el Temor y la Esperanza*, ed. O. Cárdenas (México: Centro de Estudios de Criminología Crítica de América Latina, 1991).
10. Victoria Adato de Ibarra et al., *La Mujer Delincuente* (México: Instituto de Investigaciones Jurídicas, 1983); Ma. de la Luz Lima, *Criminalidad Femenina. Teorías y Reacción Social* (México: Porrúa, 1991). Other recent works leave women on the margins; see, for example, Dolores E. Fernández, *La Pena de Prisión* (México: Unam, 1993).
11. Massimo Pavarini, *Control y Dominación* (México: Siglo XXI, 1983).
12. On the abuse of these medicines in prisons, see Mabel Burin et al., *El Malestar de las Mujeres. La Tranquilidad Recetada* (Buenos Aires: Paidos, 1991).
13. Russell P. Dobash and R. Emerson Dobash, "Community Response to Violence against Wives: Chivalry, Abstract Justice and Patriarchy," *Social Problems*, 5 (1981). See also Elena Larrauri 1994.

CHAPTER 11

Latinas and the War on Drugs in the United States, Latin America, and Europe[1]

JUANITA DÍAZ-COTTO

The impact of criminal justice policies on Latinas in the United States, Latin America, and Europe must be viewed within an international context wherein Latinas(os) are targeted for arrest and incarceration under the auspices of the U.S.-sponsored "war on drugs."[2] Whereas Latin American governments criminalize particular groups of people within their own countries, the United States criminalizes entire Latin American nations while pursuing the war on drugs. The United States highlights the role that Latinas(os) play in the production, processing, trafficking, and consumption of "illicit drugs" such as marijuana, heroin, and cocaine. At the same time, it masks the demand for such drugs in the United States and Europe[3] and the role played by U.S. government agencies,[4] law enforcement officers,[5] and private corporations[6] in the development of the drug industry.

Studies of the war on drugs in relation to the United States and Latin America have tended to focus on one region or the other. Likewise, few have analyzed the impact of such policies on Latinas or made a passing reference to them.[7] The aim of this chapter is to bring together diverse sources of information in order to compare the effects the war on drugs is having on Latinas in diverse geographic regions. Thus, we gain a deeper understanding of how the globalization of the war on drugs has affected Latina(o) communities.

Latinas(os) and U.S. Criminal Justice Policies

On December 31, 2000, there were more than two million persons imprisoned in state, federal, and local facilities in the United States.[8] These numbers were complemented by prisoners held in private jails and prisons. As of December 2003, the United States had the highest incarceration rate in the world despite declining national crime rates during the 1990s.[9] Latina(o) overrepresentation within the prisoner population was evidenced by the fact that whereas in 1999, Latinas(os) were already 15.5 percent of those held in local jails,[10] in 2000 they composed only 12.5 percent of the U.S. population.[11] At year end 2000, they were 16.4 percent of sentenced prisoners under state and federal jurisdiction.[12] When analyzed separately, findings showed that, in 1999, Latinas were one in seven of women in state prisons and one in three of women in federal prisons.[13] States such as New York and California tended to have an even greater over-representation of Latinas(os) within their jail and prisoner population, some-times composing one third of all those imprisoned.[14]

The increase in the prisoner population has been due primarily to the passage of mandatory sentencing and drug-related laws. By 1999, 57 percent of those in federal prisons[15] and 21 percent of those under state jurisdiction were sentenced for drug offenses. Latinas(os) have been particularly adversely affected by the war on drugs because of the overemphasis placed on drug crimes by criminal justice agencies,[16] the overrepresentation of Latinas(os) in drug arrests, and the fact that drug offenses are among the most harshly punished.[17]

Tougher parole board decisions and law enforcement practices have also colluded with state and federal drug-related and mandatory sentencing laws[18] to reduce defendants' ability to plea bargain, increase sentence length for some offenses, and make imprisonment mandatory for others. In New York and California, those most affected by such laws include African Americans and Latinas(os) and persons convicted for drug offenses (mainly possession) and nonviolent property crimes (e.g., theft and burglary).[19]

Elsewhere I have discussed additional factors that have contributed to the overrepresentation of Latinas(os) in rates of arrest, sentencing, and imprisonment in the United States.[20] Some of the contributing factors are that the Latina(o) population is a young population and that the young are the most likely to be arrested, criminal justice policies that target poor and working-class people for arrest and incarceration, inadequate legal representation and lack of knowledge of the inner workings of the criminal justice system, and language barriers throughout the criminal justice system. Added to these are excessive patrolling of poor and working-class neighborhoods by law enforcement personnel, discriminatory enforcement of criminal justice and immigration policies, and the fact that Latinas(os) are not as likely as whites and African Americans to be channeled into alternatives-to-incarceration programs. As a result of these facts, Latinos, but particularly Latinas, are disproportionately arrested, convicted, and imprisoned. Because of the lack of support services before, during, and after incarceration, they also have one of the highest recidivism rates.

Latinas and the War on Drugs in the United States

Men have always composed the overwhelming number of those arrested and incarcerated in the United States.[21] However, during the 1980s and 1990s, the number of women arrested for drug-related offenses increased alarmingly. By 1991, one in three women prisoners in the United States were serving sentences for drug offenses.[22] In states such as New York and California, among the most ardent supporters of drug-related and mandatory sentencing laws, women were more likely than men to be imprisoned for drug-related crimes. For example, in 1996, 32.5 percent of the men but 60.4 percent of the women in prison in New York were incarcerated for drug crimes.[23] In California, on December 31, 1999, 43 percent of the women but only 26.7 percent of the men were imprisoned for drug-related offenses.[24] Furthermore, women in federal prisons convicted for low-level drug offenses tended to receive sentences similar to those of men sentenced for serious drug-related crimes.[25]

Added to discrepancies based on gender were those based on race and ethnicity. Several studies have shown that racism plays a role in drug enforcement. For example, in New York and California, Latinas(os) and African Americans were more likely than whites to be imprisoned for drug offenses even when whites were more likely[26] or just as likely to use drugs as African Americans and Latinas(os).[27] The disproportionate impact of these combined factors is demonstrated by the fact that throughout the 1990s, Latinas in New York were more likely to be sentenced to prison for drug offenses than black but, particularly, white women. A 1990 study conducted by Coramae Richey Mann found that in New York, Latinas were 28.8 percent of women arrested for drug offenses but 41.2 percent of women imprisoned for such offenses.[28] By 1994, 82 percent of Latinas, 72 percent of black women, and 41 percent of white women imprisoned in New York were committed for drug offenses.[29]

Similarly, Mann found that whereas in California white women felons were arrested more often for drugs, theft, and burglary, they were less likely to be imprisoned for theft and drug offenses than Latina and black women.[30] Hence, Latinas made up only 18.7 percent of women arrested but 26.1 percent of women imprisoned for drug violations.[31] Latinas in California were also more likely to be imprisoned for felonies (23.8 percent) than white (16.8 percent) or black women (18.3 percent).[32]

As a result of the combination of gender and ethnic factors, Latinas in New York, for example, were more likely to be imprisoned for drug-related offenses than Latinos. Hence, 62.3 percent of Latinas but only 36 percent of Latinos were imprisoned for drug offenses on December 31, 1987.[33] By December 2001, 38.8 percent of Latinos but 61.5 percent of Latinas were imprisoned for drug-related offenses.[34] A number of additional factors could account for Latinas' overrepresentation in drug-related imprisonment rates compared with Latinos and whites. Latina drug use could have escalated significantly during the 1980s and 1990s. In fact, data compiled by the Bureau of Justice Statistics show that half of the women in state prisons on December 1999 had been using alcohol and/or other drugs while committing the offense for which they were arrested.[35]

Hence, Latina imprisonment rates could reflect their increasing drug use and subsequent arrests for drug-related crimes. Latina addicts and former addicts interviewed by the author in California seemed to think this was one possible explanation. However, they offered additional explanations for Latinas' increasing imprisonment. On the one hand, they argued that Latinos have become less willing than in the past to take full responsibility for joint drug offenses committed with Latinas. On the other hand, they felt that more Latinos now try to convince Latinas to take full responsibility for such crimes in order to avoid long prison sentences they may face because of mandatory and drug-related sentencing laws and their more extensive contacts with the criminal justice system.

Latinas were also affected by the fact that Latina and black women from Africa, South America, and the Caribbean were more likely than Latinos to be profiled as drug couriers[36] by criminal justice personnel and in the mass media. Hence, they were more likely to be stopped and searched for drugs than men or whites. This was so despite the fact that the typical drug courier was a male foreign national.[37] Moreover, Latinas were sometimes used as "decoys" on flights by drug dealers who wanted to divert attention from others on the same flight transporting larger quantities of drugs.[38]

Once arrested, Latinas did not generally have the same plea-bargaining power as Latinos. This was partly due to the fact that Latinas did not tend to play major roles in drug-trafficking networks. Thus, even when they were willing to cooperate with state authorities, Latinas seldom had the type of information most sought after by police and district attorneys.[39] When given the opportunity to plea bargain, even innocent Latinas frequently pled guilty hoping to get reduced sentences.[40] Others who could not afford to hire competent defense attorneys generally received long prison sentences when they chose trial over plea bargaining.[41] Although some Latinas who cooperated with criminal justice personnel might have been able to negotiate better sentencing terms, those who refused to become informants were frequently given harsher sentences in retaliation for their silence.[42] In all such instances, non–English-speaking Latinas were among the most vulnerable.[43]

Once imprisoned, many Latinas in New York and California, but particularly those who were Spanish monolingual, faced discriminatory treatment at the hands of the overwhelmingly white guard force. Such discrimination was compounded by overcrowded and unsanitary living conditions, economic exploitation by jail and prison administrators, and the lack of programs that would allow women to obtain adequate employment upon their release. Moreover, women prisoners had to contend with discrimination on the basis of sexual orientation; verbal, physical, and sexual abuse at the hands of jail and prison staff; and cleavages among prisoners based primarily on race, ethnicity, and sometimes class.[44]

The fact that many incarcerated women were single heads of households meant that once they were arrested, their families lost both their main caretaker and their breadwinner. The separation of children and mothers also led to the development of severe emotional and psychological problems as families tried to cope with the loss.[45] Often, the incarceration of parents, repressive criminal justice policies targeting poor youths and youth of color, and the lack of adequate social, educational, and financial support structures contributed to the eventual institutionalization and incarceration of prisoners' children.[46] Women in Latin America faced similar issues as a result of the exportation of the U.S. war on drugs to the South.

Women in Latin America and the War on Drugs

The U.S. military was enlisted into domestic law enforcement efforts[47] in 1981, when President Ronald Reagan endorsed its use to assist civilian agencies in law enforcement operations along the 2,000 mile U.S.–Mexico border. The primary objectives were to end the illegal importation of drugs, contraband, and people into the United States[48] and quash revolutionary movements in Latin America.[49] Both drug trafficking and revolutionary movements were seen as major national and international security threats.[50]

The militarization of the U.S.–Mexico border has led to incarceration of large numbers of undocumented Latinas(os), primarily Mexicans, in the United States. Once arrested for drug-related crimes, foreign nationals can be held for extended periods of time in Immigration and Naturalization Service (INS) detention facilities and private prisons. From these they can be deported to their countries of origin or detained while awaiting trial. Various human rights organizations[51] have exposed the treatment women, men, and children receive in such facilities. It will, therefore, not be discussed here. Suffice it to say that such treatment includes exposure to severely overcrowded and unsanitary living conditions as well as physical and/or sexual abuse.

Women in Mexico

The militarization of the U.S.–Mexico border has taken place alongside the push from the United States for Latin American countries to militarize their war on drugs.[52] As in the United States, the militarization of the war on drugs in Latin America has been accompanied by the passage of drug-related and mandatory sentencing laws, a drastic increase in the number of persons arrested and imprisoned for drug crimes, and the construction of more jails and prisons. It has also promoted the involvement of both the U.S. and Latin American military in civilian law enforcement efforts. The result of these joint efforts has been the weakening of Latin American civilian governments and a surge in the number of human rights violations in the region.

The Mexican government initially objected both to the militarization of the U.S.–Mexico border and to U.S. incursions into Mexican soil to pursue suspected traffickers and undocumented workers.[53] However, in response to political and economic pressure from the United States, in 1988, Mexican President Carlos Salinas announced that drug-trafficking was a "national security issue,"[54] thus placing Mexican law enforcement priorities on par with those of the United States.

War on drugs policies have resulted in an increase in the number of Mexican women arrested for low-level trafficking on both sides of the border. In some cases, Mexicans trying to cross the border have been falsely accused of drug trafficking because they were unable or unwilling to pay the bribes Mexican police officers demanded for their release.[55] Those detained in Mexico for drug-related crimes are generally held in preventive detention prior to sentencing. Those who have the money to pay the frequently exorbitant bail have sometimes been able to obtain their release while awaiting adjudication. Others have been able to obtain their freedom only through the payment of bribes to criminal justice personnel.[56] While held in detention, many Mexican women have been subjected to sexual and other forms of physical abuse, including rape and torture. Law enforcement personnel have also coerced women into signing confessions by threatening to harm family members who have also been arrested.[57] In fact, children have been tortured to make women comply with the goals of law enforcement personnel. As in the case of Latinas and other women prisoners in the United States, once sentenced and imprisoned, many of the women continued to be sexually and physically abused.[58]

A study conducted by the Women's Studies Program of *El Colegio de Mexico* during 1993 and 1994 revealed that 50 to 64 percent of imprisoned women in Mexico were being held for *delitos contra la salud* (crimes against health), that is, crimes related to the consumption and trafficking of drugs.[59] Although a small number of Mexican, Colombian, and Bolivian women have become drug lords,[60] the sexism rampant in the industry has meant that the overwhelming number of women trafficking drugs are actually transporting small amounts of drugs across national and international borders.

Ironically, a significant number of women arrested in Mexico for drug trafficking, particularly those in the larger Mexican cities, have become addicted to illegal drugs while imprisoned. Once addicted, many support their drug habit through sex work.[61] Others resort to sex work in order to support the drug habit of male partners by whom they are intimidated. As in the United States, women addicts in Mexico experience frequent incarceration both for their addiction and for the actions they take to support their habit.

Also, like most Latina prisoners in the United States, women imprisoned in Mexico face overcrowded and unsanitary living conditions. Those who are able to work while imprisoned are generally restricted to unpaid traditional women's work such as sewing, cooking, cleaning, and washing clothes. Discriminatory penal policies allow male prisoners in both countries to have a greater access to educational, vocational, and work programs than women.

As in the case of Latina prisoners in the United States, women prisoners in Mexico tend to be poor and working-class, even when they are employed prior to their incarceration. Those working outside the home tend to be employed in the service sector. Many have little or no formal education. Approximately 70 percent are between eighteen and thirty-five years old. They are overwhelmingly both mothers and single heads of households.[62]

Women in Bolivia

Indigenous peoples in the Andes have grown and consumed coca leaf safely for over three thousand years. It is used as medicine, tea, food, and in religious and social rituals.[63] Thus, initially, Bolivia, like Mexico, resisted expanding and militarizing the war on drugs.[64] However, in 1988, the Bolivian Congress, in response to economic and military threats from the United States,[65] passed Law 1008, or the Law to Regulate Coca and Controlled Substances. Although much coca production for domestic consumption remained legal, the law expanded the definition of trafficking to include areas of the country and activities not previously regulated.[66]

Law 1008 is enforced by several agencies, including the Fuerza Especial de Lucha Contra el Narcotráfico (FELCN), composed of members of the national police and the armed forces. The FELCN collaborates with the Bolivian Environmental Police[67] and several U.S. military and civilian agencies, including the Drug Enforcement Administration (DEA).[68] Thus, U.S. military forces trained and equipped Bolivian law enforcement agencies financed by the U.S. government,[69] and DEA agents have joined Bolivian officers in searches, confrontations, the destruction of coca fields and cocaine laboratories, and the bombing of roads, villages, and housing complexes. They have participated in arrests, kidnappings, detentions, and the interrogation and torture of civilians. They have helped set up houses of torture or "security houses." DEA agents have also threatened family members of detainees and, on occasion, physically abused relatives in order to force defendants to testify against themselves.

Furthermore, DEA agents have elicited bribes in exchange for the release of prisoners.[70] Ironically, the DEA collaborated with local government forces, many of whom are themselves involved in drug trafficking.[71]

The sectors of the population that have openly objected to the eradication of coca, the forced evacuation of their homes and villages, and the treatment received from local and U.S. agents have been severely repressed.[72] Leaders of peasant organizations have been particularly targeted for repression and numerous murders and massacres of men, women, and children have taken place.

> Women have been violently attacked by UMOPAR troops who have tied them to trees, cots, and have put handkerchiefs in their mouths so they will not ask for help. There are complaints of sexual harassment and rape ... They also pressure the children so that they will accuse their parents and they use them to make the parents come out of the woods.[73]

The number of women who have been threatened, arrested, beaten, raped, tortured, pressured to confess to illicit actions, and killed has risen alarmingly.[74] So has the number of children who have been subjected to physical abuse and/or killed.

The war on drugs in Bolivia has also led to an alarming increase in the number of men, women, and minors arrested and detained in Bolivian prisons as well as local detention centers.[75] By 1993, there were five thousand male and female prisoners held in Bolivian prisons.[76] The majority were incarcerated for violation of Law 1008. Minors (15- to 20-year-olds), who tend to be sentries or couriers, composed a significant percentage (16.5 percent) of those imprisoned for drug offenses.[77] Women were more likely to be imprisoned for drug-related crimes than men. Thus, in 1993, 40.5 percent of women in prison but only 23.3 percent of imprisoned men had been arrested for drug-related crimes.[78] By 1997, 16 percent of those imprisoned in Bolivia were women, an exorbitant number when compared with the United States, where women made up 6.6 percent of all prisoners under the jurisdiction of federal or state authorities at year end 2000.[79]

The involvement of Bolivian women in the drug trade has been primarily as intermediaries or as participants in lower-level activities. Some have assisted their families "in the production of coca paste by mashing the leaves and precursors with their feet."[80] Others have acted as drug couriers, transporting small amounts of coca paste or chemical precursors within national borders.[81] According to Gloria Rose M. de Achá, the majority of women imprisoned for drug trafficking in Bolivia were between the ages of twenty-five and thirty-five.[82] A significant number had little or no education. Most of them came from rural areas and spoke little or no Spanish. Like their sisters in the United States and Mexico, the majority had been victims of physical and sexual abuse prior to their arrest. Many were the sole caretaker for their children before and during imprisonment. As in the case of their counterparts in the United States, those with male partners on the outside tended to be abandoned by them when they were incarcerated.

Once people were arrested for drug crimes, Law 1008 "dangerously reduced both the evidence required to sentence the accused and the rights of the accused to a defense."[83] According to the Andean Information Network:

> The law violates principles universally recognized as fundamental rights of the accused: the presumption of innocence, the safeguards against self-incrimination, the right to a defense, the right to an impartial judge, the right to due process, the right to parole and the right to a speedy trial.[84]

Those arrested under Law 1008 were frequently detained on scant evidence provided by police and military officers who often secured confessions under duress and violence, including torture. Others were framed by the same officers. Although such procedures violated both local and international accords,[85] many pleaded guilty in order to avoid additional abuse.

In 1994, 65 percent of prisoners charged with violating Law 1008 were kept in "preventive detention" despite the fact that they were generally charged with low-level, nonviolent offenses and had not been tried by the courts.[86] Many of them claimed to be innocent of the charges. Most of those incarcerated had not been processed by the courts. A three-stage court process meant that detainees on drug-trafficking charges were generally held between one-and-a-half and three years prior to the adjudication of guilt or innocence.[87] Minimum sentencing requirements imposed sentences ranging from one to thirty years in prison.[88] To the sentences were added fines, the confiscation of property, and court costs. According to Human Rights Watch (HRW), all attempts to reform the law were initially blocked by the United States.[89]

Mandatory sentencing laws meant that once sentenced, women served long minimum sentences. The result was that all male and female prisons in Bolivia have experienced a rapid rate of overcrowding.[90] Moreover, with the financial assistance of the United States, some new prisons have been constructed.[91] Peasants in coca-growing areas who were not arrested during drug raids or those arrested and released from prison have lost everything they owned and found themselves displaced, unemployed, and forced to migrate to urban areas or other parts of the country. Sometimes they return to the illegal growing of coca leaf as a result of economic necessity.

During the 1980s and 1990s, coca-growing peasants joined other sectors of the Bolivian population to demand an end to oppression by government agencies, the redistribution of wealth, and the cessation of foreign intervention in domestic affairs.[92] Although some of these peasant communities have had a long history of activism, others have been politicized by the war on drugs. The women of the coca-growing region have become active participants in such struggles. To this end, they have confronted local police and military forces attempting to destroy their crops, demanded the release of imprisoned husbands, and held hunger strikes, marches, and demonstrations. Some have simultaneously demanded equality between the sexes and an end to the abuse of women by men inside and outside the home.

The War on Drugs and Latin American Women in Europe

According to a study conducted by María C. Dorado (1998) between 1996 and 1997, the largest number of women detained for drug trafficking in Britain and in cities such as Madrid and Frankfurt were Colombian.[93] In all three countries, imprisoned Colombian women interviewed by Dorado were predominantly single women between the ages of twenty-six and forty years who lived in urban areas in Colombia. Although most were poor, approximately 85 percent of them were financially responsible for their children and sometimes other relatives.[94] Few were illiterate, but they tended to have low educational levels.

As in the case of Latin American women couriers arrested in New York's JFK Airport, most Colombian women arrested in Europe transported drugs to support themselves and their families. Some had been tricked by friends, acquaintances, or male partners into transporting the drugs. Others had their lives or those of their children and other relatives threatened if they refused to traffic drugs. In a few cases, the children of Latinas arrested in Europe were murdered in retaliation for the women's failure to deliver the drugs.[95]

Once again, like Latina drug couriers arrested in New York, Colombian women frequently transported small quantities of drugs. Approximately 60 percent of Dorado's sample were imprisoned for transporting less than a kilo of cocaine.[96] Frequently, the women were unaware of the actual amount of drugs their were carrying, the types of drugs involved, or the value of the merchandise. Once arrested, Colombian women were subjected to long periods of questioning, isolation, and preventive detention. Those who had swallowed balloons were subjected to recurrent X-rays and physical examinations. Frequently, during this waiting period, they were given laxatives and were not allowed to eat much food, take showers, or change their clothes. Sometimes their hands and feet were shackled to their hospital beds even while sleeping.[97] As a result, they endured many days of physical pain and discomfort until they had expelled all the balloons from their bodies.

Although several international conventions (e.g., European Convention on Human Rights, Vienna Convention) stipulate that in cases involving drug trafficking, imprisonment should be used as a last resort and only for short periods of time and that sentences should be uniform across countries, Colombian and other Latin American women were arrested and quickly sentenced to various lengths of time depending on the country, the city, and the court jurisdiction involved.[98]

As in the United States, Spanish-monolingual women were provided with interpreters during some part of their criminal proceedings. Nonetheless, the lack of adequate legal representation, their unfamiliarity with the workings of the criminal justice system, and the legal restrictions imposed on their attorneys made the women unable to provide adequate defenses.[99] As a result, in countries such as England, they frequently received longer sentences than other women arrested for similar crimes.[100] Once imprisoned, they faced isolation as a result of language barriers and the fact that their families and friends were thousands of miles away. Many were unable to inform their relatives of their predicament. Others felt too ashamed to let anyone know. Even Latin American women in Spain faced cultural alienation.[101]

Like Latina couriers detained in the United States, Colombian women were first detained at the airport and questioned because, in one way or another, they fit some stereotype of a drug carrier. According to Dorado, they looked Latin, Asian, or hippie. They came from countries listed as "distributors" or "producers" of drugs. Sometimes they seemed nervous, made too many phone calls, wore certain clothes, had new luggage, carried too much cash on them, or simply walked too fast or too slow. Others carried dirty travel bags but traveled first class.[102] With few exceptions, being profiled as drug couriers was what led Latinas in Europe to be stopped for questioning in the first place.

Conclusion

The war on drugs spearheaded by the United States at the domestic and international levels has led to the increasing arrest and incarceration of Latinas in the United States, Latin America, and Europe for low-level, nonviolent, drug-related and/or economic crimes. For Latinas, such offenses are motivated by the need to support their addiction, themselves, and/or their families. Wide income disparities, ethnic and racial discrimination, and structural barriers have made it necessary for Latinas to search continuously for new ways to support themselves and their families. For many who live in coca-producing regions, the demand for cocaine from predominantly Anglo/European consumers in the United States and Europe has become an additional source of income. However, although involvement in drug-related activities has allowed some Latinas in both rural and urban areas to fare a bit better off financially than others in their countries, the minor roles they play in such enterprises have not allowed them to escape permanently the dire economic conditions under which most of them live.

Latina involvement in drug-related activities has also become one of the means by which they have become incorporated into the global market. Such incorporation, however, has placed them at the center of the international war on drugs. The globalization of the war on drugs has, in turn, led to the severe repression of entire Latina(o) communities and the incarceration of thousands of women, men, and minors throughout the United States, Latin America, and Europe. At the national and international levels the militarization of the war on drugs has led to the weakening of civil society as military authorities have encroached on areas previously reserved for civil authorities and law enforcement agencies. The militarization of the war on drugs has also been accompanied by an increase in human rights violations by law enforcement and military personnel; the growing incarceration of women, men, and minors; and the building of more jails and prisons.

During the period of time in which the war on drugs has been pursued, Latinas addicted to drugs have been repeatedly arrested and incarcerated by governments that deny them adequate access to drug rehabilitation programs and continuously interfere with Latinas' attempts to recover from alcohol and drug abuse. Ironically, the same elites who continuously arrest Latinas for low-level, nonviolent, drug-related crimes also allow drug kingpins and others working within local, state, and federal agencies to engage in illegal drug enterprises.

While governmental leaders have recognized that education and drug treatment are the most effective means of reducing the demand for illegal drugs[103] and some states have begun to carry out corrections and sentencing reforms,[104] state and federal elites continue to pursue policies that fundamentally emphasize repressive legislation and law enforcement practices as well as imprisonment. The repeal of drug-related and mandatory sentencing laws continues to be resisted by those who oppose diverting funds from law enforcement and military agencies into education and drug rehabilitation programs.

The ill-founded and intransigent nature of the U.S.-sponsored war on drugs and its total disregard for human rights abroad led to the expulsion of the United States from both the United Nations (UN) Human Rights Commission and the UN International Narcotics Control Board in May 2001,[105] a year before the U.S. invasion of Iraq. With the passage of the USA PATRIOT Act in October 2001[106] and its current use to pursue drug-related crimes, the war on drugs in the United States has reached a new level. Justice Department agents, under the guise of a terrorist threat, now frequently invoke intelligence powers to seize records and carry out surveillance of suspected drug traffickers and others involved in crimes not connected to terrorism.[107] Such actions only serve ultimately to weaken the civil rights of all.

References

1. The term "Latinas" is used in this chapter to refer to women of Latin American ancestry, including women of Mexican ancestry in the United States who define themselves as Chicanas. Although "Latinos" is commonly used as a gender-neutral plural, the author prefers "Latinas(os)" when referring to both men and women. Latin America as used here refers to the nineteen Spanish-speaking countries located in South and Central America and the Spanish-speaking Caribbean.

2. Although this chapter focuses on Latinas, African Americans in the United States continue to be among the most severely affected by the war on drugs and constitute the majority of those imprisoned nationally. See chapters by Richie, Borhman and Murakawa, Gilmore, and Smith in this volume.

3. Peter Reuter, "Foreign Demand for Latin American Drugs: The USA and Europe," in E. Joyce and C. Malamud, *Latin America and the Multinational Drug Trade* (New York: St. Martin's, 1998); Adriana Rossi, *Narcotráfico y Amazonia Ecuatoriana* (Buenos Aires, Argentina: Kohen and Asociados International, 1996).

4. Bruce M. Bagley, ed., *Drug Trafficking in the Americas: An Annotated Bibliography* (Coral Gables, FL: North South Center, University of Miami, 1996); Centro de Documentación e Información-Bolivia, *DEA y Soberanía en Bolivia* (Cochabamba, Bolivia: CEDIB, 1994); Alexander Cockburn and Jeffrey St. Clair, *Whiteout* (New York: Verso, 1998).

5. Christopher Commission, Report of the Independent Commission on the Los Angeles Police Department (Los Angeles, 1991); James G. Kolts, The Los Angeles County Sheriffs' Department: A Report (Kolts Report) (Los Angeles: Board of Supervisors, 1992); Mollen Commission, Commission Report (New York City, 1994); U.S. House of Representatives, Committee on the Judiciary, Police Misconduct, Hearings before the Subcommittee on Criminal Justice, Serial No. 50, parts 1 and 2, 98th Congress, 1st Session (Washington, D.C., 1984).

6. *Federal News Service*, U.S. Congress, Senate Governmental Committee, Permanent Investigations Subcommittee Hearing, *Drug Money Laundering* (February 27, 1992); Anthony P. Maingot, "Offshore Banking in the Caribbean: The Panamanian Case," in Joyce and Malamud 1998, 149–171.

7. See Evelin Agreda, Norma Rodríguez, and Alex Contreras, *Mujeres Cocaleras* (Cochabamba, Bolivia: Comité Coordinador de las Cinco Federaciones del Trópico de Cochabamba, 1996); Amnesty International, *Mexico, Overcoming Fear*, 1996; Elizabeth Azaola and Cristina J. Yucamán, *Las Mujeres Olvidadas* (México, D.F.: Centro Nacional de Derechos Humanos, Colegio de México, 1996); Barbara Bloom, "Triple Jeopardy: Race, Class, and Gender in Women's Imprisonment," Ph.D. diss., University of California, 1996; Correctional Association of New York (CANY), *Injustice Will Be Done* (1992); CANY, *Mandatory Injustice* (1999); Gloria R. M. de Achá, "Características de las Mujeres Encarceladas en Bolivia," in R. del Olmo, ed., *Criminalidad y Criminalización de la Mujer en la Región Andina* (Caracas, Venezuela: Nueva Sociedad, 1998); Gloria R.M. de Achá, *Violaciones a los Derechos Humanos Civiles Durante la Investigación Policial en Casos Detenidos Bajo la Ley 1008* (Cochabamba, Bolivia: Red Andina de Información, CEDIB, 1996); R. del Olmo, ed., *Criminalidad y Criminalización de la Mujer en la Región Andina* (Caracas, Venezuela: Nueva Sociedad, 1998); Juanita Díaz-Cotto, *Chicana Lives and Criminal Justice: In Their Own Words* (Austin: University of Texas, forthcoming 2006); J. Díaz-Cotto, "Latina Imprisonment and the War on Drugs," in M. Bosworth and J. Flavin, eds., *Race, Gender, and Punishment* (New Brunswick, NJ: Rutgers University Press, 2005); Human Rights Watch (HRW), *Bolivia: Human Rights Violations and the War on Drugs* (1995a); HRW, *Cruel and Usual: Disproportionate Sentences for New York Drug Offenders* 9 (2)(B), 1997a; Coramae R. Mann, "Women of Color and the Criminal Justice System," in B.R. Price and N.J. Sokoloff, eds., *The Criminal Justice System and Women* (New York: McGraw-Hill, 1995).

8. Bureau of Justice Statistics (BJS), *Census of Jails, 1999* (Washington, D.C.: Department of Justice, 2001a); BJS, *Prisoners in 2000* (Washington. D.C.: Department of Justice, 2001b).

9. Eric Lichtblau, "U.S. Crime Decrease Sets Record," *Press and Sun Bulletin* (May 8, 2000); The Sentencing Project, *New Inmate Population Figures Demonstrate Need for Policy Reform* (Washington, D.C., 2003). The combination of increasing imprisonment rates and decreasing crime rates and the manner in which private and public agencies profit from prison construction led prisoners rights advocates to speak of the "prison-industrial complex."

10. BJS 2001a: 3.

11. U.S. Census Bureau, Department of Commerce, *The Hispanic Population* (Washington, D.C.: Department of Commerce, May 2001), 1.

12. BJS 2001b: 11.

13. BJS, *Special Report: Women Offenders* (Washington, D.C.: Department of Justice, December 1999), 7.

14. California Department of Corrections, *CDC Facts: 4TH Quarter 2002* (Sacramento, 2002); California Department of Corrections, Administrative Service Division, *Historical Trends Institutions and Parole Population, 1977–1997* (Sacramento, June 1998); New York Department of Correctional Services (NYSDOCS), *The Hub System: Profile of Inmates under Custody in January 1, 1996* (Albany, 1996); U.S. Census Bureau, *The Hispanic Population: Census 2000 Brief* (Washington, D.C.: Department. of Commerce, May 2001): Table 2, p. 4.

15. BJS 2001b: 11–12.

16. Katherine Beckett and Theodore Sasson, *The Politics of Injustice* (Thousand Oaks, CA: Pine Forge, 2000).

17. CANY 1992, 1999; HRW 1997a.

18. Examples of drug-related and mandatory sentencing laws include New York's Rockefeller Drug Laws, Second Felony Offender Laws, Violent Felony Offender Laws, changes in Consecutive Sentence Provisions, California's Three Strikes Law, and Truth-in-Sentencing Laws. These laws were complemented by the 1994 Federal Crime Control Act. In 1991, there were over 100 federal crimes regulated by mandatory sentencing laws. By 1994, all fifty states had passed at least one such law (Beckett and Sasson 2000: 176). See also Barbara Bloom, Meda Chesney-Lind, and Barbara Owen, *Women in California Prisons* (San Francisco: Center on Juvenile and Criminal Justice, 1994); CANY 1992; HRW 1997a; NYSDOCS, Division of Program Planning, Research, and Evaluation, *Characteristics of Female Inmates Held under Custody, 1975–1985* (Albany, 1986a); Michael Tonry, *Sentencing Matters* (New York: Oxford University, 1996); U.S. Sentencing Commission, *Special Report to the Congress: Mandatory Minimum Penalties in the Federal Criminal Justice System* (Washington, D.C., 1991).

19. CANY, *Do They Belong in Prison?* New York, 1985; CANY 1992, 1999; Díaz-Cotto 2006; HRW 1997a; HRW, *Punishment and Prejudice: Racial Disparities in the War on Drugs* (New York, 2000).

20. See Juanita Díaz-Cotto, *Gender, Ethnicity, and the State: Latina and Latino Prison Politics* (Albany: SUNY-Press, 1996); Juanita Díaz-Cotto, "The Criminal Justice System and Its Impact on Latinas(os) in the United States," *The Justice Professional* 13 (1) (April 2000): 49–68; Díaz-Cotto, 2006.

21. U.S. Department of Justice, Federal Bureau of Investigations, *Uniform Crime Reports: Crime in the U.S.* (Washington, D.C., 1961–2002).

22. BJS, Special Report: Survey of State Prison Inmates, 1991: Women in Prison (Washington, D.C.: Department of Justice, 1994).

23. HRW 1997a: 13.

24. California Department of Corrections, Administrative Service Division, *California Prisoners and Parolees, 2000 Summary Statistics* (Sacramento, June 2000), Table 13.

25. Marc Mauer and Tracy Huling, *Young Black Americans and the Criminal Justice System: Five Years Later* (Washington, D.C.: The Sentencing Project, 1995).

26. Michael Isikoff, "Study: White Students More Likely to Use Drugs," *Washington Post*, February 25, 1991; Sam Meddis, "Whites, Not Blacks, at the Core of the Drug Crisis," *USA Today*, December 20, 1989.

27. Pettiway found that 31.2 percent of Latinas, 33.8 percent of white women, and 35 percent of black women reported heroin and opiate. Leon E. Pettiway, "Participation in Crime Partnerships by Female Drug Users," *Criminology* 25 (3) (1987): 746.

28. Mann 1995: 128.

29. HRW 1997a: 14.

30. Mann 1995: 128.
31. Mann 1995: 128. Black women were 30.5 percent of women arrested in California for drug offenses but 34.1 percent of those incarcerated for such offenses. White women were 48.5 percent of women arrested for drug violations but only 38.3 percent of those imprisoned for such offenses (Mann 1985: 128).
32. Mann 1995: 128.
33. NYSDOCS, Division of Program Planning, Research, and Evaluation. *Men and Women Under Custody: 1987–2001* (Albany, September 2002), 87.
34. Ibid.
35. BJS 1999: 8
36. CANY 1992; Penny Green, *Drug Couriers* (London: Quartet Books, 1996).
37. CANY 1992: 11. Men are also more likely to swallow "balloons" filled with drugs (CANY 12).
38. CANY 1992.
39. CANY 1999.
40. CANY 1992.
41. CANY 1992.
42. Díaz-Cotto 2006.
43. CANY 1992.
44. Díaz-Cotto 1996, 2006; HRW, Women's Rights Project, *All Too Familiar: Sexual Abuse of Women in U.S. State Prisons*, 1996; Barbara Owen, *In the Mix* (Albany: State University of New York, 1998); Katherine Watterson, *Women in Prison* (Boston: Northeastern University, 1996).
45. Zelma W. Henriques, *Imprisoned Mothers and Their Children* (Lanham: University Press of America, 1982).
46. Katherine Gabel and Denise Johnston, eds., *Children of Incarcerated Parents* (New York: Lexington Books, 1995).
47. Timothy Dunn, *The Militarization of the US-Mexico Border, 1978–1992* (Austin, TX: Center for Mexican American Studies, University of Texas, 1996).
48. Dunn 1996.
49. Carlos Alonso, *Guerra Antidrogas, Democracia, Derechos Humanos y Militarización en América Latina* (Ciudad de Guatemala, Guatemala: CEDIB, Transnational Institute, and Inforpress Centroaméricana, 1997).
50. Nicholas Dorn, J. Jepsen, and E. Savona, *European Drug Policies and Enforcement* (London: Macmillan, 1996); United Nations, *Single Convention on Narcotic Drugs* (New York: UN, 1977); UN Department of Public Information, *UN Convention Against the Illicit Traffic of Narcotics* (New York: UN, 1991); U.S. Department of State, *International Narcotics Control Strategy* (Washington, D.C., 1991); Office of National Drug Control Policy, Executive Office of the President, *The National Drug Control Strategy, 1997* (Washington, D.C., 1997).
51. Amnesty International, United States of America, Human Rights Concerns in the Border Region with Mexico (May 1998); HRW, Crossing the Line: Human Rights Abuses Along the U.S. Border with Mexico Persist Amid Climate of Impunity (1995b); HRW, Children's Rights Project, Slipping through the Crack: Unaccompanied Children Detained by the U.S. Immigration and Naturalization Service (1997b).
52. Alonso 1997; Dunn 1996; M. Jelsma and T. Ronken, eds., *Democracias Bajo Fuego* (Uruguay: TNI, Ediciones Brecha, Acción Andina, 1998); Roberto Laserna, ed., *Economía Política de las Drogas* (Cochabamba, Bolivia: Centro de Estudios de la Realidad Económica y Social-Consejo Latinoamericano de Ciencias Sociales, 1993); Rossi 1996; U.S. Congress, House Committee on Armed Services, *The Andean Drug Strategy and the Role of the U.S. Military*, 101st Congress, 1st Session (Washington, D.C., January 1990).
53. Hugo B. Margain, "The War on Drugs: A Mexican Perspective," *Voices of México* (October-December 1990): 3–8.
54. Dunn 1996: 138.
55. United Press International, "Mexican Border Police Abuse Illegal Immigrants, Report Says," February 24, 1992.
56. Azaola and Yucamán 1996.
57. Azaola and Yucamán 1996.
58. Azaola and Yucamán 1996.

59. Azaola and Yucamán 1996: 400. The second most important cause for imprisonment was property crimes, particularly theft and fraud.
60. Mario Arango, *Impacto del Narcotráfico en Antioquia* (Medellín, Colombia: J.M. Arango, 1988); Michael Levine and Laura Kavanau-Levine, *The Big White Lie* (New York: Thunder's Mouth, 1993).
61. Azaola and Yucamán 1996.
62. Azaola and Yucamán 1996.
63. Roberto Laserna, *Twenty (Mis)conceptions on Coca and Cocaine* (La Paz, Bolivia: Clave consultores, s.r.l., 1997); Rossi 1996.
64. Andy Atkins, "The Economic and Political Impact of the Drug Trade and Drug Control Policies in Bolivia," in Joyce and Malamud 1998.
65. Jelsma and Ronken 1998.
66. Andean Information Network (AIN), *The Weight of Law 1008* (Cochabamba, Bolivia: AIN, 1996).
67. Agreda et al., 1996.
68. U.S. federal agencies involved in the war on drugs have included Department of Defense (DOD), DEA, INS, Central Intelligence Agency (CIA), Federal Bureau of Investigation (FBI), Customs Service, the Federal Aviation Administration, the Bureau of Alcohol, Tobacco, and Firearms, the Department of Justice, the Department of State, and the Treasury Department (Bagley 1996).
69. HRW 1995a.
70. See: AIN 1996; CEDIB 1994; de Achá 1996; HRW 1995a.
71. Jelsma and Ronken 1998; Levine and Kavanau-Levine 1993.
72. Agreda et al., 1996; de Achá 1996.
73. Agreda et al., 1996: 19. Author's translation.
74. de Achá 1996; AIN 1996.
75. de Achá 1998: 132.
76. AIN 1997: 9.
77. Laserna 1997: 117–118.
78. Ibid., 116.
79. BJS 2001b: 1.
80. AIN 1996: 90.
81. de Achá 1998: 132.
82. de Achá 1998. For more on the conditions of women in Bolivian prisons see AIN 1997; Díaz-Cotto 2004b.
83. Atkins 1998: 108.
84. AIN 1996: i.
85. AIN 1996; AIN, *Children of Law 1008* (Cochabamba, Bolivia: AIN, 1997); United Nations Department of Public Information, *Body of Principles for the Protection of All Persons under Any Form of Detention or Imprisonment* (New York: UN, 1989).
86. Atkins 1998: 108–109.
87. Atkins 1998; AIN 1996, 1997; de Achá 1998.
88. Sentences varied depending on whether a person was convicted of planting, manufacturing, or trafficking drugs and whether the person was "found guilty of having sold drugs to someone who becomes intoxicated to the point of death" (Laserna 1997: 150).
89. HRW 1995a.
90. AIN 1997: 9–11.
91. Juan C. Pinto Quintanilla, *Cárceles y Familia* (Cochabamba, Bolivia: Terre des Hommes, 1999).
92. Agreda et al., 1996.
93. According to Dorado, in 1995, 75 percent (47) of Latin American women detained in Frankfurt were Colombian; another seven were Chilean. In 1996, all ten Latin American women detained in England were Colombian. In 1997, 71 percent of the 368 women imprisoned in Madrid were Colombian; another 4.6 percent were Venezuelan. See Maria C. Dorado, "Mujeres Latinoamericanas en Europe: el Caso de Colombia," in del Olmo 1998.
94. Dorado 1998: 80.
95. Dorado 1998: 82–84, 88.
96. Dorado 1998: 86.
97. Dorado 1998: 88–90.

98. K. Ambos, "A Comparison of Sentencing and Execution of Penalties," in CEP, ed. *European Conference on Drug Couriers* (Zurich: CEP, 1996), 25–27; Dorado 1998.
99. CANY 1992; Dorado 1998: 94–95.
100. Green 1996: 9.
101. Dorado 1998: 94–97.
102. Dorado 1998: 92–93.
103. The White House 1997.
104. Ryan S. King and Marc Mauer, *State Sentencing and Corrections Policy in an Era of Fiscal Restraint* (Washington, D.C.: The Sentencing Project, 2002).
105. *Australian Financial Review*, "U.S. Kicked off UN Drug Body" (May 9, 2001); Ian Williams, "U.S. Lost Seat on U.N. Human Rights Commission Follows Threat to Veto Mideast Resolutions," *Washington Report on Middle East Affairs* XX (5) (July 2001).
106. Richard C. Leone and Greg Anrig Jr., eds., *The War on Our Freedoms* (New York: Public Affairs, 2003).
107. Eric Lichtblau, "U.S. Uses Terror Law to Pursue Crimes from Drugs to Swindling," *New York Times* (September 28, 2003).

CHAPTER 12

From Neighborhood to Prison

Women and the War on Drugs in Portugal

MANUELA IVONE PEREIRA DA CUNHA

By the end of the twentieth century, Portugal, like most other Western nations, had experienced a dramatic inflation in prison populations.[1] The country steadily leads this trend in the European Union (EU), registering the highest carceral rate per 100,000 inhabitants throughout the last decade. In addition to its leading position in the relative general level of imprisonment, Portugal holds two other records in the EU context that are worth noticing: the highest proportion of convictions for drug-related offenses and the highest rate of women's imprisonment. These facts are not unrelated. I wish to address here some aspects of their connections as well as some of their implications as they are reflected in a Portuguese major women's penitentiary where I conducted fieldwork for two different periods of time (1986 to 1987 and 1997). Women represent 10 percent of the imprisoned population in Portugal. As far as ethnicity is concerned, the majority of the carceral population is Portuguese (86 percent). The more important non-Portuguese categories are composed of immigrants of African origin (more precisely from Portuguese-speaking countries), who represent 1 percent of the general population but amount to 9 percent of prisoners.[2]

During the past decade, a surprising reorganization of imprisoned populations in Portugal has taken place. Drug-related crime is the pivotal element that shaped this reorganization. The sudden growth of prison populations since the 1990s was accompanied by a qualitative shift. Its most fundamental aspect is the fact that these populations are now often articulated in networks of kinship and

155

neighborhood, that is, in variable clusters of preprison relations. As I will argue later, what at first sight is no more than a curious detail has in fact an enormous analytical significance for prison studies. For the moment, I am going to briefly present two main sets of reasons for this particular restructuring.

The first one lies with the specific patterns of repression that retail drug trafficking came to induce in the penal system and in law enforcement agencies. Apart from having motivated legal changes that constitute a historical regression in the general philosophy of Portuguese criminal law,[3] the war on drugs has intensified, if not created, indiscriminate mass procedures in crime control. Reported "drug-trafficking networks" frequently have in fact little sociological consistency and are no more than the artificial outcome of the way individual cases are dealt with and juxtaposed by the criminal justice system. These judicial devices can thus produce otherwise inexistent continuities between two or three dozen people. Such practices do no more than extend and compound the effects of certain law enforcement interventions favored by the war on drugs. As law enforcement became increasingly proactive instead of reactive (there are usually no drug victims' formal complaints to react to), so did the potential for selectivity and bias. These interventions are aimed more than ever at specific poor urban neighborhoods, which have become collective targets of surveillance and of routine indiscriminate sweeps. With such intense police attention, the probability of arrest is evidently higher in these territories. As in several other countries where the war on drugs has reinforced similar styles of crime control,[4] these stigmatized areas are now massive suppliers of prisoners, and the geography of imprisonment has begun to be extraordinarily predictable. It is therefore not surprising that coprisoners are often relatives and neighbors, imprisoned successively or simultaneously.

This transformation in prison populations is mainly caused by massive targeting processes, but it is also produced by the specificity of the Portuguese drug economy itself. Retail trafficking, which is the more exposed and risky scale of this activity, develops in Portugal along kinship and neighborhood ties and has benefited from the way traditional solidarities operate in underprivileged residential areas. Such is the case with *fiado*, one of the robust cultural forms of mutual assistance and interest-free informal loans that bear the circulation of both legal and illegal products. This does not mean that the drug economy is organized in the form of those extensive networks of the kind we can now find in prisons. Most of the time, in fact, it is quite the opposite. This economy evolves around small, variable circles of associates (whether kin or neighbors) that have flexible structures and work autonomously. We are far, therefore, from the stereotypical *mafia* familism. What happened was that small-scale drug trafficking brought to impoverished urban settings a booming structure of illegal opportunities in which all, regardless of age, gender, or "race," could participate.

A similar claim of social inclusiveness was also made about U.S. markets, where some authors have argued that drug retail provided an "equal opportunity" structure, albeit an illegal and unintended one.[5] And it was women's recent visibility in the drug economy that led to what seems to be an exhumation of the "new female criminal" theme. According to this view, quite popular in the 1970s, feminism had had the collateral effect of also emancipating women into crime.[6] Soon afterward, the idea was so convincingly refuted that it seemed it had been definitely buried.[7] As a matter of fact it has remained so, except for this recent partial recycling, now limited to drug-related female criminality.

This apparent gender issue deserves closer attention. The fact that the astounding proliferation of drug markets has expanded illegal opportunities is undisputed, as is the increased presence of women in those markets. However, the nature of this presence diverges significantly according to place and context. A comparative perspective can therefore be illuminating. One compelling reason for taking a comparative approach is that presence is not synonymous with equal participation, as Maher persuasively argues about U.S. drug markets, where most of the opportunities opened to women are located only in the lower, riskier, and less lucrative segments of the business.[8] In the limited way women are allowed to participate (namely as a reserve supply used when there is a shortage of male labor or an imminent risk of arrest), they occupy peripheral functions such as drug advertising, renting or selling drug paraphernalia, and assisting others' consumption. These are small niches that women have carved out for themselves in the interstices of this economy. By doing so, they have generated new, specifically female roles that did not match former typologies concerning the actors of the drug business.[9]

This sharp gender stratification is a strong argument in favor of those who see continuity rather than change in the nature of female participation in the drug economy.[10] In other words, the proclaimed change was in fact illusory; the new cornucopia was out of women's reach. Two features of these particular markets converge to produce this outcome. First, they are dominated by gender notions that confine women to domesticity and to traditional gender roles. This "underworld sexism"[11] not only seems resistant to emancipatory moves of any kind but also apparently finds fertile ground in the endemic violence that pervades most U.S. retail drug markets. Hegemonic masculinity is in fact reinforced by the fact that, in this economy, employers define employability requirements along the lines of abilities perceived as inherently male: women are assumed to lack the necessary capacity for intimidation and the mental and physical ferocity to prevail in a violent milieu.

One cannot say, however, that ideological barriers to female access are new in these settings. They became more effective during the 1990s because of a mutation in the structure of retail drug markets—a mutation that occurred not only in the United States but in European contexts as well. Such markets had by that time adopted a "business" profile that, according to the typology proposed by Johnson, Hamid, and Sanabria, consists of vertically integrated organizations, with a rigid centralized structure, involving crews of employees with nearly no autonomy.[12] Ruggiero and South characterized similar structures in Europe as "crime in organization."[13] Up until that decade the prevailing model was a different, more fluid one; with little hierarchical interdependence or permanent wage relationships, a weak functional division of labor, it rested mostly on individual entrepreneurialism. It was thus qualified as "freelance"[14] or "crime in association."[15] Even if these markets were equally oriented by male domination and by an aggressive *ethos* that also made them from the onset hostile arenas to women, their own freelance structure rendered the barriers to female participation fragile and inefficient. These permeable barriers left women more latitude as well more autonomy in the decisions they made about "where, when and how to sell."[16]

It is precisely the latter market structure that presently prevails in the Portuguese retail drug economy, where the evolution has even been opposite to the one I have so far described for European and U.S. contexts. That is, the business model evolved in the 1990s towards a freelance one. With relative ease, many women could get started on their own in dealing as freelancers, obtaining drugs on a loan or consignment basis through neighborhood networks; they often use the *fiado* female circuits, borrowing a few grams of heroin from a neighbor for resale, in the same manner as, on another occasion, they borrowed from her a few eggs or a cup of salt. Other women collaborate with male partners once in a while in a drug commercial transaction. Nevertheless, when they do, it is as kin, friends, and neighbors, not as subordinate employees of an organization led by men.

In addition to the fact that the freelance market structure prevalent in Portugal is by its very fluidity more open than the business model that became dominant in other countries, the Portuguese retail trafficking scene is also comparatively less violent. Relying more on the strategic mobilization of social relations and vicinity codes of solidarity than on conspicuous parades of virile brutality,[17] its *ethos* does not impose special qualifications of "manhood" on would-be dealers. There is, however, another reason for the relatively ungendered character of Portuguese narcowork, in other words, for the low level of filtering of participants along gender lines. This low filtering is also the counterpart, in the illegal world, of the relative frailty and ineffectiveness, in the legitimate world, of ideological obstacles to female work and to women's direct financial participation in the household budget.[18] Such frailty and ineffectiveness are especially salient among poor populations. In these contexts, the cultural definitions of gender roles also assign the realm of domestic and family responsibilities to women. However, they do not deny them the nondomestic role of provider,[19] and this circumstance is not necessarily considered as a distortion of the female cultural "script" or as an unwanted consequence of male economic failure. Poor women have always resorted to labor, not as an emancipatory or counterhegemonic option[20] but mainly as a straightforward, ordinary strategy for survival.

Women can thus be important actors in the drug economy—regardless of their ethnicity. Unlike similar drug markets elsewhere in Europe and in the United States, which are often racially stratified,[21] the Portuguese retail drug economy is occupied by both poor minorities and nonminorities. At the bottom of the market, drug dealing has become one of the vectors of ethnic social leveling. However, such leveling must be understood in the context of the retail drug economy's inscription in poor urban neighborhoods, areas with a specific interplay between categories of race/ethnicity and class. Although minorities in Portugal (mainly gypsies and immigrants from lusophone African countries such as Mozambique, Angola, Cape-Verde, and Guiné-Bissau) *are* disadvantaged, they share this disadvantage—more than is the case in other countries—with large segments of the white Portuguese population, for instance insofar as labor and the residential markets are concerned. As Machado argues, "In comparison with countries such as France, United Kingdom, Germany or Italy, in Portugal the social contrasts between 'third world' immigrant minorities and the national population are weaker, not so much because of a homogeneity in the class composition of minorities, a homogeneity which does not exist either in those countries' minorities, but mainly because in Portugal *the weight of ethnic minorities is lower within the set of underprivileged social categories.*"[22]

Referring specifically to the residential status of these minorities, and with the exception of the Cape-Verdean community, which presents higher rates of poor housing and residential concentration, this author states that "such minorities *are not comparatively more represented* than the Portuguese population in poor neighborhoods, nor are there predominantly ethnic residential areas."[23] Furthermore, as a general social gap has widened, the same social segments of both minorities and nonminorities have found themselves further removed from more affluent segments of the population. To draw a brief, if oversimplified, comparison with other contexts, it has been observed that U.S. inner-city neighborhoods tend to be racially/ethnically more uniform[24] than European ones, where more diverse populations tend to congregate in deprived locales.[25] But even here, the Portuguese case seems to present some specificities in relation to other destitute urban settings in Europe, where the poor are stratified along ethnic lines. For example, blue-collar residents resent newly arrived deprived immigrant neighbors, seeing their proximity as a sign of social demotion or an obstacle to social mobility.[26] But in Portuguese public housing neighborhoods and in the few remaining shantytowns, poverty is much more severe and survival is a priority for both minority and nonminority groups.

Such urban settings are not usually the scene of symbolic struggles around ascending or descending social trajectories.

The retail drug economy reflects this trend, which can be labeled integration within exclusion. Neither race/ethnicity nor gender determines or restricts involvement in the drug retail industry, which provides a relatively open illegal structure of opportunities. Thus, by both the specificity of its inscription in Portuguese neighborhoods and the massive repressive targeting processes it has triggered, the drug economy stands out today as the main route organizing the collective trajectories between deprived urban communities and the prison. As mentioned earlier, imprisoned networks of kin and neighbors are a central feature of this circulation, and they lie behind one of the major transformations of the contemporary prison.

This transformation is especially conspicuous in women's prisons, turning these institutions into important settings for understanding emergent phenomena, which are also widely occurring in other carceral contexts, albeit in a more diluted manner. It may well be that, for once, the study of women's institutions could set the terms of the theoretical debate about prisons, thereby inverting the asymmetries of the past: men's imprisonment has framed the debate in an universal manner, quite oblivious to gender, whereas research on its female equivalent remained invariably gender bound, unable to export its insights in a reciprocal encompassing way. In geopolitical terms the same could be said of research findings in peripheral countries, which can draw attention to phenomena whose scope is not inevitably parochial and may have a universal relevance.

Such is the case, I believe, of the kind of prison networks that have emerged in Portugal in the last decade. The prominence they gain in women's institutions stems partly from the startling homogeneity of female imprisoned populations. In the 1990s, women in prison became unified not only by a blatant impoverishment but also by a reduction of the former penal diversity.[27] Although the population of male prisoners is also fairly homogeneous (property offenses and drug-related crimes account together for the majority of convictions), its internal distribution is much more balanced than that of its female counterpart, which concentrates overwhelmingly on drug trafficking. In fact, women serve proportionally more prison sentences for drug-related crimes than men. The centrality of drug crimes in women's convictions is also what best illuminates the faster rise of female incarceration rates: these are the crimes with the highest conviction rates and which receive some of the harshest sentences. This means, as Karen Leander noticed in another context, that the present rise of women incarceration rates would owe little to a hypothetical change in the way courts deal with this gender (say, using the terms of an old controversy within the discipline of criminology, from "chivalrous" to severely punitive).[28]

Whether because of the gender inclusiveness of local drug markets or the multiple levels of its harsh repression, women occupy a central position in the processes that systematically link prisons to a small number of neighborhoods, that is, in the processes that generate carceral clusters of kin, friends, and neighbors. In the major women's penitentiary of the country, where my research was based, aunts, cousins, sisters, sisters-in-law, mothers, grandmothers, and mothers-in-law now find themselves doing time together, in a circle of kin that often amounts to more than a dozen people, sometimes encompassing four generations (when a great-grandson is born in prison to a prisoner whose daughter and granddaughter are also imprisoned). I do not include here the male kin serving their own sentences in other facilities. These circles of relatives in turn intertwine with circles of neighbors, therefore forming wide networks of prisoners who knew each other prior to imprisonment. This is to say that they reenact preprison networks of acquaintance. Hundreds of lives can thus be interwoven by these previous ties when, on the contrary, prisons are supposed to combine lives rather randomly.

These clusters of preconnected prisoners have implications that bear upon the way we think about prisons. If we were to single out one notion about the prison that could stand as a common denominator amidst the variety of views and discourses on the subject (whether scholar, expert, or lay), "a world apart" would certainly qualify.

Of course, prisons do not fit the old clichés as neatly as they used to. In the West, since World War II, they have tended to become less isolated and more open to the outside world in several ways: open to outside scrutiny and more strictly tied to a set of rules and regulations through which the state limits penitentiary managers' and wardens' margins of discretion[29]; open also by a growing flow of goods, services, and communications between the interior and the exterior. Indeed, aspects such as the penetration of the media, material exchanges, and heterocontrols have led some authors to question the adequacy of the model through which Erving Goffman depicted the prison as a "total institution."[30] Besides, it was realized long ago that prisoners do not leave their cultural background behind[31] and that what goes by the name of "prison culture" is more a contextual combination of these backgrounds than a pure endogenous product.[32]

Why, then, would I maintain that the notion of a world apart nonetheless still shapes in a fundamental manner the way we think about prisons? Because the walls of these institutions are supposed to separate prisoners from their *external* relationships, which is to say, from their *previous* social relationships. For all the increasing porosity mentioned previously, these walls would always materialize this basic social split, and even regular visits, phone calls, or letters cannot but render it more tangible. In this sense imprisonment would invariably be an interruption, a reality between brackets. As far as researchers are concerned, I do not know when this social split ceased to be an empirical question—if it ever was one—and began to be an assumption or, more important, an analytical starting point. In any case, it is this core notion that the contemporary emergence of preprison networks invites us to reconsider in a new light.

To begin with, when imprisoned, a prisoner is not detached from his or her social world anymore. Important segments of this world are transferred with him or her. So much, then, for the classical social hiatus that no prison study could fail to comment on. When one is initiated to prison life *with* kin, friends, or neighbors, or *by* kin, friends, or neighbors, personal and social identity can better resist an environment that tends to suspend or otherwise corrode them. Preestablished relations act like filters interposed between the penitentiary order and the self. Yet this is only one aspect of the continuity between the interior and the exterior world created by these particular networks. My fieldwork revealed still others.

The symbolic boundary that the prison used to represent is now eroded. The stigma that used to be associated with imprisonment is now instituted well before detention, one may say "upstream," by the very fact of belonging to certain neighborhoods. It now indicates a structural, rather than circumstantial, marginalization. In turn, the prison is already a reality embodied in the daily life of the same urban territories, where it has become an ordinary element of many biographies, a banal destiny. Everybody in those areas has an acquaintance or a relative who is or has been imprisoned. Members of different families travel together to prison facilities to visit their incarcerated relatives and friends, making the most of the opportunity of a car ride offered by a neighbor. In fact, prisoner and visitor are almost interchangeable statuses, given the frequent shift from one condition to another in different moments of one's life trajectory. More than the banality of the prison, it is its recent "normalcy" that surfaces in the way inmates dealt with my taking pictures of them, for example. When I tried to leave their faces out of the frame, they would insist in being photographed full face and would take a pose with a smile. In one case, a woman asked me for a picture because she already had had a photo taken in every single prison of the country (where she had been either a prisoner or a visitor), and this institution was the only one lacking in her collection.

But if the prison is somehow an omnipresent reality in the neighborhood, the reverse is also true. Because imprisonment can absorb one's immediate circle of relations almost entirely, this does not go without consequences, inside as well outside. The prison became in several ways an extension of neighborhood life, creating new conflicts and notions underpinning everyday sociality: for example, the notion of "respect," which does not bear upon prisoner rank but upon family values and kinship seniority, or the "no-snitching" injunction, which does not pertain to some convict or deviant code but to vicinal codes of solidarity (whereby someone who deeply abhors drug dealing, for instance, will abhor even more the idea of denouncing a "son of the neighborhood"). But above all, the inescapable general effect is that daily life in prison is not self-referential anymore. Its course is inextricably linked to the flow of outside everyday life through these wide networks of acquaintance, which not only connect prisoners between themselves but also connect them to external overlapping networks of kin, friends, or neighbors. For this reason, any intraprison event can have immediate consequences outside, and vice versa. Life inside and life outside permanently affect each other. And their respective rhythms of progression, which used to appear so discrepant in the eyes of prisoners, have become synchronized through these daily events.[33]

This mutual intrusion, this practical and symbolic continuity between two worlds, defies both goffmanian depictions of the prison as a total institution and recurrent assumptions about the prison as a world apart, as well as further undermining the very categories of "prison society" and "prison culture," which for a long time have structured prison studies. It is true that research in this area seems, for the most part, to have abandoned the prison as a subject in itself, or at least it stopped interrogating the theoretical status of these institutions. Instead, it takes the prison as a context for the study of very specific topics, nevertheless a context with given, unproblematic boundaries. But, as I argue earlier, wherever these confined networks of previous relations prevail, the material boundaries do not shape institutional life in the fundamental manner that has long been presumed. The old congruence between social and symbolic boundaries, on the one hand, and, on the other, the physical limits of the institution cannot be taken for granted anymore. It is not enough to replace the prison in the wider framework of the external forces (social, political, economical, and historical) that take part in its shaping. In order to understand inmates' perceptions, experiences, and interactions, in other words to understand imprisonment, without which debates on prisons would be pointless, it is necessary to shift the focus from the inner world of the institution toward the interface between inside and outside. In this way, we can capture the webs of meaning that constantly link both worlds. The material perimeter of the prison can provide neither the text nor the context of a social life that has become inherently translocal.

It is possible to sum up some of the general effects of the contemporary circulation between prisons and specific urban neighborhoods as follows: the former are becoming extensions of the latter. A corollary of this state of affairs is that the debate about prisons necessarily has to take into account another divide, as critical as the one that has structured these debates so far: it has to consider not merely the boundary between the imprisoned and the free but also the one between those whose lives include the prison in their horizon and those whose lives do not. Since the modern prison was born, this same divide that became salient in late modernity is not unprecedented. By the second half of the nineteenth century it was no less crucial, both in Western Europe and in the United States, as it would be a hundred years later. To put it briefly, what makes these two historical moments similar in this respect is that the object of crime control policies was, ultimately, individuals rather than populations. This is also what presently unites two apparently opposite penological trends. The repressive injunction that produced the extraordinary inflation of imprisonment rates and the defensive injunction that classifies populations according to their degree of dangerousness, simply aspiring to manage them as contained in their territories as possible,[34] have the same tendency to produce collective targets. In the end, both trends create, and are created by, a common atmosphere that is generating a new profile of prison populations, who in turn are changing, through their very characteristics, the nature of these institutions.

References

1. Vicenzo Ruggiero, Mick Ryan, and Joe Sim, eds., *Western European Penal Systems. A Critical Anatomy* (London: Sage, 1995), Loïc Wacquant, *Les Prisons de la Misère* (Paris: Raisons d'Agir Editions, 1990).
2. Anália Torres and Maria do Carmo Gomes, *Drogas e Prisões em Portugal* (Lisbon: CIES/ISCTE, 2002): 34–36.
3. Eduardo Maia Costa, "Direito Penal da Droga: Breve História de um Fracasso," *Revista do Ministério Público* 74 (1998): 103–120.
4. For example, Nicholas Dorn, Murji Karim, and Nigel South, *Traffickers. Drug Markets and Law Enforcement* (London and New York: Routledge, 1992), Dominique Duprez and Michel Kokoreff, *Les Mondes de la Drogue* (Paris: Odile Jacob, 2000).
5. For example, Philippe Bourgois and Eloise Dunlap, "Exorcising Sex for Crack: An Ethnographic Perspective from Harlem," in *Crack Pipe as Pimp: An Ethnographic Investigation of Sex-For-Crack Exchanges*, ed. M. Ratner (New York: Lexington Books, 1993): 97–132, Nancy Wilson, "Stealing and Dealing: The Drug War and Gendered Criminal Opportunity," in *Female Criminality: The State of the Art*, ed. C. Culliver (New York: Garland Publishing, 1993): 169–194.
6. Freda Adler, *Sisters in Crime* (New York: McGraw Hill, 1975), Rita Simon, *Women and Crime* (London, Lexington, and Toronto: Lexington Books, 1975).
7. Carol Smart, "The New Female Criminal: Reality or Myth?," *British Journal of Criminology* 19, no. 1 (1979): 50–59, Jane Chapman, *Economic Realities and the Female Offender* (Lexington: Lexington Books, 1980), Meda Chesney-Lind, "Women and Crime: The Female Offender," *Signs* 12, 1 (1986): 78–96, Pat Carlen, *Women, Crime and Poverty* (Milton Keynes: Open University Press, 1988).
8. Lisa Maher, *Sexed Work: Gender, Race and Resistance in a Brooklyn Drug Market* (Oxford: Clarendon Press, 1997): 18.
9. Eloise Dunlap, Bruce Johnson, and Lisa Maher, "Female Crack Sellers in New York City: Who They Are and What They Do," *Women & Criminal Justice*, 8, no. 4 (1997): 25–55.
10. Lisa Maher and Kathleen Daly, "Women in the Street-Level Drug Economy: Continuity or Change?" *Criminology* 34, no. 4 (1996): 465–491.
11. Darrell Steffensmeier and Robert Terry, "Institutional Sexism in the Underworld: A View from the Inside," *Sociological Inquiry* 56 (1986): 304–323.
12. Bruce Johnson, Ansley Hamid, and Harry Sanabria, "Emerging Models of Crack Distribution," in *Drugs, Crime, and Social Policy: Research, Issues, and Concerns*, ed. T. Mieczkowski (Boston: Allyn & Bacon, 1992): 56–78.
13. Vicenzo Ruggiero and Nigel South, "La Ville de la Fin de l'Ère Moderne en Tant que Bazar: Marchés de Stupéfiants, Entreprise Illégale et les 'Barricades'," *Déviance et Société* 20, no. 4 (1996): 315–333, 195.
14. Johnson, Hamid, and Sanabria 1992.

15. Ruggiero and South 1995, 195.
16. For examples of typical freelance markets where we can find more successful, lucrative, and less subordinate experiences than those reported by Maher 1997, see Bruce Jacobs and Jody Miller, "Crack Dealing, Gender, and Arrest Avoidance," *Social Problems* 45, no. 4 (1998): 550–569; Patricia Morgan and Jaren Ann Joe, "Uncharted Terrain: Contexts of Experience Among Women in the Illicit Drig Economy," *Women and Criminal Justice* 8, no. 3 (1997): 85–109.
17. Miguel Chaves, *Casal Ventoso: Da Gandaia ao Narcotráfico* (Lisbon: Imprensa de Ciências Sociais, 1999).
18. Virginia Ferreira, "Padrões de Segregaç'o das Mulheres no Emprego—Uma Análise do Caso Português no Quadro Europeu," in *Portugal: Um Retrato Singular*, ed. Boaventura de Sousa Santos (Oporto: Afrontamento, 1993): 233–257.
19. Sally Cole, *Women of the Praia: Work and Lives in a Portuguese Coastal Community* (Princeton, NJ: Princeton University Press, 1991).
20. Jo'o de Pina Cabral, "A Difus'o do Limiar: Margens, Hegemonias e Contradições," *Análise Social*, XXXIV, no.153 (2000): 865–892.
21. Maher 1997; Ruggiero and South 1995, 1996.
22. Fernando Luís Machado, "Etnicidade em Portugal. Contrastes e Politizaç'o," *Sociologia. Problemas e Práticas* 12 (1992): 123–136, 128. Emphasis in the original.
23. Ibid: 126. Emphasis added.
24. Robert K. Sampson and Janet L. Lauritsen, "Racial and Ethnic Disparities in Crime and Criminal Justice in the United States," in *Ethnicity, Crime and Immigration*, ed. M. Tonry (Chicago: University of Chicago Press, 1997): pp. 311–376.
25. Loïc Wacquant, "The Comparative Structure and Experience of Urban Exclusion: 'Race', Class and Space in Paris and Chicago," *Poverty, Inequality, and the Future of Social Policy: Western States in the New World Order*, ed. K. McFate et al. (New York: Russell Sage Foundation, 1995): 542–570.
26. Gérard Althabe, "La Résidence Comme Enjeu," in *Urbanisation et Enjeux Quotidiens. Terrains Ethnologiques dans la France Actuelle*, ed. G. Althabe et al. (Paris: L'Harmattan, 1993): 11–69, Monique Sélim, "Une Cohabitation Pluri-Ethnique," in G. Althabe et al., 71–111.
27. Manuela P. da Cunha, *Entre o Bairro e a Pris'o: Tráfico e Trajectos* (Lisbon: Fim de Século, 2002).
28. Karen Leander, "The Normalization of Swedish Prisons," in *Western European Penal Systems. A Critical Anatomy*, ed. V. Ruggiero, M. Ryan, and J. Sim (London: Sage, 1995): 167–193, 178–179.
29. For example, Charles Stastny and Gabrielle Tyrnauer, *Who Rules the Joint?* (Lexington: Lexington Books, 1982).
30. Erving Goffman, *Asylums. Essays on the Social Situation of Mental and Other Inmates* (Garden City, NY: Garden Books, 1961). For a critique of Goffman's position see Guy Lemire, *Anatomie de la Prison* (Montréal: Presses de l'Université de Montréal, 1990), Keith Farrington, "The Modern Prison as Total Institution? Public Perception Versus Objective Reality," *Crime and Delinquency* 38, no. 1 (1992): 6–26.
31. Clarence Schrag, "Some Foundations for a Theory of Corrections," *The Prison: Studies in Institutional Organization and Change*, ed. D. Cressey (New York: Holt, 1961): 70–90.
32. John Irwin and Donald Cressey, "Thieves, Convicts and the Inmate Culture," *Social Problems* 10 (1962): 142–155.
33. Manuela P. da Cunha, "Le Temps Suspendu. Rythmes et Durées dans une Prison Portugaise," *Terrain* 29 (1997): 59–68.
34. Jock Young, *The Exclusive Society. Social Exclusion, Crime and Difference in Late Modernity* (London: Sage, 1999); Jonathon Simon and Malcolm Feeley, "True Crime: The New Penology and Public Discourse on Crime," in *Punishment and Social Control: Essays in Honor of Sheldom Messinger*, ed. T. Blomberg and S. Cohen (New York: Aldine de Gruyter, 1995): 147–180.

CHAPTER **13**

"Mules," "Yardies," and Other Folk Devils

Mapping Cross-Border Imprisonment in Britain

JULIA SUDBURY

On October 2, 2002, Beverley Fowler, a thirty-two-year-old Jamaican woman, was found hanging from a curtain rail in her cell at Her Majesty's Prison (HMP) Durham. Beverley had served a six-year sentence for importing class A drugs and was scheduled for deportation two days after she took her life. According to prisoner advocacy group Inquest, Beverley was terrified of returning to Jamaica, where her children's father had been shot and she had been gang raped and forced to smuggle criminalized drugs by a drug-trafficking network.[1] In addition, tensions in the women's maximum-security prison were high because of a dramatic increase in the incarcerated population over the previous twelve months. Beverley's death was one of a spate of suicides, and at the time of her death, 25 percent of prisoners at HMP Durham were on special watch for self-harm.[2] Beverley's story is emblematic of the explosion in women's imprisonment in Britain. During the past twenty years, the number of women warehoused in the penal system in England and Wales has grown dramatically. Increasingly, the women hidden behind bars in Britain's scenic towns, from Durham to Winchester, are black British women and women from Britain's former colonies. In this chapter, I argue that a transnational feminist analysis provides the most effective lens through which to examine the boom in women's imprisonment. Rather than focusing on British criminal justice

167

policy in isolation from global trends, a transnational feminist lens pushes us to extend our analysis beyond national borders. Through the narratives of women imprisoned for importing drugs into Britain, the chapter explores the reasons behind the dramatic increase in the women's prison population. I suggest that a combination of four factors—the racialized feminization of poverty under neoliberal globalization, the racialized "tough on crime" agenda of successive Conservative and New Labour governments, the transnational war on drugs, and the transatlantic spread and consolidation of the prison-industrial complex in Britain—are key to understanding this dramatic expansion of coercive state violence against women at the turn of the twenty-first century.

Racialized Women in Her Majesty's Prisons

The number of people behind bars in England and Wales rose inexorably during the 1990s and continued to climb into the new millennium.[3] Throughout the 1990s, Britain's incarceration rate was second in Western Europe only to that of Portugal, a relatively impoverished nation at Europe's southernmost tip. However, in 2002, Britain surpassed even Portugal, by incarcerating 139 out of every 100,000 residents.[4] Although all European incarceration rates are far lower than North American rates, leading to a tendency by U.S. commentators to refer to Europe as a model of penal restraint, this should not obscure the striking difference between European Union members. Scandinavian countries that provide a more substantial social safety net imprison far fewer people.[5] Britain therefore represents the punitive end of the European spectrum in the treatment of poor, racialized, and criminalized communities. Britain's African Caribbean community bears the brunt of the incarceration boom. African Caribbean men are eight times more likely than whites to serve a prison sentence and, once imprisoned, serve longer sentences.[6] African Caribbean women are dramatically overrepresented in prison, making up 24 percent of women prisoners but only 1 percent of the general population.[7] The increase in the number of people behind bars has created a crisis for the prison service. Overcrowded prisons warehouse prisoners in cramped conditions and offer few opportunities for meaningful activity and limited time outside the cell. This growth in the number of prisoners has also led to an explosion in prison construction, leading commentators to comment on "the largest prison building program since the middle of the 19th century."[8] Seven new private prisons have been built since 1995, and at the time of writing, two new prisons were under construction at a cost of £111.5 million (U.S. $204 million).[9] Prison expansion has immense financial as well as social costs. By 2003, the prison system cost £2.7 billion per annum to maintain. Despite the new construction, British prisons remained dangerously overcrowded as of the time of writing.

The spate of suicides at HMP Durham is one consequence of the punishment epidemic.

Although women make up only 6 percent of those incarcerated, the women's prison population has grown at a faster rate than that of men, a phenomenon that is common to other advanced industrialized nations. In the ten years to 2002, the annual average number of women in prison increased by 173 percent, while men's incarceration grew by only 50 percent.[10] Racialized women and women from the global South account for the majority of this increase. One in five women prisoners are "foreign nationals"—non–United Kingdom passport-holders—and nearly half of these women are, like Beverley, from Jamaica.[11] In 2003, the public was shocked by newspaper reports that for the first time the majority of women in one British prison were foreign nationals. Sixty-five percent of prisoners at Morton Hall, a rural prison in Lincolnshire, were migrants, most of them of Caribbean origin.[12] Alongside black British women, migrant women have transformed the face of British prisons.

Incarcerated black women have to survive a hostile and racist environment. Black women I interviewed reported being confined to the more physically demanding work assignments, being verbally abused, and having their needs and concerns systematically ignored by guards. Between 2000 and 2003, the Commission for Racial Equality carried out a formal investigation into the prison system after serious complaints of racist victimization and discrimination. The investigation identified a culture of tolerance for racism, from everyday practices of cultural racism to "acts of intimidation and gross racial harassment."[13] Despite the launch of Respond, an antiracist initiative, and the hiring of race relations experts, racism remains endemic to the prison service. Because most attention has focused on male prisons, where racist violence and even murder have hit the headlines, racism in women's prisons remains largely unchallenged.[14] In addition to racism, migrant women face unequal treatment on the basis of their nationality. Most foreign nationals are imprisoned for their activities as "mules," low-level workers in the drug pyramid, and therefore pose no risk to the general public. However, prison service policy prevents women who do not have a British passport from entering low-security "open" prisons, where prisoners experience a less rigid regimen and are able to leave the prison on day pass to work in the community. In addition, migrant women find it extremely difficult to maintain contact with their children, who are usually left in their country of origin. Exorbitant prices charged by the telephone companies give women only a few minutes for a five pound sterling phone card and many prisons deny women the use of cheaper cards purchased on the outside by friends or family. On completion of their sentences, foreign national prisoners are deported back to their country of origin. On arrival, they face challenging economic circumstances, lack of housing, disrupted relationships with children and family, possible reprisals from drug networks, and in some instances public shaming as names of returning prisoners are announced in radio and newspaper reports. The next section discusses the crackdown on Jamaican drug couriers and explores the structural causes generating women's cross-border imprisonment.

The Creation of a "Mule"

Jamaican women hit the British headlines in December 2001, when twenty-three drug couriers were caught on an Air Jamaica flight from Kingston to London Heathrow. Commenting on the case, Phil Sinkinson, the British Deputy High Commissioner in Jamaica, whipped up public outrage with the unsubstantiated claim that one in ten passengers on flights between Jamaica and Britain were carrying criminalized drugs and that up to thirty kilograms of cocaine were being smuggled on each flight. Subsequent newspaper and television reports trumpeted the scourge of "Jamaican drug mules 'flooding' UK."[15] In their classic work on the rise of law-and-order politics in the early 1970s, Stuart Hall et al. described the confluence of events, media coverage, and official responses that created a racialized moral panic around mugging. Describing the mugger as a new folk devil, Hall argued for a shift in focus from the "deviant act" of mugging to the official and public responses it inspired, suggesting that "it is this whole complex—action and reaction—as well as what produced it and what its consequences were, which requires to be explained."[16] The public concern generated around Jamaican mules can also be described as a moral panic leading to similarly disproportionate policy responses. Like the mugging phenomenon, which was discursively constructed as a U.S. import, the image of Jamaican mules flooding Britain with dangerous drugs raises the specter of disorder carried in women's bodies from abroad, feeding nativist as well as racist sentiment. Responding to these discursive connections between migrant women, crime, and pollution, demands for action made by politicians and commentators escalated to include the introduction of visas for all visitors from Jamaica. In the light of the media frenzy, Minister for Customs and black member of parliament Paul Boateng moved to maintain New Labour's "tough on crime" image, announcing the launch of Operation Airbridge to crack down on the "lawlessness of drug trafficking."[17] The two million pound operation, including a Customs "strike force," training and equipment for Jamaican police and the Jamaica Defense Force, and enhanced policing operations designed to catch couriers at Jamaican airports before boarding, targeted black women traveling between the two countries for intensive policing and surveillance. Although newspaper reports in the broadsheet press were sometimes sympathetic, portraying Jamaican mules as mothers risking death and imprisonment in order to support their families, the government response suggests a more punitive view. Home Office Minister Bob Ainsworth gave the following rationale for the crackdown:

So called drug mules are not responsible for the majority of the cocaine that enters this country but they are a particularly serious part of the importation. They tend to be closely associated with criminals involved with the manufacture of crack which has close connections with the gun crime in our major cities and is therefore well worth extra consideration.[18]

By emphasizing the links between drug mules, the crack trade, and gun crime, Ainsworth reconceptualized the nonviolent offense of importation as a cog in the wheel of urban gang-related violence. This discursive move tapped preexisting moral panics about crack cocaine, "black on black" crime, and the transatlantic spread of gun violence and placed the burden of responsibility onto the shoulders of poor migrant women, thus legitimating harsh treatment. In the four months following the launch of Operation Airbridge, ninety-nine women "swallowers"—carrying drugs in small packages in their stomachs— were arrested at Kingston airport. Although the fifty kilos of cocaine these women carried was a relatively small proportion of the total consumed annually in Britain, harsh sentencing ensured that they will serve long sentences and swell already overcrowded prisons.[19] Meanwhile, more impoverished Jamaican women will replace them in the trade, ensuring that British demand for the drug is met.

The narratives of women prisoners interrupt the distorted political depictions and media representations of mules and "swallowers." Between 1999 and 2001, I carried out taped interviews with twenty-four women in three prisons in England—HMP Westhill, HMP Cookham Wood, and HMP Holloway—and had informal conversations and group discussions with many more. These three institutions confine large numbers of poor black British women, Caribbean women, and working class white women. In addition, there are small numbers of other European women, Colombian women and other Latinas, African, Middle Eastern, and South Asian women. Whereas many of the white women I spoke with had cycled in and out of prison on short sentences related to a drug addiction or "survival crime," most of the black women, both British residents and foreign nationals, were serving a first, often lengthy sentence for importation or possession. Migrant women drug couriers are not a homogeneous group. The women I interviewed gave three explanations for importing drugs. Some women were duped into carrying the drugs by friends or a male partner. Claims of innocence were seldom considered by judges, who tended to view the presence of the drugs as prima facie evidence of guilt. Others were coerced or intimidated into carrying drugs, usually by a male drug dealer or "gangster." In addition to threats of physical violence against the women, their children and family members were threatened with death or mutilation. The majority of the women acknowledged that they chose to carry the drugs in exchange for a few thousand pounds sterling. It is tempting to separate these women into two groups, the innocent victims of intimidation and deceit and the willing participants in crime. Indeed, organizations such as Justice for Women and Miscarriages of Justice UK are dedicated to obtaining the release of women and men who "do not deserve" to be in prison by virtue of their innocence or status as victims. However, this dualistic portrayal limits our ability to analyze the reasons why women are willing to risk their lives and liberty by swallowing condoms filled with heroin or carrying criminalized drugs in their luggage. Although some women do "choose" to import drugs, they do so in the context of limited options for survival.

Jackie's story illustrates the limited choices facing poor Caribbean women. Jackie is a thirty-five-year-old Jamaican woman serving four and a half years for importation at HMP Westhill, the women's annex of a large Victorian prison in the scenic southern town of Winchester. Before her arrest, she lived with her mother and three children. As a single mother, she found supporting herself and her children a struggle:

> Why I end up here is because of financial problem really, because I have three kids without no father and its very difficult for me. I'm from Jamaica, it's very difficult to maintain three kids, go to school, find food and pay for the house. I have to pay about [Jamaican] $3000 a month and it's just me alone. And it's very difficult to find food, light bill, water rate, very hard.

Working in the entertainment industry brought in an irregular and insufficient income that barely covered the bills. When Jackie's eldest son was accepted to a technical college, she was faced with the possibility that she would not be able to afford the tuition fee. Her desire to better her children's future, combined with concerns for the economic stability of her household, fueled her decision:

> One of the main reasons why I do the drugs is because he's supposed to go mechanical engineering and the fee is [Jamaican] $5000 a term and I just wanted to pay it one time. He's going to school and I just hope and pray I have the money.

Like Jackie's, Marta's decision to carry drugs was informed by economic insecurity. The mother of four children between four and fifteen years old, Marta embraced the chance to earn what for her was a significant sum in exchange for carrying a package that she suspected contained drugs. She did not suspect that this one trip would result in a five-year prison sentence:

> I was self-employed doing a bit of selling. I was married but my [ex]husband wasn't supportive, after sending the kids to school the money kept going down. I never knew nothing much about drugs, the only form of drugs I know is ganja, we call it weed. That's the only hard [sic] drugs I've known of in my life until I come here. And I was just asked by somebody to carry some baggage for $100,000 Jamaican dollars [US$1,650] and I just jump at it, thought it could really help out.

The past two decades have posed significant economic challenges for working class Caribbean women as the region has been incorporated into the global economy under the tutelage of the International Monetary Fund and U.S. government. Between 1980 and 1989, Edward Seaga's conservative Jamaica Labour Party (JLP) pursued the "Washington Consensus" model of neoliberal economic reforms, privatizing state-owned companies and public utilities, scaling back local government services, introducing user fees for education and health care, and obliterating an already weak social safety net. Although People's National Party candidate and former socialist Michael Manley was reelected in 1989, Manley and his successor J.P. Patterson have continued the economic path established by Seaga and his powerful international backers. These policies have led to layoffs of public sector employees, many of them women, a reduction in social service provision, and dramatic increases in the cost of basic necessities. The impact on poor women has been particularly harsh because traditional gender roles burden women with the responsibility of caring for children and sick or elderly relatives. When the state sheds its role in providing social support and public infrastructure, poor women fill the vacuum. Neoliberal social policies privilege a heterosexual couple in which the woman/wife can perform an array of unpaid tasks that enable the survival of the family unit and the production of healthy workers. The reality of childrearing for many Jamaican women bears no resemblance to this heterosexist model, as Jackie points out:

> We have a lot of young people in Jamaica need help, especially girls who get pregnant out of school and they can't afford to go back and they end up with two, three children and the father leave them. It's like me, but their father died, he didn't leave me. And they struggle to live and the quickest thing they can look upon is drugs. We need a lot of help in Jamaica financially and we can't get a good government to run the country. They come rob up the land and the poorer class of people suffer, always.

Jackie's gendered class analysis accurately describes the role of the neoliberal state. Trapped between the stick of "third world" debt and the carrot of foreign aid and investment, governments in the global South are increasingly sacrificing the working class in a bid for modernization and development. Traveling across national borders gave the women an opportunity to compare their lives with those in the global North. In so doing, they developed a gendered critique of global inequalities between advanced industrial nations and their former colonies. As Marta points out, the Jamaican women who pay the price for JLP reforms do not enjoy the benefits of a state social welfare net. It is this erosion of women's economic security under neoliberal globalization that drives many to participate in criminalized drug networks:

> We don't get child support in Jamaica, three quarters of the things that this country offers for mothers here we don't have it. And if you did have it, a lot of women wouldn't be here. This country gives you a house, they give you benefits. We get nothing in Jamaica. We have to pay for hospital. Not even education is free. Primary school used to be free under one government hand, but under another government it has been taken away.

While the Jamaican state has cut back its role in social welfare, it has stepped up its role in subsidizing foreign and domestic capital. Free trade zones established in Kingston, Montego Bay, and elsewhere offer foreign garment, electronic, and communications companies factory space and equipment, tax exemptions, a cheap female workforce, and, for the busy foreign executive, weekends of sun, sea, and sex.[20] Foreign-owned agribusiness and mining companies have also been encouraged, displacing traditional subsistence farming and causing migration from rural areas to the cities, which now account for 50 percent of the Jamaican population. Like Marta, many rural migrants turn to the informal economy for survival. Jamaican women in particular work as "higglers," petty traders buying and reselling food, cheap clothes, and other low-cost products. As the economy has shifted, women working as farmers and higglers find themselves unable to keep up with the rising costs of survival. Although younger women may find employment in the tourist industry as maids, entertainers, or sex workers or within the free trade zones assembling clothes or computers for Western markets, working class women in their thirties and older have fewer options. The failure of the legal economy to provide adequate means for survival then becomes a key incentive for Jamaican women who choose to enter the drug trade as couriers.

Women in the criminalized drug industry tend to be absorbed at the lowest level of the trade. Although Ainsworth suggests that women like Marta and Jackie work in close association with gun-using drug traffickers, the women's stories belie this depiction. Most of the women I interviewed knew very little about the crack cocaine industry and first encountered hard drugs on entering the prison system. Before their arrest, they tended to have contact with only one intermediary, usually a man, who approached them and is the person who provided the package. As Marta suggests, women's relationship with male traffickers is one of exploitation, not partnership:

> Men do it [import], but they tend to prey on the women more. Because they know that the woman in Jamaica, they care for their family, especially their kids. They would do anything to make sure their kids is looked after. So they mainly prey on the woman, especially single women.

In this sense, women are the exploited, poorly remunerated, and ultimately disposable workers of the global drug industry. Their vulnerability as primary caretakers, coupled with economic insecurity fueled by neoliberal economic reforms, creates a gendered incentive for participation in the drug trade. Rather than tackling the structural reasons for women's participation in drug trafficking, Operation Airbridge aims to deter women by a display of force and, if that fails, to apprehend and punish them. The operation has the twofold impact of channeling additional women into the Jamaican criminal justice system by catching them before they board and adding large numbers of women arrested at Heathrow and Gatwick airports to the British prison system. With such intensive policing, drug networks are likely to send more women with smaller amounts of drugs or as decoys, thus increasing the numbers of women exposed to the risk of arrest. As the remuneration for carrying a shipment of drugs worth hundreds of thousands of pounds is under . . . 5000, it is evident that targeting couriers for arrest and imprisonment will barely interrupt the supply of drugs as long as the demand, and thus the street price, remains intact. Although Operation Airbridge may shave some of the profits off the criminalized drug trade, it does nothing to address the social and economic conditions that have created endemic drug use in British inner cities or that lead Jamaican women to import drugs.

The Transnational War on Drugs

An analysis of the racialized feminization of poverty in Jamaica is essential if we are to understand the reasons why women import criminalized drugs. However, this is not sufficient to explain the detention of these women for lengthy prison terms. A variety of responses could be made to the apprehension of women with smuggled drugs. They could be sent back after confiscation of the drugs, fined, or given support in escaping the drug industry. Crime prevention initiatives targeted at poor urban Jamaican women could include poverty reduction and employment creation strategies as an alternative to the drug trade. The emphasis on policing and incarceration is the result of a particular politics of crime initiated by Margaret Thatcher three decades ago. Citing a rising crime rate accompanied by spiraling joblessness and labor disputes, the 1979 Conservative Manifesto warned: "[t]he most disturbing threat to our freedom and security is the growing disrespect for the rule of law" and promised that "[t]he next Conservative government will spend more on fighting crime even while we economize elsewhere."[21] As in the United States, the fight against crime had a racial subtext and was closely related to a crackdown on immigration. With the fascist National Front rising in popularity among the ranks of alienated unemployed white workers, Thatcher pursued the racist vote. Her statement on the television program *World in Action* in 1978 that "People are really rather afraid that this country might be rather swamped by people with a different culture" was reflected in Conservative immigration reforms: a new British Nationality Act that would strip the residency entitlements of (black) British citizens with Commonwealth passports, the end to the practice of allowing entry to male fiancés, a quota system for non–European Union citizens, and a voluntary repatriation program; all of these would have remorselessly brutal impacts on black communities.

Although immigration controls were designed to keep former colonial subjects at bay behind strictly policed borders, another mechanism was needed to control the black British population, whose discontent was demonstrated in the urban rebellions that swept Britain in 1981. This massive social control program was provided by the Americanization of drug policy. From the mid-1980s, the United States aggressively exported Reaganite drug policy. An important tool for enforcing compliance was the 1988 United Nations (Vienna) Convention Against Illicit Traffic in Narcotic Drugs and Psychotropic Substances.[22] By requiring signatories to criminalize drug cultivation, possession, and purchase for personal use; maximize the use of criminal sanctions and deterrence; and limit early release and parole in drug-related cases, the Vienna Convention represented the transnational spread of the "law and order" agenda.[23] In signing the convention, member states pledged to use criminal justice sanctions in place of medical or social solutions and turned decisively away from legalization.

British politicians have been eager partners in the U.S. war on drugs and have "gratefully accepted and sometimes sought" the "benevolence, advice, influence and leadership" of the Drug Enforcement Administration (DEA) on drug matters.[24] An infamous case involves drug enforcement agent Robert Stutman's 1988 visit to Britain. Addressing the Assistant Chief Police Officers Conference, Stutman "scared the hell" out of the participants with his apocalyptic visions of the crack epidemic in the United States and its inevitable migration to Europe as the U.S. market became saturated. Stutman's account was based on an unpublished report and anecdotal evidence. Nevertheless, a 1989

Home Affairs Committee report echoed Stutman's unsubstantiated argument that there is "no such person as a fully recovered crack addict" and that crack, by its very nature, called for a penal rather than a medical response.

The report had immediate and racialized effects. From the late 1980s, the press ran reports of crack infiltrating British cities. Crack was depicted as a foreign threat, an enemy brought into Britain by "yardies," with African Caribbean communities as the Trojan Horse enabling the foreign infiltration. As a result, resources were pumped into law enforcement activities such as Operation Dalehouse and the Crack Intelligence Coordinating Unit specifically to increase the surveillance and policing of black communities. Coinciding with the entrenchment of "Fortress Europe," the crack threat was also a justification for a heightened suspicion of black British women and men entering Britain after vacations abroad as well as Caribbean nationals entering to visit family and friends. With such targeted policing and customs attention, the numbers of African Caribbean women and men apprehended for possession, sales, and importation of both class A and lesser drugs increased dramatically. In some instances, retail of crack was largely inspired by police operations and protection of informants, as is the case in a northern city where a senior police officer admitted that undercover police buyers stimulated demand that disappeared once the police operation was over.[25] Although the belief that Britain was on the verge of a U.S.-style "crack epidemic" was found by the mid-1990s to be a "media inspired panic,"[26] the pattern of targeted surveillance has continued unabated. As public funds are poured into the high-tech policing of black suspects, a self-fulfilling cycle is generated whereby increased arrests in the black community reinforce the public fear of African Caribbean drug dealers and traffickers, legitimate the continuation of racially discrepant policing practices, and generate additional resources for the police.[27] The combination of these policing practices with racially biased trials and mandatory minimum sentencing has had a devastating impact on black women who are positioned in the lower rungs of the drug industry and are thus more vulnerable to apprehension.[28] Whereas in 1980, 4.4 percent of women serving time in prisons in England and Wales were incarcerated on drug-related offenses, by 2002 that figure had risen to 41 percent.[29] Statistics that utilize gender but not race as a category of analysis tend to underrepresent the devastating impact of the war on drugs on black women. In 2002, 75 percent of all black women in prison were there due to a drug conviction.[30]

After 14 years of Conservative rule, New Labour's 1997 election victory was viewed by many prison reformers as heralding a sea change in the politics of crime and an end to the British emulation of U.S. criminal justice policy. However, the excitement was short lived. It soon became evident that despite the promise of a more balanced approach that would be "tough on crime, tough on the causes of crime," New Labour would continue to pursue harsh policies that would fuel a U.S.-style racialized prison buildup. By locating the "causes of crime" in individual pathology and lack of discipline rather than structural inequalities, the Blair administration created a rationale for ongoing punitive interventions, setting the scene for Operation Airbridge.

The Transnational Prison-Industrial Complex

Although tough-on-crime measures generate votes in election years and serve the important function of removing discontented and disenfranchised racialized populations from the streets, they are also very expensive. It costs approximately . . . £36,000 (U.S. $66,960) per annum to warehouse a prisoner and approximately . . . 55 million to construct a new prison.[31] By the mid-1980s, the endlessly spiraling prison population and expensive prison building program began to put a strain on the Conservative commitment to mass incarceration. Although the 1987 manifesto bragged that the Conservatives had "embarked on the biggest prison building and modernisation programme this century and increased staff numbers by almost a fifth," there was a new nuance to the promise to tackle crime "by building the prisons in which to place those who pose a threat to society—*and by keeping out of prison those who do not*"[32] [emphasis added]. This more moderate support for penal sanctions was the result of two counterforces to prison growth: first, the leadership as Home Secretary of Douglas Hurd, a firm believer in rehabilitation and community reintegration for offenders; second, economic concerns—the prison boom had simply cost too much. With the cost of prison expansion projected to continue its exponential increase, ministers and civil servants were quietly raising concerns about the detrimental impact on other spending areas as well as the government's ability to deliver tax cuts. According to future Home Secretary Michael Howard, looking back on this period during a parliamentary debate in 1999:

> There was a classic conspiracy . . . between the criminal justice establishment and the civil servants in the Home Office and the Treasury to keep down the number of people in prison because prison is expensive. One of the classic objectives of criminal justice policy during most of that time . . . was to keep as few people in prison as possible.[33]

Hurd's decarceration "conspiracy" was short lived. Challenged by allegations of weak leadership, Conservative Prime Minister John Major appointed the most influential proprison home secretary in recent times. Michael Howard's much cited "Prison Works" speech at the Conservative Party conference in 1993 created the ideological framework for a turn-of-the-century prison boom. But another, less frequently noted development simultaneously removed the economic barrier to the prison buildup. This was the transatlantic spread of the private prison industry.

During the mid-1980s, Conservative and Labour politicians were aggressively courted by U.S. prison corporations and treated to tours of flagship private prisons in the United States. In 1987, a Home Affairs Select Committee was commissioned to investigate the viability of introducing privatization into the prison system. Although the committee was impressed with the new steel and glass buildings of U.S. private prisons and the glossy rhetoric of the new corrections, they were also keenly aware of the short-term economic benefits of privatization. Recommending that the private sector should be invited to bid for contracts to build and manage custodial institutions, the committee noted that privatization would *dramatically accelerate* the prison building program, which was hindered by lack of public funds.[34] Between 1991 and 1994 the mutually profitable relationship between conservative politicians and the prison industry culminated in a series of acts that allowed corporations to design, construct, manage, and finance new prisons and to bid to operate existing prisons.

Private financing for prison construction enables a sleight of hand whereby the capital costs are absorbed by the private sector and recouped through a fee per prisoner over the period of a twenty-five-year lease. Although the cost may be greater than that of public construction, it is spread over the life of the lease and thus does not appear in annual capital budgets. The introduction of competitive tenders for the operation of prisons forces the Prison Service to cut costs, with the contract going to the lowest bidder. Savings are typically found by cutting wages and benefits, reducing staff–prisoner ratios, and cutting educational programs, all of which jeopardize prisoner safety and reduce chances of successful integration after release. Even where savings on operating budgets are minimal, competitive tenders enable politicians to appear fiscally responsible while wasting enormous sums on incarcerating large numbers of prisoners for nonviolent offenses. By creating the mirage of fiscal responsibility and reducing the short-term costs of prison construction, corporate involvement has financed continued prison expansion in Britain, generating a symbiotic relationship between the state and the corporate sector. Activists and scholars in the United States have labeled this relationship "the prison-industrial complex," drawing on Dwight Eisenhower's critique of the insidious relationship between the military and the arms industry that underpinned the Cold War arms race.[35] The companies profiting from prison expansion are not limited to private prison operators but include companies supplying prisons as well as those employing prison labor. The Jamaican women who share their stories in this chapter are the raw materials that fuel this transnational prison-industrial complex.

Although drug mules have traditionally been apprehended and imprisoned in the advanced capitalist nations that generate the demand for criminalized drugs, Operation Airbridge targets both ends of the drug nexus, thus generating imprisonable bodies in Jamaica as well as Britain. At the end of 2003,

British companies were reportedly in communication with the Jamaican Ministry of National Security regarding a possible contract to build a maximum-security prison to house the growing number of mules arrested at Kingston and Montego Bay airports.[36] According to Jamaican Prison Commissioner Richard Reese, Jamaican nationals sentenced in Britain could also be housed for a fee in a form of offshore imprisonment, applying the logic of Jamaica's free trade zones to the business of warehousing prisoners.[37] In this transnational complex of political and economic interests, British tough-on-crime policies generate cross-border business opportunities for British prison companies as well as revenue-generating possibilities for the neoliberal Jamaican government. These companies in turn provide the capital investment necessary for continued prison expansion in a mutually beneficial cycle of punishment and profit.

Conclusions

What led to Beverley Fowler's death in an overcrowded prison in the north of England? The mantra of personal responsibility that dominates political opinion on both sides of the Atlantic would have us focus on the choice she made to smuggle criminalized drugs. Although drug importation does not carry a death sentence, it was certainly the precipitating act that led to her imprisonment in the harsh maximum-security regime that has taken so many women's lives. But does this not mean that Beverley's choice was the key factor that led to her death or even to her imprisonment. Instead, activists and scholars need to look at the socioeconomic conditions that present women like Beverley with "no choice" between poverty, violence, and sexual assault or work in the criminalized drug industry. We need to examine the root causes of these socioeconomic conditions, in particular the push for neoliberal social policies and free trade aggressively promoted by the United States and international financial institutions, at the expense of poor women who bear the brunt when social welfare programs are decimated and the cost of basic necessities spirals upward. And we need to expose state spending priorities that privilege the U.S.-led war on drugs and punitive law-and-order buildup over the provision of infrastructure that would provide economic security and physical safety for poor women in Jamaica and elsewhere. As more and more women, especially women of color and third-world women, are "compelled to crime" by a combination of gender violence, global inequities, and a paucity of alternatives, it is imperative that we identify and address the structural roots of women's criminalized survival strategies.[38] Women certainly do have the agency to make choices. However, following Marx, their choices are made under conditions not of their making.[39]

Having identified the causal factors underlying women's survival strategies, we also need to interrogate the state's response to these actions. The connection between crime and punishment is often taken for granted, yet the array of activities that are labeled "criminal" is contingent and shifts over time. Similarly, criminal justice priorities vary over time and what may be subject to stringent policing in one context may be considered marginal in another. The British government's punitive response to Jamaican women tricked, trapped, or compelled into the criminalized drug industry is the outcome of a three-decade-long law-and-order buildup. This bitter inheritance from the Thatcher years has been compounded by the emergence of a transnational prison-industrial complex that translates imprisonable bodies into profits for private corporations. While private interests rely on the courts to provide a constant flow of raw materials, politicians rely on private capital to underwrite the prison building boom and mask the real cost of their tough-on-crime politics. Hidden behind the moral panic about mules and yardies are the corporate and political interests that benefit from criminalization and the racialized prison buildup. A transnational feminist approach to women's imprisonment provides scholars and activists with the tools to unpack the transnational prison-industrial complex and to locate local targets for activism against global lockdown. It also deepens our analysis of women's cross-border imprisonment by examining the root causes of women's survival strategies. Using this framework, it becomes evident that any meaningful attempt to slow the pace of and ultimately end women's imprisonment must involve a fundamental transformation of the social and economic conditions that shape the life chances of women in the global South.

References

1. Inquest, "Beverley Fowler Inquest Verdict Returned" (London, 2003).
2. BBC, "Prison Criticised Over Cell Death," September 19, 2003, http://212.58.226.18/1/hi/england/3124002.stm (accessed March 30, 2004).
3. Prisoners in the United Kingdom are divided into three prison estates, England and Wales, Scotland, and Northern Ireland. This statistics cited in this chapter refer to England and Wales, which is the larger population.
4. Corrections News, "England and Wales Top Europe in Incarceration Rates," July/August 2003.
5. For example, Sweden, Finland, and Iceland incarcerate 72, 69, and 40 per 100,000 of the total population, respectively. As of 2004, England and Wales imprisoned 142 per 100,000. International Center for Prison Studies, "World Prison Brief," http://www.prisonstudies.org (accessed March 30, 2004).
6. Commission for Racial Equality, *Racial Equality in Prisons* (London: CRE, 2003), 27.
7. This figure is for 2002. Home Office, *Statistics on Women and the Criminal Justice System* (London, 2003), 44.
8. Rod Morgan, "New Labour 'Law and Order' Politics and the House of Commons Home Affairs Committee Report on Alternatives to Prison Sentences," *Punishment and Society* 1, 1, July (1999), 110.

9. HM Prison Service, "Privately Managed Prisons," http://www.hmprisonservice.gov.uk (accessed March 17, 2004).
10. Home Office, 33.
11. Of 886 foreign national women held in British prisons as of November 2003, 425 were Jamaican. Esmée Fairbairn Foundation, *A Bitter Pill to Swallow: The Sentencing of Foreign National Drug Couriers* (London, 2003).
12. Daily Telegraph, "Prisons Crisis as Foreign Inmates Soar," August 6, 2003.
13. Commission for Racial Equality, 5.
14. For example, the commission's conclusions were drawn from site visits to HMP Brixton, HMP Parc, and the Young Offenders Institution at Feltham, all of which are male institutions.
15. Audrey Gillan, "Bursting Point: The Drugs Mules Filling up UK Prisons," *The Guardian*, September 30, 2003.
16. Stuart Hall et al., *Policing the Crisis: Mugging, the State and Law and Order* (London: Macmillan, 1978), 18–19.
17. Customs and Excise, "UK and Jamaican Governments Join Forces to Crack Down on Cocaine Trafficking," London, May 22, 2002.
18. Ibid.
19. Nick Hopkins, "Mules Success Puts Squeeze on Yardies," *The Guardian*, November 22, 2002.
20. As Shirley Campbell et al. note with regard to tourism in Jamaica: "the package of sun, sand and sea is gift wrapped with the promise of sex." Shirley Campbell, Althea Perkins, and Patricia Mohammed, "'Come to Jamaica and Feel All Right': Tourism and the Sex Trade," in *Sun, Sex, and Gold: Tourism and Sex Work in the Caribbean*, ed. Kamala Kempadoo (Lanham: Rowman and Littlefield, 1999). Under the neoliberal model, foreign investors are also invited to sample Jamaica's assets.
21. Conservative Party, *The Conservative Manifesto 1979* (Conservative Party, 1979).
22. H. Richard Friman, *Narcodiplomacy: Exporting the US War on Drugs* (Ithaca and London: Cornell University Press, 1996).
23. Hans-Jorg Albrecht, "The International System of Drug Control: Developments and Trends," in *Drug War, American Style: The Internationalization of Failed Policy and Its Alternatives*, ed. J. Gerber and E. Hensen (New York and London: Garland Publishing, 2001).
24. Philip Bean, "American Influence on British Drug Policy," in Gerber and Hensen.
25. Elizabeth Joyce, "Cocaine Trafficking and British Foreign Policy," in *Latin America and the Multinational Drug Trade*, ed. E. Joyce and C. Malamud (Basingstoke: Macmillan Press, 1998), 179.
26. Joyce 181.
27. In Winter 2000, the Metropolitan Police received . . . 800,000 to carry out Operation Crackdown, targeting low-level dealers on council estates in boroughs with large black populations. The operation led to surveillance of seven hundred private properties, over eighty raids, and one thousand arrests; see Metropolitan Police, "1000 arrested in London Class A drugs offensive," press release (London, January 3, 2001). An evaluation of the operation found it had "little discernible impact" on London's crack trade, which quickly adapted to meet continuing demand. See David Rose, "Opium of the People," *The Observer*, July 8, 2001.
28. Anita Kalunta-Crumpton, *Race and Drug Trials: The Social Construction of Guilt and Innocence* (Aldershot: Ashgate, 1999).
29. Home Office, Statistics on Women and the Criminal Justice System (London, 2003), 43. HMSO, Prison Statistics England and Wales 1980 (London: HMSO, 1982).
30. Home Office, 2003, 44.
31. House of Commons, *Hansard Written Answers for July 17*, 2003, pt 42, http://www.parliament.the-stationery-office.co.uk (accessed March 18, 2004).
32. Conservative Party, The Next Moves Forward: The Conservative Manifesto 1987 (Conservative Party, 1987).
33. House of Commons, *Hansard Written Answers for May 24*, 2000, pt 11, http://www.parliament.the-stationery-office.co.uk (accessed March 18, 2004).
34. Adrian Speller, *Private Sector Involvement in Prisons* (London: Church House Publishing, 1996), 5.
35. Julia Sudbury, "Celling Black Bodies: Black Women in the Global Prison Industrial Complex," *Feminist Review* 70 (2002).

36. Caribbean Net News, "British Companies Seeking to Build Prison in Jamaica," October 2, 2003, http://www.caribbeannetnews.com/2003/10/02/prisons.htm (accessed March 17, 2004).
37. "British Prison May Be Built in Jamaica," http://www.ananova.com/news/story/sm_824719 .html (accessed March 17, 2004).
38. Beth Richie, *Compelled to Crime: The Gender Entrapment of Battered Black Women* (New York: Routledge, 1996).
39. For a classic discussion of this relationship between structure and human agency see Stuart Hall, "Cultural Studies: Two Paradigms," *Media, Culture and Society*, 2, 1 (1980).

The Daniel case problematizes the commonsense equation between crime and punishment and demonstrates that what is considered "criminal" is situational and culturally specific. In this chapter, I will suggest that this rupture does not only exist in Nigeria as an outcome of a punitive version of Islamic fundamentalism. The arbitrary and unjust punishment of Nigerian women does not occur only under Sharia. Rather the entire colonial system of criminal justice is based on the criminalization of innocent black women. The chapter starts by reviewing the theory of "victimisation as mere punishment" that I developed in my study of black women and the British criminal justice system.[1] This theory will be illustrated with recent empirical evidence from Nigeria. Finally, the implications of the problems confronting Nigerian women for the struggle to decolonize Africa will be outlined in the conclusion.

Jean Baudrillard famously asserted that Disneyland is there to conceal the fact that it is the whole of the United States that is the real Disneyland, just as the prison is there to conceal the fact that it is the social in its entirety that is the prison.[2] The implication of Baudrillard's statement is that you do not have to go to Disneyland in order to have fun in the United States. The whole country is one elaborate amusement park. Similarly, Americans don't need to enter the prison gate to become subjected to state surveillance and social control, rather the entire population is controlled as inmates of the global lockdown. Nigeria is no United States. The landmass is only a fraction of that of the United States, possibly the size of Texas alone. The population is dense in comparison—almost half the population of the United States. More to the point, U.S. prisons and jails hold more than two million people compared with the less than fifty thousand prisoners held in Nigeria. The surprising thing is that Americans feel that they can teach Nigerians better ways of running the criminal justice system when it seems that what Nigerians can learn from the United States is how to avoid the high costs of what Reiman calls the theory of the Pyrrhic defeat—the fact that after spending about four times the national budget of Nigeria on the criminal justice system alone, Americans continue to name "crime" as one of their top concerns.[3] Indeed, whereas Nigeria budgeted approximately $7 billion to run the entire country for 2003, the new U.S. Department of Homeland Security alone has been allocated more than $30 billion.

Of course, the low number of prisoners in Nigeria compared with the United States can be used as evidence that Nigerian law-enforcement agents are inefficient in comparison. They have failed to arrest the criminals who roam the streets and intimidate the ordinary citizens, whereas U.S. mayors such as Rudy Giuliani of New York can claim that zero tolerance means that the "bad guys" are all locked up. However, even the greatest enthusiasts of law and order policies cannot claim that much success because their law enforcement budgets rely on the continuing existence of criminals on the loose.[4] When people complain that Nigerian criminals are allowed to roam the streets, they more often mean the criminals in the corridors of power who cannot be touched, whereas many of the prisoners happen to be innocent poor people who lack the resources with which to bribe or influence their way out of the prison preindustrial complex.[5]

Historiography of African Women and Criminal Injustice

In my earlier work on black women in the British criminal justice system, I made a surprising discovery—that many of the black women who were placed under lockdown were completely innocent of the offense of which they had been convicted.[6] I searched in vain for criminological perspectives that could help me to explain the unexpected finding, but I was frustrated because criminology focuses almost exclusively on the punishment of individual offenders. Jurisprudence uses the term "punishment of the innocent" to describe the imprisonment of those who have been falsely convicted. However, this concept tends to view the incarceration of "the innocent" as an unfortunate error in an otherwise just and efficient criminal justice system. Thus, it fails to challenge the criminological concern with the individual and minimizes the disruptive potential of miscarriages of justice. In addition, the term "punishment" hides the fact that what is done to the innocent prisoner is a form of victimization, for which redress is required. Stuart Hall's analysis of the articulation of social relations in societies structured in dominance provides a more useful theoretical framework to understand the victimization of the innocent.[7] Hall argues that the experience of black women must be viewed through the lens of the race, class, and gender oppression to which they are subjected. These three major social relations cannot be analyzed separately, rather they are articulated, disarticulated, and rearticulated. Thus, the central point of "victimization as mere punishment" is that the criminal justice system institutionally violates the rights of certain groups of people because of the ways in which power relations are structured within society.

Historically, we can look at the African Holocaust, otherwise known as the European slave trade, for an early example of victimization as mere punishment. The works of C.L.R. James, Walter Rodney, and Angela Y. Davis alert us to the fact that our African ancestors did not have to commit any crime in order to be hunted down, chained or killed, and transported to a hostile world to be brutally exploited.[8] Race-class-gender relations were articulated in the victimization of Africans during slavery and African women suffered gender-specific inhumanities that are too well known to be recounted here. Contemporary African women and men continue to be locked down even when we have done nothing wrong. For example, the wives, mothers, sisters, or girlfriends of army officers are often arrested and detained with their children when their male relations are suspected of plotting unsuccessful coups and when they either flee or commit suicide. Sometimes, these women are harassed, maimed, killed, or detained for years even without being suspected of any crime themselves. Such cases attract immense publicity because of the prominence of the individuals involved, but research indicates that what such hostages suffer is part of the daily experience of poor men and women in Africa. Winnie Mandela had a "barometer" theory for this: she said that she was a social barometer because anything that the apartheid regime tried on her was later generalized to the oppressed in South Africa.[9] Some scholars have tried to explain the oppressive treatment of black people by analyzing the prison system as the new slave plantation or the new ghetto.[10] What they have overlooked is the fact that African Americans did not have to break any law in order to end up in the slave plantation or in the ghetto. Rather, as Reiman and Box argue, the poor end up in prison not because they are more criminal but because they lack the resources with which to free themselves even when they are falsely accused.[11] Meanwhile, the rich routinely get away with murder.

The victimization as mere punishment concept requires us to rethink the purpose of the prison. The history of prison construction in Nigeria is intricately entwined with the history of attempts to repress the popular aspirations of Nigerian masses. *African Concord*, reports that:

> Many of Nigeria's prisons are more than one hundred years old. Records show that four prisons were built between 1800 and 1850, 11 prisons were built between 1851 and 1900, 83 were built between 1900 and 1950 and 33 prisons between 1951 to date.[12]

As this article demonstrates, there was no prison in the place called Nigeria before 1800. European trading companies were the first to construct prisons in Nigeria for holding kidnapped Africans prior to the Middle Passage or for detaining Africans who resisted the banditry of Europeans in Africa. Prisons were thus first built as part of the machinery of the brutal slave economy and are closely related to the African Holocaust. In other words, the prison emerged in Nigeria not as an agency of the criminal justice system but as a tool for organized crimes against humanity. The Africans who were kidnapped and detained before being sold into slavery had committed absolutely no offense. The biological fiction of racial inferiority, not criminality, was used to justify their loss of liberty. The period 1850 to 1900 covers the first few decades of the official colonization of Nigeria after the 1860 Berlin conference for the partition of Africa. In this short period the number of prisons in Nigeria nearly trebled, reflecting increasing resistance to European penetration of the interior regions. The geometrical progression in the development of the prison preindustrial complex in Nigeria continued; 1900 to 1950 represents the period of nationalist struggles when the gunboat criminology of imperialism failed to silence the call for independence and many patriots were thrown into jail. Following independence in 1960, the rate of the growth of the prison establishments slowed somewhat, reflecting the relative legitimacy of neocolonial regimes, but the rate remained high enough to reflect their continuing reliance on the colonial methodology for stifling popular protests in Nigeria. I am not suggesting that all prisoners are freedom fighters. Some of the prisoners may have committed violent or unsocial acts. However, I am convinced that this correlation between the history of repression in Nigeria and the history of the expansion of penal institutions needs to be studied more closely. As Michel Foucault informs us, there were hardly any prisons in Europe until the late eighteenth century.[13] Prior to that, punishment in Europe took the form of public display of torture. Foucault's genealogy of the prison implies that the prison is not an enduring feature of human society but a repressive technology of modernity. In the Nigerian context, the birth of the prison cannot be separated from the histories of slavery, colonialism, and neocolonialism.

Political independence from the British has not ushered in a golden era of postcolonial justice. M.K.O. Abiola, who established *African Concord*, was one of the few rich and powerful people to suffer victimization as mere punishment in Nigeria. After claiming victory in the June 1992 presidential elections that were annulled by the military, he was jailed and ultimately murdered in prison. While he was in detention, one of his wives, Kudirat Abiola, was executed by an assassination squad set up by the bloody dictator General Sani Abacha, who also hanged Kenule Saro-Wiwa and eight other Ogoni environmental activists after framing them for the murder of four chiefs in Ogoniland. Abacha also sentenced to death several past military rulers of Nigeria, including the present president, General Obasanjo, following a trumped-up charge of complicity in a coup plot against him. Luckily for many of them but too late for General Shehu Yaradua, who was killed in detention, General Abacha died suddenly and they were released by his successor, General Abubakar. This close shave with death made Obasanjo pledge to support the campaign for the abolition of the death penalty worldwide.[14]

The first time that rich and powerful people found themselves behind bars in Nigeria was when Chief Obafemi Awolowo and leaders of the opposition were framed and convicted of plotting to overthrow the government by force in the First Republic. Following his imprisonment, a group of army officers attempted a coup with the aim of handing over power to Chief Awolowo, but they failed and were also detained in prison. A countercoup followed and facilitated a genocidal pogrom in the north against easterners. This led to the attempted cessation by the east and the release of Chief Awolowo and the military officers from prison before the onset of the Nigeria–Biafra war of 1967 to 1970. The second time large numbers of the members of the elite saw themselves in prison was after the abortive military coup against the government of

General Murtala Muhammad, which saw dozens of top army officers and several civilians executed for their role in the coup attempt under General Obasanjo as the succeeding head of state. Again following the overthrow of the Second Republic government of Shehu Shagari in 1983, the military rulers prosecuted and convicted many of the Second Republic politicians of high levels of corruption and embezzlement. They were given long prison sentences ranging from twenty-five years to life. However, in 1985 the military government was overthrown and all the rogue politicians jailed by Generals Idiagbon and Buhari were released by General Babangida. Babangida did not hesitate later to execute dozens of top military officers suspected of involvement in several abortive coups against his own military regime.

Recent Empirical Reports on Nigerian Women in Prison

In the fall of 1998, I collaborated on a study of the militarization of Nigerian civil society.[15] During the fieldwork, we learnt that social institutions such as the family, educational institutions, religious establishments, trade and commerce, the justice system, and community relations were permeated by the militaristic ethos of a society that had experienced long terms of military rule. Husbands assumed the role of the commanders in chief of the family, beating wives and children; educational institutions witnessed authoritarian styles of administration while students formed secret cults with which to commit murder or gang rapes of female students; religious and ethnic violence was the order of the day; and due process was almost nonexistent. Militarism promoted violent means for settling quarrels in civil society; for example, traders would hire armed soldiers to murder their rivals. The militarism of Nigerian society is also reflected in policing and the prisons, which are feared as institutions imbued with violence, including sexual violence, corruption, and the rule of force.

Police Violence and Detention

The economic desperation of most families due to the Structural Adjustment Programs decreed by the World Bank and the International Monetary Fund (IMF) means that families are forced to choose which children should be educated and which should be left in ignorance. This leads to the continued undereducation of girls, who are then more vulnerable to injustices and exploitation as young women. Moreover, the crushing poverty imposed on Nigerians as part of this "global lockdown" has led to popular protests by the masses of the people resulting in the widespread arrest of women either for participation in such protests or for being family members of suspected men. In 2001, Nigerian women stripped naked to intimidate oil workers and seize control of the facilities of Chevron Texaco to press home their demand that the company, which polluted the environment from which they could no longer earn their living as peasants, should pay reparations to the community and provide jobs for their sons (not surprisingly, given patriarchy, the women did not also demand jobs for the daughters, the wives, and the mothers of the community). The women decided to lead the protest after the young men who had previously engaged in direct action were arrested and jailed. Although the women were not arrested, the disdainful response of the politicians was to ignore them and punish them with the bitter cold air of the open seas, where some of them reportedly caught pneumonia. Thus, the women did not have to go to prison in order to experience the cruelty of the global lockdown. In 1984 Maroko slum was demolished on the orders of the governor of Lagos state. Three hundred thousand ghetto dwellers became instantly homeless. Some were forced to sleep under bridges, but a few found refuge in some uncompleted housing estates that the government was developing. Again, the state military governor ordered armed police to eject the refugees and in the process as many as seventeen women and young girls were forcibly raped by the officers.

On the topic of arrest and detention, Akumadu reports that women are treated in a crude and unconstitutional manner.[16] Many women were not told that they were under arrest until they were lured to the police station under the pretext of helping police with investigations, and some are not told of the charge against them until they appear in court. To make matters worse, the police are given wide discretion by the law to make arrests without a warrant under various circumstances. A prostitute, Miss Adizat Mohammed, who was detained at the Kano police post, reported that the police raid prostitutes only when they were broke and that those who pay the three hundred Naira "fine" or bribe demanded by the police are released immediately. Another woman who was a trader reported that she displayed her wares in front of her house once during a compulsory national environmental sanitation exercise when police officers arrested her and confiscated her wares. She was released on bail after two days in detention, but her wares were never returned to her. Another woman, Mrs. Kemi (last name withheld) had a quarrel with her neighbor and was arrested with her infant baby. Both were held in detention for a week without any provision for child-care facilities. She suspected that the police officers must have been "settled" or bribed by her neighbor to torture her and her baby. The result of the overzealous use of detention by the police is that their tiny police cells are always overcrowded and the only toilet facility in such crowded cells is usually a bucket.

In the cells, older inmates extort "state money" or taxes from new inmates and refusal to pay may result in physical abuse by other inmates. This is more common among the male detainees, but they also extend their demands to the female detainees and any resistance is met with threats to throw the woman into a cell occupied by men. Such psychological torture was usually enough to make the women acquiesce to extortion. In addition, food is rarely served to the detainees and, when served, it is often not fit for human consumption. Thus, the detainees are expected to bribe police officers in order to be allowed to buy their own food from food vendors at the police station. During interrogation, women reported being tortured by having a candlestick or the neck of a bottle inserted into their private parts by the male police officers in an attempt to get them to confess to crimes that they did not commit. The suspects were usually not allowed access to an attorney, and the illiterate ones were not even read their rights only to have police officers write up statements for them to sign with a thumbprint without realizing that they were signing a confession. One woman, Mrs. Esther Ayorinde, went to a police station to complain that by moving her husband from one police station to another that was far, it was difficult for her to visit him in detention. Her husband had earlier been arrested following a quarrel with his elder brother over the sale of their father's land by the brother. The police officers arrested the wife for complaining and proceeded to detain her in the same cell where suspected male armed robbers were held. She was gang raped. Women rarely report cases of rape in custody out of a feeling of shame. Theresa Akumadu reports that women seeking redress for sexual harassment at work are often subjected to further violence by the police.[17] She gives the example of a typist, Miss Uzoma Okorie, who was maliciously accused of theft by her boss after rebuffing his advances. During her interrogation, police officers gave her what they called the "V.I.P. treatment" by stripping her naked, cuffing her hands behind a pillar, and inserting the neck of a bottle in her vagina while flogging her bare buttocks until she bled so much that she fainted only to recover in the police hospital days later.

Prisons

Recent research on Nigerian prisons focuses on overcrowding and concerns about a growing population. Agomoh et al. reported that there are currently "148 prisons and about eighty-three satellite prisons or lock-ups (where few prisoners are held in court buildings), 10 prison farms and nine cottage industries for the training of inmates."[18] In 1999, the prison population was 40,899 and out of this 21,579 or 52.8% were prisoners awaiting trial. While these figures appear much fewer than the two million Americans behind bars, it should be noted that Nigerian prisons have a combined capacity of 25,000 and are therefore significantly overcrowded. If the number of people awaiting trial were given bail, more than half the prisoners would be released and the prisons would be nearer their full capacity. If the innocent people who are wrongly convicted were also released from prison, the Nigerian prison population would be much lower still. And if nonviolent offenders were corrected in the community, Nigeria would not be in need of many prisons at all. Moreover, some of the prisoners are too young to be in prison. For example, in 1991, out of a total of 52,129 prisoners, 1,204 were below the age of sixteen. These young children were housed with adult prisoners and they were thereby exposed to sexual and physical abuse by the older male prisoners and guards. Agomoh et al. gave the sex distribution of the population of Nigerian prisons by state as shown in Table 14.1 (note that Bayelsa did not record any prisoners probably because it was a newly created state that was yet to construct its own prison facility).

From the statistics in Table 14.1, we could see that Nigerian prisons reflect the global phenomenon that incarcerated populations are mainly male. The major difference between these findings and my study of black women and the British criminal justice system is that in Nigeria, social relations of race are almost irrelevant given the relative homogeneity of the population.[20] In the place of race, the politics of ethnicity is articulated with gender and class to explain the preponderance of women from certain parts of the country in women's prisons. The fact that the prisons in the predominantly Muslim north and those in the predominantly Christian south of the country are not remarkably different in the gender composition of prisoners is an indication that religion and ethnicity are not significant variables for the explanation of the prison population. Whether the prisoners are male or female, young or old, they are more likely to be poor, uneducated, and unemployed. However, more recent reports of the use of Sharia law to oppress Nigerian women in the northern parts of the country are an indication that women do not have to be in prison to qualify as inmates of the global lockdown. Similar oppressive gender social control is also found in the south, where inhumane treatment is reserved for poor widows and the practice of female genital mutilation remains widespread. The high populations of women in the prisons of Rivers State, Lagos State, and Kaduna State may be a reflection of the fact that these are trouble spots of recent ethnic/religious conflicts that law enforcement agents have tried to repress through mass arrests and detention without trial. Women do not have to riot in order to become suspects to be detained because the police use the practice of holding women as hostages when they cannot find a son, husband, brother, or boyfriend who is wanted as a suspect.

In 1996, the Civil Liberties Organisation published a report on life *Behind the Wall*.[21] The report documented the cruel condition of Nigerian men in prison but hardly commented on the plight of women and children. The focus on men alone is in common with the tradition of "malestream" criminology whereby women remain invisible. To their credit, the CLO saw the shortcomings of their first edition and decided to issue a revised edition in which women and children were mentioned in addition to the dedication of a second volume exclusively to the issue of women and children who appear to be hidden in the shadows of the prison walls. The report quotes Nigerian State High Court Judge Justice Alhassan Idoko, who describes Nigerian prisons as ghettoes and

TABLE 14.1 Distribution of Prisoners by Sex and State, June 1999[19]

State	Males	Females	Total
Abia	1,117	27	1,144
Abuja	356	8	425
Adamawa	1,527	20	1,547
Akwa-Ibom	1,323	28	1,351
Anambra	1,720	22	1,742
Bauchi	1,048	4	1,052
Bayelsa	—	—	—
Benue	603	3	606
Borno	1,609	9	1,618
Cross River	875	18	893
Delta	1,535	58	1,593
Ebonyi	709	16	725
Edo	1,744	67	1,811
Ekiti	273	6	279
Enugu	1,278	27	1,305
Gombe	586	7	593
Imo	1,401	40	1,441
Jigawa	647	5	652
Kaduna	2,016	22	2,038
Kano	1,431	40	1,471
Katsina	1,063	12	1,075
Kebbi	946	11	957
Kogi	286	3	289
Kwara	309	5	314
Lagos	5,442	92	5,534
Nasarawa	567	4	571
Niger	970	5	975
Ogun	689	11	700
Ondo	725	1	726
Osun	305	10	315
Oyo	745	16	761
Plateau	1,012	16	1,028
Rivers	2,064	67	2,131
Sokoto	854	19	873
Taraba	1,149	19	1,168
Yobe	631	2	633
Zamfara	681	6	687
Total	**40,260**	**726**	**40,986**

shanty towns where inmates are forced to live on top of one another because of congestion.[22] The use of mass release or amnesty by politicians who are trying to save money or seeking cheap popularity makes it difficult to assess overcrowding or to predict future trends. For example, the total prison population was 25,622 in 1979 and 31,000 in 1990 but the average monthly prison population grew from 32,000 in 1979 to 60,000 in 1990. The fact that the average monthly prison population was nearly twice the annual prison population in 1990 is indicative of the practice of mass arrests and mass releases by the military government that was facing a crisis of hegemony from a people who refused to be intimidated. Overall, prison congestion in male and female prisons is illustrated by Ehonwa with Table 14.2. The rate of overcrowding appears in parentheses.

Other prisons are even more overcrowded than the few examples from Lagos State shown in Table 14.2. For instance, Ado-Ekiti prison is overpopulated at a rate of 557.58%; Ogwashi-Uku prison—456.86%; Auchi—398.75%; Benin—349.55%; Lafiagi—318.18%; Sapele—285.31%; Biu—285.00%; Potiskum—274.67%; Ilorin—238.84%; Kirikiri Medium Security—236.36%; Kwale—222.73%; Enugu—221.16%; Nguru—213.98%; Warri—202.69%; Okene—183.33%; and Owo—179.33%. Most of these highly congested prisons are in the southern part of the country.

It is evident that the female prison in Kirikiri is much less congested than the male prisons. The temptation here is for malestream criminologists to deny that the women are undergoing repressive and inhumane conditions in prison. As Pat Carlen argues with reference to female prisons in the United Kingdom, the fact that they are relatively less overcrowded than the male ones often leads to the suggestion that female prisons are more like college campuses or hotels.[23] That would be grossly mistaken because there is evidence that women are more likely to end up in prison as hostages of the law when men close to them are suspected of doing something wrong. The patriarchal assumption that conditions in female prisons are good derives from the use of male imprisonment as the false standard with which to measure how women should be treated. The consequence is that even when innocent women are being unlawfully held as hostages in prison, there is little outrage because the difference between the capacity of the only women's prison in the country and the actual prison population is seen to be "so marginal that it is practically of no consequence."[24]

TABLE 14.2   Selected Prison Capacities and Actual Prison Populations in Nigeria

PRISON	KIRIKIRI MAX	IKOYI	KIRIKIRI WOMEN
CAPACITY	956	800	105
POPULATION	2,596 (171.55%)	2,861 (257.63%)	137 (130.47%)

The report goes on to indicate that women make up 3.4% of the prison population in Nigeria but adds that when women were kept in rooms within male prisons, their rooms were "reasonably spacious" even when thirty-one women are forced to share two rooms. However, the report warns that if there are no plans to tackle congestion, the female prison and the female wings in male prisons might soon become as overcrowded as the male ones. The report tends to consider women only as an afterthought; nevertheless, Table 14.3 and Figure 14.1 indicate the reasons for overcrowding in Nigerian prisons.

The figures suggest that if the prisoners who were awaiting trial were given bail, the prison population would be nearer its normal capacity. Moreover, if children who were illegally detained in prison and nonviolent offenders were corrected in the community rather than being held in prison, Nigerian prisons would be almost entirely empty. The category of "Others" in prison was not explained in the report, but they could include those who were detained without being charged with any offense and so they could not be said to be convicts or remand prisoners. From all the preceding discussions, we can predict that the proportion of women who were awaiting trial or those convicted of nonviolent offenses or those simply held as hostages or as "Others" would be extremely high.

TABLE 14.3   Categories of Prisoners in Nigeria; 1988–1995

Category	1988	1989	1990	1991	1992	1995
Remand	19,745	21,063	19,219	21,615	19,985	35,750
Convict	31,871	31,193	28,448	30,511	21,767	17,902
Others	1,592	1,640	6,412	7,874	8,210	1,348

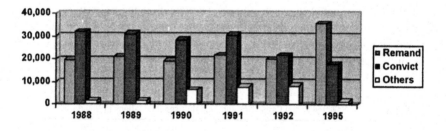

Figure 14.1   Bar Chart of Categories of Nigerian Prisoners: 1988–1995

In 1993, the Civil Liberties Organisation published a report on *Prisoners in the Shadows*. These children and women are hidden behind the walls of the prison and are also hidden from public curiosity about prison conditions, partly because prison authorities restrict access to women in prison even by researchers. This report shows that although women prisoners are fewer in number, the rate of increase in the female population far outstrips that of male populations in prison. This is partly due to a media panic in Nigeria that suggests that women's liberation is leading to women committing as much crime as men.

That was part of the reason why the military government introduced the double jeopardy decree in the early 1990s to seek the retrial of Nigerians who served prison sentences for drugs offenses and their sentencing to a fresh term of imprisonment following their deportation.[25] Apparently, the inhumane conditions of the prison-industrial complex in Europe and North America were regarded by brutal dictators in Nigeria as child's play and not proper punishment. However, Olurentimehin and Ogedengbe reported that patriarchal oppression of women is responsible for increasing substance abuse among women in Nigeria.[26] The same patriarchal and imperialist oppression is also noticeable in the huge number of women being trafficked to Europe to work as prostitutes in order to earn money with which to support their family at home.

Toward Countercolonial Criminology

This chapter has demonstrated that Nigerian women do not have to commit any crime in order to fall under the repressive gaze of the global lockdown. Although Nigeria has a relatively low rate of incarceration, its prisons are significantly overcrowded. In part, this is due to the large numbers of imprisoned men and women who have not been convicted of any offense, as well as children and significant numbers of women held as hostages for men wanted as suspects. The crisis of Nigerian prisons reflects the larger crisis of underdevelopment in Nigeria. I will therefore conclude with a discussion of policies that African leaders are touting as the solution to the problems of underdevelopment, including mass poverty and preventable death, mass illiteracy, and political repression.

According to the African heads of state who met in Abuja, Nigeria, to adopt the New Economic Plan for African Development (NEPAD), these problems are due to a lack of foreign investment in Africa. They argue that NEPAD will be the African equivalent of the Marshall Plan, which helped to stabilize Europe at the end of World War II. There are three main problems with NEPAD. First, although African leaders promote it as an original African initiative that will involve the masses in the development of the continent, ordinary people were not consulted when the plan was drafted. Second, when these leaders promise that NEPAD will be to Africa what Marshall was to Europe, they conveniently forget that Marshall was a government grant given to Europe by the United States, whereas NEPAD involves private foreign investment, not aid. Third, NEPAD is promoted as being gender sensitive when it is based on the same economic policies of structural adjustment that the World Bank and IMF have been imposing on African countries to the detriment of women.[27] Contrary to these predictions, NEPAD will lock African people more tightly into the cells of the imperialist global lockdown. A more viable policy for Africa is that championed by Kwame Nkrumah—a People's Republic of Africa would immediately eliminate the conditions of neocolonialism and halt the multiplication of military budgets in Africa. This alone would free up enormous resources for education, health care, and social security planning. A People's Republic of Africa would also pursue reparations for the African Holocaust, thus generating an alternative source of income.

Whereas the crafters of NEPAD view the integration of Africa into the global economy as a panacea for social and economic underdevelopment, critics of neoliberal globalization have developed a different analysis. Fidel Castro, in his address to the United Nations conference on the financing of development in Mexico (2002), proposed that global economic integration was in fact a key reason for underdevelopment. According to him:

> The existing world economic order constitutes a system of plundering and exploitation like no other in history . . . . [In the year 2001] more than 826 million people were actually starving; there were 854 million illiterate adults; 325 million children do not attend school, 2 billion people have no access to low cost medications and 2.4 billion people lack the basic sanitation conditions. Not less than 11 million children under age 5 perish every year from preventable causes, while half a million go blind for lack of vitamin A; the life span of the population in the developed world is 30 years higher than that of the people living in Sub-Saharan Africa . . . . In the face of the present deep crisis, a still worse future is offered where the economic, social and ecological tragedy of an increasingly ungovernable world would never be resolved and where the number of the poor and the starving would grow higher, as if a larger part of humanity were doomed.

While most criminologists busy themselves theorizing the punishment of offenders (as if anyone who is "punished" is necessarily an offender), Castro has proved himself a better criminologist by highlighting crimes of genocidal proportions that result from the global economic lockdown. The silence of criminologists on such massive criminal policies around the world is actually underdeveloping criminology as a discipline. Criminal injustice systems worldwide have contributed to the inhumane treatment of people of color, especially people of African descent. The battle of ideas has been a critical component of the criminal justice apparatus. This is why criminology is a common discipline in universities located in Europe and North America whereas the discipline is hardly existent in Africa (apart from South Africa), Asia, and South America, for criminology was developed to serve imperialism as a tool for the repression of others.[28]

An old African proverb says, if you hold someone on the ground, you too will not be able to rise until you let the person go. The prison officer is also a prisoner of some sort. This saying provides insight into the nature of the global lockdown—we are all inmates of the global prison whether we are behind bars or in front of bars or branded with bar codes. Our collective responsibility for imperialism (as the workers, investors, and consumers who oil its machines and the teachers who train its troops) means that we need to ask ourselves what we can do to reverse the process of recolonization perpetrated by free trade agreements and IMF-led socioeconomic policies. Criminologists need to study the history of the solidarity between their discipline and imperialism in order to learn from global struggles for decolonization and to develop a new methodology. Only in this way can we use what Amilcar Cabral called the weapon of theory to strengthen anti-imperialist struggles around the world.[29]

References

1. Biko Agozino, *Black Women and the Criminal Justice System: Towards the Decolonisation of Victimisation* (Aldershot: Ashgate, 1997).
2. Jean Baudrillard, *Simulations* (New York: Semiotext(e), 1983): 25.
3. Jeffrey Reiman, *The Rich Get Richer and the Poor Get Prison* (New York: Wiley, 1979).
4. Increasingly those "criminals" include police officers such as the killers of Amadou Diallo and the brutal attackers of Abner Louima and fraudulent corporate executives.
5. I use the term "prison preindustrial complex" to underline the premedieval conditions that are prevalent in Nigerian prisons, the fact that the prisoners are not engaged in any meaningful industrial activity, and the fact that the government has yet to privatize prisons, which are still represented as a social service. In common with the prison-industrial complex in the United States, Nigerian contractors earn huge profits from keeping human plantations supplied with commodities at monopoly prices.
6. Agozino 1997.
7. Stuart Hall, "Race, Articulation and Societies Structured in Dominance," in UNESCO ed., *Sociological Theories: Race and Colonialism* (Paris: Unesco, 1980).
8. C.L.R. James, *The Black Jacobins: Toussaint l'Ouverture and the San Diego Revolution* (London: Allison and Busby, 1980); Walter Rodney, *How Europe Underdeveloped Africa* (London, Bogle l'Ouverture, 1972); Angela Davis, *Women, Race and Class* (London: The Women's Press, 1981).
9. Winnie Mandela, *Part of My Soul*, ed. A. Benjamin (Middlesex: Penguin, 1984).
10. Loïc Wacquant, "Deadly Symbiosis: When Ghetto and Prison Meet and Merge," *Punishment & Society* 3, 1 (2001): 95–134.
11. Reiman 1979; Steve Box, *Power, Crime and Mystification* (London, Tavistock, 1983).
12. Quoted in Osaze L. Ehonwa, *Behind the Wall: A Report on Prison Conditions in Nigeria and the Nigerian Prison System* (Lagos: Civil Liberties Organisation, 1996).
13. Michel Foucault, *Discipline and Punish: The Birth of the Prison* (London: Allen Lane, 1977).

14. Close to the end of his first term in office as an executive president in Nigeria, he was yet to sign a bill for the abolition of capital punishment in Nigeria. Such a bill was introduced only during the campaign for Obasanjo's reelection in 2003.
15. Biko Agozino and Unyierie Idem, *Nigeria: Democratising a Militarised Civil Society* (London, CDD, 2001).
16. Theresa Akumadu, *Patterns of Abuse of Women's Rights in Employment and Police Custody* (Lagos, Civil Liberties Organisation, 1995).
17. Akumadu 1995.
18. Uju Agomoh, A. Adeyemi, and V. Ogbebor, *The Prison Service and Penal Reform in Nigeria: A Synthesis Study* (Lagos: PRAWA, 2001): 6.
19. Agomoh et al., 2001: 18.
20. Agozino 1997.
21. Osaze L. Ehonwa, *Prisoners in the Shadow: A Report on Women and Children in Five Nigerian Prisons* (Lagos, Civil Liberties Organisation, 1993).
22. In Nigeria, the term "congestion" is used to mean overcrowding.
23. Pat Carlen, *Women's Imprisonment* (London: Routledge & Kegan Paul, 1983).
24. Ehonwa 1996: 19.
25. Agozino 1997.
26. Olufunmilayo Oloruntimehin and R.O. Ogedengbe, "Women and Substance Abuse in Nigeria," in L. N. Tsu, ed., *Women and Substance Abuse*, 1992 Interim Report, Geneva, WHO/PSA/92.9 (1992): 30–41.
27. Gwendolyn Mikell (ed.), *African Feminism: The Politics of Survival in Sub-Saharan Africa* (Philadelphia: University of Pennsylvania Press, 1997).
28. For a more detailed discussion of this point see Biko Agozino, *Counter Colonial Criminology: A Critique of Imperialist Reason* (London: Pluto, 2003).
29. Amilcar Cabral, *Unity and Struggle* (New York: Monthly Review Press, 1979).

CHAPTER 15

Occupied Territories, Resisting Women

Palestinian Women Political Prisoners[1]

ELHAM BAYOUR

Palestinian women have been the backbone of the Palestinian national liberation struggle for over seventy years, well before the birth of the Palestinian Liberation Organization in the mid-1960s. Their contributions and sacrifices have been overlooked locally and ignored by Western social scientists. Palestinian female political prisoners have been detained since the mid-1970s,[2] and yet no comprehensive research has been conducted to make visible their political involvement. In this chapter, I discuss Palestinian women's contributions to the national liberation struggle and their experiences of imprisonment as a result of their political activity. I argue that occupation policies toward these women constitute sexual terrorism. Palestinian women from three refugee camps in the Gaza Strip describe their experiences of detention and torture and lives after imprisonment in their own words. Palestinian women face a Western colonial bias at the hands of Western writers and feminists, by whom they have been repeatedly labeled controlled and oppressed subjects. This chapter aims to deconstruct the scholarly misrepresentation that erases Palestinian women's political activities.

Palestinian women under occupation face a dual struggle: the nationalist struggle to liberate their land from multilayered colonization and occupation and, in addition to this territorial and internal colonization, the inequity of life under patriarchal Arab traditions. When we discuss the social and political issues facing Palestinian women, it is important to recognize the sociohistorical impact of military occupation. Territorial colonization of Palestinian land for the past fifty-six years, loss of sovereignty and freedom of movement, and the internal colonization of Palestinian politics and economics have all been devastating for women's social and political situation and for their health.

Historically, Palestinian women, like women in the rest of the Arab world, have been victims of customs and traditions inherited from the feudal bourgeois structure that dominated the area.[3] They have also suffered national oppression and occupation by the Ottoman Empire, the British Mandate, and Zionism.[4] Patriarchy and religious doctrines intertwined to form oppressive societal controls that stunted women's mental capacities. This affected their educational, economic, and political aspirations. Anyone setting out to examine the situation of Palestinian women must confront the fact that they are oppressed both as Palestinians and as women. Theorists must analyze the relationship between national liberation and women's independence. This dilemma has both practical and ideological dimensions. The complexity of this problem has led both feminists and nationalists to circumvent it. However, any attempt to escape this predicament leads either to a feminism that ignores the effects of colonial oppression on Palestinian social and family structures or to a sterile nationalism without social content.[5]

Palestinian Women's Resistance

Palestinian women began organized political activity in the early 1900s. They demonstrated against British colonization and the growth of Zionist settlements in Palestine. Women were among forty thousand Arab citizens who gathered and marched in the streets of Jerusalem in the great uprising against the British on January 27, 1920.[6] This demonstration, planned in the utmost secrecy, was unprecedented in the history of Jerusalem.[7] Women set up charitable associations to care for children, the needy, and the sick. They collected aid and foodstuffs and opened girls' schools in rural areas. In 1921, the Arab Palestinian Women's Union was established in Jerusalem. Their goals were to increase union membership and to unify women's efforts to develop the social and political struggle against the British Mandate and Zionist settlements in Palestine.[8] In 1929, a particularly turbulent year in Palestine, the first Arab Women's Congress of Palestine was attended by over two thousand Palestinian women, who presented their resolutions and demands to the British high commissioner. The congress declared that the 1917 Balfour Declaration, whereby Britain was to help the Zionists acquire a national home in Palestine, was the sole cause of social unrest in the country and predicted that it might cause more bloodshed in the future.[9]

As well as participating in demonstrations, peasant women were openly involved in a more active and dangerous way.[10] Palestinian women joined the peasant revolution that erupted in 1936.[11] During the six-month general strike, initiated on April 21, 1936, markets and stores were closed and transportation stopped. All activities came to a standstill except for organized demonstrations in which people carried empty coffins marked "British Justice Is Buried Here." Bloody battles took place everywhere, students went on strike, and schools were closed. In retaliation, the government of the British Mandate issued orders to bomb houses of revolutionaries and jailed leaders and demonstrators. On May 4, 1936, about six hundred female students held a meeting in Jerusalem and decided to launch a general strike in all educational establishments in Palestine. They organized a mass demonstration on May 6 in which many Palestinian women participated. The demonstrators called for an end to British colonization and Zionist settlement and urged the adoption of measures to boycott British products.[12]

Struggling to protect their villages and their land, Palestinian women also participated in armed campaigns in rural areas as supporters and fighters. A few fought and died, such as Fatemeh Ghazzal, who was killed in battle on June 26, 1936 in Wadi Azzoun, near Lydda. She is the first known Palestinian woman killed in combat.[13] On April 9, 1948, 137 combatant women participated in resistance to the infamous massacre of Deir Yassin. Jamila Ahmad Salah and Dibeh Atiya were shot and wounded while they distributed arms and ammunition to fighters defending their village.

During the first Intifada (Palestinian uprising), which started in 1987 and ended in 1993 with the Oslo Accord, Palestinian women's participation positively affected the entire society. They fought the occupation forces on the streets; navigated the roads for the youth; transported messages, money, and arms from the leadership to the local committees; took care of the injured; and initiated popular committees and grassroots cooperatives. They broke curfews imposed on their camps by leading food conveys, and they started underground schools for children in order to break the educational ban that the occupation imposed on the Palestinian populace.

Women's Narratives of Occupation and Resistance

In 1998, 1999, and 2000, I traveled to the Gaza Strip to conduct research on Palestinian women refugees who were former political prisoners. This research took place in Shat', Rafah, and Khan Younis refugee camps. I interviewed fifty-two women who had been prisoners of conscience. They were eager to share their experiences of resistance in their refugee camps, their brutal detention, and their lives after prison in order to raise awareness among international audiences. I conducted the interviews in Arabic with an emphasis on the Palestinian dialect that the women and I share. Our dialect was not the only common factor that brought us closer together. Our experiences of living in different refugee camps provided an important basis for mutual understanding, as well as our shared customs and cultural sensitivities. I translated the testimonies into English with the aim of keeping the women's expressions and the meanings as close to the Arabic/Palestinian dialect as possible.

Most of the women requested that I use their real names. However, because the women's decisions about this may have changed as a result of intensified aggression, I decided to use pseudonyms to protect their identities. The names I use in this chapter are adopted from the 534 villages that were destroyed in 1948.

The women I interviewed gave several interrelated reasons for becoming involved in the national liberation struggle. These included being uprooted from their villages in Palestine, the destitution of refugee life, and the arbitrary punishment imposed on them by the armed forces. For these women, the liberation of Palestine meant the liberation of the whole Palestinian population and the return of the refugees to their original villages. Jameila's[14] explanation of her motivation to become politically involved is typical of many of the women I interviewed:

Nobody influenced or encouraged me to be involved in the national struggle. I did it by myself. It was a protest again the situation, a protest against the society. It is from poverty and misery. I was fed up of the bugs and the dirt hay walls we had. We lived in tents; the insects and bugs infested our dirt floors. We suffered from polluted water, rain, cold winters, hot summers, and collective bathrooms. Open sewage became small puddles full of diseases, insects, and bad smells. Plague attacked us once. Rats, roaches, and mice were rampant. The poverty and the suffering pressed me to be political. I was a person who wanted to run from the suffering. It was a way to flee from my own suffering. This is why I became involved in the struggle to free myself and my people.

For many Palestinian women, political engagement meant making the difficult choice to jeopardize their family responsibilities and risk the disapproval of their male kin. Nevertheless, these women saw political involvement as the only way to achieve true security and well-being for their families. Bisan, a 75-year-old former political prisoner, describes her husband's response to her activism:

I used to transport the leadership money from the West Bank in fruit baskets. I covered it with dried figs. I used to walk along the beach from Yaffa to Gaza, transporting messages and guns under my traditional Palestinian dress. My husband would ask me, "Where have you been? Where did you come from?" I never told him that I was active because I knew he would not let me. He used to lock me in the house and take the keys with him. I used to jump out of the window and go to my meetings.

My two sons and my daughter were in prison before me. We were four family members in prison together. They tortured my son in front of me. I did not cry one tear. I said to them, "Palestine is precious and he has to pay the price for her freedom." You know, sometimes I feel guilty because I missed my daughters while in prison, but it is very hard to balance your fight for your country and your family responsibilities.

For women like Bisan, gender and nationality are inextricably interconnected in their experiences of resistance.

Palestinian Women Political Prisoners

As punishment for their participation in resisting the occupation, over two thousand Palestinian women were imprisoned, humiliated, sexually assaulted, and physically and mentally tortured between 1970 and 1993.[15] Palestinian women political prisoners were targeted by policies designed to dispossess and disempower the Palestinian population. These policies humiliate women through physical, mental, and sexual torture. They seek to exercise control over women's spirits as well as their bodies, sexuality, and reproduction. These policies are designed to dishonor Palestinian men through the brutalization of Palestinian women's bodies.

The military's treatment of Bisan and Sirin was designed to dishonor them as pious elderly Palestinian women. When they were arrested they were wearing traditional Palestinian embroidered dresses. Both women were forced to take off their clothes and fit into tight, short, sleeveless dresses. By stripping the women of their traditional clothing, the soldiers attempted to undermine the women's cultural identity, symbolically erasing the women's adherence to their national cultural heritage. The women's clothing became a battleground for the struggle over sovereignty and a location for the telling or erasing of history. The stitching, design, and color of the women's dresses serve as a reminder of both unlawful occupation and the tenacity of Palestinian culture and heritage.

Sexual violence against Palestinian women political prisoners is a manifestation of the close relationship between occupation and sexism. Sexual terrorism is a fundamental part of Palestinian women's prison experiences and imprisoned women's bodies are used as the battleground on which the occupier wages war. Women political prisoners reported repeated incidents of sexual retaliation and threats of sexual assault. Female soldiers were reportedly no less brutal than their male counterparts, as Hitten explained:

They brought Safad at midnight. I knew her but our secret policy was to act like we did not know each other. They ordered her to take off her clothes in front of the soldiers. She refused. The Jewish woman soldier started beating her up. Safad grabbed her hair and hit her on the back. Safad had an ulcer and was very scared because they threatened to rape her.

During interrogation, Palestinian women's personal and private sexual lives were made public. Their interrogators accused them of being prostitutes or of being pregnant at the time of their imprisonment, so that their families would disown them.[16] In order to manipulate gendered cultural taboos regarding honor and sexual purity, the women's interrogators threatened to shame or rape them. In so doing, they hoped to achieve multiple goals at the individual and collective levels. First, they aimed to make the women admit their participation in political organizations. Second, they hoped to discourage them and other women from future nationalist activities. Third, they attempted to shame them and their families within their own communities. And finally, because women are culturally constructed as emblems of their nation, the occupying forces aimed to control women's bodies in order to conquer their culture and land.

The sexual violence reported by interviewees includes repeated threats of rape, sexual assault, beating women's breasts and genitals, fondling, verbal sexual abuse, and bringing the woman's father and/or a Palestinian male political prisoner and ordering him to rape her. Their assailants would frequently strip women or remove their own clothes, at times reaching sexual climax while torturing the woman. Salama, an eighteen-year-old, described the physical, mental, and sexual torture she endured in prison:

I remember Steve, the interrogator. His specialty was beatings. He is blond and tall, very ugly. They said, "We have a surprise for you." I wondered what this surprise might be, maybe another man confessed about me. All of a sudden Steve kicked the door with his feet. They all laughed and said, "This is the surprise." He grabbed me by my clothes, at the collar, and carried me as you might carry a hen by her wings so her feet do not touch the floor. This is how he carried me from room to room. He started to strangle me. I remember when he was choking me he used to look at his watch, until I was close to suffocating and stuff started coming out of my mouth. He would release me for a minute and then he would do it again. He repeated this six times. He continued doing this every other day. He used to beat my head at the front, on the forehead. Light continuous beatings until I lost my concentration and my balance. I felt my ears were empty and I started feeling dizzy.

After this Steve took off his clothes and stood naked in front of me. He showed me a naked picture of himself and said, "I am going to go inside you now. Look at me when I am small. Imagine when you see me big."

Women's prison experiences demonstrate the connection between occupation and sexual violence. Although sexual abuse is designed to dehumanize and disempower women, this practice is also targeted at Palestinian men, for whom the protection and control of women are a core part of their socially constructed masculinity.[17] The sexual torture experienced by Jameila is one example of this practice:

> During interrogations they brought in an African Palestinian male political prisoner and ordered him to rape me. They beat him near death because he refused. I asked him to do it to stop his torture. They put a bag on my head and ordered me to climb up on rows of tables assembled over each other to the electric chair, still naked. They electrocuted me for four hours. The electric shocks were administered until I turned blue. Then they threw me in extremely cold water, and then more beatings. They forced me to stand up on one leg with my hands raised upward and they covered my head with a burlap bag full of feces.
>
> During my first imprisonment I had my first menstrual blood. I was very scared. I thought that they had raped me. A male soldier heard my screams and told me, "Yes, we have raped you." They left me for three days covered with blood, without napkins or underwear. My whole body was swollen from the beatings. I could not open my eyes. When the Red Cross came to visit the prison, the guards hid me in a different prison, Ramleh.[18] I developed two personalities. I became very violent, and beat up everybody who stood in my way. I was put away in an isolated cell for six years. My family only visited me five times during my imprisonment because I was in solitary confinement all the time. I was never allowed to go out, exercise, walk, or see the sun. After my first release I did not leave my room for one year. I had to see a psychiatrist for help.

Jameila's harrowing experience is evidence of how the interrelated practices of occupation and sexual violence disrupt Palestinian society. In this instance, both actors in the act of sexual violence were Palestinians. A Palestinian man was forced to assault and debase a Palestinian woman's body, spirit, and dignity. Moreover, the guard's racialized agenda in choosing an African Palestinian male political prisoner to rape Jameila raises another set of alarming questions. Jameila concluded that the guards intended to promote animosity and hostility between different Palestinian communities. The strategy of divide and conquer has been practiced since 1948 in order to diminish social unity and national solidarity.

Rape or threats of rape attack the integrity of the woman as a person as well as her identity as a woman. They render her homeless in her own body. Sexual abuse strikes at a woman's power; it seeks to degrade and destroy her; its goal is domination and dehumanization.[19] The 1988 United Nations Convention against Torture defines torture as the willful infliction of severe physical pain and mental suffering not only to elicit information but also to punish, intimidate, discriminate, or to obliterate the victim's personality and diminish her personal capacities. It is not simply or necessarily the infliction of terrible physical pain, it also includes the use of pain, sensory deprivation, isolation, and humiliation as a pathway to the mind. Degradation is both vehicle and goal.[20] Hafia testified that:

> My cell was called a grave or a closet. It was 2 meters by 1 and half meters. It is exactly your size standing. You have to stand all the time in it. When you go to the bathroom voices and noises follow you, so you are scared to take off your clothes. They make you feel that you are watched all the time. When the Red Cross came I told them about the noises, but the occupiers said, "Do not listen to her, she is imagining it." I started to question my sanity. Physical torture is much easier than mental torture. I'd prefer to have broken hands, arms, and legs rather than doubting my mental capacity.

In addition to the detrimental psychological and health effects of sexual violence experienced in the course of interrogations, women suffered from harsh living conditions, including appalling sanitation, inadequate nutrition, and denial of family visits and medical treatment.

Another tactic used to humiliate women is to handcuff pregnant women prisoners when they go into labor, a graphic expression of occupation as the control of women's fertility. Because pregnant women are perceived as carriers of their race and bearers of the nation, the torture and control of their bodies are particularly symbolic. When Zeeb was arrested, she was seven months into her pregnancy:

> I was in my third trimester when I was arrested and they wanted to perform an abortion on me. I did not let them. They took me to Majdal prison and did an ultra-sound to check the gender of the baby. When they knew that the baby was a boy, they started screaming at me, "You are going to bring a *Fedae*" (freedom fighter). They put me in a cell that was one and a half by two meters. They kicked my stomach with their huge military boots, spitting and cussing at me. They left me there for four days with no food or water. They did not allow me to use the bathroom for one week. I was very weak, my feet were swollen, and my entire body was aching.

Zeeb did not abort. She delivered her son in prison with her hands and feet shackled to the bed, and she stayed shackled for three days after her delivery because the guard went on vacation and took the keys with him. This lack of re-gard for Zeeb's health and for the survival of her child is not an anomaly. Rather it is indicative of the devastating impact of military policy on Palestinian women and children.

Colonial military violence against Palestinian women prisoners should be viewed within the context of violence against Palestinian women as a whole and is one result of the Palestinians' overall loss of political status since 1948. Control of Palestinian women is central to colonial nationalist ideology. As the reproducers of the despised race, Palestinian women are targets of control. During the first Intifada, hundreds of women miscarried after being tear-gassed. The military tear-gassed a nursery in Gaza and threw tear gas bombs into Palestinian homes, a strategy that was clearly designed to reduce the Palestinian population through the brutalization of women's bodies. Occupation authorities view the control of Palestinian women's reproductive capacity as a matter of security. In January 2001, for example, recommenda-tions to control Palestinian women's bodies and their reproductive decisions were adopted at a conference in Tel Aviv entitled "National Strength and Security in Israel." The rationale given was Palestinian women's high birth rate of 4.6 children, compared with 2.6 children for Jewish women in the area. Conference participants recommended that population control measures should be made a condition of donations by the international community to the Palestinian Authority. In the current Intifada, 176 women have been killed in two years and fifty-one have had to give birth at roadblocks.[21]

Women's Experience After Imprisonment

After their release, former prisoners continued to experience physical and psy-chological suffering as well as defamation and harassment. Women were watched and ordered to report to the police center more than once a week. Zeeb testifies:

> When I arrived in Gaza, I found that they had demolished my house and my kids were living in a tent donated by UNRWA [United Nations Relief and Work Agency]. I stayed with them in the tent. A Jewish judge came to my tent and told me that if I stayed in the tent they will burn it while we are in it. He came to collect the five thousand Shekels bail that I had to pay for my release.

> I rebuilt my house and now I am living with my five boys. My husband is a political prisoner. He was imprisoned before me. During interrogations they told me that my husband had confessed about me. They wanted to create problems between us so we would divorce each other, but I did not believe them.

Majdal also experienced harassment after her release:

They monitored my house daily. They came each night and sat in this room until morning. I used to make them coffee and tea. We did not have a sewage system. We had a well for the sewage. One morning while I was having breakfast, they came with two dogs and two women soldiers. They started shooting at the walls. They said that they saw a fedae (freedom fighter) who came with a box. My brother in-law came to visit and brought the box of a video cassette recorder. This is how closely I was watched.

Jameila described the lasting physical impact of imprisonment:

After my third release I was paralyzed for three months and had back surgery. I have diabetes and am waiting to have another back surgery. I cannot perform hard work or hold heavy things. I suffer from continuous back pain, chest and stomach pain. As you see, I have black spots all over my face from torture, cigarette burns and stress.

Palestinian women political prisoners suffered not only from their experiences in prison but also from the reaction of their own community, which responded by blaming them. During the first Intifada young men offered to marry women political prisoners in an effort to support and encourage them, so that other women would continue the struggle. Palestinian families responded to state sexual abuse by imposing greater control over women, by forbidding them to leave home, and by curbing their studies, sometimes violently.[22] Salama explained how the wider community attempted to deal with women returning home:

Views regarding us women political prisoners in the Palestinian communities depend on the times and the political situation of the revolution. There were girls who were seriously crushed and their lives were ruined. To counteract girls political activities and to stop problems, some parents forced their daughters to be married as second wives, before they go back to prison and create problems.

The experience of imprisonment became a permanent stigma that affected Jenin's future marriage prospects. She said:

After my release a man came and wanted to marry me. When he and his family knew I had been detained they changed their mind because I was a political prisoner. I married my husband, a chemist. He married me because his sister was a political prisoner and he is sympathetic towards me.

But do not think that because he is educated and a chemist he is not backward and traditional. We always fight over my job. He does not want me to work but his salary is not enough for the six of us. I do not listen to him. I keep on working. He can control me if he keeps me at home. No job, no economic freedom. But I know all this and fight with him.

The age, strength of character, and determination of women who have survived detention are also a threat to some prospective male partners, as Jenin suggests:

We women political prisoners are facing an age problem. All men like to marry young girls. When a woman was imprisoned for a long period of time she became over twenty years of age and nobody wants to marry her. All men look for seventeen- and eighteen-year-old girls to marry in order to control them. When you are working together with men politically they all theorize about ideas of freedom and equality, but when it comes down to the bottom of the matter, they do not want to marry a knowledgeable woman who fought and who has experience. They want an inexperienced girl to control as they wish. Women who were detained are strong and might not obey them.

As these women's experiences demonstrate, colonization reinforces patriarchal gender relations and religious fundamentalism. In the face of dispossession and loss of land, colonized men and women hold fiercely onto their heritage, at times adhering to cultural dogmas that negatively affect women and children.

Recent Women Political Prisoners

Over 650,000 Palestinians have been detained under the occupation since 1967. Detainees are held in overcrowded prison tents that are often threadbare and do not offer adequate shelter against extreme weather. Prisoners are not provided with adequate food rations, in terms of quantity or quality, nor are they provided with clean clothes or adequate cleaning supplies. Many of the detainees currently being held in military detention camps were injured during their arrests and have not received necessary medical attention. Those who suffer from chronic illnesses are in a similar situation.[23]

The women interviewed for this chapter were arrested, imprisoned, and released during the first Intifada. Women continue to be injured, killed, and sent to prison for their political activities. Since the Intifada that erupted in September 2001, Palestinian women have experienced an escalated arrest campaign by the occupation forces. At the time of writing, five Palestinian women had been arrested during this recent Intifada. Among them are two minors,

Su'ad Ghazal (seventeen) and Sara 'Issa Amro (fourteen). Su'ad was placed in an isolation cell, two meters square and with an open toilet, for a period of four days. During that time she was prevented from any contact with others and prohibited from leaving the cell. Sara, the fourteen-year-old, was brought before the court on April 24, 2001, when the military prosecutor offered a plea bargain that required her to serve a three-year sentence. The current situation of Palestinian female prisoners in Al-Ramla prison, particularly the conditions of juvenile detainees, is extremely brutal.

The Palestinian news agency WAFA reported on August 17, 2003 that "There are seventy three Palestinian female prisoners still held at the Israeli prison of Al-Ramla, suffering from maltreatment and deteriorating human conditions at the hands of the Israeli occupation authorities." According to a statement issued by the Palestinian Ministry of Prisoners Affairs, a number of Palestinian female prisoners were being held without trial, and several others were detained as a means of pressure against their husbands or relatives for extracting confessions. According to testimonies gathered from female prisoners themselves by the ministry's advocates, the detention conditions of female prisoners have become increasingly bad as occupation authorities have tightened restrictions on them.[24] Of the seventy-three Palestinian women in detention, ten are minors under the age of eighteen. These children are held in conditions that contravene international standards of detention as well as the UN Convention on the Rights of the Child. The UN convention stipulates that all individuals under the age of eighteen are considered children. They must not be submitted to torture, or cruel, inhuman and degrading treatment, nor deprived of their liberty except as a last resort. The youngest of the detainees, Zainab Al Shouly and 'Aisha Abeyat, both turned fifteen while in prison.

Six Palestinian women are currently being held under administrative detention orders, meaning that they are imprisoned without charge or trial. One of them, Tahani Al Titi, has been serving continuously renewed administrative detention orders since June 13, 2002. The use of administrative detention for Palestinian women dramatically increased at the end of 2003, paralleling similar use during the first Palestinian Intifada. Detainees include mothers of young children, including Mervat Taha, who was pregnant when she was arrested on June 13, 2002. She is serving a twenty-month sentence and gave birth to her child in prison.[25]

Conclusion

Palestinian women's testimonies of survival and resistance demonstrate that they are not subjugated and silenced but that they are active in demanding their rights. The women's words reveal a multilayered struggle against the occupation and against internal patriarchal controls within Palestinian society. Male

Palestinian leaders should realize that the battle against occupation cannot be separated from women's dependence on men. A country cannot become liberated when half of its inhabitants are subordinated. Palestinian women cannot achieve social consciousness without achieving a consciousness of self. Egyptian feminist El-Sa'adawi asks, "Can a woman who is dependent on her husband liberate her children, other women, or her nation from occupation?"[26] The testimonies of Palestinian women political prisoners demonstrate that freedom cannot be less than whole, and Palestinian women's rights will never be given to them but must be acquired through struggle. While women struggle against patriarchal attitudes in their own communities, gender inequality in Palestinian society cannot and should not be divorced from the violence of political oppression and occupation.

This chapter has demonstrated that sexual terrorism is an integral part of women's experiences of political imprisonment. Sexual violence against women in prison cannot be viewed in isolation from widespread sexual assaults and human rights violations of Palestinian women that take place at checkpoints and during home searches, as well as in prison. Body searches, strip searches, and other public acts of humiliation are all forms of state violence systematically deployed against women. It is not only men who carry out human rights violations; female soldiers also violate Palestinian women's rights in prison, on the streets, or in their homes. Palestinian women are positioned in the front line of brutal, gendered occupation policies. Yet their mistreatment under the occupation has garnered little attention or outrage from the international community. Western feminists, who often display considerable concern for global women's issues, have frequently failed to challenge the sexual terrorism deployed by the occupation forces. In part, this may be due to the widespread perception that any critique of Zionist policies is inherently anti-Semitic, leading many feminists to remain silent for fear of being so labeled. The challenge for feminists and progressives is to listen to the testimonies of Palestinian women and to commit themselves to supporting the women's struggles for self-determination.

References

1. This paper was first presented at the Third International Conference on Women in Africa and the African Diaspora, Antananarivo, Madagascar, October 8–17, 2001.
2. In this chapter, the term "political prisoner" is used to describe all Palestinian women who are imprisoned as a result of the occupation of Palestine.
3. Laila Jammal, "Contributions by Palestinian Women to the Struggle for Liberation," *Palestine Liberation Organization Bulletin* 7, 13 (1981): 30–40.
4. Zionism describes the political movement for the establishment and maintenance of a Jewish state in Palestine.
5. Rosemary Sayigh, "Encounters with Palestinian Women under Occupation," in *Occupation: Israel over Palestine*, ed. Naseer Aruri (Belmont, Massachusetts: Association of Arab American Press, 1983), 269.
6. Jammal 1981, 30.

7. Matiel Mogannam, *The Arab Woman and the Palestine Problem* (London: Hyperion Press, 1937), 96.

8. Jammal 1981, 30.

9. Nadia Hijab, *Womanpower: The Arab Debate on Women at Work* (Cambridge: Cambridge University Press, 1988), 146; Mogannam 1937, 74–5.

10. Julie Peteet, *Gender in Crisis: Women and the Palestinian Resistance Movement* (New York: Columbia University Press, 1991), 53,

11. The fact that peasant women were among the casualties at street demonstrations early in the Mandate directs our attention to nineteenth-century peasant uprisings—against Ottoman taxes and the first Zionist settlers—in which women certainly took part. See Adel Sammara and Rosemary Sayigh, *Profile of an Occupation* (London and New York: Zed Books, 1989), 155.

12. Jammal 1981, 31.

13. Peteet 1991, 55.

14. The name Jameila is used to honor the Algerian political prisoner, Jameila Bou Heired, who was tortured to death in the 1950s when the French colonized Algeria.

15. Personal interview with Khalida Jarrar, director of Addameer Prisoners Support and Human Rights Association, 2000. Addameer is a nonprofit organization based in Ramullah, Palestine.

16. Tamar Mayer (ed), *Women and the Israeli Occupation: The Politics of Change* (New York and London: Routledge, 1994), 79.

17. Elise Young, *Keepers of the History: Women and the Israeli-Palestinian Conflict* (New York: Teachers College Press, 1992), 184.

18. Also known as Al-Ramla prison.

19. Rhonda Copelon, "Surfacing Gender: Reconceptualizing Crimes Against Women in Time of War," in *The Women And War Reader*, ed. A. Lorentzen and J. Turpin (New York: New York University, 1998), 76.

20. Amnesty International, "Amnesty International Report on Torture," in *The Women and War Reader*, ed. A. Lorentzen and J. Turpin (New York: New York University Press, 1988).

21. Al-Awda News, "Israel killed 176 Palestinian women in two years, 51 had to give birth at Israeli roadblocks" (March 8, 2003). http://www.miftah.org/Display.cfm?DocId=1839& CategoryId=2. Accessed April 10, 2004.

22. Nabila Espanioly, "Palestinian Women in Israel: Identity in the Light of the Occupation," in *Women and the Israeli Occupation: The Politics of Change*, ed. T. Mayer (New York and London: Routledge, 1994), 116.

23. Palestine Monitor, "Palestinian Prisoners in Israeli Detentions" (February 2003). http://www.palestinemonitor.org/factsheet/Palestinian_Prisoners.html. Accessed April 10, 2004.

24. Ministry of Prisoners Affairs, "Female Palestinian Prisoners of Al-Ramla Israeli Prison Face Harsh Conditions," International Press Center and WAFA (August 17, 2003), http://www.ipc-ps.info/ipc_e/ipc_e-1/e_News%20Reports/2003/reports-024.html. Accessed April 12, 2004.

25. Addameer Prisoners Support and Human Rights Association, "International Women's Day: 65 Palestinian women remain in Israeli detention camps," press release (March 8, 2003). http://electronicIntifada.net/v2/article1229.shtml. Accessed April 10, 2004.

26. Nawal El Saadawi, *The Nawal El Saadawi Reader* (London and New York: Zed Books, 1997), 16.

CHAPTER 16

Playing Global Cop

U.S. Militarism and the Prison-Industrial Complex

LINDA EVANS

The disintegration of the former Soviet Union and the alternative economic system embodied in the socialist bloc has allowed the United States to establish absolute economic and military hegemony. Wielding uncontested power, the United States is rapidly recreating the world in its own image, establishing a global police state. The purpose of U.S. militarization is to impose a new world order: neoliberal capitalism for everyone, whether they want it or not. This imposition of global capitalism requires the crudest forms of social control, including mass imprisonment, political repression, proxy wars, and outright military takeovers. Women are affected in a variety of ways by militarization and increasing repression, including political surveillance and mass incarceration. This chapter will examine how domestic and external wars waged by the "global policeman" affect women, particularly women of color and women from the global South. It will also explore the connections between militarism and the prison-industrial complex and discuss the ways in which increased surveillance, policing, and mass incarceration are militarizing U.S. society.

Preemptive Strikes: Mass Incarceration and Social Control

Since the onset of the economic restructuring that we now know as globalization, communities of color in the United States have experienced increasing repression. The Nixon years introduced the "war on crime," outlined in Nixon's 1973 State of the Union address.[1] Reagan dramatically increased spending on

215

policing and prisons through the intensification of the "war on drugs." Both the war on crime and the war on drugs scapegoated and targeted poor communities of color. In many ways, these "wars" were preemptive strikes. As economic conditions deteriorate, the strategy for social control is to put poor people away before they pose a serious threat to social order. The goal is to incarcerate and immobilize people oppressed by these social conditions—those at the bottom, the helpless, the hopeless—before they organize to demand change. Communities of color that are already ravaged by drug addiction, poverty, and related violence have been further decimated by the war on drugs and mass imprisonment. These social conditions, compounded by intensive policing and punitive penal policies, have severely compromised the ability of people in these communities to organize and take action against economic and social injustice.

Successive administrations from Reagan to Bush Jr. have adopted mass incarceration as the primary strategy to maintain social control. This is directly reflected in the large numbers of people of color who are currently in prison. Over two million people are in U.S. prisons and jails, most of them poor and people of color—African Americans, Latinos, Native Americans, and immigrants from the global South.[2] The growth of the prison population in the United States has had a devastating impact on women of color. The incarceration rate is increasing even more rapidly for women than for men. Of the approximately 100,000 women now in U.S. prisons and jails, 60 percent are women of color.[3] Thousands of people of color are in prison for violations of immigration law, many of them women and the mothers of U.S. citizens. Under the Illegal Immigration Reform and Immigrant Responsibility Act of 1996, these women are involuntarily deported after serving prison sentences, permanently separated from their children and families who continue to live in the United States.[4] Often women are deported to countries where they have no remaining family, cultural ties, or resources. It is no wonder that these women risk serial arrests, additional prison sentences, and successive deportations to reunite with their families.

Punishment for Profit

In addition to enforcing control over communities of color, continuing prison expansion has been adopted as part of a strategy for economic recovery. In the 1960s, the military-industrial complex emerged as a partnership between the U.S. military and private corporations that profited from U.S. military incursions around the world. Similarly, the prison-industrial complex is an interweaving of private business and government interests, extremely profitable when the end of the Cold War signaled a decline in military spending. Although the military-industrial complex is reemerging as a result of Bush's military agenda, the growth of the prison-industrial complex has been a profitable interim strategy for numerous corporations. Comparing 1998 spending on crime control ($210 billion) with government spending on defense ($256 billion), Nils Christie notes, "The costs of the war against the enemies within is now approaching the costs against the enemies outside the country. While military spending is going down, the spending on crime is going up. It evens out."[5]

In the lull between wars during the last twenty-five years, defense industry giants such as Westinghouse retooled and lobbied Washington for their share of the domestic law enforcement market. "Night Enforcer" goggles used in the Gulf War, electronic "Hot Wire" fencing ("so hot NATO chose it for high-risk installations"), and other equipment once used by the military are now being marketed to the criminal justice system. A growing "specialty item" industry sells fencing, handcuffs, drug detectors, protective vests, and other security devices to prisons.

With over two million people currently inside U.S. prisons and jails, the construction and maintenance of prisons are big business, just like the arms industry and maintenance of armed forces. Increasingly, private corrections companies are building and running prisons. One of the largest private prison companies, Corrections Corporation of America (CCA), operates internationally with more than sixty-eight facilities in the United States, Puerto Rico, Australia, and the United Kingdom.[6] Under contract by state and federal governments to run jails and prisons, corporations such as CCA are paid a fixed amount per prisoner, so they operate as cheaply as possible in order to make the greatest profit. Prison owners are raking in billions of dollars by cutting corners, which harms prisoners. Substandard diets, inadequate healthcare, unsafe conditions, and abuses by poorly trained personnel have all been documented in these institutions, which are unabashedly about making profits.[7]

Communications companies such as AT&T, Sprint, and MCI are also profiting by gouging prisoners and their families with exorbitant phone calling rates—up to six times the normal long-distance charges. Some firms, such as Corrections Communications Corporation, operate phone systems only in prisons and provide systematic surveillance services for prison administrations. These companies are reaping huge profits at the expense of prisoners and their families; prisoners are often effectively cut off from communications because of the excessive cost of phone calls. Because 80 percent of women prisoners are mothers, this makes developing and maintaining relationships with their children even more difficult, if not impossible. This is heartbreaking to women inside and destroys the family and community structures in communities of color.

Another source of profit for private companies is prison labor. Companies that use prison labor include IBM, Motorola, Compaq, Texas Industries, Honeywell, Microsoft, Boeing, Starbucks, Victoria's Secret, Revlon, and Pierre

Cardin.[8] Nordstrom's department stores market "Prison Blues" jeans as well as T-shirts and jackets made in Oregon prisons. Prisoners around the United States produce curtains and bedspreads, furniture, electronic components, security glass, stainless steel tanks, and cables and perform computerized telephone messaging, data entry, dental equipment assembly, and many other tasks for the profit of private industry. They are paid pennies per hour—in UNICOR, the prison industry operated by the federal prison system, wages start at twenty-two cents per hour.

As with any industry, the prison economy needs raw materials. In this case the raw materials are prisoners, including increasing numbers of women of color. The prison-industrial complex can grow only if more and more people are incarcerated, even if crime rates drop. Increasing corporate profits has been an incentive for the growth of the prison-industrial complex in the United States.

Life Inside a Police State

Over the past two decades, any pretense of rehabilitation in U.S. prisons has been replaced by pure punishment and warehousing. As a result, these institutions have become the embodiment of a militarized society. Women in U.S. prisons are truly experiencing life inside a police state. As a federal prisoner from 1985 to 2001 at FCI-Dublin and other prisons and jails, I experienced this militarized existence firsthand.

Every action of every day is strictly regimented, with rules enforced by a prison military hierarchy complete with lieutenants and captains. Prisoners' individual identities are purposely diminished: they wear uniforms, move only at prescribed times under strict supervision, and are subject to random and sexually abusive pat or strip searches. Women prisoners live in a compound surrounded by chain-link fences and razor wire; usually their only view is of other prisons. They are isolated from their communities—prisons are typically sited on military bases or in remote rural areas, which makes visiting difficult to impossible. Most states have only one women's prison, which virtually guarantees that visitors will have to travel long distances at great expense to visit. Women prisoners are separated from their loved ones for years on end, sometimes literally ripped apart from their children by police or prison guards in the visiting room. Their compliance is reinforced with behavior modification and harsh punishment, including disciplinary segregation and long periods of twenty-four-hour lockdown. Rehabilitative vocational and educational programs have virtually disappeared in recent years. Cutbacks in budgets for these programs have been severe, while guards' salaries and allocations for increased security measures continue to rise. For example, in 2003, when Governor Gray Davis of California faced massive protests about budget cuts to social services without cuts to his prison budget, he responded by firing every teacher in the entire California prison system. This repressive atmosphere leaves life-long scars on women, most of whom already suffer from histories of domestic violence and abuse.

Besides the permanent damage done to individuals, the mass incarceration of women has an incalculable cost to our communities. In the United States today, ten million children have one or more parents who have been in prison.[9] When a mother is imprisoned, children end up in foster care, looked after by grandmothers or aunts—still more women of color who are suffering real hardships from the expansion of the prison state. Rosalie Davis, for instance, is a sixty-two-year-old African American woman in Oakland, California, raising her third set of children—her great-grandchildren.[10] Rosalie's daughter was locked up in California's prisons when her children were young, and Rosalie rescued them from the notorious abuses of the foster care system. Years later, Rosalie's adult granddaughter was murdered, a victim of street violence. So Rosalie stepped in once again, this time to rescue her great-grandchildren. Typical of many African American women in the United States, Rosalie worked two jobs while raising her children, grandchildren, and great-grandchildren as a single mother. Her story reflects just one way in which the voracious expansion of the U.S. prison system affects women of color. This expansion has not made women in poor urban communities any safer. On the contrary, incarceration, racism, and poverty generate a mutually reinforcing cycle of violence and social disintegration.

The Permanent Stigma of Imprisonment

As attitudes toward criminalized populations have hardened, previously covert practices of discrimination have been converted into public policy. Numerous measures have been passed that cumulatively exclude millions of former prisoners from political, social, or economic participation in society. In eighteen states, women convicted of drug felonies can never again receive welfare benefits or food stamps.[11] They are ineligible for student loans, denying them access to education, one of the most effective deterrents to recidivism. Felons are denied employment in a multitude of occupations that require certification or licensure, such as nursing and other medical professions, teaching, real estate, and the law. People with felony convictions are also excluded from access to any job requiring a security bond, such as nighttime janitor jobs. For example, Rashida Johnson had been employed as an x-ray technician for over ten years before her arrest and imprisonment. Her felony conviction means that now she is permanently banned from employment in her chosen profession.[12] Nearly four million people have lost their right to vote because of felony convictions—democratic rights are a permanent casualty of the war on crime.[13]

Women who have been in prison over fifteen months may permanently lose custody of their children under provisions of the 1997 Adoption and Safe Families Act. In many states, women must repay child support payments made by the state to foster care families—often amounting to thousands of dollars—before they can regain custody of their children. Inability or failure to pay court-imposed fines and restitution may also result in termination of parental rights. Children of incarcerated parents are five times more likely to be arrested as juveniles than other children.[14] Women watch their own children imprisoned at skyrocketing rates and mourn for the future of their families. Their communities are being torn apart by the war on drugs and the war on crime—which women experience as a war on their families, their neighbors, and themselves.

"One-strike eviction" policies in public housing mean that women convicted of drug felonies are not eligible for public housing. In fact, the U.S. Supreme Court recently ruled that whole families may be evicted because of suspected criminal activity by any member of the family.[15] These policies also mean that women living in public housing cannot legally take in and care for their children returning from prison. As a result in part of one-strike evictions, thirty to fifty percent of parolees in urban areas become homeless, many of them women and children.[16]

After September 11: The Surveillance State

The militarization of U.S. society and the drive for social control extend beyond mass imprisonment. The gradual erosion of civil rights for people of color over the last thirty years has intensified since the attacks of September 11, 2001, through legislation such as the USA PATRIOT Act (Uniting & Strengthening America through Providing Appropriate Tools Required to Intercept and Obstruct Terrorism). Government surveillance of the populace has been expanded through the consolidation of existing video surveillance networks and widespread installation of new surveillance cameras in public places. New wiretapping laws allow interception of telephone and computer communications without evidence of criminal activity or even suspicion that any laws have been broken. A "Total Information Awareness system" is being instituted at untold cost by John Poindexter, whose ties to the Iran-Contragate scandal have been officially buried. There is news every day of more special surveillance apparatus being put into place in cities and small towns all over the United States. This expanded repressive apparatus is legitimated by a culture of fear fueled by federal terror alerts and reinforced by constant media coverage of "terrorism preparedness."

Expanding the domestic war on terrorism has also required a major expansion of the political police. Just a few months after the September 11 attacks on the World Trade Center and the Pentagon, the Bush administration established the Department of Homeland Security. This Cabinet-level department consolidates surveillance operations of over one hundred government agencies. Its budget—$38.1 billion—is 10 percent more than the combined budgets of all the agencies it enfolded.[17] This money is desperately needed for social programs, drug rehabilitation, education, and health care, particularly in poor communities and communities of color. The FBI's Joint Terrorism Task Force has been expanded to thirty-four cities and includes a full one quarter of the FBI's active personnel, with fighting terrorism as its official priority. The definition of "domestic terrorism" has been broadened to include "groups or individuals operating entirely inside the U.S., attempting to influence the U.S. government or population to effect political or social change by engaging in criminal activity."[18] The pretext of "suspected criminal activity" is no longer a requirement for surveillance of political activists or organizations. The CIA's new mission, which allows it to conduct surveillance against people inside the United States, is a significant break with previous policy. This heralds the return of the controversial Counter Intelligence Program (COINTELPRO) that conducted illegal covert operations in the 1960s and 1970s against the Black Panther Party, the American Indian Movement, the Puerto Rican Independence Movement, and also organizations from the socialist left. Prisoner advocates are not immune from this renewed drive to police political activism. For example, the New York offices of Critical Resistance, a prison abolitionist organization, were raided by police in November 2003, leading to numerous arrests under spurious charges. Police accountability activists in San Francisco have also been targeted for investigation as part of the antiterrorism drive. These arrests and interrogations demonstrate that police powers allowed in the fight against so-called domestic terrorism will actually be used to suppress political dissent and undermine community efforts to challenge the impunity of the police and prison authorities.

Criminalizing Immigration

The U.S. Citizenship and Immigration Service (formerly Immigration and Naturalizations Service, INS), part of the Department of Homeland Security, has also expanded its participation in the "war against terrorism." Practices of racial profiling such as police stops for "driving while Black and Brown," once denied by law enforcement, have now been expanded and legitimized as public policy, including a requirement that Arab men from over twenty-five nations register and submit to INS interrogation.[19] Arab and Arab American women have lost their sons, brothers, and husbands with no notice because these men have been detained and held incommunicado. Although widespread resistance resulted in a temporary halt to registration procedures, Arab Americans and those assumed to be Muslim continue to be profiled, both by law enforcement officials and by a general public encouraged to be vigilant in search of "terrorist" suspects.

The militarization of the U.S. border initiated in the 1990s has been enhanced by the war on terror. At the same time, state border enforcement has been supplemented by white supremacist vigilantes who hunt down undocumented immigrants, uninhibited and often encouraged by Border Patrol agents.[20] The fact of being an economic refugee has been criminalized. Women from Mexico, Central America, and South America seeking employment as domestic servants or service sector workers are the invisible victims of the xenophobic drive for secure borders; thousands of these women are arrested and imprisoned every year for illegal border crossings. Border walls complete with infrared cameras and high-intensity lights have been installed at key border crossing points, forcing migrants to cross at more dangerous locations. This increased militarization of the border has resulted in additional deaths from exposure and dehydration.

"Free trade" has also had significant implications for the criminalization of immigrants in the United States. North American Free Trade Agreement (NAFTA) regulations have drastically increased imports of food produced by U.S. agribusiness, destroying traditional agriculture throughout Mexico. Millions of campesinos/as have been driven off their land into poverty and the slums surrounding Mexico City. They are refugees in their own country, victimized by U.S. policies of free trade that are enforced by the World Trade Organization. Mexico's economic policies are directly controlled by the U.S.-dominated International Monetary Fund (IMF) and the World Bank, making sovereignty an illusion. Mexican women in particular are suffering profound economic insecurity under the neoliberal regime[21] As a result, more women are driven to seek work in the United States, many of them crossing illegally and risking imprisonment, deportation, and death.

The criminalization of immigration is the direct result of economic globalization. Policies dictated by the IMF, World Bank, and World Trade Organization have caused the deterioration of economic sovereignty and of living conditions in developing nations. Racist immigration quotas and the difficulty of obtaining legal entry into the United States have forced undocumented workers into dangerous illegal border crossings. Millions of people have migrated from their homelands to the United States, simply struggling for basic survival for themselves and their families.

Exporting the War against Terrorism

The expansion of domestic surveillance in the war against terrorism has been mirrored in the expansion and consolidation of antiterrorism forces worldwide, under the leadership of the United States. After September 11, the United States was quick to define the terms: "Every nation, in every region, now has a decision to make. Either you are with us, or you are with the terrorists," President Bush expounded just a few days after the attacks.[22] The Bush administration has threatened and coerced nations to join the war against terrorism or face severe reprisals, including the withdrawal of military aid. Nations around the globe have fallen into line, instituting antiterrorism measures modeled after U.S. laws. Through its control over World Bank and IMF policy, the United States has ensured that indebted nations increase their police and military while severely cutting government spending on social services.[23] The United States dominates the International Association of Chiefs of Police, providing ideological leadership, technical assistance, and training for police forces internationally. The FBI has a presence in numerous countries, including legal attaches in thirty-two countries, including Thailand, Russia, the Ukraine, Italy, and countries in South America. Its international training program has trained over thirteen thousand members of law enforcement from over sixty countries.[24] U.S. control over police forces internationally has long been an unrecognized adjunct to overt military strategy.

One of the fundamental requirements of structural adjustment loans made by the IMF and World Bank is the privatization of government services, which may include the privatization of prisons. The United States has also proposed new regulations in the World Trade Organization that will require international bidding competitions for the provision of government services, such as the operation and maintenance of prisons.[25] These provisions will open the international market to the U.S. private prison industry.

The Legacy of a Global Police State

The U.S. military strategy for global hegemony has been in place for decades. U.S. imperialism—political and economic global domination—is based firmly on U.S. military might. The 2003 U.S. Defense Department budget was $379 billion—more than $1 billion a day.[26] The United States operates permanent military bases in over fifty countries, with thousands of U.S. troops permanently stationed on foreign soil. At the time of writing, the United States is already waging war in Iraq, Colombia, the Philippines, Afghanistan, and by proxy in Palestine through an annual $3 billion in U.S. aid to Israel. Economic sanctions are in place against Cuba. Special operations by U.S. armed forces and U.S.-funded paramilitaries are ongoing and take many forms. "Plan Colombia," instituted ostensibly to fight "narco-terrorists," enables the United States to intervene in a decades-old civil war with the goal of eliminating the leftist Fuerzas Armadas Revolucionarias de Colombia (FARC). "Training exercises" involving hundreds of U.S. troops were recently reinitiated in the Philippines after decades of struggle by the Filipino people had finally eliminated U.S. bases.

Women's everyday lives have been devastated by U.S. militarism and imperialism. In Iraq, for example, women have been seriously affected by economic sanctions since 1990, even before the war intensified and the U.S. occupation began. They watched their children die because medicines were unavailable for a multitude of treatable diseases, including diarrhea, respiratory diseases, and malnutrition. Thousands of children die from leukemia, cancers, and other effects of depleted uranium left by U.S. missiles and bombs. Even before the 2002 invasion of Iraq, one in four Iraqi children was born at under five pounds. These children are part of what foreign medical teams refer to as the "stunted generation," small and vulnerable to disease, their life expectancy reduced by 30 percent.[27] In the 2003 invasion, thousands of Iraqi men, women, and children were killed by the U.S. military, and thousands more will suffer as a result of the wholesale destruction of their society's infrastructure.

Enforced by the global policeman, IMF/World Bank structural adjustment loans require the sale of national resources and public utilities to private corporations. This results in incredible hardship for the women of indebted nations. When drinking water suddenly starts to cost money, women have to walk farther to get water or risk drinking contaminated water. When electricity prices triple because a public utility is privatized, the price of basic necessities increases. When even elementary schools start charging tuition, children, especially girls, do not learn to read. When hospitals charge for medical care and medicines, children die. Conditions imposed by structural adjustment loans have drastically cut back government health, social service, and education budgets, resulting in increases in infant mortality and illiteracy and shortening peoples' lives in developing nations. Families have been separated by the need for family members to work in the city or in another country to earn money to send home. Subsistence agriculture has been taken over by international agribusiness, causing families to become landless, hungry, refugees. These conditions have caused people in many countries to resist in every way imaginable. World Bank riots have taken place all over Latin America, Africa, and Asia. Massive demonstrations against privatization of public resources are commonplace. Women of color have led many of these struggles—from India to Nigeria to Mexico—demanding what their communities need for survival and rebirth and resisting the militarization of their societies.

Resistance to U.S. militarism also brings women of color into conflict with the law. In Puerto Rico, the U.S. Navy has enforced its continuing colonial domination over the island of Vieques by using the island for practice bombing runs, despite a Puerto Rican plebiscite that mandated immediate withdrawal of U.S. armed forces from its territory. Over a thousand men and women have been arrested in the last three years for "trespassing" on land that the U.S. Navy stole from the islanders, struggling to end the cancers and other health problems related to pollution from these "war games." Nilda Medina, one of the leaders of the Comité pro el Rescate y Desarollo de Vieques (Committee for the Rescue and Development of Vieques), has been arrested numerous times for "trespassing" on the U.S. military bases on the island, attempting to stop the bombardment of the island with her body and her life. In just two weeks, from January 13 to February 1, 2003, over 100 tons of bombs were dropped on the tiny island—bombs that left heavy metals of uranium oxide and other military toxics.[28] Massive protests succeeded in making military use of the island impractical and unmanageable, and the U.S. Navy abandoned its war games as of May 1, 2003. But after May 1, Nilda Medina and other protesters were arrested once again.

Conclusion: Building a Feminist Internationalist Justice Movement

Inside the United States and in nations around the world, women are actively opposing mass incarceration, the growth of the international prison-industrial complex, and the imposition of the prison/police state as a model of governance. These phenomena are intricately connected to broader political and economic agendas. The imposition of neoliberal capitalism on developing nations, for example, requires intensified social control mechanisms such as increased imprisonment and surveillance of internal resistance movements. Global domination by U.S.-led capitalism is constantly strengthening its hegemony over the people of the world through military, economic, and political strategies. U.S. imperialism has never been stronger. The war on terrorism is another cover for expanding the power of the police state—a sequel to the war on crime and the war on drugs

In order to be effective, women who are fighting for racial justice and to dismantle the prison-industrial complex must base our movement on an understanding of the complex connections between warfare against communities of color inside the United States, international and domestic effects of economic globalization, and the international war against terrorism. Worldwide resistance to globalization has mandated the political development of the war against terrorism, just as surely as suppressing revolutionary movements in the United States during the 1960s and 1970s required mass incarceration of people of color to ensure social control. The attacks of September 11 simply provided a convenient rationale for imposing previously prepared scenarios of repression.

The growth of the global police state is unprecedented, and the survival of our communities requires an urgent and united response. In the 1960s and 1970s, women fought in national liberation movements, successfully challenged the hegemony of U.S. imperialism, and won independence and self-government. Women in the anti-imperialist movement allied ourselves with people fighting for their freedom and self-determination. We emulated the example of women freedom fighters in liberation movements around the world. We participated in armed actions against U.S. political and military targets, believing that building a revolutionary struggle for socialism could bring about equality and liberation for all women. Many women of color were revolutionary leaders—members of the Black Panther Party and Black Liberation Army, Puerto Rican independentistas, members of the American Indian Movement fighting for sovereignty for Native American nations. Some white women were allies with these struggles, believing that solidarity in action could defeat U.S. empire building. In the course of the struggle, many women were arrested for our actions. We were sentenced to the maximum sentences allowed by law and prosecuted in consecutive trials when the maximum sentences did not guarantee life imprisonment. Like women resistance fighters around the world, we became political prisoners. Some of us are still in prison, and most of us continue to fight against the imperialist system that oppresses the entire world in the guise of the global policeman. Perhaps the most important lesson we can communicate is that the struggle continues and will continue until our children and grandchildren can one day be free. The future awaits us all, but we can win only if we dare to struggle. And it is imperative that we unite internationally. Capitalist globalization is an international phenomenon, and it requires internationalist resistance.

References

1. Richard Milhous Nixon, "Message on Crime Control," in *State of the Union Message*, 1973.
2. Editorial, *New York Times*, April 9, 2003.
3. National Women's Law Center, "Women in Prison," in *Walkin' Steel '95*, ed. Committee to End the Marion Lockdown (Chicago: Committee to End the Marion Lockdown, 1995).
4. Center for Law and Social Policy and Community Legal Services, *Every Door Closed: Barriers Facing Parents with Criminal Records* (Washington, D.C.: Center for Law & Social Policy, 2002), 91–104.
5. Nils Christie, *Crime Control as Industry: Towards Gulags, Western Style* (London: Routledge, 2001), 140.
6. Avery F. Gordon, "Globalism and the Prison Industrial Complex: An Interview with Angela Davis," *Race and Class* 40 (October 1998–March 1999), 150.
7. Judith Green, "Bailing out Private Jails," *The American Prospect* 12, No. 6 (September 10, 2001).
8. Ibid 149. See also Eve Goldberg and Linda Evans, *The Prison-Industrial Complex and the Global Economy* (Montreal: Kersplebedeb Publishing, 2003), 11–14.
9. Charlene Wear Simmons, *Children of Incarcerated Parents*, 7(2) California Research Bureau Note 2 (March 2000).
10. Adair Lara, "To Grandmother's House They Go," *San Francisco Chronicle*, December 29, 2002.
11. Patricia Allard, *Life Sentences: Denying Welfare Benefits to Women Convicted of Drug Offenses* (Washington, D.C.: The Sentencing Project, 2002), 3.
12. Personal testimony to the author, January 2004.
13. The Sentencing Project and Human Rights Watch, *Losing the Vote: The Impact of Felony Disenfranchisement Laws in the United States* (Washington, D.C.: The Sentencing Project, 1998), 1.
14. Women's Prison Association and Home, Inc., *Family to Family: Partnerships between Corrections and Child Welfare* (New York: Women's Prison Association and Home, 1998), 8.
15. Supreme Court, Department of Housing and Urban Development v. Rucker, Oakland Public Housing Authority v. Rucker, #00-1770, 00-1781, March 26, 2002.
16. Southern California Criminal Justice Consortium, *Los Angeles in Lockdown* (Los Angeles: Criminal Justice Consortium, 2001).

17. Center for Arms Control and Non-Proliferation, *Homeland Security Budget* (Washington, D.C.: Center for Arms Control and Non-Proliferation, 2003).
18. Federal Bureau of Investigation, "If You Encounter Any of the Following, Call the Joint Terrorism Task Force" (Phoenix, AZ: FBI, 2002).
19. The National Security Entry-Exit Registration System was announced on June 6, 2002 by Attorney General Ashcroft. Stating that the USA PATRIOT Act called for the establishment of an entry-exit registration system, Ashcroft announced that men over sixteen, primarily from Muslim countries, would be required to register and submit to fingerprinting and photographs. Countries affected include Afghanistan, Algeria, Armenia, Bahrain, Egypt, Eritrea, Indonesia, Iran, Iraq, Jordan, Kuwait, Libya, Lebanon, Morocco, North Korea, Oman, Pakistan, Qatar, Saudi Arabia, Somalia, Sudan, Syria, Tunisia, United Arab Emirates, and Yemen. U.S. Department of Justice, *Fact Sheet: National Security Entry-Exit Registration System* (Washington, D.C.: Department of Justice, June 6, 2002).
20. Border Action Network, *Hate or Heroism: Vigilantes on the Arizona-Mexico Border* (Tucson: Border Action Network, 2002).
21. Lynn Stephen, "Democracy for Whom? Women's Grassroots Political Activism in the 1990s, Mexico City and Chiapas," in *Neoliberalism Revisited: Economic Restructuring and Mexico's Political Future*, ed. G. Otero (Boulder, CO: Westview Press, 1996).
22. George W. Bush, "President's speech to Joint Session of Congress," September 20, 2001.
23. 50 Years Is Enough Network, *Economic Justice News* (New York: 50 Years Is Enough Network, October 2001 and January 2004). See also publications of the International Forum on Globalization.
24. Federal Bureau of Investigations, http://www.fbi.gov, accessed February 23, 2003.
25. Working Group on the WTO/MAI, "A Citizen's Guide to the World Trade Organization" (Washington, D.C.: Public Citizen, July 1999), 19–20.
26. International Network of Engineers and Scientists against Proliferation, *U.S. Defense Budget Request for Fiscal Year 2003*, Bulletin 19. http://www.inesap.org, accessed November 30, 2003.
27. Ramsey Clark, "Report to the UN Security Council re Iraq," January 26, 2000.
28. Comité pro Rescate y Desarollo de Vieques, Press Release, January 26, 2003. www.prorescatevieques.org, accessed November 30, 2003.

Part III
From Criminalization to Resistance

CHAPTER 17

Pierce the Future for Hope

Mothers and Prisoners in the
Post-Keynesian California Landscape

RUTH WILSON GILMORE

[W]hen the woes of the poor press most dangerously upon the rich, then an age searches most energetically to pierce the future for hope.[1]

Introduction

Under the surface of sweeping political, economic, and social changes—the sum effects of neoliberal globalization's forces and abandonments—many oppositional grassroots groups have emerged. This chapter details such a group situated in 1990s Los Angeles. The chapter's purpose is to demonstrate the inverse mirror image of globalization and particularly to show how crises, at various scales, also present—sometimes surprising—opportunities for organizing and action.

Mothers Reclaiming our Children (Mothers ROC) began to organize in November 1992 in response to a growing crisis: the intensity with which the state was locking their children of all ages into the criminal justice system.[2] At the outset, the ROC consisted of only a few mothers and others, women and men, led by founder and president Barbara Meredith and life-long activist Francie Arbol. The initial project was to mobilize in defense of Meredith's son, an ex-gangster, who had been instrumental in the now-historic Los Angeles gang truce. The ROC lost his case but gained the makings of a movement. By the spring of 1993, when the LA Four went to trial, Mothers ROC had developed a network throughout greater Los Angeles and achieved recognition as an organization devoted to action rather than to commentary.[3]

The Mothers ROC mission is "to be seen, heard, and felt in the interest of justice." To achieve this goal, Mothers ROC convenes its activism on the dispersed stages of the criminal justice system. The group extends an unconditional invitation to all mothers struggling on behalf of their children, and it reaches its audience in various ways. The primary method is leafleting public spaces around jails, prisons, police stations, and courthouses to announce the group's existence and purpose. When distributing flyers and business cards, members try to engage people in conversations to explain further what Mothers ROC is and does. ROCers give talks and workshops at elementary and secondary schools, colleges and universities, churches, clubs, and (with decreasing frequency) prisons and jails. They also appear on regional and local radio and television programs. Using these means, Mothers ROC has established a presence at many locations throughout the political geography of the penal system.

ROCers have attracted hundreds of mothers who want to fight on behalf of their own children in the system. Many were already performing in solitude the arduous labor of being on the outside for someone—trying adequately to switch among the many and sometimes conflicting roles required of caregivers, waged workers, and justice advocates. Some attend one meeting and never return, and others persist whether their person's case loses or wins. Often newcomers bring someone to the meeting for moral support—marriage or other partner, relative, child, friend from church or neighborhood, and that person also becomes active. Usually twenty-five women and men participate in each weekly gathering. Most of them learned about the ROC from one of the outreach practices just noted or from an acquaintance who had direct contact with a member. The rest, however, were guided to the organization by their persons in custody. Among the tens of thousands awaiting trial or doing time in juvenile detention camps and centers, in county jails throughout the Southland, and in State prisons, knowledge of Mothers ROC circulates by word of mouth, and a standard part of the message is that the women are willing to help with even apparently hopeless cases.

The ROC's principle is printed on every flyer: "We say there's no justice. What are we going to do about it? . . . EDUCATE, ORGANIZE, EMPOWER." Mothers ROC makes no judgment about the innocence of charged persons whose families turn to the group. The group does not provide services to mothers but rather helps them learn how each part of the system works and, as we shall see, to grasp the ways in which crisis can be viewed as an opportunity rather than a constraint. In the process of cooperative self-help, the mothers transform their reproductive labor as primary caregivers into activism; the activism expands into the greater project to reclaim all children, regardless of race, age, residence, or alleged crime. Experienced ROCers team up with newcomers to call on investigators and attorneys. They research similar cases and become familiar with the policies and personalities of prosecutors and judges. In addition, ROCers attend each others' hearings or trials. They also observe courtroom practices in general and monitor individual officers of the court or state's witnesses believed to promote injustice. The group's periodic demonstrations outside courthouses and police stations bring public attention to unfair practices. Finally, ROCers sponsor monthly legal workshops with activist attorneys and request research reports from scholar-activist members, to help mothers become familiar with the bewildering details of the system in action.

Never an exclusively Black organization, Mothers ROC presumed at first that it would appeal most strongly to African American women because the state seemed to concentrate its energies on taking their children. However, the sweeping character of the State's new laws, coupled with the organization's spatially extensive informational campaigns, brought Chicanas, other Latinas, and White women to Mothers ROC for help, and the group eventually came to consist of Black, Brown, Yellow, and White women, and some men. Most participants currently have persons in custody. People come to meetings from all over Los Angeles County, western San Bernardino and Riverside Counties, and northern Orange County. Their loved ones are in detention throughout California.

Mothers ROC self-consciously identifies with other Third-World activist mothers, the name deliberately invoking South African, Palestinian, and Central and South American women's struggles. As we shall see, the organization is neither spontaneous and naive, nor vanguard and dogmatic, but rather, to use Antonio Gramsci's formulation of a philosophy of praxis, "renovates and makes critical already-existing activities" of both action and analysis to build a movement.[4]

From Military Keynesianism to Post-Keynesian Militarism

The stories I will tell about Mothers ROC are evidence of how people organize against their abandonment and disposal within oppositional spaces delimited by gender, race, class, and violence. The crisis that Mothers ROC encounters is not unique to the group or the communities they represent. Rather, the crisis emerges from the objective conditions produced by changes in the forces, relations, and geography of capital accumulation in California. These changes, in turn, have produced surpluses of land, labor, finance capital, and state capacity.[5] Since the early 1980s, power blocs have resolved great portions of these surpluses into the state's enormous and costly prison system. In expanding and coordinating its capacities to monitor, to coerce, and to punish, the state at all levels is in process of restructuring its own form and purpose. I call this restructuring the transition from military Keynesianism to post-Keynesian militarism.

Gender, Power, Race, and Space

Huge and powerful structural adjustments are not simply determinate of all social processes and outcomes. The rapid expansion of prison *also* derives from the political, social, and ideological operations of the U.S. racial state.[6] Racism alone does not, however, adequately explain for whom, and for what, the system works. The state's attempt to produce a geographical solution (incarceration) to political economic crisis is informed by racialized contradictions that are also gendered. These contradictions, in all of their everyday messiness, and the attempts by mother-activists to resolve them are this chapter's narrative.

The political and analytical importance of the chapter coheres in three major themes that all have to do with breaking boundaries. The first theme centers on how African American practices of social mothering produce a group of diverse women working toward common goals. The second theme explores how outreach projects successfully permeate the organization of highly segregated social space and in some measure start a process of sociopolitical reintegration. And the final theme concerns mobilizing the symbolic power of motherhood to challenge the legitimacy of the changing state. As we shall see, Mothers ROC refuses to be bound and isolated by the normative limitations of California's gender, class, and race hierarchies. Presenting us a glimpse of utopia's work, Mothers ROC enacts both the possibilities and the difficulties of organizing across the many boundaries that rationalize and reinforce Apartheid America.[7]

Free Gilbert Jones: The Early Political Geography of Mothers ROC

> Mothers suffer a special pain when their children are incarcerated (lost to them). It was from this pain and suffering that Mothers ROC was born! We are an organization of mothers (and others) whose children have been arrested and incarcerated. We fight against the police abuse, the false arrests and convictions, and the unfair treatment throughout the justice system. We educate ourselves and our young about the workings of the criminal justice system.[8]

Nobody disputes that on November 29, 1991 the Los Angeles Police Department shot George Noyes to death at the Imperial Courts public housing project, outside the homes of his mother and grandmother. The still-raging controversy concerns whether he was armed, whether he was kneeling, and whether he was begging for his life. According to members of the George Noyes

Justice Committee, he was executed by a notoriously brutal policewoman. According to LAPD, he was a gangster run amok. No charges have ever been filed in the case.

The killing provoked the beginning of a grassroots realignment of power throughout South Central Los Angeles, producing along the way both the LA Gang Truce and Mothers ROC. Formerly an active gang member, George had recently moved to Sacramento to get out of the life. He died while home for the Thanksgiving holidays. For his family members and friends who began organizing, the nature of George's violent end epitomized their collective experience and dread of the LAPD.[9]

Two of the dead man's cousins, Gilbert and Jocelyn, and their mother Barbara initiated the inquiry into and institution of the means by which those most vulnerable to state violence could begin systematically to shield themselves from it.[10] Family, neighbors, and visitors at Imperial Courts, including George's mother, grandmother, siblings, aunt, and cousins, began to testify among themselves about what they had seen, what they had heard, and how the death could be explained only as murder. Such practice is typical wherever poor people are harassed, hurt, or killed by police.[11] The political problem centers on what to do with the energy that fears and traumas produce. Does the state's discipline work? Does it terrorize everyone into silence, by dividing the "good" from the "bad," by intensifying anxieties that lead to premature deaths due to alcoholism and drug addictions (including cigarettes), heart disease, suicide, crimes of passion, and other killers of the urban working and workless poor?[12]

In order to persuade as many residents as possible that the death concerned them all, the family formed the George Noyes Justice Committee. The committee started meeting at Imperial Courts in the all-purpose room to figure out ways to fight the wrongful death. To mark the moment further, Barbara, Gilbert, and Jocelyn decided to walk the neighborhood. They started with the three South Central public housing projects and asked gangs to declare a one-day truce so that all of George's family and friends—who lived scattered about the area—could attend the funeral. Los Angeles has a steady history of making and remaking itself along highly segregated lines; and material pressures and limits that did not originate with gangs keep certain kinds of people stuck in specific deindustrialized areas.[13]

The dangers of the pilgrimage were many: Gilbert was a well-known gang member who could not pass the streets freely. His sister Jocelyn and mother Barbara could not identify themselves as George's or Gilbert's relatives without simultaneously revealing their familial connections to, and therefore exposing themselves as, potential enemies. And finally, because neither Jocelyn nor Barbara lived in the public housing projects, residents might easily view them as outsiders making trouble in locations intensely surveilled by helicopters, on-site security, caseworkers from income assistance programs, and periodic LAPD raids.[14]

To reassure residents that she was not an "outside agitator" but rather a grieving aunt, fearful mother, and good sister, Barbara started holding meetings for women, especially mothers, at Imperial Courts. She explains:

> I believed we had to start taking care of our children. The police would not think they could get away with shooting our children down in cold blood if we took better care of them. So I started [what eventually became] Mothers ROC at Imperial Courts. We would meet once or twice a week. We talked about grooming, about how to brush and braid your daughter's hair. How your children should look when they leave your house. How they should talk to the police, to strangers, to each other. It seemed to me it was up to us to change things, by doing what we already knew how to do. Our mothers had taught us everything. And our grandmothers, and our aunts, and the ladies next door. They all taught us so we could have a better life. So we have to teach our children for them to have a better life. I think we let them down because we stopped teaching them and talking to them. . . . My [late] husband and I both worked, all day, every day, so our kids could have the things we never had. We thought it was the right thing to do, to work hard and to make our children's lives easier than our lives. But we didn't make their lives easier, we made them harder. And now we have to teach them, and let them teach us where we went wrong.

Born on the eve of World War II, Barbara grew up in Louisiana, enmeshed by formal and informal community networks of family and friends.[15] She married a career military man, lived on bases around the United States including Alaska, and eventually settled in Los Angeles, where she was widowed as her four children reached adulthood. Although many African Americans in Los Angeles achieved modest prosperity during the defense boom of World War II, their segregation from good jobs started at the war's end, and every subsequent recession has hit the community with lasting severity. When the old heavy industries (steel, tire, auto, and to some degree oil) cut workers or closed plants and the waterfront delaborized, direct loss of those jobs, in combination with the disappearance of jobs reliant on that industrial core, left the city's Black working class men without access to alternative, high-wage, local, industries.[16]

Many women from the "stranded communities"[17] concentrated in the projects enthusiastically welcomed Barbara's meetings. They could talk about themselves, their hopes and disappointments, their interrupted life plans. As many as sixty mothers and daughters (and sometimes young sons, but rarely any boys more than four or five years old) might attend one of the sessions, and they eagerly put themselves to the tasks of doing each other's hair and staging fashion shows, while talking about their loved ones who had died violently, who were in prison, or who had simply disappeared. According to Barbara, most of the women were engaged in the informal economy, selling legal goods or providing lawful services for unreported income.[18] At the same time, concern about joblessness—their own, their children's fathers', their children's, and especially their sons'—dominated the discussions that did not focus on grooming, nutrition, or violently premature deaths. The women reported from experience what scholars prove again and again: in the United States, certain types of people have access to certain types of jobs. For Black people looking out from the jail-like complex of the Courts, the landscape of legitimate work is an expanse of big, empty factories; minimum wage service jobs in retail or home health care; unreliable, slow, and expensive public transportation; and bad schools leading, in terms of education and skills, nowhere.[19]

Before Barbara had become deeply involved with the women, but after she had held an organizational meeting to propose her strategy for action, she, Jocelyn, and Gilbert achieved the one-day truce for George's funeral. As they walked and talked with people they emphasized how everyone could relate to a family who had lost a loved one to police violence. Rodney King's beating in March of that year provided a ready and politically charged referent that even extremely hostile listeners could recognize, and it transformed highly segmented groupings into a provisional "we" who might mediate the gang-ontrolled divisions of Los Angeles' streets. Little by little, the older male gang members began to acknowledge their collective power and what it could mean for Rodney King, for George Noyes, for many others, and for themselves, should they decide to allow everyone free passage through the streets of South Central for one day.

The men also agreed to a truce in the name of grieving mothers. They extended their commonsense notion of gangs as "kin" and thereby recognized a central familial figure's claim on their care. "Mother" became, in name, George's mother for whom Barbara, her sister, was a stand-in. Barbara's ability to speak from her heart, to express a mother's pain at losing a child, and to acknowledge her own son's gangster status without glorification or shame, touched men for whom George's death was, at least at first, of minimal importance. On behalf of Barbara, of George's mother, of "mothers," the men agreed to redirect their power and to instruct the gangs to police their streets and themselves in order for the dead man's family to gather for a big, peaceful funeral.

Thus, Barbara forged an alliance among women in the projects, in spite of her own outsider status, by appealing to a power achieved through coordinated maternal practices; they made critical the activities of mothering as necessary, social, and consequential by doing, as a group, what they already knew how to do as individuals.[20] At the same time, she, Gilbert, and Jocelyn persuaded the gangs to rearticulate South Central's divisions and shift their everyday capacity to act as extralegal "shadow states" by realigning their practices from small-scale "interstate" rivalries to an area-wide alliance.[21]

Both groups—mothers and gangs—quite rapidly developed a process of identification focused, at the outset, on realizing a common interest—a nonviolent funeral for a man many of them did not know. But although they came together in the name of children and of mothers, their goal became actionable in the context of their more general interest to struggle against the conditions that required so much organizing to precede so homely an affair as a burial. The everyday brutality that provoked Barbara and her children to bring this particular funeral to the foreground of consciousness provided material and symbolic shape for what was to follow. The interest embodied by those who attended, or who enabled, George's peaceful services gave way to a sense of purpose not bounded by a gravesite or a day. The developing identity of purpose cast the spatially unified legal state as the legitimate object of resistance and opposition against which to organize future actions.

The next stage of organizing shortly followed George's December 9 funeral. During the services, mothers and others who spoke in his memory called for a rally to protest the police murder. At the same time the Imam of a nearby independent mosque offered his house of worship as a sanctuary where the gangsters could work to extend the truce across time and space. The gang reconciliation first embraced the rally: more than five hundred people turned out at the 108th Street Station to accuse the police of murder and to announce the end of the community's passivity, vulnerability, and complicity with respect to brutal treatment too often doled out by the hands of the law.

Gilbert and a number of other gang members, inspired by the turn of events, continued the peacemaking process, each day bringing in more people from a wider and wider region of South Central. Word went out through all sorts of networks alerting Black gangsters everywhere to the possibilities of the historic moment. Barbara attended every meeting at the mosque and continued to hold the self-help discussion groups at the Courts—where sometimes women from other projects would show up to see what was going on. Gang members from the truce meetings would come to report their progress, and women other than Barbara would also attend meetings at the mosque to monitor the proceedings. The George Noyes Justice Committee also continued to meet, with the object of finding an opening in fortress LAPD through which they could successfully lob their charges of wrongful death.

In the middle of February 1992, just as a Justice Committee fundraising dance at the Imperial Courts all-purpose room was about to end, LAPD showed up to arrest Gilbert. They charged him with taking ten dollars during an armed robbery that allegedly occurred outside the building moments earlier. The problem of justice for George immediately widened to include his cousin Gilbert. Barbara, convinced that the purpose of her son's arrest was to stop the work she and her children had started, began to organize on his behalf as well.

While Gilbert was in custody, fighting for his freedom, the Los Angeles uprising (April 29 to May 2) significantly shifted the prevailing political mood of the city. Three days of "multicultural riots"[22] produced both new unities and new divisions. The uprising began in the afternoon, after a suburban jury acquitted the four LAPD officers who had beaten Rodney King. Millions had viewed the four policemen in action, because the beating, videotaped by eyewitness George Holiday, had been extensively and intensively broadcast for more than a year.[23] Several weeks before the verdict became public knowledge, the peacemakers of the Los Angeles gang worlds had signed the truce. Indeed, the riots did not produce the truce; rather, the truce, Mothers ROC, and the uprising were all expressions of the same conditions that characterized relations between the state and stranded Black, Brown, and other poor communities throughout deindustrializing Los Angeles.

Like the four policemen's trial, Gilbert's also changed venue. But, unlike the movement of the officers' trial to Simi Valley, where they would be more likely to have a jury of their peers (police, retired military), the state resited Gilbert's case from Compton—where seating a Black jury is quite easy—to the Long Beach courtroom of a notoriously "antigang" judge. Despite the testimony of numerous witnesses who were with him at the time of the robbery, the jury found Gilbert guilty, and, despite further testimony at the sentencing hearing by former Governor Jerry Brown, Congresswoman Maxine Waters, and others concerning the young man's peacemaking achievements, the judge bound him over to the custody of the California Department of Corrections (CDC) to serve seven years for a ten dollar robbery.

For Barbara, the injustice in both the four policemen's and Gilbert's cases made clear that the object of struggle was not only the South East station house of the LAPD Southern Division. It was the state, at many levels, that took her son away, just as it was the state, at many levels, that enabled the police to take her nephew's life. The CDC assigned her son to Susanville, a prison located more than five hundred miles from Los Angeles, near Reno, Nevada, where the White Aryan Brotherhood reputedly dominated the prisoner population. This assignment terrorized the family on two accounts: First, they feared that his notoriety as a Black gang peace activist would bring him into conflict with the Aryans. Second, Barbara had suffered a heart attack during the fall of 1992, and she was not able to make the long journey to visit him. Mothers ROC launched a successful political campaign to have Gilbert moved closer to home, and he spent about half his time in Tehachapi, about 150 miles north of home, and was released on parole after serving three years and eleven months.[24]

The project to "Free Gilbert Jones" also marks the beginning of the formal organization of Mothers ROC. In alliance with a number of other South Central mothers, many of whom had children in custody as a result of the uprising, Barbara started to hold regular sidewalk protests downtown, at the main Los Angeles County Courthouse, and at Parker Center—the LAPD headquarters. During this phase, in November 1992, Los Angeles activist Francie Arbol met Barbara through the intervention of an LA-based writer/activist who had been impressed both by Gilbert's accomplishments and by Barbara's eloquent persistence. Together, Francie and Barbara founded Mothers ROC.

From Imperial Courts to the State Courts

The formation of Mothers ROC as a political group seeking justice coincided with the restructuring of a disbanded communist tendency that started organizing in several U.S. cities during the 1950s. Nelson Peery, an African American revolutionary, founded the small party. The group was renowned in radical Los Angeles circles for grassroots, issue-oriented organizing with nonparty folks.

Francie Arbol joined the party as a teenager in the 1960s. She always worked on both workplace and community-based issues arising from exploitation and injustice, while raising her two daughters—mostly alone—on a bookkeeper's wages. She brought to Mothers ROC a systematic analysis of social structures and political economy, cast in colloquial terms, and a keen sensibility for how to get things done. Unafraid to engage in spirited debate, she also carries through on any project the group decides to pursue, regardless of her opinion of it.

When Francie and Barbara sat to shape an action-oriented group of mothers, they met in the garage office of the disbanded party's ongoing umbrella organization, the Equal Rights Congress (ERC). The office is about a mile north of the infamous intersection where Reginald Denny and the LA Four had their fateful encounter and seventy-five blocks northwest from the site of George Noyes's murder. The garage sits on property belonging to the Society of Friends, and the living room of the small front house became Mothers ROC's regular meeting place. The house has long been a location for activists to meet, a surprisingly pacific oasis in the midst of a neighborhood in constant flux. People who live in South Central, as well as those from outlying communities, are not afraid to go there because the house is not "of" any particular group's turf.

Mothers ROC announced a regular Wednesday evening meeting beginning in November, and kept it constant. African American mothers came—six, then ten, then twenty, then twenty-five or more. They came to talk about the injustice of the LAPD case compared with that of the LA Four; they came to talk about their own children's cases; they came because there was someone, at last, to talk with about what concerned and frightened them most.

Who did not come? Most of the women who so enthusiastically participated in Barbara's mothering sessions down at Imperial Courts did not make the journey north. Mothers ROC's central premise did not change. Barbara has always been consistent in her invocation of collective mothering as the practice from which activism springs. However, the outright politics of the formal organization seems to have deterred some, especially given its dedication to confronting the state head-on. This aspect seemed dangerous to people who, as noted earlier, live intensively policed lives. Francie's role discouraged others who will not trust White people as a matter of course. And finally, some came and left because rumors that communists controlled the new group spread rapidly, thanks to the inadvertently strategic intervention of two Black policemen.

According to the story that circulated widely through the organization and beyond, the two policemen called on the mother of an LA Four defendant to warn her that her son's case would go much better if she disassociated herself from "those communists" in Mothers ROC. The purpose of the visit is open to dispute: some say the police were trying to break up the group, and others say they were trying to help a struggling Black woman, known personally to one of them, who did not understand the consequences of her activism.[25] The news provoked a crisis in the ROC. Some women wanted Francie expelled; others, including the mother in question, quit. Barbara and Francie held special meetings one weekend at several locations in the city and county, where they fielded questions and engaged in fiery debates about communists, racism, and justice.

Francie candidly discussed her reasons for having become a communist and also described how the party had, in her experience, outlived its usefulness. She also refused to quit the ROC and made clear to those who planned to flee her influence that if she was the biggest problem in their lives they would not have joined the ROC in the first place. The brutality of policemen, the menace of prosecutors, and the meanness of judges with respect to their children were not a response to communism. But could the specter of communism make things worse? Barbara reminded the group that its purpose did not preclude any kind of person from joining and being active—as long as they worked toward the goal of justice for the children.

The debates followed an intricate pattern, demonstrating the rich complexities of common sense in this particular time and place.[26] The systematic critique of state power with respect to criminalized children required the mothers also to question the authority of the state's representatives—police, judges, prosecutors, and other lawyers. If communism were bracketed the mothers would agree in one voice that their problem was, indeed, state violence and systemic injustice. Yet, when confronted by the post-1989 fact of a (former) communist in their midst, many of the women absolutely embraced the state's definition of *the* collective enemy for whom Francie, a tiny Anglo activist, was a stand-in. Most of the women had attended elementary school during the cold war buildup in the 1950s, and the lessons they learned—whether lining up for civil defense drills or studying the geography of "the free world"—informed their current evaluation of possibility and danger. Further, the connection of communism with atheism sits ill with women for whom, as we shall see, God and prayer are vital sources of guidance and strength.

What Barbara and Francie and their allies had to do was help the women see and say that their own children—not "communists"—were "the enemy" now.[27] Even if the policemen represented authentic African American anticommunist fears, rather than the designs of the county prosecutor, the outcome would not change. The ROC's children already labored under the greatest liability—that of having been designated "human sacrifice"[28] in the ongoing drama of a state struggling and restructuring in the context of its own delegitimation at the "end of history." Others versed in radical traditions spoke up during the agonizing debates, but the heat stayed mainly on Francie, who stalwartly took it. Francie was not the only Anglo in the group at the time, but the combination of her whiteness, her radical roots, and her refusal to yield—plus her blunt confrontational style—kept her downstage center during the crisis.

The crisis resolved into a truce among those who stayed, forcing the group to mature quickly into an organization *for* itself despite substantial internal differences. The process heightened suspicions but also enhanced everybody's sense of political identity. That is, while disagreeing with the "politics" figured by Francie and others, the women enacted an alternative political vision by remaining in the fight *as* the ROC. They made clear to all who inquired that *mothers*, not some hidden cadre of White or Black communists, openly and deliberately set the agendas for action. Severance of the ROC from the ERC gave symbolic emphasis to the organization's insistence on autonomy, even though the meeting place, office, and telephone number did not change.

In this period, the group's actions, formerly centered on the Gilbert Jones and the LA Four cases, became generalized so that the ROC could act quickly and consistently on new cases. The ROC set up the systems of court monitoring and initiated the legal workshops. The workshops became primary centers for people to learn about topics such as self-representation, sentence enhancement, and related issues. One crucial item emerged consistently in the workshops: the assumption that a private attorney is preferable to a public defender. Such thought is rooted in U.S. commonsense assumptions that "you get what you pay for." The fact that working people including the mothers "pay" for all the public defenders via taxation is invisible in this schema. However, in the ROC, automatic distrust of public defenders has gradually given way to a view of how sectoral growth in industrialized punishment produces both overworked public defenders and a concomitant expansion of unscrupulous private lawyers looking to make a sure dollar.[29]

The shift in membership—from the proto formation at Imperial Courts to the fully fledged Mothers ROC poised to do battle in the state courts—represented a change in the social position of the women as a group. Nearly all current ROCers perform waged work in the formal economy, and if they do not it is because they are disabled (generally by ailments of poverty and stress such as heart disease and cancer) or they are retired. Many are homeowners who live in modest stucco or frame bungalows or condominiums. They are keenly conscious that they have *something* to lose.[30] The structure of Mothers ROC gives them a framework for hope as well as for action—thus purpose—and it provides the basis for an expansion of their attention from seeking remedies in the courtroom (law) to exposing and changing the ways the system operates (politics).

One State + Two Laws = Three Strikes

Every Mothers ROC meeting is framed by prayer. At the beginning and end of each session the group holds hands in a circle and asks for protection and guidance. The women who lead the prayers have a gift for preaching. Their invocations set and summarize the seemingly endless agenda of reclaiming the children, within a material context of spiritual hope realized through human action. Prayer helps span the visible and invisible social distances among ROCers for whom, in most cases, organized religion is a vital aspect of life. Prayer also demonstrates the power of attentive listening for group building. Anyone in the group may comment affirmatively on the leader's devotional trajectory, and such encouragement of the speaker encourages the collectivity. And finally, by emphasizing the difficulty and urgency of the situation that has brought them together, prayer renews and strengthens the mothers' provisional unity. Individual differences, which occasionally produce incidents, need not become persistent organizational impediments—in a church or in the ROC.

The group meditation on power and powerlessness establishes the scene in which mothers are able to identify with each other. Arrest and incarceration are common in the United States, yet those who are touched by law enforcement are so segregated in many different ways that the experience of confrontation with the legal system does not produce collective oppositional activities. In the ROC and elsewhere, the similarity of mothers' stories can produce a sense of commonalty, but there are no guarantees that such a sensibility will serve as the basis for collective action. Within a social order of wide and deep inequality—most forcefully recognized as racial inequality—mothers are cautious because they know not all children are equally vulnerable to the law's harsh punishments.

When Pearl Daye's thirty-one year-old son called from the police station to say he had been arrested for allegedly shoplifting a package of razor blades from a discount drugstore, she was confused—he had a steady job—and distressed—he had not been in any kind of trouble for more than eight years. Going to the station to post bail, Pearl found it set at an absolutely unattainable $650,000 because the Los Angeles County District Attorney's office charged Harry Daye with a third-strike felony rather than a petty theft misdemeanor. Suddenly, then, the African American man who seemed successfully to have put his life in order faced a mandatory minimum sentence of twenty-five years to life without possibility of parole.

As Pearl related the compounding events of Harry's arrest and accusation at her first Mothers ROC meeting, she often paused because of the almost unendurable anxiety of retelling and revealing seemingly unbelievable adverse family circumstances to strangers. However, the roomful of women recognized the Daye's drama as neither bureaucratic error nor bad dream but rather as an increasingly ordinary conflict between families like theirs and the law. The plot had already become so familiar, one year into implementation of California's Three Strikes Act, that at certain moments a number of women, as though they were a chorus, recited with Pearl what the public defender and others had told her—especially the (street name of the) guaranteed sentence: "Twenty-five to . . . without."

Harry Daye faced the death of freedom because at that time the Los Angeles County District Attorney's written policy was to enforce the three strikes law vigorously. Such vigor includes charging defendants to ensure the longest possible prison sentences, regardless of the current character of the defendant's life. Harry's alleged petty theft constituted what California law designates a "wobbler"—an offense that can be classified, and punished, as either a misdemeanor or a felony. Three strikes and other minimum mandatory sentence laws, conventionally portrayed to work with a machine-like disregard for individual circumstance, actually explicitly allow prosecutors and judges to use discretion "in the interest of justice." However, throughout California—especially in the southern counties where most prisoners are produced—the practice of prosecutorial or judicial discretion in favor of second- or third-strike defendants is so rare as to be newsworthy.[31]

Pearl ended her introductory testimony to Mothers ROC with an observation about the entire system: "The way I see it there are two laws, one for the Black, and one for the White." Leticia Gonzales, a Chicana whose husband had started a "twenty-five to . . . without" sentence some months earlier disagreed. "No. I think there is one law for the People of Color, and another law for the White." By this time, everyone was talking. Francie Arbol proposed another structure: "Poor people, and rich people." But poor versus rich failed to explain the State versus O.J. Simpson: Why was the Los Angeles County District Attorney's office spending so much time and money to convict one Black defendant? Therefore, the distinction could not be rich versus poor. At the same time, because virtually all the prisoners anyone in the room knew or could imagine were people of modest means from working-class families, the money question could not simply be dropped. Anti-Black racism seemed to explain a great deal but could not account for all extreme vulnerability before the law.

In the year or so before Pearl Daye brought her case to the ROC, Latino (mostly Chicano and Mexicano) prisoners surpassed African Americans as the largest group, in absolute numbers, in CDC custody. The unevenness in outcome for people of color lies in the offense with which defendants are charged. Both federal and California laws allow radically different treatment of people who have done essentially the same thing. Such police, prosecutorial, and judicial prerogative—which, since its introduction in the early 1980s, has remained fundamentally impervious to challenges based on "equal protection," "cruel and unusual punishment," and other constitutional principles—provides both the means and the encouragement for application of substantively different rules and punishments to various kinds of defendants.

It is not surprising, then, that the ROCers had a hard time developing a brief characterization of how the law discriminates. The law's ability to wobble makes routinely unequal punishments possible. At the same time, the wobble makes developing a commonsense definition of how such inequality is achieved and reproduced on a case-by-case basis very difficult indeed. Everyone who spoke—nearly everyone in the room—had no doubt that the system operates on a dual track. But how is each defendant routed?

Leticia Gonzales could match Pearl's story horror for horror. Her husband had been tried and convicted for shoplifting a pair of pants during the Christmas shopping rush. She is convinced that either nobody took anything or that somebody else, who looks like her husband, took the things. "Why would he take some pants? He could buy them. And at Christmas, there are guards everywhere around at the stores. He's not stupid." However, since in his deep past he had been convicted on two counts of robbery, the petty theft of a pair of inexpensive trousers became, in his case, robbery, sending him down for "twenty-five to . . . without."

Leticia heard about the ROC from her husband, who heard in the county jail. She was afraid to come to the meeting at first, because she did not know anybody, lived down in San Pedro, and was afraid she might not be welcomed. Much to her surprise, the group, still composed predominately of African Americans, did welcome her, and as the months went by, more and more Latinas showed up at the door. Mothers of sixteen-year-olds charged with murder. Wives of second- and third-strike defendants. Grandmothers of kids charged under the Street Terrorism Enforcement and Protection (STEP) Act of 1998.

Indeed, the Black and Brown cadres of *abuelas* began to hold occasional caucuses—after the manner of the grandmothers of Argentina's *Plaza de Mayo*— to discuss their unique problems, which often centered on their status as undocumented primary caregivers to their children's children.

The number of Latinas attending meetings increased, as the Los Angeles County prosecutor extended vigorous enforcement of California's rapidly expanding body of criminal legislation to Brown as well as Black defendants. The night of Pearl Daye's first visit, the ROC's debate about the law's unequal application continued well into the evening and spilled out onto the sidewalk after the regular meeting came to a close. The crucial issue in resolving the question had to do with maintaining organizational solidarity. Finally, one of the women proposed this solution: There are, as Pearl had said, two laws—one for Black people and one for White people. Given how the prosecutors had started charging more and more Brown, and other poor defendants, under the new laws, especially three strikes, then perhaps the explanation could be put this way: You have to be White to be prosecuted under White law, but you do not have to be Black to be prosecuted under Black law. The resolution satisfied that evening's debaters, as it provided a way to recognize the extension of prosecutorial practices without displacing the African Americans' measurable experience of the most intensive application of the laws.

Situating a Conclusion: The History of Future Struggle

> We think organizations have to be the first step toward a social movement.
>
> Myles Horton, founder, Highlander Center[32]

Mothers ROC is part of a rich history of oppositional struggle and may be compared with several kinds of twentieth-century movements whose systems, organizations, and/or practices resonate with the Los Angeles grassroots women's understanding of social conditions and approach to social change. As with Mothers ROC, the organizations briefly examined in this section mingle reformist and radical ideologies and strategies; in the vision and substance of their political projects, they pose challenges to the oppressive system in question *and* to dominant structures of antisystemic organizing. I believe such complexity expresses an organic relation between these struggles and the specific context of the crises from which they emerge. Here, I differentiate specificity from a narrow conception of localism.[33] The way conflict emerges in a social structure is not inevitable, even though it may be understood, at a higher level of abstraction, to be an expression of a fundamental antagonism—such as class conflict. What happens at the local level has everything to do with forces operating at other scales.

For Mothers ROC, then, three major conditions of existence—and categories of analysis—form the heart of the group's specific response to crisis. These consist of the embeddedness of African American and other working-class mothers in a world only minimally circumscribed by home; the problem of organizing the unorganized in the United States according to strategies other than singular, insular identities (e.g., occupation, race, parental status); and the potential power of "motherhood" as a political foundation from which to confront an increasingly hostile state.

Women whose paid labor is crucial to the household economy and who are normatively measured, in the dominant discourse and the gross domestic product, according to their performance in the gender-segmented labor market, embody different roles with respect to production, reproduction, and politics than women who evade such material and ideological constraints.[34]

In this historical context, motherhood functioned through, and as an attribute of, the woman-as-laborer, enacted as collective, or social, rather than individualized practice.[35] Most children might learn strictly to labor in whatever niche constituted their generation's labor market enclave.[36] At the same time, however, the constant restructuring of labor markets—most notably during wartime—meant that mothers were also educating their daughters and sons in ways of thinking that might lead to more radical consciousness of what change *without* progress meant, given the material and ideological positioning of Black people in the racial state.[37]

Organizing is always constrained by recognition: How do people come actively to identify in and act through a group such that its collective end surpasses reification of characteristics (e.g., identity politics), or protection of a fixed set of interests (e.g., corporatist politics), and instead extends toward an evolving, purposeful social movement (e.g., class politics)?[38]

In a few instances U.S. labor activists have broadened their practices by engaging in a class rather than corporatist approach. Whereas most such efforts resulted in failure—crushed by the capitalist state's coercive and ideological apparatuses—some attempts along this way produced surprising results.[39] An areal approach, dedicated to organizing both workers' clients and workers' communities, is a bottom-up strategy to develop comprehensive regional plans, in which the struggle for outcomes also raises expectations. These raised expectations produce solidarity between households and among waged workers and their dependents.

The divisions between home and work, private and public, on the stage of capitalist culture constitute for many the normative limits to particular kinds of conflict. When the political dimensions of breaches in those limits become apparent in crises, new possibilities for social movements unfold. As we have seen, Black working-class women politicized the material and ideological distance between their paid and unwaged labor by traversing the streets. More recently, janitors around the United States have taken their clandestine exploitation public on a number of fronts, combining community-based organizing with front-line, public sphere militancy led by immigrants. In Argentina, under the fascist military government (1977 to 1983), the Madres of the Plaza de Mayo defied the expectation that women should not meddle in affairs of the state—which is to say the male, or public sphere—by organizing on the basis of a simple and culturally indisputable claim that mothers ought to know where their children are.

The ROC's solutions to the problems constituting the daily struggle to reclaim the children draw from the structural features of radical self-help, from the strategies of organizing on every platform where conflict occurs, and from the argument that mothers should extend their techniques as mothers beyond the mystifying veil of traditional domestic spheres. In a word, they enact the "consciencization" of motherhood.[40] The solutions are grounded in, but not bounded by, local conditions. Indeed, the organicism of Mothers ROC has to do precisely with its attention to the specific sites and scales of power that produce prison geographies *and* to the ways those sites and scales might be exploited for oppositional ends.

A small, poor, multiracial group of working-class people, mostly prisoners' mothers, mobilize in the interstices of the politically abandoned, heavily policed, declining welfare state. They come forward, in the first instance, because they will not let their children go. They stay forward, in the spaces created by intensified imprisonment of their loved ones, because they encounter many mothers and others in the same locations eager to join in the reclamation project. And they push further, because from those breaches they can see, and try to occupy, positions from which to challenge collectively the individualized involuntary migration of urban "surplus population" into rural prisons.[41]

"Arrest is the political art of individualizing disorder."[42] Such individualization produces again and again, for the millions arrested in the United States each year, fragmentation rather than connection as each person and household, dealing with each arrest, must figure out how to undo the detention—which appears to be nothing more than a highly rationalized confrontation between the individual and the state. The larger disorder is then reified in typologies of wrongdoing and formalized as "crime"—which, like unemployment, is alleged to have a "natural" if changing rate in a social formation.[43] ROCers gradually but decisively refuse both the individualized nature of their persons' arrests and the "naturalness" of crime, of working-class poverty, of the coercive (versus caring) power of the state.[44] They arrive at their critique through action. Action, crucially, includes the difficult work of identification—which entails production, not mere discovery, of a "suture"[45] among people whose ties might not be based in blood or soil. Through the socially and spatially complex processes of identification that are attentive to racial, class, and gender specificities as well as commonalties, the ROCers transform themselves and the external world.

By enlivening African American practices of social mothering, the ROCers engage a broadening community in their concern for the circumstances and fate of prisoners. That social opening provides avenues for all kinds of mothers (and others) to join in the work, as the enormous labor confronting each mother tends to encourage all both to accept and to extend help. I make no claim for "social mothering" as an exclusively or universally African American cultural practice; it is neither. However, Barbara Meredith's commonsense invocation of mothering as collective action makes possible the group's integration of mothers with similar or quite different maternalist assumptions (Kaplan 1982; see also Traugott 1995).[46] In other words, techniques developed over generations, on behalf of Black children and families within terror-demarcated, racially defined enclaves, provide contemporary means to choreograph interracial political solidarity among all kinds of mothers losing their loved ones into the prison system. These mothers and others can and do identify each other in the small "public" spaces between their socially segregated residential living places and the "unitized" carceral quarters in which their children are caged. Some members are shy about jumping into the process, and others come to the ROC for help on their individual case only; but all who persist practice the "each one teach one" approach.[47]

The process of integrating different kinds of mothers and others into the ROC involves extensive outreach designed to permeate social boundaries. These projects catch people in the "betweens" of segregated lives: at work, for example, or on the bus. Such areal permeation raises a more general problem of identification. The ROCers easily recognize each other in the spaces of the criminal justice system. Outside those areas, what constitutes resemblance? If we are not all Black, and if all activists are not mothers, and if all prisoners are not (young) children, then who are we? Poor people who work. As a community of purpose, Mothers ROC acts on the basis of a simple inversion: We are not poor because our loved ones are in prison; rather, our loved ones are in prison because we are poor. It follows that outreach should target working poor people and their youth. Class, then, constitutes the context for this analysis and action, but does not displace or subsume racism: poor people of color have the most persons in prison.[48]

Nor does gender disappear, on two accounts; first, women who work to support their families and to free their loved ones encounter each other as laborers with similar triple workdays—job, home, justice. In addition, mothers who reject the disposal of their children, and ask why they themselves should not be compensated for struggling against the state, raise a challenge to both their children's and their own devaluations from the vantage of reproductive labor.[49] The communist organizational and analytical influences in the ROC help keep these overdetermined antagonisms in the foreground of activism. As a result, Mothers ROC is building an alliance that women and men may enter from a number of positions and where they stay because the group's primary purpose retains clarity—even as members repeatedly clash when trying to produce an adequately comprehensive account of the world in which they struggle. In the context of shared antagonism, the activists produce the values they share; in turn, that collective work produces community solidarity, or political integration, enabling further action. Solidarity increases with increased knowledge concerning the complexity with which the state, as a contradictory social actor, works. The alliance tends toward a scale of resolution at which, for example, any individual police precinct house ceases to be the total presence of the state and shrinks back toward its systemic position—the neighborhood outpost of what the ROCers characterize as a military occupation that will require a political movement to disband. As Mothers ROC seeks a wider regional membership, it also seeks to locate itself in a wider community of activism, reaching out nationally and internationally. Such movement heightens the potential for connections between Mothers ROC and women throughout the global workforce who struggle daily against the actual processes and effects of worldwide structural adjustments.

The ineluctable salience of dominant notions of gender and generation shapes the means through which Mothers ROC critically employs the ideological power of motherhood to challenge the legitimacy of the changing state. All prisoners are somebody's children, and children are not alienable.[50] The racial and gendered social division of labor requires mothers of prisoners to live lives of high visibility; ROCers turn that visibility to a politically charged presence, voice, and movement against injustice, such that their activism becomes the centerpiece of their socially productive reproductive labor.[51] As with mothers' movements in Latin America, South Africa, and Palestine, Mothers ROC's front-line relation to the state is not as a petitioner for a share in the social wage but rather as an antagonist against the state's form and purpose with respect to the life chances of their family members and those like them. The insistence on the rights of mothers to children, and children to mothers, is not a defense of "traditional" domesticity as a separate sphere; rather it represents political activation around rising awareness of the ways that the working-class "domestic" is a site saturated by the racial state.

References

1. Peter Linebaugh, *The London Hanged* (Cambridge: Cambridge, 1992), 65.
2. A note on terms: When "State" is capitalized, it refers to California; in lowercase, "state" refers to the political-geographic category, which I will discuss at a number of levels: U.S. federal, California, Los Angeles County, Los Angeles City, and so forth. The state is not a monolith; the conflicts, coordinations, and compromises within and between various scales of the state are the subject of a different segment of this project. However, I do wish to underscore here

that readers who find structural analysis debilitating might (ironically) find reassurance in the indisputable fact that "agency" figures in state practices just as in grassroots movements.

3. The LA Four were the young African American men charged with the widely televised beating of White truck driver Reginald Denny on April 29, 1992, the first day of the Uprising. Denny himself objected to the railroading of the Four.

4. Antonio Gramsci, *Selections from the Prison Notebooks* (New York: International Publishers, 1971), 330–331.

5. For theoretical and empirical elaboration of these surpluses, see Ruth Wilson Gilmore, "Globalization and U.S. Prison Growth," *Race and Class* 40, 2/3 (1998): 171–188 and *Golden Gulag* (Berkeley: University of California, forthcoming).

6. Michael Omi and Howard Winant, *Racial Formation in the United States* (New York: Routledge, 1986).

7. Douglas Massey and Nancy Denton, *American Apartheid* (Cambridge: Harvard, 1993); cf Leela Fernandes, *Producing Workers* (Philadelphia: University of Pennsylvania, 1997).

8. 1995 Flyer, Mothers Reclaiming Our Children

9. Helicopters are the premier symbol of Los Angeles's capitalized, militarized police force; choppers pulse and hover overhead day and night, coordinating motorized ground forces from a superior and flexible vantage point—mobilely panoptic, although lacking the stealth Bentham envisioned. Bear in mind LAPD invented the Special Weapons and Tactics (SWAT) team specifically to police politically organized Black people; see Walton E. Bean, *California: An Interpretive History*, 2nd Edn. (New York: McGraw-Hill, 1973).

10. Cf Joy L. James, *Resisting State Violence* (New York: Routledge, 1997).

11. See, for example, Frances Fox Piven and Richard A. Cloward, *Regulating the Poor* (New York: Vintage, 1971); Stuart Hall et al., *Policing the Crisis* (New York: Holmes & Meier, 1978).

12. Michael Greenberg and Dona Schneider, "Violence in American Cities: Young Black Males Is the Answer, But What Was the Question?" *Social Science and Medicine* 39, 2 (1994): 179–187.

13. B. Marchand, *The Emergence of Los Angeles* (London: Pion Ltd, 1986); Melvin L. Oliver et al., "Anatomy of a Rebellion: A Political-Economic Analysis," in *Reading Rodney King/Reading Urban Uprising*, ed. R. Gooding-Williams (New York: Routledge, 1993), 117–141.

14. Mike Davis, *City of Quartz* (New York: Verso, 1990).

15. Cf bell hooks, *Yearning* (Boston: South End Press, 1990), chs. 5–6.

16. David Grant et al., "African Americans: Social and Economic Bifurcation," in *Ethnic Los Angeles*, ed. Roger Waldinger and Mehdi Bozorgmehr (New York: Russell Sage Foundation, 1996); Oliver et al. 1993; Nelson Peery, *Black Fire* (New York: The New Press, 1994).

17. Jacqueline Jones, *The Dispossessed* (New York: Basic Books, 1992).

18. Cf Heidi Hartmann, "The Family as the Locus of Gender, Class and Political Struggle: The Example of Housework," *Signs* 6, 3 (1981): 366–394.

19. Holly Sklar, *Chaos or Community?* (Boston: South End Press, 1995).

20. Patricia Hill Collins, *Black Feminist Thought* (Boston: Unwin Hyman, 1990).

21. Wolch developed the "shadow state" concept to theorize the rise of nongovernmental organizations in neoliberalism's context. Jennifer Wolch, *The Shadow State: Government and Voluntary Sector in Transition* (New York: The Foundation Center, 1989).

22. Mike Davis, "Uprising and Repression in L.A.," in R. Gooding-Williams ed., 1993, 142–154.

23. Gilmore Ruth Wilson, "Terror Austerity Race Gender Excess Theater," in R. Gooding-Williams ed. 1993, 23–37; Haki R. Madhubuti, *Why L.A. Happened* (Chicago: Third World Press, 1993); Robert Gooding-Williams, ed., *Reading Rodney King, Reading Urban Uprising* (New York: Routledge, 1993).

24. Prisoners are "unitized"—which is CDC jargon for "segregated."

25. A recurring irony in Mothers ROC cases—especially African Americans'—is how frequently the (extended) family knows, or is related to, a police officer (the frequency is related, of course, to the battle by Black people to gain access to state jobs). The fact helps mothers take a systemic, rather than individualized, view of their struggle.

26. Gramsci 1971; Stuart Hall, "Gramsci's Relevance for the Study of Race and Ethnicity," *Journal of Communication Inquiry* 10, 2 (1986): 5–27.

27. Gilmore 1993.

28. Wilmette Brown, *No Justice, No Peace: The 1992 Los Angeles Rebellion from a Black/women's Perspective* (London: International Black Women for Wages for Housework, 1992).

29. Many new Mothers tell the same story—they mortgage the house, or sell the car, in order to pay a lawyer whose contract, it turns out, is only to take the case through the most routine rounds of court filings and appearances. Further, the magnitude of wealth thus depleted is historically low due to racist state and private lending rules (Melvin L. Oliver and Thomas M. Shapiro, *Black Wealth/White Wealth* [New York: Routledge, 1995]; Massey and Denton 1992).

30. A. Sivanandan, *A Different Hunger* (London: Pluto Press, 1982).

31. Cf Tom Gorman, "Lawyer Fired over '3 Strikes' Switches Sides," *Los Angeles Times*, April 25, 1996: A-3.

32. Myles Horton and Paulo Freire, *We Make the Road by Walking* (Philadelphia: Temple, 1990): 124.

33. Gramsci 1971; Doreen Massey, *Space, Place, and Gender* (Oxford: Blackwell, 1994).

34. Eileen Boris, "The Power of Motherhood: Black and White Activist Women Redefine the Political," *Yale Journal of Law and Feminism* Fall (1989): 25–49.

35. Collins 1990; see also Deborah Gray White, *Ar'n't I a Woman? Female Slaves in the Plantation South* (New York: Norton, 1985); Temma Kaplan, "Female Consciousness and Collective Action," *Signs* 7, 3 (1982): 545–566.

36. Paul Willis, *Learning to Labor: How Working Class Kids Get Working Class Jobs* (New York: Columbia, 1997).

37. Clyde Woods, *Development Arrested* (New York: Verso, 1996); George Lipsitz, *A Life in the Struggle: Ivory Perry and the Culture of Opposition* (Philadelphia: Temple, 1987); Chester Himes, *If He Hollers* (New York Y: Thunder's Mouth, 1986 [1945]); Omi and Winant 1986

38. Doracie Zoleta-Nantes, conversation with author, 1995; Gramsci 1971; Hall 1986 and "Cultural Identity and Diaspora," in *Identity: Community, Culture and Difference*, ed. L. Rutherford (London: Lawrence and Wishart, 1990).

39. Phillip Foner, "The IWW and the Negro Worker," *Journal of Negro History* (1970): 45–64; Robin D. G. Kelley, *Hammer and Hoe* (Chapel Hill: University of North Carolina, 1990); Howard Wial, "The Emerging Organizational Structure of Unionism in Low-Wage Services," *Rutgers Law Review* 45 (1993): 671–738.

40. Paulo Freire, *Pedagogy of the Oppressed* (New York: Seabury, 1970).

41. James O'Connor, *The Fiscal Crisis of the State* (New York: St. Martin's, 1973).

42. Allen Feldman, *Formations of Violence* (Chicago: University of Chicago, 1991): 109.

43. See Peter W. Greenwood et al., *Three Strikes and You're Out: Estimated Costs of California's New Mandatory-Sentencing Law* (Santa Monica: The Rand Corporation, 1994); James Q. Wilson and Richard Herrnstein, *Crime and Human Nature* (New York: Simon and Schuster, 1985); Anwar Shaikh, *The Current Economic Crisis: Causes and Implications* (Detroit: Against the Current Pamphlet, 1983 [reprinted 1989]). "Inflation and Unemployment," paper presented at the Brecht Forum (New York, March 1996).

44. See also David Anderson, *Crime and the Politics of Hysteria* (New York: Times Books, 1995); Charles Derber, *The Wilding of America* (New York: St Martins, 1996).

45. Hall 1990.

46. Kaplan 1982; see also Mark Traugott, *Repertoires and Cycles of Collective Action* (Durham: Duke, 1995).

47. A recurrent theme in discussions among many of the shyer mothers is their avowal of, and explanation for, their own unfitness. They refute the dominant explanations—they don't take drugs, rely on welfare, or work in the sex industry. But what lingers is a doubt whether they as women (and men) who might have trouble reading, or who have been afraid to stand up to the law, can ever be fit parents for loved ones caught in a system in which book knowledge and various types of intimidation—intellectual as well as physical—feature centrally in outcomes of cases. Many ask me to accompany them to meetings with officials because they feel stronger knowing that I know all the *words*—as well as the demographics, statistics, history, etc. As they teach each other what they learn, all of the ROCers gain confidence; indeed, those who cannot read well flourish by using their substantial memories to chart and compare cases.

48. Stuart Hall, "Race, Articulation and Societies Structured in Dominance," in UNESCO *Sociological Theories: Race and Colonialism* (Poole: UNESCO, 1980): 305–346.

49. Mariarosa Dalla Costa and Selma James, *The Power of Women and the Subversion of the Community* (London: Falling Wall Press, 1972); Leopoldina Fortunati, *The Arcane of Reproduction: Housework, Prostitution, Labor and Capital* (Brooklyn: Autonomedia, 1995). According to the United Nations International Labor Organisation, women do two thirds of the world's work, receive 5 percent of the income, and own 1 percent of the assets. Activist Margaret Prescod of the Wages for Housework Campaign interprets these figures as illuminating both sexism and racism on a global scale (see Gilmore 1993).
50. Drucilla Cornell, *The Imaginary Domain* (New York: Routledge, 1995).
51. Jo Fisher, *Mothers of the Disappeared* (Boston: South End Press, 1989).

CHAPTER 18

The Justice for Women Campaign
Incarcerated Domestic Violence Survivors in Post-Apartheid South Africa

LISA VETTEN AND KAILASH BHANA

Introduction

Annemarie Engelbrecht is a twenty-nine-year-old South African women currently awaiting trial at Johannesburg Women's prison for the murder of her abusive husband. Interviewed by one of the authors, she observed wryly that nine years in an abusive relationship had prepared her well for imprisonment; her husband's death had not ended the coercive control she was subjected to but merely changed the source of that control. Like many women who kill in order to defend themselves against violent men, Engelbrecht was not protected by the state. Indeed, in the last few months of his life the deceased would offer to call the police himself, taunting her with their repeated failure to come to her aid. In June 2002, after yet another assault, Engelbrecht handcuffed her husband while he was sleeping and smothered him. This response needs to be placed in the larger context of state obligations to address domestic violence, set out in the Constitutional Court judgment *S v Baloyi*:

> Indeed, the State is under a series of constitutional mandates which include the obligation to deal with domestic violence: to protect both the rights of everyone to enjoy freedom and security of the person and to bodily and psychological integrity, and the right to have their dignity respected and protected, as well as the defensive rights of everyone not to

255

be subjected to torture in any way and not to be treated or punished in a cruel, inhuman or degrading way.[1]

In Annemarie Engelbrecht's case, the state did not exercise its mandate "to deal with domestic violence." What are the consequences of the state's failure to meet its obligation to women such as Ms. Engelbrecht? Does such failure affect the moral culpability of women who kill their abusive partners—particularly when they do so following years of indifference on the part of the criminal justice system to the violence inflicted upon them? Further, is imprisonment of such women (possibly for life) an appropriate response by the state to domestic violence?

In this chapter we present a case study of a project that grapples with these questions by challenging the imprisonment of survivors of domestic violence. The Justice for Women Campaign aims to reform law and sentencing practices applied to women such as Annemarie Engelbrecht and to obtain early release for women already serving a sentence for killing their abuser. We begin the chapter with a short, contextualizing description of race and gender inequality in South Africa. This is followed by a statistical outline of the incidence of domestic violence in the country as well as a brief discussion of research investigating conviction and sentencing patterns in cases of domestic violence that have culminated in a killing. We then sketch patterns of imprisonment in South Africa, highlighting the effects of gender and race upon imprisonment. We end with an account of the strategies and activities constituting the Campaign and some reflections on our progress and the challenges we have faced.

Race and Gender Inequality in South Africa

South African society is marked by deep inequalities, and the intersections of race and gender produce particularly egregious disadvantages and losses in individuals' lives. Apartheid, the cornerstone of the National Party, institutionalized four major "race" groups in South Africa: whites, Asians, coloreds, and blacks.[2] This artificial categorization of people on the basis of skin color created a discriminatory hierarchy of advantages and disadvantages, with white people enjoying a disproportionate share of privileges and benefits and people classified as "black" (the indigenous African population) subjected to the greatest hardships and inequality. Sandwiched between these two extremes were "Asians" (or people originating from India) followed by those classified as "colored" (of mixed race descent). Although South Africa's first democratic elections held in 1994 formally signaled the end of apartheid, inequality persists, despite the strides made by the African National Congress (ANC) government. For instance, white men earn almost five times more per hour than African women.

Race also affects the nature and extent of help available to women living in violent circumstances. The Group Areas Act, a key piece of apartheid legislation, designated where people could live on the basis of race. Areas reserved for Black people were allocated fewer hospitals, clinics, and police stations than white areas. In 1994, for instance, 74 percent of the country's police stations were located in white suburbs or business districts.[3] Feminist domestic violence organizations and shelters were first started by white women and, as a consequence, also located within white areas, which effectively placed them out of the reach of the majority of women.[4] With the political shifts initiated in the 1990s, this situation began changing as Black women started setting up township-based organizations. However, many of these community-based organizations remain disadvantaged by their struggle for funds and other resources.[5]

Domestic Violence, Homicide, and Sentencing

Because there is no category of crime termed "domestic violence" in South Africa, few statistics are available recording how many cases of such violence are reported to the police annually.[6] However, a community-based prevalence study conducted in 1997 in three of South Africa's nine provinces found that 26.8 percent of women in the Eastern Cape, 28.4 percent of women in Mpumalanga, and 19.1 percent of women in the Northern Province had been physically abused in their lifetimes by a current or ex-partner. The same study also investigated the prevalence of emotional and financial abuse experienced by women in the year prior to the study. This was found to have affected 51.4 percent of women in the Eastern Cape, 50 percent in Mpumalanga, and 39.6 percent in Northern Province.[7] A study of 1,394 men working for three Cape Town municipalities found that approximately 44 percent of these men were willing to admit to the researchers that they abused their female partners.[8]

It is clear that domestic violence is a major problem that, in one form or another, affects as many as one in two women in some parts of South Africa. Given this prevalence, it is remarkable how few women kill their abusive partners. Indeed, research finds that the risk of being killed by an intimate partner is far greater for women than it is for men.[9] A review of 144 cases in the province of Gauteng found that for every one woman who killed her male partner, four men killed their female partners. More than half of the women killed under circumstances in which they were being abused. The same was not true for male perpetrators, at least a third of whom had a history of abusing their female partner before finally killing her.[10]

Fifty-eight percent of the women were acquitted or given a noncustodial sentence, compared with only 10 percent of the men.[11] However, the study also points to a small group women who received considerably lengthier sentences than almost all of their male counterparts. This was the group of women who killed their abusive partners while they were asleep or otherwise vulnerable or employed third parties.[12] Because there was a delay between the last attack or threat and the killing, the women's actions appeared premeditated. Because their actions did not take place in the heat of the moment, such women could not claim that they were acting in self-defense or responding to an unbearable provocation.[13] It is this group of women who are the focus of the Justice for Women Campaign. In the next section we outline the world that abused women enter once sentenced to a prison term.

Race, Gender, and Imprisonment in South Africa

There are 229 functioning prisons in South Africa, holding 165,217 prisoners as of July 31, 2003. In addition to 180,991 male prisoners, South African prisons hold 4,032 children and 4,226 women with 228 infants. Constituting less than 3 percent of South Africa's prison population, women represent the minority of South Africa's prison population, as they do the world over. As such, they are utterly absent from almost all South African writing on prisons and imprisonment and really emerge from the shadows only when they are mentioned, in passing, as the mothers of "babies behind bars."[14] In all other respects it is the conditions and circumstances of men's imprisonment that define and shape policy and discussion around imprisonment in South Africa.

The past decade has witnessed the growth of a punitive "tough-on-crime" agenda in advanced industrialized nations in response to the increasing inequalities and social disorder caused by neoliberal globalization. South Africa has not been immune to this trend, exemplified by the introduction of sentencing guidelines (the Criminal Law Amendment Act, no. 105 of 1997) that reduce judicial discretion and impose mandatory minimum terms. These mandatory minimum sentences have resulted in a significant increase in the number of sentenced prisoners. By September 2002, 7,885 prisoners were serving sentences in excess of twenty years; seven years earlier, 1,885 people had been serving such sentences. Those serving sentences of fifteen to twenty years rose from 2,660 in 1995 to 8,355 in January 2003. During the same time period, those serving ten to fifteen years rose from 6,168 to 18,956. As a result of these shifts in sentencing policy, South African prisons are significantly overcrowded, holding 164 percent of capacity.[15] The backlog in cases is also a significant source of overcrowding, and the most overcrowded sections of South Africa's prisons are those housing awaiting-trial prisoners. Of the 57,858 prisoners awaiting trial on March 28, 2003, 19,592 (or 34 percent) had been granted bail but could not afford to pay the amount set. The amounts ranged from as little as R50.00 (U.S.$8).[16]

Information about prisoners and conditions in prisons is rarely disaggregated by gender. It is even more difficult to obtain data disaggregated by both race and gender. Indeed, while trying to source information from prison officials we were informed that race-disaggregated data were "too sensitive" for general release and could be provided only to high-ranking officials. Inevitably, our analysis of the intersections between race, gender, and imprisonment is limited. Women's and girls' imprisonment has increased by 68 percent during the period 1995–96 to 2002–03, with the figures rising from 2,535 to 4,253. Men's imprisonment has increased by 69 percent during the same period, from 107,512 to 181,553.[17] Women in South Africa's prisons are accommodated either at one of the eight women's prisons that house only women or in one of the further seventy-two prisons accommodating both women and men separately. Half of all sentenced women and girls are currently imprisoned for crimes involving some form of aggression. A further 32 percent are serving time for economic crimes. Six percent of sentenced women and girls were in prison for crimes related to narcotics and 1 percent for sexual crimes.[18] In relation to the length of sentence generally, 62 percent of women were serving sentences of five years and less as opposed to 41 percent of men.[19]

Differences along both race and gender lines are visible in imprisonment patterns. On May 31, 2003, Africans constituted 69.7 percent of the female prison population, coloreds 21.2 percent, Asians (or Indians) just under 1 percent, and whites 8.3 percent. African men made up 76.6 percent of the male prison population, coloreds 20.7 percent, whites 2.2 percent, and Indians 0.5 percent.[20] According to the 2001 census, Africans constitute 79 percent of the population, coloreds 8.9 percent, Asians 2.5 percent, and whites 9.6 percent. Colored women and men are most overrepresented among the prison population, being imprisoned at more than double their rate in the South African population. Of all race and gender groups, white men have the lowest rates of imprisonment in proportion to their presence in the population. These racial and gendered disparities form the backdrop to the founding of the Justice for Women Campaign.

The Justice for Women Campaign

The Justice for Women Campaign (JFWC) owes its existence to a male prison warder, Sandy Ramontoedi, who shot and killed his estranged wife Yvonne at the Johannesburg Regional Court. He was subsequently sentenced in 1997 to three years correctional supervision, which he served while continuing to work at Johannesburg Prison. At about the same time, one of the authors was contacted for help by a journalist asking if she could assist Elizabeth Phala, a woman serving a twenty-five-year sentence for killing her abusive partner. The stunning disparity in sentences, as well as the judges' responses to the abuse present in both cases, provided the impetus for the Campaign, which is based at the Centre for the Study of Violence and Reconciliation (CSVR), a nongovernmental organization (NGO). In 1998 we began seeking out women who had killed abusive partners and were now incarcerated at Johannesburg Women's Prison. To date, eleven such women have been identified.

Organization and Structure of the Justice for Women Campaign

From the outset, the organizers formed networks with similar NGOs. Our purpose in doing so was twofold: to strengthen our advocacy and activism and to bring together the range of skills and resources required to carry out the Campaign's strategies. At this point we called ourselves the Justice for Women Alliance and comprised a mix of legal organizations (such as Tshwaranang Legal Advocacy Centre, the Centre for Applied Legal Studies, the Legal Resources Centre), domestic violence service providers (the Nisaa Institute for Women's Development), and the National Institute for Crime Prevention and Reintegration of Offenders (NICRO). We were also supported by the Commission for Gender Equality, an institution established in 1997 under Chapter Nine of the Constitution.

In 2001, the Alliance was restructured and became the basis for the present-day Campaign. This was a strategic shift as well as a pragmatic response to changing staffing, capacity, and organizational priorities. As an alliance, we were in danger of becoming an end in and of ourselves rather than a means to an end. The Campaign now has a more fluid structure with partnerships forming around particular issues or events, such as trials or vigils, rather than being established on a permanent basis. The Campaign has three main goals: reforming legal defenses to murder and sentencing guidelines/provisions; establishing a review mechanism to allow the early release of women who have killed abusive partners; and providing a variety of legal and other support services to women assisted by the Campaign. We describe each of these in the sections that follow.

Reforming Legal Defenses to Murder and Sentencing Guidelines

A number of studies inform the Campaign's legal reform goals. The first is the comparison of conviction and sentencing patterns handed down to men and women convicted of killing an intimate partner;[21] the second, an examination of comparative law and legal literature on legal defenses to murder;[22] and the last an examination of how defenses to murder are applied under South African law, which includes identifying the obstacles preventing women from using the traditional defenses to murder when they kill their abusers, particularly in nonconfrontational situations.[23]

It is important to focus on sentencing guidelines and practices for two reasons. First, the conviction and sentencing study demonstrated that there is no paradigmatic battered woman against whom all others must be measured. Remedies must therefore be crafted to reflect women's diversity of experiences and responses to domestic violence. For instance, it may not always be possible under all circumstances to expand the definition of self-defense to fit all battered women's actions.[24] Thus, some convictions for murder may be unavoidable, making it important that domestic violence assume significance as a mitigating factor for sentencing purposes. Second, the Criminal Law Amendment Act (no. 105 of 1997) obliges courts to hand down life sentences for murders found to be planned or premeditated. This provision guarantees severe consequences for the group of women who do not kill their abusers during confrontations. However, if courts find that "substantial and compelling" circumstances exist justifying a lesser sentence, the mandatory minimum need not be imposed. It is essential to establish that domestic violence does indeed constitute one such substantial and compelling circumstance. Although legal reform will benefit women in the future, it is of limited benefit to women already serving sentences for killing their partners. The second goal of the Campaign therefore addresses the early release of already convicted women.

Establishing a Review Mechanism to Allow Early Release

Under South African law both judicial and nonjudicial remedies exist to alter sentences. Judicial remedies include reviews of, or appeals against, both conviction and sentence; nonjudicial remedies include parole, the conversion of a custodial sentence to one of correctional supervision, and presidential pardon. We have utilized all of these remedies with varying degrees of success, and three women have been released already (with a fourth awaiting a date for her parole hearing). Five women have, however, exhausted all legal remedies and have not served sufficient time to be eligible for parole yet. This is where Section 84 (2) (j) of the Constitution, which grants the President of South Africa the power to pardon or reprieve a person from punishment, has become relevant. Pardon is a discretionary executive power that is both legal and political in nature. Typically, it is a measure of last resort available to convicted persons once all other legal remedies have been exhausted.

As our international precedent for a review process, we have referred to the Canadian Self Defence Review, initiated in 1995 following the Supreme Court of Canada's decision in *R v. Lavallee* (1990) 1 SCR 852.[25] To ensure that the outcome of *Lavallee* benefited women convicted and sentenced prior to this decision, the Canadian government appointed Judge Ratushny to lead a national review of cases involving women convicted of killing abusive partners, spouses, or guardians.[26]

Some local precedent for reviews or early releases also exists in South Africa, the most well-known being the amnesties awarded by the Truth and Reconciliation Commission to those who made a full disclosure of political crimes committed during apartheid. Another set of pardons was granted by former president Mandela to women prisoners who were the primary caretakers of children younger than eleven years. The latter group of pardons have some bearing on our arguments for early releases. In pardoning this category of women, the president took into account the fact that it would serve the interests of children, given that mothers are generally responsible for child care; that the group of female prisoners in question constituted a very small portion of the prison population; and that the early release of the category of women in question would not bring the administration of justice into disrepute.[27]

Another factor to be taken into account in exercising mercy toward women who kill their abusive partners is the quality of legal assistance afforded to them. A judge interviewed for one of the research reports stated that he had rarely seen proper arguments and proper evidence of domestic violence put before him in cases involving women who had killed their abusive partners.[28] Criminal law experts interviewed for the same study made a similar point about the quality of trial advocacy, observing that legal defenses to murder would open up to battered women if the evidence was adduced and argued properly.[29] Thus, these various points, taken together with the state's positive duties outlined earlier in the *Baloyi* decision, constitute the basis for appealing to the president to extend mercy toward this group of domestic violence survivors. Once it is established that this is a group deserving of mercy, decisions would then need to be made on a case-by-case basis, depending on the facts of individual women's cases.

On April 23, 2001 the Campaign for the women's early release was officially launched with the submission of Maria Scholtz's application for presidential pardon to the Department of Justice and Constitutional Development, through which such applications are customarily first routed before being sent to the President's Office. Applications for Elsie Morare, Harriet Chidi, Sharla Sebejan, and Meisie Kgomo were also filed.[30] In all, a total of five applications were filed for three African, one white, and one Indian woman. The women were selected on the basis that they had exhausted all legal remedies; their abuse could be corroborated, preempting accusations that claims of abuse had been conveniently manufactured to escape responsibility; and that they represented a diverse sample of imprisoned domestic violence survivors, challenging race- and class-based stereotypes about who is victimized by and who perpetrates domestic violence. The applications were supported by the National Network on Violence Against Women and the Commission for Gender Equality.

Advocacy and Mobilization to Support Early Release

The National Network on Violence against Women chose the Campaign as its focus for the annual Sixteen Days of Activism to End Violence Against Women in 2001.[31] The Network hired a train to transport its members from Johannesburg to Cape Town, where a public rally was held at Robben Island. Currently a popular tourist destination, Robben Island is the site of the prison where former President Nelson Mandela was incarcerated as a political prisoner for twenty-four years. As such, it was a potent symbol highlighting that injustices in the penal system have not ended with the dismantling of the apartheid regime. At each stop along the route, women would get off the train and hold a short public demonstration against the custodial sentences imposed on women who kill abusive partners. In addition the eight other provincial networks on violence against women held events at the prisons in their provinces as part of the Campaign. The petition supporting the women's early release was signed by approximately one thousand people. On the December 8, 2003, we held a candlelight vigil outside the Johannesburg Central Prison, where the five women are serving their sentences. Members' of the women's families read speeches written by the women while partner organizations spoke about the purpose and goals of the Campaign.

The issue has proved popular with the media, who continue to give it regular coverage. Informal polls suggest that sections of the South African public favor the women's early release. A vote conducted after the screening of a short program about the women and the Campaign by *Carte Blanche* (a national investigative news show) in November 2002 found that 89 percent of callers were in favor of releasing the women. Another telephone vote conducted in May 2003 during the airing of a televised debate about the issue on the program *Asikhulumi* recorded 67 percent of callers as supporting the women's release. The *Carte Blanche* program had another, more individual catalyzing effect. After the program, one of the women was contacted by her in-laws for the first time in many years. This particular family member showed a willingness to understand the woman's motivation for killing her abusive husband and the circumstances under which he was killed.

Support Services to Women Supported by the Campaign

Women in prison have more than legal concerns on their minds. Siblings and parents fall ill or die; children run away, fail school, or are raped. When such circumstances arise, there is little women can do from behind bars, particularly when the state services that should assist them are not functioning effectively. This state of affairs led us to embark on a series of actions to encourage (and put pressure on) government departments to fulfill their mandated tasks. This included obtaining urgent court orders compelling the Department of Correctional Services (DCS) to allow two women to attend family funerals and undertaking five case studies detailing the impact on children of long-term maternal incarceration.[32]

Although all the children's lives had been adversely affected by their mother's imprisonment, some children's circumstances were particularly dire. Two closely interlinked problems contributed to these negative effects: the quality of care some children received following their mothers' imprisonment and the nature of prison visiting arrangements. Who children live with while their mother is in prison affects both the well-being of the children and the type and quality of relationship they are likely to enjoy subsequently with their mother. In terms of African customary law (a colonial reconstruction of previous cultural mores), women become part of a man's family.[33] The children are considered to belong to the father too. Thus, when African children lose both parents, they are most often seen as the responsibility of the father's family.

Our case studies found that children living with paternal relatives were more likely to experience neglect and emotional and physical abuse than children living with maternal relatives. Indeed, the animosity that paternal relatives harbored toward the mother for killing their family member was often displaced onto the children. For example, Lerato Chidi, who bears a strong physical resemblance to her mother Harriet, was accused by her paternal relatives of having taken part in her father's killing, although there is no evidence to support this claim. They refused to care for her and chased her from their home. She was sixteen at the time and spent the next five years living with whomever would take her in. Paternal relatives also deliberately attempted to alienate the children from their mothers and had to be compelled to bring the children to see their mothers. One child was told that his mother was a witch who would kill him just as she had killed his father. Two sets of paternal relatives also abused money held in trust for the children by their father's estates.[34]

Although maternal relatives tried much harder to ensure that the children were well cared for, particular features of imprisonment nonetheless militated against the maintenance of good relationships. Because the women are long-term prisoners, they are held at a maximum security facility. As a result, many of the women were imprisoned some distance away from where their children live, with four out of the five sets of children constituting the case studies living outside Gauteng, where Johannesburg prison is located. Prohibitive public transport costs have reduced visits to the bare minimum that can be afforded. Visiting conditions also work against inmates. A-category prisoners (into which the women fall by virtue of the length of time they have served and record of good behavior) are permitted forty-five contact visits of one hour each per year. These visits take place in one of two communal visiting sections. As a result, there is little opportunity for private conversation. Overcrowding also means that the prison has forgone the creation of any play area for the children. Visiting times are thus too brief and infrequent and the visiting environment too child-unfriendly to support close relationships between the women and their children. Inevitably, mothers and children are losing contact with one another.

The publication of the report's findings produced some immediate outcomes. The Department of Social Development launched investigations into some of the children's circumstances, resulting in the removal of at least two children from the care of abusive family members. One woman's children also began visiting her for the first time in eight years. A task team comprising representatives of the Department of Social Development, DCS, the CSVR, the social work department of the University of the Witwatersrand, and Heartworks was also established to develop a pilot dual-purpose intervention that would coordinate government services to such children and devise a program to reestablish and maintain regular contact between the women and their children. However, this program is yet to be implemented.

Addressing the Effects of Domestic Violence and Imprisonment

Sharla Sebejan, reflecting on her experience of imprisonment, wrote:

> In this insane hell-hole, where I share a cell with thirty-five other women, I have actually found a little haven, for the hardships, suffering and emotional abuse I now undergo, is nothing compared to living with my husband—being too afraid to talk, eat or even smile, being constantly crippled with fear that I might be doing something wrong, for which I'd get a beating and thrown out of the house, to spend the night in the car.[35]

From her point of view, the loss of liberty entailed by imprisonment also represents a kind of freedom. Yet the difference between Sebejan's marriage and imprisonment is only one of degree. Her words, like those of Annemarie Engelbrecht, point to similarities between imprisonment and abusive relationships. Both are characterized by authoritarianism, a marked power imbalance, enforced restrictions of movement and activities, lack of freedom of association, violence, and the enforcement of arbitrary and trivial demands. It is therefore difficult for women to work through and heal from the damaging effects of domestic violence. Indeed, many of the strategies used to cope in an abusive relationship, such as compliance with others' demands, denial of one's own wishes and thoughts, defensive violence, suppression of feelings, may be very necessary to surviving in prison. Limited therapeutic assistance to deal with these effects is available from the DCS, which employs a total of thirty-one psychologists nationally to attend to the needs of all sentenced prisoners.[36]

More recently, DCS introduced restorative justice programs at its various facilities. The Department describes restorative justice as an approach "based on the understanding of crime as an act against the victim and community and it (*sic*) aims to remedy the fundamental shortcomings in the criminal justice process. . . . It emphasizes the importance of the role of the victims, families and community members by more actively involving them in the justice process. It is also aimed at holding offenders directly accountable to the people they have violated and at the restoring of the losses and harm suffered by the victims."[37] There may well be many benefits to this program. However, in practice, when prison authorities implement the program, they require women to ask forgiveness for their crimes. This clearly fails to recognize the ambiguous position abused women occupy, being simultaneously offender and victim. As a consequence, the wrongs done to the women remain invisible and denied.

To address these unique gaps, we proposed a program developed in consultation with the women to DCS. The program aimed to explore both the effects upon the women of the domestic violence as well as their subsequent imprisonment. It was also intended to create opportunities for the women to discuss their actions with their children (some of whom harbored very real, but strongly suppressed feelings of anger toward their mothers). Another component of the program aimed to focus on preparing women for life on the outside, such as finding housing and employment, dealing with people, in the event of their release. However, like the children's proposal, this program has never been implemented.

Successes and Challenges along the Way

The campaign has presented us with a blend of strategic and practical challenges. With the exception of the research, much of this work has been unfunded. Lawyers willing to do *pro bono* work in this area are rare; even more unusual are lawyers familiar with both criminal law and feminist thinking in this area. As a consequence, extensive reliance is sometimes placed on the goodwill of already-busy people with the result that work was not always completed on time, particularly in relation to compiling the pardons. Many of the individuals first associated with the Campaign also left their organizations, which affected continuity and decision making. In addition to being both labor and resource intensive, this work is emotionally draining. As a result, we have had to limit the number of women we are able to assist.

Activists and researchers who neglect to familiarize themselves with the minutiae of DCS bureaucracy and hierarchy do so at their peril, as we discovered when an acrimonious relationship developed between ourselves and the management structure of Johannesburg Women's prison. Although matters have improved, these difficulties played a clear role in preventing the implementation of both psychoeducational programs and stopped communication with the women—who then began wondering if they had been forgotten.

Advocacy is also vulnerable to the unpredictable vagaries of the larger political context. In May 2002, President Mbeki provided "clandestine" pardons to 33 male prisoners said to have taken part in the liberation struggle. Less than two weeks later, Dumisani Ncamazana, a former Azanian People's Liberation

Army cadre, murdered Martin Whitaker.[38] A number of political parties called for a review of the pardoning process, with the leader of the official opposition going so far as to submit a private member's bill to parliament proposing to prescribe and regulate the process. Another politician quoted unsourced, unverified statistics "showing that 94 percent of people pardoned got involved in crime again."[39] Advocating for the women's release was, understandably, made difficult while so much public opinion was opposed to presidential pardons.

Media representation of the women's actions represents another key challenge, with women generally falling somewhere between the two extremes of pathetic victims or ruthless schemers. For example, articles submitted to us before publication by journalists covering the Campaign described one woman as a "cold-hearted, calculating bitch" and another as "a woman whose self-esteem is so thin it could be scraped off with a teaspoon." Although it may be easier to garner public support by depicting the women as the helpless and suffering victims of their beastly, monstrous men, such crude and sensational characterizations obscure the complexity of abusive relationships, as well as the couple concerned.

Conclusions

When women kill their abusive partners in ways that resemble those of men, they enjoy the benefit of the law. The women who behave differently are failed in a multitude of ways—through laws that discriminate and invalidate their experiences of abuse, by legal counsel unable or unwilling to prepare and argue their cases adequately, and through presiding officers unable to comprehend the realities of abuse. With imprisonment, coercive control of the women shifts from their partners to the state; and although imprisonment may prompt some women to discover a certain resilience within themselves, more frequently it exacerbates underlying problems and difficulties. In some instances it extends the women's punishment to their children. The Justice for Women Campaign challenges the DCS, as well as the Department of Justice and Constitutional Development, to consider their roles in perpetuating some of the dynamics of violent relationships in battered women's lives.

To date, the Campaign has made its greatest impact on the legal profession, with attorneys increasingly requesting information and assistance in this area of law.[40] There are also signs indicating that we are making some inroads into judicial thinking. On the strength of the legal research we conducted, a retired Constitutional Court judge who now trains other judges committed himself to including the issues and arguments in future training. In addition, in late 2003 the CSVR and the Centre for Applied Legal Studies (CALS) were called by a judge to appear in court in terms of section 186 of the Criminal Procedure Act and testify about domestic violence in South Africa. To the best of our knowledge, this is the first time a South African judge has admitted to not being an expert on domestic violence and requested education on this topic via expert testimony.

In 2004 many of the rights' arguments we have been developing around sentencing will finally be tested in the Supreme Court appeal of Anieta Ferreira, who was sentenced to life imprisonment for the murder of her abusive common-law partner. The other rights argument we have been evolving applies to parole eligibility. Broadly, prisoners may be considered eligible for parole after they have served at least one third of their sentence—unless they are classified aggressive offenders. At least two thirds to three quarters of the sentence must be served first by this category before they are considered eligible for parole. Women who have killed their abusive partners are classified as aggressive offenders by virtue of their having been convicted of murder. We hope to challenge this with a substantive equality argument. Essentially, we will argue that abused women's right to equality is being violated by treating them in exactly the same manner as individuals who commit violent acts, including rape and murder, in very different contexts. Because the moral culpability assigned to these various crimes is not equivalent, differential treatment is warranted.

The testing of these various rights' arguments will need to be accompanied by the strengthening of our arguments for mercy, particularly as we intend stepping up public mobilization in support of the women's early releases. This is where transnational networking may be useful. Certainly, being able to refer to the precedent of the Canadian Self Defence Review has helped our arguments, most notably by reassuring government officials and members of the public that we are not wandering into uncharted waters. Further, because there now seem to be a number of initiatives to release women who kill their abusive partners in the United Kingdom, Canada, the United States, and Australia, the time may be ripe for some cross-country discussion and sharing of lessons.

The Campaign has also made us very aware of the problem of women's imprisonment generally. Working at a prison, it is impossible to ignore how widespread experiences of rape, child abuse, and domestic violence are in the lives of women and girls in conflict with the law generally; research interviews we are currently conducting only confirm and quantify this view. It is an indictment of South African society that the only "help" we offer some survivors of rape and domestic violence is imprisonment.

References

1. Minister of Justice and Another Intervening (2000) (2) SA 425.
2. In this chapter "black" refers to an apartheid racial category. Where uppercase "Black" is used, it refers to a political identity shared by all those people designated "non-white" by the former apartheid government.

3. Department of Safety and Security, White Paper on Safety and Security: In Service of Safety 1999–2004 (Pretoria, 1998). http://www.gov.za/whitepaper/1998/safety.htm. Accessed December 2003.

4. Lisa Vetten, "Paper Promises, Protests and Petitions: South African State and Civil Society Responses to Violence Against Women," in *Reclaiming Women's Spaces: New Perspectives on Violence Against Women and Sheltering in South Africa*, ed. Y. Park, J. Fedler, and Z. Dangor (Johannesburg: Nisaa Institute for Women's Development, 2000).

5. Lisa Vetten and Zohra Khan, "We're Doing Their Work for Them": *An Investigation into Government Support to Non-profit Organisations Providing Services to Women Experiencing Gender Violence* (Johannesburg: Centre for the Study of Violence and Reconciliation, 2003).

6. Acts that constitute domestic violence may be reported in a range of criminal categories such as "assault with intent to cause grievous bodily harm" (GBH), pointing a firearm, attempted murder, intimidation, and indecent assault.

7. Rachel Jewkes et al., "He Must Give Me Money, He Mustn't Beat Me" *Violence Against Women in Three South African Provinces* (Pretoria: CERSA [Women's Health] Medical Research Council, 1999).

8. Naeema Abrahams, Rachel Jewkes, and Ria Laubsher, "I Do Not Believe in Democracy in the Home": *Men's Relationships with and Abuse of Women* (Tygerberg: CERSA [Women's Health] Medical Research Council, 1999).

9. Lisa Vetten and Collet Ngwane, "I Love You to Destruction": *An Analysis of Convictions and Sentences in Cases of Spousal Homicide* (Johannesburg: Centre for the Study of Violence and Reconciliation, forthcoming).

10. These figures probably underestimate the actual number of cases involving abuse. In the absence of any other supporting evidence, we did not include within these totals relationships described as "stormy" or "unhappy," although these are often euphemisms for abuse.

11. These disparities are to be expected, given how many women killed their partners either in accidents (referring to struggles over a gun or knife) or through defending themselves.

12. This pattern is by no means unique to South Africa. McGuigan's review of 223 U.S. cases involving abused women who kill their partners found that these killings occurred most often in the course of an attack upon the woman by her partner, with 75 percent of the deaths having occurred during a confrontation. Nonetheless, a significant minority of abused women (20 percent) also killed their abusers when the abuser was asleep or drunk or otherwise vulnerable, or hired a third party to perform the killing, when no imminent danger was apparent.

13. For self-defense to succeed, an accused person must show that the attack against which they were defending has commenced or was imminently threatened. A person cannot defend against an attack that will happen some time in future or respond to an attack that is already over. Jonathon Burchell and John Milton, *Cases and Materials on Criminal Law*, 2nd edition (Johannesburg: Juta, 2000).

14. In terms of the Correctional Services Act (no. 111 of 1998), children may remain with their mothers in prison until their fifth birthday. On July 31, 2003 there were 228 such children in prison with their mothers.

15. In the late 1990s, two U.S.-style private prisons were built in South Africa. However, neither of the two private prisons, Mangaung and Kutama-Sinthumule, is subject to overcrowding as they take no more prisoners than the number determined by their contracts. At the time of writing, women were not housed in either private facility.

16. Judicial Inspectorate of Prisons, Annual Report for the Period 1 April 2002 to 31 March 2003 (Cape Town, 2003), 27. Available at http://judicialinsp.pwv.gov.za. Accessed September 2003.

17. Department of Correctional Services, Annual Report 1 April 2002 to 31 March 2003 (Pretoria, 2003).

18. On September 31, 2003. Ibid.

19. On July 31, 2003. Judicial Inspectorate of Prisons.

20. Department of Correctional Services 2003.

21. Vetten and Ngwane forthcoming.

22. Hallie Ludsin, *Legal Defense for Battered Women Who Kill Their Abusers: Discussion Document 1* (Johannesburg: Centre for the Study of Violence and Reconciliation, 2003a).

23. Hallie Ludsin, *South African Criminal Law and Battered Women Who Kill: Discussion Document 2* (Johannesburg: Centre for the Study of Violence and Reconciliation, 2003b).
24. At this point it seems unlikely that self-defense can be expanded sufficiently to include women who involve third parties in the killing of their husbands.
25. Prior to *Lavallee*, an accused could not raise self-defense in a context in which he or she anticipated future harm; self-defense could be used only when the accused acted while in the process of being victimized or harmed. The court upheld that battered women, after experiencing the cycle of violence repeatedly, become attuned to the cycle and are thus able to anticipate accurately when they are likely to be victimized again. Under such circumstances, requiring battered women to wait to be abused before permitting them to defend themselves would be "tantamount to sentencing her to 'murder by installment'." The court held that consideration should be taken of the cumulative effect of abuse on the woman.
26. Ultimately, seven remedies were recommended out of the ninety-eight applications reviewed. The Minister of Justice and Solicitor General of Canada announced in 1997 that they would provide remedies for five of the seven women. Two of the women would receive remission of their sentences, two women would receive conditional pardon, and one woman would have her case referred to the Court of Appeal under s.690 of the Canadian Criminal Code.
27. Karisha Pillay, *Battered Women Who Kill: Avenues for Legal/Political Recourse* (Centre for the Study of Violence and Reconciliation, 2002), 33.
28. Ludsin, 2003b.
29. Ludsin 2003b, 64.
30. Sentenced respectively to 21 years, 21 years, 15 years, 21 years, and death (Meisie is still waiting for her sentence to be commuted following the abolition of the death penalty in South Africa).
31. This is the period from November 25, the International Day of No to Violence Against Women, and December 10, International Human Rights Day.
32. Kailash Bhana and Tessa Hochfeld, "Now We Have Nothing": *The Impact of Long-term Maternal Imprisonment on Children Whose Mothers Kill an Abusive Partner* (Johannesburg: Center for the Study of Violence and Reconciliation, 2001).
33. Winnie Kubayi, "The Major Sources of Children's Legal Rights," in *Children and the Law*, ed. A. Skelton (Pietermaritzburg: Lawyers for Human Rights, 1998).
34. Kubayi 1998.
35. This excerpt is taken from a speech Ms. Sebejan wrote in 2001 to be read on her behalf at the Robben Island function described earlier.
36. Department of Correctional Services, 2003.
37. Department of Correctional Services, *Restorative Justice, Healing the Wounds of Crime, Working for a Safer Community* (2003). Available at: http://www.dcs.gov.za/restorativejustice/. Accessed December 2003.
38. SAPA and African Eye News Service, "Ncamazana brothers get life in jail," *The Star*, December 13, 2002.
39. Christelle Terreblanche and SAPA, "Call to revisit pardoning after freed prisoner kills," *The Star*, December 12, 2002.
40. In recognition of the Campaign's work reintegrating released prisoners, the Campaign received the NICRO Whistle Blowers' Award in 2001.

CHAPTER 19

Reproductive Rights in Nepal

From Criminalization to Resistance

MELISSA UPRETI

I was sick during my pregnancy with a fever almost every other day. I did-
n't receive any treatment. I didn't have a job. I was eight months pregnant
when I started bleeding and had a miscarriage. I was in my room and
called out to my mother and neighbors for help. Some villagers accused
me of killing my child! My parents tried to defend me and said that I had
been ill for a while. The villagers kept arguing among themselves about
what really happened. Finally, three days later, a few men reported the incident to the police. I suspect my husband of having instigated them to
report me. He had already married another woman.

Kali Maya[1]

Nepal occupies a very special place in contemporary abortion rights and antiprison discourse. It is one of the few countries in the world where women
have routinely been imprisoned for having abortions. As such, Nepal provides
an opportunity to understand the policing and criminalization of women's
sexuality and to identify strategies for resistance. This chapter offers a glimpse
into the impact of the former abortion ban in Nepal by looking at who was
punished for making the reproductive choices that many of us take for granted.
It also analyzes the recent historic advancement toward the recognition of
women's reproductive rights in Nepal and describes how local and international efforts converged to bring about this groundbreaking change, transforming Nepal from a country with one of the most restrictive abortion laws in

271

the world to one with a law that now ranks among the most liberal. Finally, this chapter reflects upon the transnational aspect of the abortion movement in Nepal and considers current challenges, particularly the continuing imprisonment of women sentenced under the now defunct ban and U.S. foreign policy, which is threatening to defeat the impact of this huge gain for women's rights.

Imprisonment for Abortion

Transnational collaborations have played a critical role in challenging women's imprisonment for abortion. In 2000, The Center for Reproductive Rights (U.S.) collaborated with the Forum for Women, Law and Development (FWLD, Nepal) to conduct the first comprehensive human rights fact-finding mission on abortion in Nepal with a focus on the impact of the ban on women's reproductive rights and the rights of prisoners.[2]

This report established for the first time that Nepal's law on abortion violated nationally and internationally protected human rights. Nepal's punitive approach to abortion, combined with its weak protections for women who were incarcerated under the law, resulted in further human rights violations of women as prisoners. The report established key findings that lent critical support to the movement for decriminalizing abortion in Nepal and established a basis for demanding the release of women imprisoned for abortion. It demonstrated that the criminalization of abortion violated women's right to life, equality, health, privacy, physical integrity, and reproductive decision making in a context where women's reproductive self-determination was already weakened by their low social status, widespread early marriage, poverty, and lack of access to family planning. Women's rights to due process and a fair trial were routinely violated by those entrusted with the duty to safeguard their rights. Nepali women's right to be free from arbitrary arrest and detention was routinely violated by inconsistent application of the criminal abortion law. Low-income and rural women faced the greatest discrimination under the abortion ban. Women who were convicted faced harsh conditions in prison and inadequate access to health care.[3]

These findings were successfully used to demonstrate the impact of the former abortion ban and to support the legalization of abortion in 2002. However, no action was taken by the government to release the women imprisoned for abortion or even to investigate the claims of violations of due process that essentially brought the legitimacy of their imprisonment into question.

The Victims of the Ban

The punitive approach to abortion in Nepal stems from the legal and social characterization of the procedure as an act of murder unless performed for a benevolent purpose. However, benevolence was never legally defined. This approach has been reinforced by social and religious views that deem the practice a sin and fail to recognize women's autonomy in matters of reproduction. The following case study is illustrative of how these factors come into play when a pregnancy fails:

> Kumari was in the fifth month of her pregnancy when she unexpectedly went into labor while digging in the fields and had a miscarriage; she couldn't afford to rest, someone had to do the work. Later, when she told the village elder what had happened, he responded by saying that she had "killed her child." She insisted that she had not done anything to "kill her child," but he said that what she had done was "considered to be murder." He reported her to the police. She was arrested and charged with infanticide.

> Kumari did not undergo a medical examination; however, the fetus was examined to determine the "cause of death." She did not have a lawyer and was not informed about her right to legal representation. She was produced before a judge, and when she told him that she did not kill her child, she was confronted with the question, "If you didn't, who did?"

> Kumari was 30 when she had the miscarriage and has four children. Her husband had been away for almost 10 years and she lived with her parents. Kumari says that family planning services were offered in her village but she never used contraception because she felt "awkward" and was "scared of what others would think if they found out."[4]

One of the most disturbing aspects of abortion-related prosecutions in Nepal has been the practice of charging women who have allegedly had abortions with the more severe crime of infanticide. This has resulted in harsher sentencing extending to life imprisonment, when in fact the maximum sentence for abortion was 3 years. The failure of individuals, law enforcement agents, and judicial officers to distinguish between spontaneous abortion (miscarriage), induced abortion, and infanticide at the time of reporting an alleged crime and during the different stages of investigation and prosecution has led to inconsistent application of the abortion ban, making a woman's criminal liability a matter of chance.

The rights of women as criminal defendants have been routinely violated in Nepal. In cases involving charges of abortion or infanticide, the likelihood of a fair trial has been undermined by utter disregard for standard procedures and guarantees of due process. Women suspected of terminating their pregnancies have been routinely denied the right to legal counsel, the right to remain silent, and the right to prompt proceedings. Few women are subjected to proper medical examination immediately after an alleged abortion, which is key to determining the true cause of the termination of a pregnancy. The biases that pervade the justice system in Nepal have also resulted in women being consistently denied the right to be presumed innocent until proved guilty. Together, these violations represent not only violations of the internationally recognized rights of criminal defendants but also violations of the constitutional rights of criminal defendants under Nepali law. The following statement by a police officer is illustrative of the biases pervading the justice system: "[W]omen lie about what happened and always say that the fetus was spontaneously expelled before nine months to save themselves. . . ."[5]

Trends in imprisonment for abortion also reveal a gender and a class bias. Men have rarely been convicted for aiding, abetting, or even performing illegal abortions. Low-income, rural women have faced the most discrimination under the former ban and have the least access to legal information and representation. Most of them—up to 60 percent—have never attended school.[6]

Women imprisoned for abortion in Nepal are frequently victims of circumstance. The harsh realities of rural life predispose women in Nepal to failed pregnancies involving spontaneous miscarriages and still-births. Because of their poor economic and social status, it is common for pregnant women in Nepal to continue to engage in high levels of work-related physical activity, regardless of the consequences for their pregnancy, whether it be digging in the fields or collecting firewood to cook their next meal; they simply do not have a choice. In addition, most women do not have access to basic reproductive health care services, including family planning and pre- and postnatal care; often where services are available, women do not use them because of their own apprehensions about contraception and the social pressures to bear children—preferably sons. Long-standing social practices such as child marriage, which are clearly detrimental to the health of women and girls and undermine women's reproductive autonomy, have compromised women's ability to protect themselves from unplanned and unwanted pregnancies. None of these factors are taken into consideration during prosecutions for abortion. Women are treated as criminals regardless of the fact that they are themselves victims of government neglect and the cultural suppression of their reproductive and sexual freedom.

Women accused of abortion and pregnancy-related crimes are sentenced even before they are tried. Clearly, *Kumari* never had a chance—she was convicted by society for allegedly "killing her child" long before she was sentenced to prison by a court of law. Most women do not receive any legal assistance at all during a criminal trial.[7] They are hauled through the criminal justice system without any genuine attempt by law enforcement agents to find out the truth and without any concern for their well-being or rights. In the words of one prisoner, "I have been sentenced to life in prison . . . . In court, no one asked me any questions or let me tell my side of the story."[8]

The former abortion ban was an inherently flawed law as it clearly violated a broad range of nationally and internationally protected human rights. However, it was also a widely abused law, as it was frequently misapplied and misused by individuals to punish women for their personal decisions related to their reproductive behavior or sexuality. The following case study illustrates the tragic story of a young woman who tried to protect herself by making her own choices:

> *Durga* was 17 when she eloped with a man whom she later married. Her husband wanted her to go to India with him but she wanted to go back to her village. This refusal apparently angered her husband and their friends.
>
> Meanwhile Durga became pregnant and one day during the eighth month of her pregnancy, she experienced severe stomach pain. When she asked her husband and friends to take her to a doctor, they refused to help! Later, Durga went into labor and delivered a dead fetus. Her friends immediately called the police alleging that she had killed her baby.
>
> Durga was arrested and taken to the police station where the police asked her if she did it. She did not have legal representation and was not examined by a doctor. Furthermore, she was kept at the police station for 17 days.
>
> Durga has been sentenced to life in prison. The two friends who reported her did make official statements alleging her guilt but they did not appear in court. Durga was taken to court twice but on both occasions was late for the hearings.
>
> Durga has never had visitors. She is not sure if her parents know she is in prison. She says they'd probably come to see her if they did. She now firmly believes that her husband and their friends wanted to take her to India so that they could sell her to a brothel. She was only trying to protect herself by saying "No!"[9]

This story reveals the true nature of the former abortion ban in Nepal. The former law did not simply represent an expected moral standard of behavior, it also reinforced the negation of women's agency and reproductive freedom.

Once imprisoned, women have also experienced violations of their right to human treatment in detention. Conditions in Nepal's prisons are appalling. Supplies of food and water are generally inadequate. Access to routine health care and emergency health care is extremely limited, and women are often expected to pay for their own medical treatment.[10] Interviews with women during the 2001 study revealed that 74 percent of women felt ill and needed medical attention, and 35 percent said they had not even bothered to ask for help. Very often, men and women were housed in the same facility and even required to share the same toilets, despite rules requiring the strict segregation of male and female prisoners. In some prisons, income-generating programs were available for men but not for women.[11] In the words of a lawyer who works very closely with prisoners in Nepal, "Prisoners are not people, they have no identity; they're neglected by the management . . . the management is entirely male dominated and there is no one to pay attention to female issues."[12]

The imprisonment of women for abortion has often had far-reaching implications for their families, especially their children. In numerous cases documented over the years, children have been forced to accompany their mothers to prison because of the absence of an alternative caregiver.[13] Some children have been forced to work as domestic servants in order to avoid destitution, leading to their exploitation and abuse.[14] The implications for these children have been tragic. The lack of education, loss of family security, exposure to harsh conditions in prison, and the stigma of being the children of alleged criminals has led to violations of their human rights as children.

The Decriminalization of Abortion

Abortion was legalized in 2002, following many years of advocacy and campaigning by national and grassroots activists and more recently by international advocates. The decriminalization of abortion in Nepal came about as a result of a combination of different forces over a period of three decades.

Developments at the National Level

In 1967, the Nepal Medical Council introduced a rule that would allow physicians to perform abortions if the pregnancy posed a risk to the woman's health. However, this rule was never applied.[15] Six years later recommendations for legalizing abortion were made by a formal body appointed by the government to reform the criminal code, on the following conditions: within the first 12 weeks of pregnancy with a woman's consent; if in the opinion of a medical practitioner, the pregnancy posed a risk to the life of the pregnant woman or there was a risk of fetal abnormality; or if the pregnancy was a result of rape or incest.[16] However, these recommendations were not adopted, nor did they lead to any major advocacy initiatives.

In 1990, Nepal made the transition from an absolute monarchy to a democracy. This created a new political environment for civil society and especially for the women's rights movement. The transition was marked by the adoption of a new constitution, which clearly established the right to equality and enshrined nondiscrimination as a fundamental right. In response to the staggering maternal death rate in the country, in 1994 the government adopted a National Safe Motherhood Policy, which, among other things, recognized the need for legal reforms to reduce the incidence of maternal deaths resulting from factors including unsafe abortion.[17] In 1996, under the leadership of a member of parliament who was also the chairperson of the Family Planning Association of Nepal, experts drafted the "Protection of Pregnancy Bill," which aimed to legalize abortion on certain grounds.[18] This bill was registered and debated in parliament; however, it eventually lapsed when the parliamentarian's term came to an end. The abortion question surfaced once again in the same year with the registration of the 11th Amendment Bill, 1997, which proposed sweeping reforms to the National Civil Code by amending several discriminatory laws including unequal property laws.[19] By this time, the movement to legalize abortion had become part of a broader antidiscrimination movement led by women's rights activists. Because of growing pressure from the grassroots and civil society, the government decided to take on the responsibility of drafting a comprehensive bill that would address women's concerns. The bill finally adopted by parliament in March 2002 represented a consensus between women's rights groups and the government. It brought about an end to centuries of formal discrimination in many aspects of the law and marked a significant first step toward the official recognition of women's reproductive rights.

Developments in International Law and Policy

Advancements toward abortion law reform at the national level were greatly influenced and informed by legal and policy developments at the international level. Shortly after Nepal's transition to democracy, the newly elected government signed and ratified a number of major international treaties, including the International Covenant on Civil and Political Rights, 1976; the International Covenant on Economic, Social and Cultural Rights, 1976; and the Convention for the Elimination of All Forms of Discrimination Against Women, 1979. In 1994, representatives of the government participated at the International Conference on Population and Development at Cairo, where 179 governments, including the Nepali government, adopted through consensus a program of action that recognized reproductive rights as human rights. In 1995, the Nepali government participated at the Fourth World Conference on Women and formally adopted the Beijing Platform for Action, which affirmed women's reproductive rights as human rights and placed upon governments the responsibility for creating an enabling legal environment for promoting women's equality and empowerment. It noted the need for governments to eliminate discrimination in criminal prosecutions against women and to consider reviewing laws containing punitive measures against women who have undergone illegal abortions.[20]

During the 1990s, a number of international treaty-monitoring bodies also expressed their concern about the high number of deaths due to unsafe abortion and the incarceration of women for illegal abortion. In 1994, the Human Rights Committee voiced its concern about the "high proportion of women prisoners sentenced for offences resulting from unwanted pregnancies."[21] The Committee on the Elimination of Discrimination Against Women (CEDAW), in 1999, expressed deep concern about the ban on abortion and its alarming link to the high maternal mortality rate in Nepal.[22] In 2001, expressing similar concern about unsafe abortion as a cause of high maternal mortality and the incarceration of women for illegal abortion, the Committee on Economic, Social and Cultural Rights urged the government of Nepal to "take remedial action to address the problems of clandestine abortions, unwanted pregnancies and the high rate of maternal mortality" and "to allow abortions when pregnancies are life threatening or a result of rape or incest."[23] Although the pronouncements of international treaty monitoring bodies are not strictly binding, they do have enormous persuasive value. These pronouncements were used by advocates in Nepal to pressure their government to demonstrate greater respect for human rights and to comply with international law.

In August 2003, the Sub-Commission for Human Rights in Geneva decided to commission a general study on the situation of women in prison in response to a letter submitted jointly by the Center and FWLD describing in detail the situation of women in prison for abortion in Nepal.[24]

International Support for the Movement in Nepal

International collaborative efforts also contributed to the debate on abortion in Nepal. The International Planned Parenthood Federation, through its affiliate the Family Planning Association of Nepal (FPAN), has been a long-standing supporter of the legalization of abortion in Nepal and a key advocate for legal change. More recently, a number of other organizations in the global north such as Ipas, Equality Now, and Amnesty International have bolstered the efforts of advocates in Nepal by providing financial support, through public education, and by lobbying the Nepali government.

The Campaign for the Release of Women in Prison

In response to the government's failure to take responsibility for the profound injustices suffered by women imprisoned for abortion under the former ban, on March 8, 2003, International Women's Day, the Forum for Women, Law and Development and the Center for Reproductive Rights launched an official campaign calling for the release of women imprisoned for abortion and alleged infanticide. The campaign included a variety of interventions including court appeals and pleas for amnesty to the king on certain days of the year when formal appeals for the release of prisoners are entertained by the government. Numerous public appeals were made to the government seeking the release of women in prison by publishing the facts about the women in prison in leading newspapers, with the support of key organizations including the Family Planning Association of Nepal (FPAN), the Center for Research on Environment, Health and Population Activities (CREHPA), and Ipas.[25] As a result of these efforts, twenty-eight women have been released from prison so far.[26]

Threats That Undermine Recent Gains

The transformation of Nepal from a country with one of the most restrictive abortion laws in the world to a country with one of the most liberal laws was a groundbreaking event celebrated by activists worldwide. However, law reform is just the first step in women's struggle for equality and social justice. Now that the right to safe and legal abortion has formally been incorporated into Nepali law, transforming this right into a reality has become a challenge for activists in Nepal, especially because of the continuing imprisonment of women for abortion and the subversive impact of U.S. foreign policy.

Thirty women prosecuted under the former ban are still in prison. Although the persistent efforts of national and international advocacy groups have resulted in the release of almost half the women who were in prison two years ago, it has been a time-consuming process. Gender discrimination is endemic in Nepal and garnering support for the release of women imprisoned for abortion has been an enormous challenge. However, securing the release of these women is critical for a number of reasons: these women have suffered violations of human rights as women seeking to exercise their reproductive freedom, as criminal defendants, and as prisoners, and the government must be held accountable for these violations; the continuing imprisonment of these women reinforces the stigma against abortion and is unfavorable to the successful implementation of the new abortion law.

U.S. Foreign Policy

Many international organizations—including a number of U.S.-based groups—came to the aid of women's rights activists in Nepal by supporting the advocacy for the release of women in prison. Yet, the official policy of the U.S. government on abortion threatens to subvert the gains achieved by women by imposing unreasonable restrictions on abortion-related activities through the imposition of the "Global Gag Rule." This policy restricts foreign nongovernmental organizations (NGOs) that receive U.S. family planning funds from using their own, non-U.S. funds to provide legal abortion services, lobby their own governments for abortion law reform, or even provide accurate medical counseling or referrals regarding abortion.[27] As a result of the chilling effect of this policy, USAID does not even fund the abortions it can technically support, such as when a woman's life is in danger or in cases of rape or incest. Prior to the amendment of the former ban, USAID-funded health NGOs were not able to support or participate in the movement for decriminalization. The restrictions imposed by USAID, which included censorship of free speech, resulted in their exclusion from the democratic process. The continuing imposition of this policy is now preventing reproductive health NGOs in Nepal, which depend on USAID funding for their survival, from providing safe abortion services in a manner consistent with their own law. More important, by condemning abortion, this policy demonizes women who have abortions and condones the incarceration of women imprisoned for abortion, making it even more difficult for advocates to mobilize support for their release.

Reflections

Although the movement for abortion law reform in Nepal is primarily an indigenous movement, it also represents a successful example of transnational collaboration. The imprisonment of women for abortion in Nepal became a global concern because of the impunity with which the government of Nepal carried out its mandate to criminalize abortion at a time when most governments across the world have progressed toward the adoption of liberal abortion laws[28] and reproductive rights have become established as human rights. Through international collaboration, advocates were able to mobilize resources and talent to expose the unfair and degrading treatment extended to women incarcerated for abortion in the dilapidated prisons scattered across the tiny and largely obscure kingdom of Nepal, and this eventually helped build international support for ending the discrimination and abuse.

The challenges facing activists in Nepal as a result of the gag rule place a particular responsibility on activists in the United States, who have a very important role to play in exposing the fallacies of this policy and condemning the imprisonment of women for abortion in Nepal. The involvement of advocates from the global north is critical because the activists and women in Nepal who bear the brunt of the gag rule do not have the ability or legal standing to challenge it. Moreover, certain parallels can be drawn between the situation of women at the receiving end of the gag rule and low-income women in the United States. The latter are particularly affected by the Hyde Amendment, which bans the use of federal Medicaid dollars and other federal funds for almost all abortions, obstructing the provision of safe abortion services for low-income women in the United States.[29] This law clearly violates women's right to safe abortion services in a country where the right to choose has been constitutionally guaranteed.

A greater threat to women's health and rights in the United States has recently emerged in the form of a federal ban on a broad range of abortion procedures through the introduction of the so-called Partial Birth Abortion Ban.[30] In this country, partial birth abortion is frequently referred to by its supporters as partial birth infanticide. This trend is strikingly similar to that in Nepal, where abortion has frequently been equated with infanticide, resulting in devastating consequences for women and their rights.[31] The situation of women imprisoned for abortion in Nepal provides a glimpse of what life could become like for disadvantaged and disempowered women in the United States, if they surrender to this attack on their reproductive rights by allowing the ban come into effect, and if officials and prison activists fail to take into account the broader political issues that contribute to criminalizing women's behavior and the gender bias that pervades the criminal justice system.

Many of the factors that have resulted in the incarceration of women in Nepal, such as lack of access to family planning services, poverty, and discrimination, are experienced by a significant proportion of women in the United States, especially women of color, including immigrant minority women.[32] Women's access to health care in the United States is significantly influenced by race and nationality, which also determine lifestyles and cultural practices that may predispose pregnant women to certain health risks. For example, studies reveal that black women in the United States are four times more likely to die during pregnancy and childbirth than white women.[33] Laws that criminalize women's behavior during pregnancy also tend to have a disparate impact on minority groups, resulting in higher rates of imprisonment of women belonging to a certain social class and race.[34] The needs of minority groups have been largely ignored by policymakers in the United States and the impact of existing laws and policies on these vulnerable groups has not been evaluated. The rights violations and social deprivation experienced by these women are no less egregious than those experienced by women in the global south.

Conclusion

Many of the challenges confronting women in the global south are experienced by women in the global north because gender-based discrimination, which is often compounded by race or nationality, is a global phenomenon. It follows that there is much to be gained through transnational organizing and exchanging strategies to challenge the injustices facing women in different parts of the world. Although an understanding of the local social and political context must inform a particular strategy, international coalitions can strengthen local struggles, especially if resources are used strategically and leveraged according to the respective strengths of the participants. The case of Nepal provides a model of effective transnational organizing against women's criminalization and human rights violations. It also suggests a new direction for prison activists and advocates, by revealing the linkages between gender discrimination, the policing of women's sexuality, and women's imprisonment.

References

1. Center for Reproductive Rights (CRR) and Forum for Women, Law and Development (FWLD), *Abortion in Nepal: Women Imprisoned* (New York: CRR and FLWD, 2002), 43.
2. The study was based on in-depth interviews with nineteen women imprisoned on charges of abortion and infanticide who were selected from a pool of fifty-seven prisoners profiled in a preliminary round of research. Judges, police officers, public prosecutors, officials belonging to various government ministries, health care providers, lawyers, and representatives of NGOs working on women's rights and the rights of prisoners from across the country were also interviewed.
3. CRR and FLWD 2002, 13–14.
4. Center for Reproductive Rights, "Case Studies for Advocacy Kit" (case study, filed with the Center for Reproductive Rights, 2001).
5. CRR and FLWD 2002, 72.
6. CRR and FLWD 2002, 13.
7. CRR and FLWD 2002, 68.
8. Excerpt from interview with Sarita (pseudonym), inmate, Dilli Bazaar Khor Jail, Kathmandu Nepal; *Abortion in Nepal: Women Imprisoned* (CRR and FLWD 2002, 76).
9. Center for Reproductive Rights, 2001.
10. CRR and FLWD 2002, 81.
11. CRR and FLWD 2002, 82.
12. CRR and FLWD 2002, 79, 82.
13. CRR and FLWD 2002, 22.
14. CRR and FLWD 2002, 22; details on file with CRR.
15. FWLD and Planned Parenthood Global Partners, *Struggles to Legalize Abortion in Nepal and Challenges Ahead* (Kathmandu: FWLD, 2003), 13–14.
16. FWLD and Planned Parenthood Global Partners, 2003, 18.
17. Nepal Ministry of Health, *Nepal Demographic and Health Survey 2001* (Calverton, ML: Ministry of Health, New ERA, and ORC Marco, 2002), 139.
18. FWLD and Planned Parenthood Global Partners 2003, 28.
19. FWLD and Planned Parenthood Global Partners 2003, 29.
20. UN, Department of Public Information, Platform for Action and Beijing Declaration: Fourth World Conference on Women, Beijing, China, 4–15 September 1995 (New York: UN, 1995), paras. 106 (k).
21. UN, Human Rights Committee, *Concluding Observations on Nepal* (Geneva: UN, 1994), UN Doc. CCPR/C/79/Add.42 at para. 8.
22. UN, Committee on the Elimination of Discrimination Against Women, *Concluding Observations on Nepal* (New York: UN, 1999), UN Doc. CEDAW/A/54/38 at para. 147.
23. UN, Committee on Economic, Social and Cultural Rights, *Concluding Observations on Nepal* (Geneva: UN, 2001), UN Doc. E/C.12/1/Add.66 at para. 55.
24. David Weissbrodt, e-mail message to Laura Katzive, August 29, 2003.
25. Copies of appeals on file with the Center for Reproductive Rights.
26. Forum for Women, Law and Development, e-mail message to author, May 6, 2004.
27. Center for Reproductive Rights, *The Bush Global Gag Rule: A Violation of International Human Rights and the U.S. Constitution* (New York: CRR, 2003), 1.
28. Abortion Advocacy Kit, Center for Reproductive Rights

29. Center for Reproductive Rights, *Roe v. Wade and the Right to Privacy* (New York: CRR, 2003), 12.
30. CRR 2003.
31. See Human Life of Washington, Infanticide/Partial-Birth Abortion/Born-Alive Abortion, http://www.humanlife.net/infanticide.html; cited on May 25, 2004.
32. Lora Jo Foo, *Asian American Women: Issues, Concerns, and Responsive Human and Civil Rights Advocacy* (New York: Ford Foundation, 2002).
33. Centers for Disease Control and Prevention, "State-Specific Maternal Mortality Among Black and White Women—United States, 1987–1996," *Morbidity and Mortality Weekly Report* 48, 23 (June 18, 1999): 492–496. Available online: http://www.cdc.gov/epo/mmwr/preview/mmwrhtml/mm4823a3.htm cited on May 25, 2004.
34. See www.reprorights.org for more information.

CHAPTER 20

Sisters Inside

Speaking Out Against Criminal Injustice

DEBBIE KILROY

For over a decade, women prisoners, former prisoners, and their allies in Queensland, Australia, have been organizing to challenge the brutal treatment of women inside and to advocate the abolition of women's prisons. Formed in 1992, Sisters Inside is unique in involving the leadership of women prisoners who make decisions about service delivery and help to determine our political agenda for change. Unlike many prison reform organizations that speak *on behalf of* prisoners, Sisters Inside provides a platform for women inside to speak for themselves. This chapter first explores prison culture in Australian women's prisons. It is important to understand women's prison culture in order to appreciate why it is essential that women prisoners should have the opportunity to speak for themselves. Second, the chapter discusses the many aspects of coercive control, discipline, and abuse that women experience during their incarceration. Finally, the chapter describes the structure and goals of Sisters Inside, as a model for organizing alliances between women inside and outside the prison walls.

The Culture of Women's Prisons

In order to understand what women experience while they are incarcerated, readers need to be aware of the women's prison culture in Australia. Because prison culture silences and disempowers women, it is crucial that women prisoners gain a voice and are heard by the general public. The culture within the prison walls that women live in, day in and day out, is their survival. It is impossible to present a complete picture of this multifaceted complex and dynamic system in a short chapter. What follows is a brief synopsis of the culture that structures the lives of incarcerated women. In Australian prison culture, prison staff are named "screws." In order to be consistent with this culture, I use this term throughout the chapter. The term screw does not include professional staff and management; it refers only to custodial officers. To explain where women and screws fit into the culture is very complex as there are many overlaps and subsystems; however, I will attempt to give you some sense of Australian prison culture and its impact.

On entering the prison you are inducted into prison culture, although you are usually unaware that this process is taking place. Your crime and length of sentence will usually determine how you are treated and where you are placed within the culture. They will prescribe how you will survive or not survive your prison sentence. They will determine whether you are accepted by the prison system or ostracized. There are no clear boundaries about who is a long-termer and who is a short-termer. However, there are clear cultural norms that identify where a woman will be placed within this system. If you are a lifer—a woman sentenced to life—you will usually be accepted into the long-termers group. A life sentence is approximately sixteen years before you can apply for parole. However, if you are actually sentenced to sixteen years but not a life sentence, this does not automatically mean you are accepted into this group. There is a clear delineation between the two sentences. Once the lifers "suss you out" and believe that "you're okay," you will be accepted and initiated into the long-termers group. There are a number of criteria that a woman would have to meet in order to be accepted. First, she must demonstrate that she can stay in control of her feelings. She must prove that she will not show anger outwardly unless directed toward management in a controlled manner on issues that affect other women. Her crime must not be against children and she must not be a "dog"; that is, she must not betray confidences and must adhere to the code of silence.

Women serving short-term sentences usually show grief once imprisoned; however, they learn quickly that this is not accepted within the culture. A woman who shows her emotions through crying in prison will be labeled a "sook" or weak and told to "snap out of it 'cause you only have a short sentence." She will receive little sympathy from long-termers, who are likely to ask her impatiently: "what are you whingeing about, how long you got?" The short-termer woman who shows emotion through crying will gain very limited support from other women in prison or screws. Within this culture there is very little respect given to a "short-termer whinger." A woman who shows emotion through anger will also be isolated. This will prove to the other women and the screws that you are not "together," you are not in control. It is crucial that you stay in control in this culture, as the consequences for losing control are severe. The consequence of showing anger is to be breached, a disciplinary procedure involving punishment and isolation. Breaches are used as a behavior modification technique; basically, a woman is punished for her behavior if it is not acceptable by the screws. When she is breached for expressing anger outwardly, a woman can be locked away in isolation in the detention unit (DU) for up to 7 days. Anger can also be expressed inwardly, in ways that are detrimental to short-termers, for example, through "blood letting" (self-harm). Through self-harm, the anger can be released through the slices cut into the woman's arms. Total desensitization of the whole body is another way of dealing with anger. Anger is rarely expressed in overt physical violence, a fact that distinguishes women's prisons from their male counterparts.

Desensitization is the primary coping method that long-termers use to prove that they are in control so that they are accepted within the culture. Ironically, long-termers are allowed emotions of anger and sorrow while short-termers are ostracized. However, these emotions can only be controlled and not overtly shown to everyone in the prison. Individual anger can be shown within the long-termers group, and the group will offer support to the woman and attempt to resolve the problem generating the anger. Individual sorrow through crying is also allowed if it is pain and grief that is shared by most of the long-termers. For example, if a child is ill, the expression of sorrow is acceptable because the loss of their role as mother is shared by the other women. This display of emotion is controlled, and outsiders—short-termer women or screws—are not privy to the discussion or allowed to share what their grief and pain is like for them as mothers. If an outsider tries to join the process, desensitization will take over and the long-termers will shut down their emotions. Exclusion from the long-termers' group is once again enforced through protective mechanisms.

Screws and Long-Termers: Resistance to Change

Women prisoners and screws are responsible for maintaining the life force of the prison. A woman prisoner or a screw who tries to bring about change will be isolated, eventually silenced, and in some cases threatened with passive or overt violence. If a screw tries to make changes to the culture, protective mechanisms will be used to isolate the screw or the screw will be threatened. The screw will choose to either resign or conform to the culture. In 1990, when a murder happened in Brisbane Women's Correctional Centre, many staff who were affected emotionally by the murder were labeled "weak." They took stress leave for lengthy periods of time, and because they knew they could not survive this harsh culture most of these staff resigned. There is very limited respect and support for the weak from other screws and the women in prison.

There are different sorts of power within the culture. There is official power, which is attached to a person's position of employment, and there is real power, which is usually unofficial and held by the long-termers and screws. A screw has more immediate power than a person in a management position. A person in a middle management role told me:

> When I was a screw years ago, I had more power within the prison—now that I am in a management role I have hardly any real power. I have the power within my role but I am made accountable for everything I do and I can lose my job if I f . . . up. Years ago I knew who was doing what, where and when and we had the run of the show, we could breach women; lock them up when we choose and lose things like the mail and requests from the women as we choose. No one could do a thing to us because we had the 'real' power. Management would make their threats to us and say they were going to change the prison culture but they never could because we knew we would be around a lot longer than them and we held the power.[1]

As another screw said with regard to new managers coming into the prison and having changes planned, "it doesn't matter, they come and they go just like all the rest and we'll still be here—nothing has changed in the 20 years I've been around."[2] When I continued to explain that the manager is determined to change the culture and asked if anything is changing, he replied, "look nothing changes. It's the same shit, different depths." There is a huge resistance from long-termer screws to change the culture.

Within the culture the screws also maintain separation between the short-termers and the long-termers. They play the women off against each other, and this maintains the constant tension between the two groups of women. Screws who have been part of the prison for many years and are accepted by the other screws ensure that constant harassment is inflicted on short-term women. The long-term screws' role is to maintain pressure on the short-term screws so that they also conform to the culture. However, the screws (short-termers and long-termers) will not harass the long-termer women. They behave differently in all their interactions with them. The long-termer women will usually be shown respect and left to their own devices as long as what they do does not impinge on the screws. The principle is, you stay out of my way I'll stay out of yours.

The process screws use to play off long-termer women against short-termer women is to carry stories about who is whingeing and who is being breached for anger-related behaviors, for example, self-harm and suicide attempts. One of the many other ways screws play each group off is by telling the long-termers who is "dogging on" other women in prison, whether it is true or not. The word can travel at a speed faster than light in the women's prison. The stories are made up to suit their power play in maintaining the culture through separation of the groups. This creates a strong bond between long-termer women and the long-termer screws.

Punishment, Surveillance, and State Sexual Abuse

Legal frameworks and policies also ensure the maintenance of the women's prison culture of desensitization. Three legal provisions are critical here. First, section 86 of the *Corrective Services Act 2000* gives the legal framework for the use of breaching, which, as discussed earlier, is a form of punishment involving severe isolation. Second, section 26A of the Corrective Services Act 2000 allows strip searches. The invasive and abusive nature of strip searching carried out on women prisoners has led Sisters Inside to campaign against this practice, which we label "sexual assault by the State." Finally, section 42 of the Corrective Services Act 2000 allows the use of Crisis Support Units, which are a form of torture and seclusion.

Breaches are an internal prison discipline in which women are placed in total isolation in a DU. Cameras are used on a twenty-four-hour basis for surveillance. Women are not given privacy for using the toilet or showering. No communication of any form is permitted. This includes no books, television, radios, or any form of contact with other women. Although the practice of isolation is horrific, women say that the most horrendous part of the experience is that they know that male screws may be observing them. This invasive surveillance escalates the trauma of the whole experience. A breach may be meted out for offenses including assault, drug use, insubordination toward prison authorities, hanging towels on cell doors, smoking in cells, obscene language, or walking on the grass. Alarmingly, in some cases women are punished for self-harming behavior.

In September 1999 a woman on remand was driven to suicide the night after her release from the DU. Sisters Inside was informed that she had been placed in the DU for two days because she was in possession of "prohibited articles." These articles were incense sticks that were sent to her through the prison mail system and a towel with a hole in it. She was released and then returned to the DU for a further twenty-four hours for swearing at a senior officer. After the alarm was first raised, screws were reluctant to open the door because they thought she was in the corner and about to attack them. One and a half hours later they finally gained entry and found her dead, hanging with plaited wool. It was reported to us that a senior member of staff was heard to lament repeatedly: "My new jail, how could she do this to me." This whole incident indicates that prison authorities were totally lacking any consideration or empathy for the disastrous impact of severe isolation.[3]

Section 26A of the Corrective Services Act 2000 provides for mandatory strip searching after every personal contact visit. This runs counter to the preservation of basic human rights of prisoners. According to the Department of Corrective Services, visitors pass illicit drugs to prisoners. Authorities have therefore justified strip searches of prisoners as a necessary precaution in keeping the prison drug and contraband free. Since August 1999, strip searches have been conducted as a matter of mandate after all visits to the women's prison at Wacol. According to records obtained by Sisters Inside under the Freedom of Information Act, between August 1999 and August 2002, 15,942 full body searches, including a strip search of a baby, were conducted on women and children in Brisbane Women's Correctional Centre. In addition, 17,191 non-strip searches were conducted. Contraband reported by authorities included tobacco, jewelry, cigarettes, "pad no blood," "foul odour," "scratch," and two incidents of drugs over a three-year period.[4] It is difficult to understand how the pad, the scratch, and the foul odor can be considered contraband but prison records have identified them as such.

In spite of the comprehensive practice of strip searching, drugs still get into the prison. Furthermore, it has been identified that because of mandatory searches, numbers of visitors have decreased drastically. This is due to women asking their children and families not to visit them because they cannot face being sexually assaulted through the mandatory strip search after a family visit. Strip searching is an abusive practice that is effectively a criminal assault and revictimizes women who have been sexually abused. Sisters Inside statistics indicate that 89 percent of women in prison have experienced sexual abuse.[5] Furthermore, Australia is signatory to United Nations covenants that prohibit torture and other cruel, inhuman, or degrading punishment or treatment. Because mandatory strip searching has no effective outcome, it must be seen as simply a mechanism for punishment, control, and sexual assault by the state.

Under section 42 of the Corrective Services Act 2000, women who are considered at risk of self-harm or likely to harm others will experience a further level of isolation and torture. They are sent to the Crisis Support Unit (CSU), which was located in a male prison until only a few months ago. Crisis Support Unit orders can be up to five days in length if the woman is identified by a screw as being at risk of self-harm and up to three months if the woman is identified by a doctor or psychologist as being at risk of self-harm or suicide. However, Sisters Inside is in contact with a young woman who has been on consecutive CSU orders for over five years.

The staff in the CSU are predominantly male, and women have reported that "they were asked by a male officer monitoring the cells to perform sexual acts for the entertainment of male officers."[6] In another incident in Townsville three women reported that they were placed in straight jackets, denied water for long periods of time, given no access to toilet facilities, and forced to drink their own urine.[7] These incidents may not be the norm for the CSU, but if any such incidents occur it is a clear and undeniable violation of the human rights of prisoners and is indicative of the sort of abuses that inevitably occur within isolated institutions. Furthermore, the women are strip searched every time they come in contact with any person other than screws in the CSU. Therefore, they could be strip searched five, ten, or fifteen times a day. The greater the isolation, the greater propensity for abuse.[8]

Raising Our Voices

Sisters Inside works with women in prison to challenge the injustices faced by incarcerated women, their children, and families. Our mission statement explains that:

> *Sisters Inside* is an independent community organisation which exists to advocate for the human rights of women in the criminal justice system in Queensland, and to address gaps in the services available to them. We will work alongside women in prison in determining the best way to fulfil these roles.

Our primary focus is the abolition of women's prisons. This value underlies all actions of the organization. Sisters Inside has two areas of activity: first, legal reform, and second, service provision. Sisters Inside works predominantly with women in Queensland. There are five women's prisons in Queensland— Brisbane Women's Correctional Centre, Townsville Women's Correctional Centre, Numinbah Women's Correctional Centre, Helena Jones Community Correctional Centre, and Warwick WORC Program. These prisons hold a total of five hundred women. Indigenous women are disproportionately incarcerated in Australia and make up 30 percent of all women prisoners but only 2 percent of the nation's imprisonable population. In addition, immigrant women are increasingly adding to the imprisoned population. In the past two decades, the number of women in prison in Australia has skyrocketed because of "tough-on-crime" policies and the "war on drugs," which has imposed long sentences on women. In addition, tough parole policies have swelled prison populations. Women sentenced to two years or fewer are not eligible for parole but must serve two thirds of their sentence. At that point, prison authorities make the decision as to whether to release them or not. Under this arbitrary system, most women serve their sentence in full. The increase in women's imprisonment is reflected in the total prison population, which grew by 102 percent between 1982 and 1998.[9] Sisters Inside is a crucial voice of opposition to prison expansion and tough-on-crime political rhetoric.

Sisters Inside has a management committee made up of women in prison, ex-inmates, and other interested women from the community. Management members include indigenous women, women from non–English-speaking backgrounds, and young women. We believe it is important to be representative of the population of women in prison. The management committee meets regularly inside Brisbane Women's Correctional Centre and identifies gaps and high-need areas within the prison system and ways of meeting these needs. The committee also make day-to-day decisions about running the organization, including finances, employment of staff, legal reform focus, and funding. Sisters Inside is overseen and managed by women for women, including presently eight women in prison. The organization emphasizes the value of the knowledge and experience of women in prison. We recognize the expertise of women inside to identify their own needs, both within the prison environment and in transition to the general community. All of Sisters Inside's programs are underpinned by the considerable experience of women inside and the information that women inside have about prison culture and systems. Sisters Inside exists entirely for the benefit of the women in prison; its staff and culture are not an end in themselves. Our values and vision statement assert that the organization is directed by women. We are committed to valuing women within the prison system and trusting the judgment of women inside to know what they want. Sisters Inside is autonomous; that is to say, we are directed by the needs of the women and not the needs of the criminal injustice system.

Conclusion

Women living in the prison culture face terror on a daily basis. Their human rights are infringed by being breached for petty reasons, they are sexually abused by the state through the practice of mandatory strip searching, and they are tortured for being at risk of self-harm. For these traumatic practices to end, it is crucial that the testimonies of women inside should be heard. During our many discussions, members of Sisters Inside have identified a key to any successful prison activism, that is, that women in prison must have a voice about who they are and what their needs are. The voices of women prisoners are rarely if ever heard in the broader community. Sisters Inside has been a crucial vehicle for empowerment, allowing women to have a voice and to be heard. All activities undertaken by the organization ensure that the women inside take the lead in speaking out and making decisions. *Global Lockdown* is one avenue for the women inside to be heard. For change to happen, there needs to be a commitment from the wider community to continue to listen.

References

1. Kate Warner, *Walkin' the Talk: A History of Sisters Inside* (Queensland: Sisters Inside, 2001).
2. Ibid.
3. Debbie Kilroy and Anne Warner, "Deprivation of Liberty, Deprivation of Rights," in *Prisoners as Citizens: Human Rights in Australian Prisons*, ed. D. Brown and M. Wilkie (Annandale, NSW: Federation Press, 2002).

4. Department of Corrective Services, *Freedom of Information Records: Strip Searching* (DCS: Queensland, 1999–2002).
5. Debbie Kilroy, "When Will You See the Real Us? Women in Prison," *Women in Prison Journal* 2 (October 2001): 13–15.
6. Tony Koch, "Women Locked in with men," *Courier Mail* (September 9, 2000).
7. John Anderson, "Prisoners' Horror Claim: Women Drank Urine in Cells," *Townsville Bulletin* (June 21, 2000).
8. Debbie Kilroy and Anne Warner, 2002.
9. In 1982 the incarceration rate was 89.9 per 100,000; by 1998, it had increased to 139 per 100,000. Australian Institute of Criminology, *Imprisonment in Australia: Trends in Prison Populations and Imprisonment Rates* (Canberra: Australian Institute of Criminology, 2000).

Contributor Biographies

Biko Agozino is associate professor in social and behavioral sciences at Cheyney University of Pennsylvania, the oldest historically black college in America. He is author of *Black Women and the Criminal Justice System: Towards the Decolonisation of Victimisation* (Ashgate Publishing, 1997) and editor of the Ashgate Interdisciplinary Research Series in Ethnic, Gender and Class Relations. He has a Ph.D. in law from the University of Edinburgh, M.Phil. in criminology from the University of Cambridge, and a B.Sc. in sociology from the University of Calabar.

Asale Angel Ajani is assistant professor of anthropology at the Gallatin School, New York University. Her areas of research include globalization, diasporic studies, feminist theory, and critical race theory, as well as state and political violence. Asale is currently working on a book entitled *Negotiating Small Truths: Incarcerated African Women and Other Forms of State Violence* based on extensive fieldwork in the Rebibbia Women's Prison in Rome, Italy. She is also the founder of Texas Prison Watch and has worked for Women Care for women returning home from prison.

Elham Bayour was born and raised in Dbayeh Palestinian refugee camp in Lebanon. Elham is a national board member of Incite! Women of Color Against Violence. She has presented papers on Palestinian refugees at conferences in Belgium, Jerusalem, Palestine, Turkey, and the United States. Her work is published in the proceedings of the International Oral History Association and in *50 Years of Palestinian Human Rights Violations*.

Kailash Bhana is a senior trainer/researcher in the Gender Unit at the Centre for the Study of Violence and Reconciliation. Her research areas include the impact of maternal imprisonment on children, gender violence against women with disabilities, and the costs of gender-based violence to South African women. Kailash has been an expert witness in the High Court of South Africa regarding women who kill their abusive partners and has participated in the Justice for Women Campaign. Currently, she is facilitating a capacity building program on HIV/AIDS and gender-based violence. Kailash holds a degree in social work from the University of Witwatersrand.

Rebecca Bohrman is a doctoral candidate in the political science department at Yale University and a fellow at the University of Virginia's Miller Center of Public Affairs. Her dissertation, entitled *Sifting Immigrants: The Political and Historical Roots of Administrative Failure in the Immigration and Naturalization Service*, argues that patterns of political conflict around immigration issues have impeded effective immigration administration. She has taught English as a Second Language at El Centro de Educacion y Cultura in Chicago.

Manuela Ivone Pereira da Cunha teaches anthropology at the University of Minho (Portugal) and is a member of IDEMEC (France). She did extensive fieldwork in different periods in a major women's prison, which resulted in two books and several articles. Her more recent book was distinguished in Portugal with a prize for the social sciences, awarded by an international jury. Manuela was also the recipient of a Wenner-Gren Foundation for Anthropological Research fellowship. Her current research focuses on prisons, crime and criminalization, urban neighborhoods, and the structure of drug markets.

Juanita Díaz-Cotto is a Black Puerto Rican lesbian, feminist socialist who is active in various progressive social movements. She is the author of *Gender, Ethnicity and the State: Latina and Latino Prison Politics* and editor, under the pseudonym of Juanita Ramos, of *Compañeras: Latina Lesbians*. Juanita is an Associate Professor of Sociology, Women's Studies, and Latin American and Caribbean Area Studies at the State University of New York at Binghamton. She is currently working on a book entitled *Chicanas Lives and Criminal Justice: In Their Own Words*.

Linda Evans is an anti-imperialist who served sixteen years of a forty-year federal prison sentence for actions against the U.S. government. While in prison she was a founding member of the prisoner organizations Pleasanton AIDS Counseling and Education and the Council Against Racism. She also completed both her B.A. and M.A. in humanities and coauthored *The Prison-Industrial Complex and the Global Economy*. On January 20, 2001, President Clinton commuted her sentence. Linda is cofounder of All Of Us Or None, an organization that works to end discrimination against people with felony convictions.

Ruth Wilson Gilmore is an associate professor in geography at the University of Southern California. She is a member of Critical Resistance, the Prison Activist Resource Center, and the California Prison Moratorium Coalition. Her study of small prison towns in rural California debunks the myth of prison expansion as a driver of economic prosperity. Her forthcoming book, *Golden Gulag: Labor, Land, State, and Opposition in Globalizing California* (University of California Press), explores the political economy of California's prison expansion since 1982 and discovers urban and rural grassroots opposition.

Cristina Jose-Kampfner is a professor in psychology and women's studies at Eastern Michigan University. She is a Latina activist who has worked on behalf of women in prison and their children for the past twenty years. She has written several publications on women doing life sentences in the United States and Mexico. Cristina is the founder of a mother/child visitation program in Michigan women's prisons and the Washtenaw County Jail. She has studied the emotional and academic consequences of maternal incarceration on children's school performance and children living inside prisons in Mexico.

Kamala Kempadoo is associate professor in social science at York University. She is author of *Sexing the Caribbean: Studies of Gender, Race and Sexual Labor* (Routledge 2004), and editor of *Sun, Sex and Gold: Tourism and Sex Work in the Caribbean* (Rowman and Littlefield 1999) and *Global Sex Workers: Rights, Resistance and Redefinition* (Routledge 1998). She works closely with the Global Alliance Against Traffic in Women (GAATW) and is a Diaspora member of the Caribbean Association for Feminist Research and Action (CAFRA). For several years she was an organizer and activist in the Black and Migrant women's movement in the Netherlands.

Shahnaz Khan is an assistant professor in global studies and women's studies at Wilfrid Laurier University, Waterloo, Canada. She is the author of *Aversion and Desire: Negotiating Muslim Female Identity in the Diaspora* as well as numerous articles in journals including *Signs: Journal of Women in Culture and Society, Feminist Review, Feminist Studies, Canadian Journal of Women and the Law,* and the online journal *Genders*. Her research interests include women in Pakistan, Muslim women in the diaspora, and images of Afghan women in the west.

Debbie Kilroy is the director and cofounder of Sisters Inside, a unique organization that involves both women in prison and ex-prisoners on its management committee. She has spent many years in prison. Over the last twelve years Sisters Inside has addressed the needs identified by women prisoners through service provision and law reform, including sexual assault counseling and campaigns against systemic gender discrimination and strip searching. In 2003, Debbie was awarded the Order of Australia Medal. She has a degree in social work, is a qualified gestalt therapist, and is completing a degree in law.

Robbie Kina is an Aboriginal artist and prison activist from Queensland, Australia. In 1988, she went to jail for killing her de facto husband. Six years later, she was freed after the Queensland Court of Appeal set aside her conviction, concluding that her partner's brutal abuse should have been included in her defense. Robbie's case drew national attention and became central to feminist efforts to reform the criminal justice system. Robbie is Aboriginal Support Worker with Sisters Inside, a Queensland-based organization working on behalf of women in prison.

Naomi Murakawa is an assistant professor in the political science department at the University of Washington. She has a Ph.D. from Yale University and is completing a manuscript entitled *Electing to Punish: Congress, Race, and the Rise of the American Criminal Justice State.* She was the Co-Director of Research at A Better Way Foundation, an organization working to shift Connecticut's drug policy from a paradigm of criminal justice to one of public health.

Lisa Neve is an Aboriginal woman who recently successfully appealed her designation, at age 21, of dangerous offender, a designation that is accompanied by an indefinite sentence. In 1994 she was called the most dangerous woman in Canada by Justice Murray and was sent to a maximum security prison. At the appeal, it was ruled that instead of an indeterminate sentence, she should have received a three-year sentence. Lisa's case was supported by the Canadian Association of Elizabeth Fry Societies and the Native Women's Association of Canada. She is a currently a writer and activist.

Stormy Ogden is Kashaya Pomo, from Stewart Point, and a recognized member of the Tule River Yokuts tribe. She is a prison rights activist who has worked with the American Indian Movement for several years. While serving a five-year sentence at the California Rehabilitation Center at Norco, Stormy campaigned for the first sweat lodge to be built in a women's state prison in California. Stormy is active on domestic violence, recovery, protection of spiritual traditions, and Native women in prison. She is coauthor of *The American Indian Within the White Man's Prison: A Story of Genocide* (Uncompromising Books).

Kim Pate is the executive director of the Canadian Association of Elizabeth Fry Societies. In addition to her work with and on behalf of criminalized women and girls, Kim has been a strong advocate for social justice and has been involved with criminal justice and penal reform matters for two decades. A teacher and a lawyer by training, she has worked on a range of issues including child welfare, social services, mental health and educational reform, First Nations issues, and individual and systemic discrimination on the basis of gender, race, class, income, age, ability, and sexual orientation.

Sapana Pradhan-Malla is a lawyer who has worked for the legal recognition of women's human rights in Nepal for over a decade. Much of her career has been spent documenting the human rights violations of women persecuted under Nepal's brutal abortion law. She is coauthor of the study "Discriminatory Laws in Nepal and the Impact on Women: A Review of the Current Situation and Proposals for Change," which highlighted the injustices of the Nepali abortion laws before their revision. Sapana is president of the Forum for Women, Law and Development in Nepal.

Beth E. Richie has been active in the movement to end violence against women and against women's incarceration for the past twenty years. Her work focuses on the experiences of African American battered women and sexual assault survivors and women in prison. Beth is head of the Department of African American Studies and is on the faculty of the Departments of Criminal Justice and Gender and Women's Studies at the University of Illinois at Chicago. She is the author of *Compelled to Crime: The Gender Entrapment of Black Battered Women* and articles on women, violence, and imprisonment.

Kemba Smith was convicted as a college student of conspiracy for drug involvement and sentenced to 24.5 years in a federal prison. During her incarceration, the Kemba Smith Justice Project fought to secure her release and to invoke public outrage at the impact of mandatory minimum sentencing on battered women defendants. On December 22, 2000, President Clinton granted her clemency and issued a pardon. Since her release she has been awarded a Soros Justice Fellowship. She currently works with the Kemba Smith Foundation to promote drug law reform and justice for young people of color in the United States.

Julia Sudbury is Canada Research Council Chair in Social Justice, Equity and Diversity in the Faculty of Social Work at the University of Toronto and is on leave from the department of ethnic studies at Mills College. She is the author of *Other Kinds of Dreams: Black Women's Organizations and the Politics of Transformation* (Routledge 1998). Her current research focuses on women, criminalization, globalization, and the transnational prison-industrial complex. She is a national board member of Critical Resistance and Incite! Women of Color Against Violence and is an editorial board member of *Social Justice*.

Melissa Upreti is a Nepalese lawyer currently working as the Legal Adviser for Asia at the Center for Reproductive Rights, New York (www.reproductiverights.org). Melissa went to law school in India and the United States and worked as a program officer at the Asia Foundation in Nepal. After joining the Center in 2000, she led a fact-finding mission to investigate human rights violations of women imprisoned for abortion in Nepal. She is coauthor of *Abortion in Nepal: Women Imprisoned* and coordinator and editor of a regional report entitled *Women of the World: Laws and Policies Affecting their Reproductive Lives—South Asia* (2004).

Lisa Vetten is the manager of the gender program of the Centre for the Study of Violence and Reconciliation, a nongovernmental organization dedicated to peaceful and fundamental transformation in South Africa. She is currently a contributing editor to the South African newspaper *The Star*. She is also a member of the steering committee of the South African Gender-Based Violence and Health Initiative (SAGBVHI). Lisa first began working in women's prisons in 1998 with a focus on women who kill their abusive partners and is a founder member of the Justice for Women Campaign.

Selected Bibliography

Aboriginal and Torres Strait Islander Commission (ATSIC). *The Royal Commission into Aboriginal Deaths in Custody: An Overview of its Establishment, Findings and Outcomes.* Canberra: ATSIC, 1991, http://www.atsic.gov.au.

Abrahams, Naeema, Rachel Jewkes, and Ria Laubsher. *"I Do Not Believe in Democracy in the Home": Men's Relationships with and Abuse of Women.* Tygerberg: CERSA (Women's Health) Medical Research Council, 1999.

de Achá, Gloria R. M. *Violaciones a los Derechos Humanos Civiles Durante la Investigación Policial en Casos Detenidos Bajo la Ley 1008.* Cochabamba, Bolivia: Red Andina de Información, CEDIB, 1996.

____. "Características de las Mujeres Encarceladas en Bolivia." In *Criminalidad y Criminalización de la Mujer en la Región Andina,* edited by R. del Olmo. Caracas, Venezuela: Nueva Sociedad, 1998.

Adler, Freda. *Sisters in Crime: The Rise of the New Female Criminal.* New York: McGraw Hill, 1975.

Agomoh, Uju, A. Adeyemi, and V. Ogbebor. *The Prison Service and Penal Reform in Nigeria: A Synthesis Study.* Lagos: PRAWA, 2001.

Agozino, Biko. "Changes in the Social Construction of Criminality among Immigrants in the United Kingdom." In *Immigrant Delinquency: Social Sciences,* edited by European Commission. Luxembourg: European Commission, 1996.

____. *Black Women and the Criminal Justice System: Towards the Decolonisation of Victimisation.* Aldershot: Ashgate, 1997.

____. *Counter Colonial Criminology: A Critique of Imperialist Reason.* London: Pluto, 2003.

Agozino, Biko and Unyierie Idem. *Nigeria: Democratising a Militarised Civil Society.* London: CDD, 2001.

Agreda, Evelin, Norma Rodríguez, and Alex Contreras. *Mujeres Cocaleras.* Cochabamba, Bolivia: Comité Coordinador de las Cinco Federaciones del Trópico de Cochabamba, 1996.

Ahmad, Aijaz. "Of Dictators and Democrats: Indo-Pakistan Politics in the Year 2000." In *Lineages of the Present: Ideology and Politics in Contemporary South Asia,* edited by A. Ahmad. London: Verso Press, 2000.

Akumadu, Theresa. *Patterns of Abuse of Women's Rights in Employment and Police Custody.* Lagos: Civil Liberties Organisation, 1995.

Albrecht, Hans-Jorg. "The International System of Drug Control: Developments and Trends." In *Drug War, American Style: The Internationalization of Failed Policy and Its Alternatives,* edited by J. Gerber and E. Hensen. New York and London: Garland Publishing, 2001.

Alexander, Jacqui and Chandra Talpade Mohanty (eds). *Feminist Genealogies, Colonial Legacies, Democratic Futures.* New York: Routledge, 1997.

Allard, Patricia. *Life Sentences: Denying Welfare Benefits to Women Convicted of Drug Offenses.* Washington, DC: The Sentencing Project, 2002.

Alonso, Carlos. *Guerra Antidrogas, Democracia, Derechos Humanos y Militarización en América Latina.* Ciudad de Guatemala, Guatemala: CEDIB, Transnational Institute, and Inforpress Centroamericana, 1997.

301

Althabe, Gérard. "La Résidence Comme Enjeu." In *Urbanisation et Enjeux Quotidiens. Terrains Ethnologiques dans la France Actuelle*, edited by G. Althabe, C. Marcadet, M. de la Pradelle, and M. Sálim (eds.), Urbanisation et Enjeux Quotidiens. Paris: L'Harmattan, 1993.

Ambos, K. "A Comparison of Sentencing and Execution of Penalties." In *European Conference on Drug Couriers*, edited by CEP. Zurich: CEP, 1996.

American Association of University Women. *Hostile Hallways: The AAUW Survey on Sexual Harassment in America's Schools*. Washington, DC: Harris/Scholastic Research, 1993.

Amnesty International. "Amnesty International Report on Torture." In *The Women and War Reader*, edited by A. Lorentzen and J. Turpin. New York: New York University Press, 1988.

_____. *Mexico, Overcoming Fear*. New York, 1996.

_____. *United States of America, Human Rights Concerns in the Border Region with Mexico*. May 1998.

_____. *"Not Part of my Sentence:" Violations of the Human Rights of Women in Custody*. New York, 1999.

_____. *Italy: Alleged Torture and Ill Treatment by Law Enforcement and Prison Officers*. London: Amnesty International, 1995.

Anastasia, Stefano. "Il vaso di Pandora. Carcere e pena dopo le riforme." In *Il Vaso di pandora: Carcere e pena dopo le riforme*, edited by Mauro Palma. Roma: Istituto della Enciclopedia Italiana, 1997.

Andean Information Network. *The Weight of Law 1008*. Cochabamba, Bolivia: AIN, 1996.

_____. *Children of Law 1008*. Cochabamba, Bolivia: AIN, 1997.

Anderson, David. *Crime and the Politics of Hysteria*. New York: Times Books, 1995.

Arango, Mario. *Impacto del Narcotráfico en Antioquia*. Medellín, Colombia: J.M. Arango, 1988.

Atkins, Andy. "The Economic and Political Impact of the Drug Trade and Drug Control Policies in Bolivia." In *Latin America and the Multinational Drug Trade*, edited by E. Joyce and C. Malamud. Basingstoke: Macmillan Press, 1998.

Australian Institute of Criminology. *Imprisonment in Australia: Trends in Prison Populations and Imprisonment Rate*. Canberra: Australian Institute of Criminology, 2000.

Australian Law Reform Commission (ALRC). *Equality Before the Law: Justice for Women*. ALRC 69. Sydney, Australia: ALRC, 1994, http://www.austlii.edu.au.

Azaola, Elena and Cristina José Yacamán, *Las Mujeres Olvidadas: Un Estudio Acerca de la Situación de las Cárceles Para Mujeres de la República Mexicana*. México: Programa Interdisciplinario de Estudios de la Mujer, El Colegio de México/Comisión Nacional de Derechos Humanos, 1996.

Bagley, Bruce M. (ed). *Drug Trafficking in the Americas: An Annotated Bibliography*. Coral Gables, FL: North South Center, University of Miami, 1996.

Bales, Kevin. *Disposable People: New Slavery in the Global Economy*. Berkeley/Los Angeles: University of California Press, 1999.

Baratta, Alessandro. *Criminología Crítica y Crítica del Derecho Penal*. México: Siglo XXI, 1986.

_____. "Resocialización o Control Social? Por un Concepto Crítico de Reintegración Social del Condenado." In *El Sistema Penitenciario: Entre el Temor y la Esperanza*, edited by O. Cárdenas. México: Centro de Estudios de Criminología Crítica de América Latina, 1991.

Barrios, Sharon A. "Is the Immigration and Naturalization Service Unreformable? Past Experience and Future Prospects." *Administration and Society* 34 (2002): 370–388.

Barron, Christie, L. *Giving Youth a Voice: A Basis for Rethinking Adolescent Violence*. Halifax, Nova Scotia: Fernwood Publishing, 2000.

Barry, Kathleen. *Female Sexual Slavery*. New York: New York University Press, 1984.

Baudrillard, Jean. *Simulations*. New York: Semiotext(e), 1983.

Bean, Philip. "American Influence on British Drug Policy." In *Drug War, American Style: The Internationalization of Failed Policy and Its Alternatives*, edited by J. Gerber and E. Hensen. New York and London: Garland Publishing, 2001.

Bean, Walton E. *California: An Interpretive History*, 2nd Edn. New York: McGraw-Hill, 1973.

Beckett, Katherine. *Making Crime Pay: Law and Order in Contemporary American Politics*. New York: Oxford University Press, 1997.

Beckett, Katherine and Theodore Sasson. *The Politics of Injustice*. Thousand Oaks, CA: Pine Forge, 2000.

Belknap, Joanne. *The Invisible Woman: Gender, Crime and Justice*. Belmont, CA: Wadsworth Publishing Company, 1996.

Bello, Walden. "Building an Iron Cage: Bretton Woods Institutions, the WTO and the South." In *Views from the South: The Effects of Globalisation and the WTO on Third World Countries*, edited by S. Anderson. Chicago: First Food Books, 2000.

Bernstein, Laurie. *Sonia's Daughter: Prostitutes and Their Regulation in Imperial Russia.* Berkeley/Los Angeles: University of California Press, 1995.

Bhana, Kailash and Tessa Hochfeld. *"Now We Have Nothing": The Impact of Long-term Maternal Imprisonment on Children Whose Mothers Kill an Abusive Partner.* Johannesburg: Center for the Study of Violence and Reconciliation, 2001.

Bhandari, Neena. "Aboriginal Violence Against Women." *Contemporary Review* 283, 1655 (2003): 353–356.

Bhattacharjee, Anannya. "Private Fists and Public Force: Race, Gender and Surveillance." In *Policing the National Body: Race, Gender and Criminalization*, edited by J. Silliman and A. Bhattacharjee. Cambridge, MA: South End Press, 2002.

Biglan, Anthony J., J. Noelle, L. Ochs, K. Smolkowski, and C. Metzger. "Does Sexual Coercion Play a Role in the High-Risk Sexual Behavior of Adolescent and Young Adult Women?" *Journal of Behavioral Medicine* 18 (1995): 549.

Bloom, Barbara. "Triple Jeopardy: Race, Class, and Gender in Women's Imprisonment." Ph.D. dissertation, University of California, 1996.

Bloom, Barbara, Meda Chesney-Lind, and Barbara Owen. *Women in California Prisons*. San Francisco: Center on Juvenile and Criminal Justice, 1994.

Border Action Network. *Hate or Heroism: Vigilantes on the Arizona-Mexico Border.* Tucson: Border Action Network, 2002.

Boris, Eileen. "The Power of Motherhood: Black and White Activist Women Redefine the Political." *Yale Journal of Law and Feminism* Fall (1989): 25–49.

Bosworth, Mary. *Engendering Resistance: Agency and Power in Women's Prisons.* Aldershot: Ashgate, 1999.

Bourgois, Philippe and Eloise Dunlap. "Exorcising Sex for Crack: An Ethnographic Perspective from Harlem." In *Crack Pipe as Pimp: An Ethnographic Investigation of Sex-For-Crack Exchanges*, edited by M. Ratner. New York: Lexington Books, 1993.

Bowman, Cynthia G. "Street Harassment and the Informal Ghettoization of Women." *Harvard Law Review* 106 (1993): 517.

Box, Steve. *Power, Crime and Mystification.* London, Tavistock, 1983.

Boyer, Debra and David Fine. "Sexual Abuse as a Factor in Adolescent Pregnancy and Child Maltreatment." *Family Planning Perspectives* 24 (1992): 4–11, 19.

Brennan, Denise E. "Everything Is for Sale Here: Sex Tourism in Sosúa, the Dominican Republic." Ph.D. dissertation, Yale University, 1998.

Brown, Jodi M. and Patrick A. Langan, *State Court Sentencing of Convicted Felons 1994.* Washington, DC: Bureau of Justice Statistics, 1998.

Brown, Wilmette. *No Justice, No Peace: The 1992 Los Angeles Rebellion from a Black/women's Perspective.* London: International Black Women for Wages for Housework, 1992.

Browne, Angela and Shair Bassuk. "Intimate Violence in the Lives of Homeless and Poor Housed Women: Prevalence and Patterns in an Ethnically Diverse Sample." *American Journal of Orthopsychiatry* 67, 2 (1997): 261–278.

Burchell, Jonathon and John Milton. *Cases and Materials on Criminal Law*, 2nd Edn. Johannesburg: Juta, 2000.

Bureau of Justice Statistics. *Special Report: Survey of State Prison Inmates, 1991: Women in Prison.* Washington, DC: Department of Justice, 1994.

____. *Special Report: Women Offenders.* Washington, DC: Department of Justice, December 1999.

____. *Prisoners in 2000.* Washington, DC: Department of Justice, 2001.

____. *Prisoners in 2003.* Washington, DC: Department of Justice, 2003.

____. *Census of Jails, 1999.* Washington, DC: Department of Justice, 2001.

Burin, Mabel, Esther Moncarz, and Susana Velázquez. *El Malestar de las Mujeres. La Tranquilidad Recetada.* Buenos Aires: Paidos, 1991.

Burki, Shahid Javid. "The State and the Political Economy of Redistribution in Pakistan." In *The Politics of Social Transformation in Afghanistan, Iran, and Pakistan*, edited by M. Weiner and A. Banuazizi. Syracuse, NY: Syracuse University Press, 1994.

Cabezas, Amalia Lucía. "Women's Work Is Never Done: Sex Tourism in Sosua, the Dominican Republic." In *Sun, Sex, and Gold: Tourism and Sex Work in the Caribbean*, edited by K. Kempadoo. Lanham: Rowman and Littlefield, 1999.

Cabral, Amilcar. *Unity and Struggle*. New York: Monthly Review Press, 1979.

Cabral, Jo'o de Pina. "A Difus'o do Limiar: Margens, Hegemonias e Contradições." *Análise Social* XXXIV, 153 (2000): 865–892.

California Department of Corrections. *Historical Trends Institutions and Parole Population, 1977–1997*. Sacramento, June 1998.

____. *California Prisoners and Parolees, 2000 Summary Statistics*. Sacramento, June 2000.

____. *CDC Facts: 4TH Quarter 2002*. Sacramento, 2002.

Campbell, Ann. "Girls' Talk: The Social Representation of Aggression by Female Gang Members." *Criminal Justice and Behavior* 11, 2 (1984): 139–156.

Campbell, S., A. Perkins, and P. Mohammed. "'Come to Jamaica and Feel All Right': Tourism and the Sex Trade." In *Sun, Sex, and Gold: Tourism and Sex Work in the Caribbean*, edited by K. Kempadoo. Lanham: Rowman and Littlefield, 1999.

Canadian Human Rights Commission. *Protecting Their Rights: A Systemic Review of Human Rights in Correctional Services for Federally Sentenced Women*. Ottawa: CHRC, 2003.

Carcach, Carlos and Anna Grant. *Imprisonment in Australia: Trends in Prison Populations and Imprisonment Rates*. The Australian Institute of Criminology, 1999.

Carlen, Pat. *Women's Imprisonment*. London: Routledge & Kegan Paul, 1983.

____. *Women, Crime and Poverty*. Milton Keynes: Open University Press, 1988.

____. *Sledgehammer: Women's Imprisonment at the Millennium*. London: Macmillan Press, 1998.

Carter, Donald Martin. *States of Grace: Senegalese in Italy and the New European Immigration*. Minneapolis: University of Minnesota Press, 1997.

Center for Arms Control and Non-Proliferation. *Homeland Security Budget*. Washington, DC: Center for Arms Control and Non-Proliferation, 2003.

Center for Law and Social Policy and Community Legal Services. *Every Door Closed: Barriers Facing Parents with Criminal Records*. Washington, DC: Center for Law & Social Policy, 2002.

Center for Reproductive Rights. *Breaking the Silence: The Global Gag Rule's Impact on Unsafe Abortions*. New York: CRR, 2003. Available online: http://www.reproductiverights.org.

____. *Roe v. Wade and the Right to Privacy*. New York: CRR, 2003.

Center for Reproductive Rights and Forum for Women, Law and Development. *Abortion in Nepal: Women Imprisoned*. New York: CRR and FLWD, 2002.

Center on Juvenile and Criminal Justice. *California Prison Growth*. http://www.cjcj.org.

Centers for Disease Control and Prevention. "State-Specific Maternal Mortality Among Black and White Women—United States, 1987–1996," *Morbidity and Mortality Weekly Report* 48, 23 (June 18, 1999): 492–496.

Centro de Documentación e Información-Bolivia. *DEA y Soberanía en Bolivia*. Cochabamba, Bolivia: CEDIB, 1994.

Chakravarthi, Raghhavan. *Recolonisation*. Penang: Third World Network, 1990.

CHANGE. "Combatting Trafficking in Persons: A Directory of Organisations." CHANGE Anti-trafficking Programme, London, 2003.

Chapkis, Wendy. *Live Sex Acts: Women Performing Erotic Labor*. New York: Routledge, 1997.

____. "Trafficking, Migration and the Law: Protecting Innocents, Punishing Immigrants." *Gender and Society* 17 (2003): 923–937.

Chapman, Jane. *Economic Realities and the Female Offender*. Lexington: Lexington Books, 1980.

Chaves, Miguel. *Casal Ventoso: Da Gandaia ao Narcotráfico*. Lisbon: Imprensa de Ciências Sociais, 1999.

Chesney-Lind, Meda. "Women and Crime: The Female Offender." *Signs* 12, 1 (1986).

____. *The Female Offender: Girls, Women and Crime*. Thousand Oaks: CA: Sage Publications, 1997.

Chigwada-Bailey, Ruth. *Black Women's Experiences of Criminal Justice: A Discourse on Disadvantage*. Winchester: Waterside Press, 1997.

Ching Yoon Louie, Miriam. *Sweatshop Warriors: Immigrant Women Workers Take on the Global Economy*. Cambridge, MA: South End Press, 2001.

Chiodi, Milena. "Immigrazione, Devianza e Percezione d'Insicrezza: Analisi del Quatiere Crocetta a Modena." In *Dei Delitti e Delle Pene [special issue]: Immigrazione e insicrezza*, edited by Dario Melossi. Napoli: Edizioni Scientifiche Italiane, 1999: 115–140.

Christianson, Scott. *With Liberty for Some: 500 Years of Imprisonment in America*. Boston: Northeastern University Press, 1998.

Christie, Nils. *Crime Control as Industry: Toward Gulags, Western Style*. London: Routledge, 1993.

Christopher Commission. *Report of the Independent Commission on the Los Angeles Police Department*. Los Angeles, 1991.

Chuang, Janie. "Trafficking in Women: The United States as Global Sheriff." In *University of Toronto Feminism and Law Workshop Series*. Toronto, 2004.

Churchill, Ward and Jim Vander Wall. *The COINTELPRO Papers: Documents from the FBI's Secret Wars Against Dissent in the United States*. Cambridge, MA: South End Press, 2002.

Coalition Against the Trafficking in Women. "Fact Book on Global Sexual Exploitation: Italy." 1999. http:www.uri.edu/artsci/wms/hughes/catw/italy.html.

Cockburn, Alexander and Jeffrey St. Clair. *Whiteout*. New York: Verso, 1998.

Cole, Sally. *Women of the Praia: Work and Lives in a Portuguese Coastal Community*. Princeton, NJ: Princeton University Press, 1991.

Collins, Patricia Hill. *Black Feminist Thought: Knowledge, Consciousness and the Politics of Empowerment*. Boston: Unwin Hyman, 1990.

Comack, Elizabeth. *Women in Trouble: Connecting Women's Law Violations to Their Histories of Abuse*. Halifax: Fernwood Publishing, 1996.

_____. "Women and Crime." In *Criminology: A Canadian Perspective*, edited by R. Linden. Toronto: Harcourt, 2000.

Commission for Racial Equality. *Racial Equality in Prisons*. London: CRE, 2003.

Commission of Enquiry on the Status of Women. *Report*. Islamabad, Pakistan: Government of Pakistan Publication, August 1997.

Cooke, Sandy and Susanne Davies. *Harsh Punishment: International Experiences of Women's Imprisonment*. Boston: Northeastern University Press, 1999.

Copelon, Rhonda. "Surfacing Gender: Reconceptualizing Crimes Against Women in Time of War." In *The Women and War Reader*, edited by Ann Lorentzen and Jennifer Turpin. New York: New York University, 1998.

Cornell, Drucilla. *The Imaginary Domain*. New York: Routledge, 1995.

Correctional Association of New York. *Do They Belong in Prison?* New York, 1985.

_____. *Injustice Will Be Done*. New York, 1992.

_____. *Mandatory Injustice*. New York, 1999.

Costo, Rupert and H. Jeannette Costo. *Natives of the Golden State: The California Indian*. Riverside: The Indian Historian Press, 1995.

Cunha, Manuela P. da. "Le Temps Suspendu: Rythmes et Durées dans une Prison Portugaise." *Terrain* 29 (1997): 59–68.

_____. *Entre o Bairro e a Pris´o: Tráfico e Trajectos*. Lisbon: Fim de Século, 2002.

Currie, Elliott. *Crime and Punishment in America*. New York: Henry Holt and Co., 1998.

Dalla Costa, Mariarosa and Selma James. *The Power of Women and the Subversion of the Community*. London: Falling Wall Press, 1972.

Danielson, Kirstie K., Terrie E. Moffitt, Avshalom Caspi, and Phil A. Silva. "Co-morbidity Between Abuse of an Adult and DSM-III-R Mental Disorders: Evidence From an Epidemiological Study." *American Journal of Psychiatry* 155, 1 (1998): 131–133.

Davila, Alberto, Jose A. Pagan, and Montserrat Viladrich Grau. "Immigration Reform, the INS, and the Distribution of Interior and Border Enforcement Resources." *Public Choice* 99 (1999): 327–345.

Davis, Angela Y. "Race and Criminalization: Black Americans and the Punishment Industry." In *The Angela Y. Davis Reader*, edited by J. James. Malden: Blackwell Publishers, 1998.

_____. *Women, Race and Class*. London: The Women's Press, 1981.

_____. "Reflections on Race, Class, and Gender in the USA." In *The Angela Y. Davis Reader*, edited by J. James. Malden: Blackwell Publishers, 1998.

_____. *Are Prisons Obsolete?* New York: Seven Stories Press, 2003.

Davis, Angela Y. and Cassandra Shaylor. "Race, Gender and the Prison Industrial Complex: California and Beyond." *Meridiens* 2, 1 (2001): 1–24.

Davis, Mike. *City of Quartz*. New York: Verso, 1990.

_____. "Uprising and Repression in L.A." In *Reading Rodney King/Reading Urban Uprising*, edited by R. Gooding-Williams. New York: Routledge, 1993.

d'Aquino, Niccolo. "Immigrants Supplanting Emigration." *Europe* (April 2000): 47.

dal Lago, Alessandro. "The Impact of Migration on Receiving Societies: Some Ethnographic Remarks." In *Immigrant Delinquency: Social Sciences*, edited by European Commission. Luxembourg: European Commission, 1996.

Demleitner, Nora V. "The Law at a Crossroads: The Construction of Migrant Women Trafficked into Prostitution." In *Global Human Smuggling: Comparative Perspectives*, edited by D. Kyle and R. Koslowski. Baltimore: John Hopkins University Press, 2001.

Department of Correctional Services. *Restorative Justice, Healing the Wounds of Crime, Working for a Safer Community* (Pretoria, 2003). http://www.dcs.gov.za/restorativejustice/. Accessed December 2003.

Department of Safety and Security. *White Paper on Safety and Security: In Service of Safety 1999–2004* (Pretoria, 1998). http://www.gov.za/whitepaper/1998/safety.htm. Accessed December 2003.

Derber, Charles. *The Wilding of America*. New York: St Martins, 1996.

Derby, C. Nana. "The Causes and Character of 'Contemporary Slavery'." *Canadian Woman Studies* 22, 3–4 (2003): 60–65.

Díaz-Cotto, Juanita. *Gender, Ethnicity and the State: Latina and Latino Prison Politics*. New York: State University of New York Press, 1996.

____. "The Criminal Justice System and Its Impact on Latinas(os) in the United States," *The Justice Professional* 13, 1 (April 2000).

____. *Chicana Lives and Criminal Justice: In Their Own Words*. Austin: University of Texas, forthcoming 2006.

____. "Latina Imprisonment and the War on Drugs." In *Race, Gender, and Punishment*, edited by M. Bosworth and S. Bush-Baskette. Boston: Northeastern University, forthcoming 2004.

Dobash, Russell P. and Rebecca E. Dobash. "Community Response to Violence against Wives: Chivalry, Abstract Justice and Patriarchy." *Social Problems* 5 (1981).

____. *Rethinking Violence Against Women*. Thousand Oaks: CA. Sage Publications, 1998.

Doezema, Jo. "Loose Woman or Lost Women? The Re-emergence of the Myth of White Slavery in Contemporary Discourse of Trafficking in Women." *Gender Issues* Winter (2000):23–50.

Dorado, Maria C. "Mujeres Latinoamericanas en Europe: el Caso de Colombia." In *Criminalidad y Criminalización de la Mujer en la Región Andina*, edited by R. del Olmo. Caracas, Venezuela: Nueva Sociedad, 1998.

Dorn, Nicholas, Murji Karim, and Nigel South. *Traffickers. Drug Markets and Law Enforcement*. London and New York: Routledge, 1992.

Dorn, Nicholas, J. Jepsen, and E. Savona. *European Drug Policies and Enforcement*. London: Macmillan, 1996.

Dua, Enakshi and Angela Robertson. *Scratching the Surface: Canadian Anti-Racist Feminist Thought*. Toronto: Women's Press, 1999.

Dunlap, Eloise, Bruce Johnson, and Lisa Maher. "Female Crack Sellers in New York City: Who They Are and What They Do." *Women & Criminal Justice* 8, 4 (1997): 25–55.

Dunn, Timothy. *The Militarization of the US-Mexico Border, 1978–1992*. Austin, TX: Center for Mexican American Studies, University of Texas, 1996.

Duprez, Dominique and Michel Kokoreff. *Les Mondes de la Drogue*. Paris: Odile Jacob, 2000.

Dworkin, Andrea. "The Women Suicide Bombers." *Feminista* 5, 1 (2002). http://www.feminista.com/v5n1/dworkin.html.

Dyer, Joel. *The Perpetual Prisoner Machine: How America Profits from Crime*. Boulder, CO: Westview Press, 2000.

Eades, Diana. "Legal Recognition of Cultural Differences in Communication: The Case of Robyn Kina." *Language and Communication* (1996): 215–31.

Ehonwa, Osaze L. *Prisoners in the Shadow: A Report on Women and Children in Five Nigerian Prisons*. Lagos, Civil Liberties Organisation, 1993.

____. *Behind the Wall: A Report on Prison Conditions in Nigeria and the Nigerian Prison System*. Lagos: Civil Liberties Organisation, 1996.

Elkins, Mike, Carly Gray, and Keith Rogers. *Prison Population Brief England and Wales April 2001*. London: Home Office Research Development Statistics, 2001.

El Saadawi, Nawal. *The Nawal El Saadawi Reader*. London and New York: Zed Books, 1997.

Esmée Fairbairn Foundation. *A Bitter Pill to Swallow: The Sentencing of Foreign National Drug Couriers*. London, 2003.

Espanioly, Nabila. "Palestinian Women in Israel: Identity in the Light of the Occupation." In *Women and the Israeli Occupation: The Politics of Change*, edited by T. Mayer. New York and London: Routledge, 1994.

Espenshade, Thomas J. "Does the Threat of Border Apprehension Deter Undocumented United-States Immigration?" *Population and Development Review* 20 (1994): 871–892.

Esposito, John. *Women in Muslim Family Law*. Syracuse, NY: Syracuse University Press, 1982.

Faccioli, Franca. "Il carcere in Italia: appunti su un dibattito." In *Donne in Carcere: Ricerca sulla detenzione femminile in Italia*, edited by E. Campelli, F. Facciolo, V. Giordano, and T. Pitch. Milano: Feltrinelli, 1992.

Faith, Karlene. *Unruly Women: The Politics of Confinement and Resistance*. Vancouver: Press Gang Publishers, 1993.

Farley, Melissa and Howard Barkan, "Prostitution, Violence and Posttraumatic Stress Disorder." *Women and Health* 23, 3 (1998): 37–49.

Farrington, Keith. "The Modern Prison as Total Institution? Public Perception Versus Objective Reality." *Crime and Delinquency* 38, 1 (1992): 6–26.

Feeley, Malcolm and Jonathon Simon. "The New Penology: Notes on the Emerging Strategy of Corrections and Its Implications." *Criminology* 30, 4 (1992).

Feldman, Allen. *Formations of Violence*. Chicago: University of Chicago, 1991.

Fernandes, Leela. *Producing Workers*. Philadelphia: University of Pennsylvania, 1997.

Fernández, Dolores E. *La Pena de Prisión*. México: Unam, 1993.

Ferreira, Virginia. "Padrões de Segregaç'o das Mulheres no Emprego—Uma Análise do Caso Português no Quadro Europeu." In *Portugal: Um Retrato Singular*, edited by Boaventura de Sousa Santos. Oporto: Afrontamento, 1993.

Fisher, Jo. *Mothers of the Disappeared*. Boston: South End Press, 1989.

Foner, Phillip. "The IWW and the Negro Worker." *Journal of Negro History* (1970): 45–64.

Foo, Lora Jo. *Asian American Women: Issues, Concerns, and Responsive Human and Civil Rights Advocacy*. New York: Ford Foundation, 2002.

Fortunati, Leopoldina. *The Arcane of Reproduction: Housework, Prostitution, Labor and Capital*. Brooklyn: Autonomedia, 1995.

Forum for Women Law and Development and Planned Parenthood Global Partners. *Struggles to Legalize Abortion in Nepal and Challenges Ahead*. Kathmandu: FWLD, 2003.

Foucault, Michel. *Discipline and Punish: The Birth of the Prison*. London: Allen Lane, 1977.

Freedman, Estelle. *Their Sisters Keepers*. Ann Arbor: University of Michigan Press, 1981.

Freire, Paulo. *Pedagogy of the Oppressed*. New York: Seabury, 1970.

Friman, H. Richard. *Narcodiplomacy: Exporting the US War on Drugs*. Ithaca, NY and London: Cornell University Press, 1996.

Frymer, Paul. *Uneasy Alliances: Race and Party Competition in America*. Princeton, NJ: Princeton University Press, 1999.

Gabel, Katherine and Denise Johnston (eds). *Children of Incarcerated Parents*. New York: Lexington Books, 1995.

Gallagher, Anne. "Human Rights and the New UN Protocols on Trafficking and Migrant Smuggling: A Preliminary Analysis." *Human Rights Quarterly* 23 (2001a): 975–1004.

Garland, David. *Mass Imprisonment: Social Causes and Consequences*. London: Sage Publications, 2001.

Gibson, Mary. *Prostitution and the State in Italy, 1860–1915*. New Brunswick, NJ: Rutgers University Press, 1986.

Gilman, Sander L. *Difference and Pathology: Stereotypes of Sexuality, Race, and Madness*. Ithaca, NY: Cornell University Press, 1985.

Gilmore Ruth Wilson. "Terror Austerity Race Gender Excess Theater." In *Reading Rodney King/Reading Urban Uprising*, edited by R. Gooding-Williams. New York: Routledge, 1993.

____. Globalization and U.S. Prison Growth. *Race and Class* 40, 2/3 (1998): 171–188. Forthcoming.

____. *Golden Gulag*. Berkeley: University of California, forthcoming.

Gilroy, Paul. *Ain't No Black in the Union Jack: The Cultural Politics of Race and Nation*. Chicago: Chicago University Press, 1991.

Goffman, Erving. *Asylums. Essays on the Social Situation of Mental and Other Inmates*. Garden City, NY: Garden Books, 1961.

Goldberg, Eve and Linda Evans. *The Prison Industrial Complex and the Global Economy*. Berkeley, CA: Agit Press, 1998.

Gooding-Williams, Robert (ed). *Reading Rodney King, Reading Urban Uprising*. New York: Routledge, 1993.

Gordon, Avery F. "Globalism and the Prison Industrial Complex: An Interview with Angela Davis." *Race and Class* 40 (October 1998–March 1999).

Government Research Bureau. *Justice in South Dakota: Does Race Make a Difference?* State of South Dakota, 2002.

Gramsci, Antonio. *Selections from the Prison Notebooks*. New York: International Publishers, 1971.

Grant, David, Melvin L. Oliver, and Angela D. James. "African Americans: Social and Economic Bifurcation." In *Ethnic Los Angeles*, edited by Roger Waldinger and Mehdi Bozorgmehr. New York: Russell Sage Foundation, 1996.

Green, Judith. "Bailing Out Private Jails." *The American Prospect* 12, 6 (September 10, 2001).

Greenberg, Michael and Dona Schneider. "Violence in American Cities: Young Black Males Is the Answer, But What Was the Question?" *Social Science and Medicine* 39, 2 (1994): 179–187.

Greenfeld, Lawrence A. and Steven K. Smith. *American Indians and Crime*. Bureau of Justice Statistics, NCJ 173386, 1999.

Greenfeld, Lawrence A. and Tracy L. Snell. *Women Offenders*. Washington, DC: Bureau of Justice Statistics, 1999.

Greenwood, Peter W., C. Peter Rydell, Allan F. Abrahamse, Jonathon P. Caulkins, Jonathon Chiesa, Karyn E. Moder, and Stephen P. Klein. *Three Strikes and You're Out: Estimated Costs of California's New Mandatory-Sentencing Law*. Santa Monica: The Rand Corporation, 1994.

Grewal, Inderpal and Caren Kaplan. *Scattered Hegemonies, Postmodernity and Transnational Feminist Practices*. Minneapolis: University of Minnesota Press, 1994.

Grittner, Frederick K. *White Slavery: Myth, Ideology and American Law*. New York: Garland Press, 1990.

Guild, Elspeth. "The Legal Framework of Citizenship of the European Union." In *Citizenship, Nationality and Migration in Europe*, edited by D. Cesarani and M. Fulbrook. London: Routledge, 1996.

Hall, Stuart. "Cultural Studies: Two Paradigms." *Media, Culture and Society* 2, 1 (1980).

_____. "Gramsci's Relevance for the Study of Race and Ethnicity." *Journal of Communication Inquiry* 10, 2 (1986): 5–27.

_____. "Race, Articulation and Societies Structured in Dominance." In UNESCO *Sociological Theories: Race and Colonialism*. Poole: UNESCO, 1998.

_____. "Cultural Identity and Diaspora." In *Identity: Community, Culture and Difference*, edited by L Rutherford. London: Lawrence and Wishart, 1990.

Hall, Stuart, James Critcher, Tony Jefferson, John Clarke, and Brian Robert. *Policing the Crisis: Mugging, the State and Law and Order*. London: Macmillan, 1978.

Hancock, Linda. "Aboriginality and Lawyering." *Violence Against Women* 2, 4 (1996): 429–447.

Hannah-Moffat, Kelly. *Punishment in Disguise: Penal Governance and Federal Imprisonment of Women in Canada*. Toronto: University of Toronto Press, 2001.

Hartmann, Heidi. "The Family as the Locus of Gender, Class and Political Struggle: The Example of Housework." *Signs* 6, 3 (1981): 366–394.

Himes, Chester. *If He Hollers*, New York: Thunder's Mouth, 1986 [1945].

Hooks, Bell. *Yearning*. Boston: South End Press, 1990.

Horton, Myles and Paulo Freire. *We Make the Road by Walking*. Philadelphia: Temple, 1990.

Hijab, Nadia. *Womanpower: The Arab Debate on Women at Work*. Cambridge: Cambridge University Press, 1988.

HM Prison Service. "Privately Managed Prisons." http://www.hmprisonservice.gov.uk

[The Holy] Qur'an, trans. Abdullah Yusuf Ali. Beirut: Dar al-Arabia, 1968.

Home Office. *Statistics on Women and the Criminal Justice System*. London, 2003.

Howe, Adrian. *Punish and Critique: Towards a Feminist Analysis of Penality*. London: Routledge, 1994.

Human Rights Commission of Pakistan. *State of Human Rights in Pakistan in 1997*. Lahore, Pakistan: Maktaba Jadeed Press, 1997.

Human Rights Watch. *Police Brutality in the United States*. New York, 1991.

_____. *Bolivia: Human Rights Violations and the War on Drugs*. New York, 1995.

____. *Crossing the Line: Human Rights Abuses Along the U.S. Border with Mexico Persist Amid Climate of Impunity.* New York, 1995.

____. *Slipping through the Crack: Unaccompanied Children Detained by the U.S. Immigration and Naturalization Service.* New York, 1997.

____. *Cruel and Usual: Disproportionate Sentences for New York Drug Offenders* 9 (2)(B). New York: 1997.

____. *Punishment and Prejudice: Racial Disparities in the War on Drugs.* New York, 2000.

Humphries, Drew. *Crack Mothers: Pregnancy, Drugs and the Media.* Columbus: Ohio State University Press, 1999.

Hynes, H. Patricia and Janice Raymond. "Put in Harm's Way: The Neglected Health Consequences of Sex Trafficking in the United States." In *Policing the National Body: Race, Gender and Criminalization,* edited by J. Silliman and A. Bhattacharjee. Cambridge, MA: South End Press, 2002.

International Center for Prison Studies. "World Prison Brief." http://www.prisonstudies.org.

International Helsinki Federation for Human Rights. "IHF Focus," 1999. http://www.ihf-hr.org/reports/italy.

International Organization for Migration. *Trafficking in Women to Italy for Sexual Exploitation.* Washington, DC: International Organization for Migration, 1996.

Irwin, John and Donald Cressey. "Thieves, Convicts and the Inmate Culture." *Social Problems* 10 (1962): 142–155.

Jacobs, Bruce and Jody Miller. "Crack Dealing, Gender, and Arrest Avoidance." *Social Problems* 45, 4 (1998): 550–569.

Jahangir, Asma and Hina Jilani. *The Hadood Ordinances: A Divine Sanction?* Lahore: Rhotas Books, 1988.

Jalal, Ayesha. "The Convenience of Subservience: Women and the State of Pakistan." In *Women, Islam and the State,* edited by D. Kandiyoti. Philadelphia: Temple University Press, 1991.

____. "The State and Political Privilege in Pakistan." In *The Politics of Social Transformation in Afghanistan, Iran, and Pakistan,* edited by M. Weiner and A. Banuazizi. Syracuse, NY: Syracuse University Press, 1994.

James, C. L. R. *The Black Jacobins: Toussaint l'Ouverture and the San Diego Revolution.* London: Allison and Busby, 1980.

James, Joy L. *Resisting State Violence.* New York: Routledge, 1997.

Jammal, Laila. "Contributions by Palestinian Women to the Struggle for Liberation." *Palestine Liberation Organization Bulletin* 7, 13 (1981): 30–40.

Javier Pina y Palacios (ed). *La Mujer Delincuente.* México: Instituto de Investigaciones Jurídicas, 1983.

Jeffreys, Sheila. *The Idea of Prostitution.* Melbourne: Spinifex, 1997.

Jelsma, M. and T. Ronken (eds). *Democracias Bajo Fuego.* Uruguay: TNI, Ediciones Brecha, Acción Andina, 1998.

Jewkes, Rachel, Loveday Penn-Kekana, Jonathon Levin, M. Ratsaka, and M. Schrieber. "*He Must Give Me Money, He Mustn't Beat Me*" *Violence Against Women in Three South African Provinces.* Pretoria: CERSA (Women's Health) Medical Research Council, 1999.

Johnson, Bruce, Ansley Hamid, and Harry Sanabria. "Emerging Models of Crack Distribution." In *Drugs, Crime, and Social Policy: Research, Issues, and Concerns,* edited by T. Mieczkowski. Boston: Allyn and Bacon, 1992.

Johnson, Kevin R. "The Case Against Race Profiling in Immigration Enforcement." *Washington University Law Quarterly* 78 (2000): 676–736.

Jones, Jacqueline. *The Dispossessed.* New York: Basic Books, 1992.

Joyce, Elizabeth. "Cocaine Trafficking and British Foreign Policy." In *Latin America and the Multinational Drug Trade,* edited by E. Joyce and C. Malamud. Basingstoke: Macmillan Press, 1998.

Judicial Inspectorate of Prisons. *Annual Report for the Period 1 April 2002 to 31 March 2003* (Cape Town, 2003), 27. Available online: http://judicialinsp.pwv.gov.za. Accessed September 2003.

Justice Policy Institute. *Cellblocks or Classrooms? The Funding of Higher Education and Corrections and Its Impact on African American Men.* Washington, DC: Justice Policy Institute, 2000.

____. *New Prison Statistics: Nation's Use of Incarceration on the Rise Again.* July 25, 2003. http://www.justicepolicy.org.

Kalunta-Crumpton, Anita. *Race and Drug Trials: The Social Construction of Guilt and Innocence.* Aldershot: Ashgate, 1999.

Kandiyoti, Deniz. "Bargaining with Patriarchy." *Gender and Society* 2 (1988): 274–290.

Kaplan, Temma. "Female Consciousness and Collective Action." *Signs* 7, 3 (1982): 545–566.

Keith, Michael. "From Punishment to Discipline? Racism, Racialization and the Policing of Social Control." In *Racism, the City and the State*, edited by M. Cross and M. Keith. New York: Routledge, 1993.

Kelley, Robin D. G. *Hammer and Hoe.* Chapel Hill: University of North Carolina, 1990.

Kempadoo, Kamala (ed). *Sun, Sex and Gold: Tourism and Sex Work in the Caribbean.* Lanham: Rowman and Littlefield, 1999.

_____. "Women of Color and the Global Sex Trade: Transnational Feminist Perspectives." *Meridians* 1 (2001): 28–51.

_____. (ed) *Shifts in the Debate: New Approaches to Migration, Trafficking, and Sex Work in Asia.* Boulder, CO: Paradigm Publishers, forthcoming.

Kempadoo, Kamala and Jo Doezema (eds). *Global Sex Workers: Rights, Resistance, and Redefinition.* New York: Routledge, 1998.

Kilroy, Debbie. "When Will You See the Real Us? Women in Prison." *Women in Prison Journal* 2 (October 2001): 13–15.

Kilroy, Debbie and Anne Warner. "Deprivation of Liberty, Deprivation of Rights." In *Prisoners as Citizens: Human Rights in Australian Prisons*, edited by D. Brown and M. Wilkie. Annandale, NSW: Federation Press, 2002.

King, Ryan S. and Marc Mauer. *State Sentencing and Corrections Policy in an Era of Fiscal Restraint.* Washington, DC: The Sentencing Project, 2002.

Klein, Naomi. *Fences and Windows: Dispatches from the Front Lines of the Globalization Debate.* New York: Picador USA, 2002.

Klinkner, Philip A. and Rogers M. Smith. *The Unsteady March: The Rise and Decline of Racial Equality in America.* Chicago: University of Chicago Press, 1999.

Kolts, James G. *The Los Angeles County Sheriffs' Department: A Report (Kolts Report).* Los Angeles: Board of Supervisors, 1992.

Kubayi, Winnie. "The Major Sources of Children's Legal Rights." In *Children and the Law*, edited by A. Skelton. Pietermaritzburg: Lawyers for Human Rights, 1998.

Kyle, David and Rey Koslowski. *Global Human Smuggling: Comparative Perspectives.* Baltimore: John Hopkins University Press, 2001.

Latta, F. F. *Handbook of the Yokuts Indian.* Bakersfield: Bear State Books, 1949.

Larrauri, Elena. *Mujeres, Derecho Penal y Criminología.* México: Siglo XXI, 1994.

Laserna, Roberto (ed). *Economía Política de las Drogas.* Cochabamba, Bolivia: Centro de Estudios de la Realidad Económica y Social-Consejo Latinoamericano de Ciencias Sociales, 1993.

_____. *Twenty (Mis)conceptions on Coca and Cocaine.* La Paz, Bolivia: Clave consultores, s.r.l., 1997.

Leander, Karen. "The Normalization of Swedish Prisons." In *Western European Penal Systems. A Critical Anatomy*, edited by V. Ruggiero, M. Ryan, and J. Sim. London: Sage, 1995.

Lemire, Guy. *Anatomie de la Prison.* Montréal: Presses de l'Université de Montréal, 1990.

Leone, Richard C. and Greg Anrig Jr. (eds) *The War on Our Freedoms.* New York: Public Affairs, 2003.

Levine, Michael and Laura Kavanau-Levine. *The Big White Lie.* New York: Thunder's Mouth, 1993.

Lima, Ma. de la Luz. *Criminalidad Femenina. Teorías y Reacción Social.* México: Porrúa 1991.

Lindsley, Syd. "The Gendered Assault on Immigrants." In *Policing the National Body: Race, Gender, and Criminalization*, edited by J. Silliman and A. Bhattacharjee. Cambridge, MA.: South End Press, 2002.

Linebaugh, Peter. *The London Hanged.* Cambridge: Cambridge University Press, 1992.

Lipsitz, George. *A Life in the Struggle: Ivory Perry and the Culture of Opposition.* Philadelphia: Temple, 1987.

Ludsin, Hallie. *Legal Defense for Battered Women Who Kill Their Abusers: Discussion Document 1.* Johannesburg: Centre for the Study of Violence and Reconciliation, 2003.

_____. *South African Criminal Law and Battered Women Who Kill: Discussion Document 2.* Johannesburg: Centre for the Study of Violence and Reconciliation, 2003.

Machado, Fernando Luís. "Etnicidade em Portugal. Contrastes e Politizaç'o." *Sociologia. Problemas e Práticas* 12 (1992): 123–136.

Madhubuti, Haki R. *Why L.A. Happened.* Chicago: Third World Press, 1993.

Maher, Lisa. *Sexed Work. Gender, Race and Resistance in a Brooklyn Drug Market.* Oxford: Clarendon Press, 1997.

Maher, Lisa and Kathleen Daly. "Women in the Street-Level Drug Economy: Continuity or Change?" *Criminology* 34, 4 (1996): 465–491.

Maher, Vanessa. "Immigration and Social Identities." In *Italian Cultural Studies: An Introduction,* edited by D. Forgacs and R. Lumley. Oxford: Oxford University Press, 1996.

Maia Costa, Eduardo. "Direito Penal da Droga: Breve História de um Fracasso." *Revista do Ministério Público* 74 (1998): 103–120.

Maingot, Anthony P. "Offshore Banking in the Caribbean: The Panamanian Case." In *Latin America and the Multinational Drug Trade,* edited by E. Joyce and C. Malamud. New York: St. Martin's, 1998.

Mandela, Winnie. *Part of My Soul,* edited by A. Benjamin. Middlesex: Penguin, 1984.

Mann, Coramae R. "Women of Color and the Criminal Justice System." In *The Criminal Justice System and Women* edited by B. R. Price and N. J. Sokoloff. New York: McGraw-Hill, 1995.

Marchand, B. *The Emergence of Los Angeles.* London: Pion Ltd, 1986.

Margain, Hugo B. "The War on Drugs: A Mexican Perspective," *Voices of México* (October–December 1990): 3–8.

Marshall, Phil. "The Trojan Horse and Other Worries." *Stop by Stop: Newsletter of the UN Inter-Agency Project on Trafficking in Women and Children in the Mekong Sub-region,* Third Quarter, 2001.

Marshall, Phil and Susu Thatun. "Miles Away: The Trouble with Prevention in the Greater Mekong Sub-region." In *Shifts in the Debate: New Approaches to Migration, Trafficking and Sex Work in Asia,* edited by K. Kempadoo. Boulder, CO: Paradigm Publishers, forthcoming.

Martinez, Elizabeth "Betita." "Where Was the Color in Seattle?: Looking for Reasons Why the Great Battle Was So White." *Colorlines* 3, 1 (2000).

Massachusetts Governor's Commission on Gay and Lesbian Youth. *Making Schools Safe for Gay and Lesbian Youth.* 1993.

Massey, Doreen. *Space, Place, and Gender.* Oxford: Blackwell, 1994.

Massey, Douglas and Nancy Denton. *American Apartheid.* Cambridge, MA: Harvard, 1993.

Mauer, Marc and Tracy Huling. *Young Black Americans and the Criminal Justice System: Five Years Later.* Washington, DC: The Sentencing Project, 1995.

Mayer, Tamar (ed). *Women and the Israeli Occupation: The Politics of Change.* New York and London: Routledge, 1994.

Medhi, Rubya. "The Offence of Rape in the Islamic Law of Pakistan." *Women Living Under Muslim Laws, Dossier 18* B.P. 23, 34790. Grabels, France, 1991: 98–108.

Melossi, Dario. "'In a Peaceful Life': Migration and the Crime of Modernity in Europe/Italy." *Punishment and Society.* Vol 5 No. 4.

Mikell, Gwendolyn (ed). *African Feminism: The Politics of Survival in Sub-Saharan Africa.* Philadelphia: University of Pennsylvania Press, 1997.

Milasin, Ljubomir. "Illegal Immigrants Are Easy Prey for Pimps." Agence France Presse, 2000.

Miles, Angela. *Integrative Feminisms: Building Global Visions 1960s–1990s.* New York: Routledge, 1996.

Miller, Jerome. *Search and Destroy: African-American Males in the Criminal Justice System.* Cambridge: Cambridge University Press, 1996.

Mirza, Heidi. *Black British Feminism: A Reader.* London: Routledge, 1997.

Mogannam, Matiel. *The Arab Woman and the Palestine Problem.* London: Hyperion Press, 1937.

Mohanty, Chandra Talpade. *Feminism without Borders: Decolonizing Theory, Practicing Solidarity.* Durham, NC: Duke University Press, 2003.

Mohanty, Chandra Talpade, Ann Russo, and Lourdes Torres. *Third World Women and the Politics of Feminism.* Bloomington: Indiana University Press, 1991.

Mollen Commission. *Commission Report.* New York City, 1994.

Moraga, Cherrie and Gloria Anzaldua. *This Bridge Called My Back: Writings by Radical Women of Color.* Watertown, MA: Persephone Books, 1981.

Morgan, Patricia and Jaren Ann Joe. "Uncharted Terrain: Contexts of Experience Among Women in the Illicit Drug Economy." *Women and Criminal Justice* 8, 3 (1997): 85–109

Morgan, Rod. "New Labour 'Law and Order' Politics and the House of Commons Home Affairs Committee Report on Alternatives to Prison Sentences." *Punishment and Society* 1, 1 (1999).

Morris, Milton. *Immigration—The Beleaguered Bureaucracy*. Washington, DC: The Brookings Institution, 1985.

Motivational Educational Entertainment Productions. *The MEE Report 2: In Search of Love: Dating Violence Among Urban Youth* Philadelphia: Center for Human Advancement, 1996.

Mumola, Christopher J. *Incarcerated Parents and Their Children*. Washington, DC: Bureau of Justice Statistics, 2000.

Munoz, Gema Martin. "Islam and the West, an Intentional Duality." In *Islam, Modernism and the West*, edited by G.M. Munoz. London: I. B. Tauris, 1999.

National Council of La Raza. *The Mainstreaming of Hate: A Report of Latinos and Harassment, Hate Violence, and Law Enforcement Abuse in the 90's*. Washington, DC: National Council of La Raza, 1999.

National Criminal Victimization Survey. *Preventing Violence Against Women*. June 1995.

National Women's Law Center. "Women in Prison." In *Walkin' Steel '95*, edited by Committee to End the Marion Lockdown. Chicago: Committee to End the Marion Lockdown, 1995.

Nepal Ministry of Health. *Nepal Demographic and Health Survey 2001*. Calverton, ML: Ministry of Health, New ERA, and ORC Marco, 2002.

New York Department of Correctional Services. *Characteristics of Female Inmates Held Under Custody, 1975–1985*. Albany, 1986.

_____. *The Hub System: Profile of Inmates Under Custody in January 1, 1996*. Albany, 1996.

_____. *Men and Women Undercustody: 1987–2001*. Albany, September 2002.

New York Gay and Lesbian Anti-Violence Project. *Annual Report* (1996).

Nicholas, Margaret. "Bisexuality in Women: Myths, Realities and Implications for Therapy." In *Women and Sex Therapy, Closing the Circle of Sexual Knowledge*, edited by E. Rothblum. Harrington Park Press, 1988.

Norton, Jack. *Genocide in Northwestern California: When Our Worlds Cried*. San Francisco: The Indian Historian Press, 1997.

O'Connor, James. *The Fiscal Crisis of the State*. New York: St. Martin's, 1973.

Office of National Drug Control Policy, Executive Office of the President. *The National Drug Control Strategy, 1997*. Washington, DC, 1997.

Oliver, Melvin L. and Thomas M. Shapiro. *Black Wealth/White Wealth*. New York: Routledge, 1995.

Oliver, Melvin L., James H. Johnson, and Walter C. Farrel Jr. "Anatomy of a Rebellion: A Political-Economic Analysis." In *Reading Rodney King/Reading Urban Uprising*, edited by R. Gooding-Williams. New York: Routledge, 1993.

Oloruntimehin, Olufunmilayo and R. O. Ogedengbe. "Women and Substance Abuse in Nigeria." In *Women and Substance Abuse*, Interim Report, edited by L. N. Hsu. Geneva, WHO/PSA/92.9, 1992: 30–41.

Omi, Michael and Howard Winant. *Racial Formation in the United States*. New York: Routledge, 1986.

O'Neill, Amy Richard. "International Trafficking in Women to the United States: A Contemporary Manifestation of Slavery and Organized Crime." Center for the Study of Intelligence, DCI Exceptional Intelligence Analyst Program, U.S. Government, 1999.

O'Neill, Maggie. *Prostitution and Feminism: Towards a Politics of Feeling*. Cambridge: Polity Press, 2001.

Owen, Barbara. *In the Mix: Struggle and Survival in a Women's Prison*. New York: SUNY, 1998.

Palidda, Salvatore. "La construction sociale de la déviance et de la criminalité parmi les immigré: Le cas Italien." In *Immigrant Delinquency: Social Sciences*, edited by European Commission. Luxembourg: European Commission, 1996.

Pattullo, Polly. *Last Resorts: The Cost of Tourism in the Caribbean*. Kingston: Ian Randle, 1996.

Pavarini, Massimo. *Control y Dominación*. México: Siglo XXI, 1983.

_____. "The New Penology and Politics in Crisis: The Italian Case." In *Prisons in Context*, edited by R. D. King and M. Maguire. Oxford: Clarendon Press, 1994.

Pearson, Elaine. "Human Traffic, Human Rights: Redefining Victim Protection." Anti-Slavery International, London, 2002.

Peery, Nelson. *Black Fire*. New York: The New Press, 1994.

Peteet, Julie. *Gender in Crisis: Women and the Palestinian Resistance Movement*. New York: Columbia University Press, 1991.

Pettiway, Leon E. "Participation in Crime Partnerships by Female Drug Users," *Criminology* 25, 3 (1987): 746.

Pillay, Karisha. *Battered Women Who Kill: Avenues for Legal/Political Recourse*. Centre for the Study of Violence and Reconciliation, 2002.

Pinto Quintanilla, Juan C. *Cárceles y Familia*. Cochabamba, Bolivia: Terre des Hommes, 1999.

Piven, Frances Fox and Richard A. Cloward. *Regulating the Poor*. New York: Vintage, 1971.

____. Capitalism and the Origins of Domestic Labor. *Review of Radical Political Economics* 24, 2 (1992): 1–7.

Pollock, Shoshana. "Moving Inside: The Role of Lawbreaking in Black Women's Attempt to Gain Economic Independence." Paper presented at American Society of Criminology, November 1999.

Raeder, Myrna. "Gender and Sentencing: Single Mom, Battered Women, and Other Sex-Based Anomalies in the Gender-Free World of the Federal Sentencing Guidelines." *Pepperdine Law Review* 20, 3 (1993).

Rafter, Nicole Hahn. *Partial Justice: Women, Prisons, and Social Control*. New Brunswick, NJ: Transaction Press, 1992.

Rafter, Nicole and Frances Heidensohn (eds). *International Feminist Perspectives in Criminology*. Buckingham: Open University Press, 1995.

Raphael, Jody. *Trapped by Poverty, Trapped by Abuse: New Evidence Documenting the Relationship Between Domestic Violence and Welfare*. Project for Research on Welfare, Work and Domestic Violence, Taylor Institute and the University of Minnesota Research Development Center on Poverty, Risk and Mental Health, 1997.

Reed, Adolph Jr. (ed.) *Without Justice for All*. Boulder, CO: Westview Press, 1999.

Reed, Little Rock. *The American Indian in the White Man's Prisons: A Story of Genocide*. Taos, NM: Uncompromising Books, 1993.

Reiman, Jeffrey. *The Rich Get Richer and the Poor Get Prison*. New York: Wiley, 1979.

Remafedi, Gary, S. French, M. Story, M. Resnick, and R. Blum. "The Relationship Between Suicide Risk and Sexual Orientation: Results of a Population-Based Study." *American Journal of Public Health* 88 (1998): 57–60.

Reuter, Peter. "Foreign Demand for Latin American Drugs: The USA and Europe." In *Latin America and the Multinational Drug Trade*, edited by E. Joyce and C. Malamud. New York: St. Martin's, 1998.

Reyes, Belinda I., Hans P. Johnson, and Richard Van Swearingen. *Holding the Line?: The Effect of the Recent Border Build-Up on Unauthorized Immigration*. San Francisco: Public Policy Institute of California, 2002.

Reyneri, Emilio. "Migrant Insertion in the Formal Economy, Deviant Behaviour and the Impact on Receiving Societies: Some Hypotheses for a Cross-National Research." In *Immigrant Delinquency: Social Sciences*, edited by European Commission. Luxembourg: European Commission, 1996.

Richie, Beth. *Compelled to Crime: The Gender Entrapment of Battered Black Women*. New York: Routledge, 1996.

____. "Coming Up in the Boogie Down: The Role of Violence in the Lives of Adolescents in the South Bronx." *Health Education and Behavior* 26, 6 (1998): 788–805.

Roberts, Dorothy. *Killing the Black Body: Race, Reproduction, and the Meaning of Liberty*. New York: Pantheon Books, 1997.

____. *Shattered Bonds: The Color of Child Welfare*. New York: Basic Books, 2002.

Rodney, Walter. *How Europe Underdeveloped Africa*. London: Bogle l'Ouverture, 1972.

Ross, Luana. *Inventing the Savage: The Social Construction of Native American Criminality*. Austin: University of Texas Press, 1998.

Rossi, Adriana. *Narcotráfico y Amazonia Ecuatoriana*. Buenos Aires, Argentina: Kohen and Asociados International, 1996.

Rouse, Shahnaz. "Sovereignty and Citizenship in Pakistan." In *Appropriating Gender*, edited by P. Jeffery and A. Basu. New York: Routledge, 1998.

Rubin, Gayle. "The Traffic in Women." In *Toward an Anthology of Women*, edited by R. Reiter. New York: Monthly Review Press, 1975.

Ruggiero, Vicenzo, Mick Ryan, and Joe Sim eds. *Western European Penal Systems. A Critical Anatomy*. London: Sage, 1995.

Ruggiero, Vicenzo and Nigel South. "La Ville de la Fin de l'Ère Moderne en Tant que Bazar: Marchés de Stupéfiants, Entreprise Illégale et les 'Barricades'." *Déviance et Société* 20, 4 (1996): 315–333, 195.

Russell, Susan, with the Canadian Federation of University Women. *Take Action for Equality, Development and Peace: A Canadian Follow-Up Guide to Beijing'95*, edited by Linda Souter and Betty Bayless. Ottawa, ON: CRIAW, Canadian Beijing Facilitating Committee, 1996.

Safe Schools Coalition of Washington. *Safe Schools Anti-Violence Documentation Project: Third Annual Report.* 1996.

Sammara, Adel and Rosemary Sayigh. *Profile of an Occupation.* London and New York: Zed Books, 1989.

Sampson, Robert K. and Janet L. Lauritsen. "Racial and Ethnic Disparities in Crime and Criminal Justice in the United States." In *Ethnicity, Crime and Immigration*, edited by M. Tonry. Chicago: University of Chicago Press, 1997.

Sanchez Taylor, Jacqueline. "Tourism and 'Embodied' Commodities: Sex Tourism in the Caribbean." In *Tourism and Sex: Culture, Commerce and Coercion, Tourism, Leisure and Recreation Series*, edited by S. Carter and S. Clift. London: Pinter, 2002.

Sardar Ali, Shaheen. *Gender and Human Rights in Islam and International Law: Equal Before Allah, Unequal Before Man?* The Hague: Kluwer Law International, 2000.

Sassen, Saskia. *The Global City: New York, London, Tokyo.* Princeton: Princeton University Press, 1991.

Sayigh, Rosemary. "Encounters with Palestinian Women under Occupation." In *Occupation: Israel over Palestine*, edited by Naseer Aruri. Belmont, MA: Association of Arab American Press, 1983.

Scalia, John. *Noncitizens in the Federal Criminal Justice System, 1984–94.* Washington, DC: U.S. Department of Justice, Bureau of Justice Statistics, 1996.

Scalia, John and Marika F. X. Litras. "Bureau of Justice Statistics Special Report: Immigration Offenders in the Federal Criminal Justice System, 2000." U.S. Department of Justice, Office of Justice Programs, 2002.

Schechter, S. *Women and Male Violence: The Vision and Struggles of the Battered Women's Movement.* Boston: South End Press,1983.

Schofield, Victoria. *Kashmir in Conflict: India, Pakistan and the Unfinished War.* New York: I. B. Tauris, 2000.

Schrag, Clarence. "Some Foundations for a Theory of Corrections." In *The Prison: Studies in Institutional Organization and Change*, edited by D. Cressey. New York: Holt, 1961.

Scully, Eileen. "Pre-Cold War Traffic in Sexual Labor and Its Foes: Some Contemporary Lessons." Pp. 74–106 in *Global Human Smuggling: Comparative Perspectives*, edited by D. Kyle and R. Koslowski. Baltimore: Johns Hopkins University Press, 2001.

Sélim, Monique. "Une Cohabitation Pluri-Ethnique." In *Urbanisation et Enjeux Quotidiens. Terrains Ethnologiques dans la France Actuelle*, edited by G. Althabe et al. Paris: L'Harmattan, 1993.

The Sentencing Project. *New Inmate Population Figures Demonstrate Need for Policy Reform.* Washington, DC, 2003.

The Sentencing Project and Human Rights Watch. *Losing the Vote: The Impact of Felony Disenfranchisement Laws in the United States.* Washington, DC: The Sentencing Project, 1998.

Shaikh, Anwar. *The Current Economic Crisis: Causes and Implications.* Detroit: Against the Current Pamphlet, 1983 [reprinted 1989].

Sivanandan, A. *A Different Hunger.* London: Pluto Press, 1982.

Sklar, Holly. *Chaos or Community?* Boston: South End Press, 1995.

Skrobanek, Siriporn, Nattaya Boonpakdi, and Chutima Janthakeero. *The Traffic in Women: Human Realities of the International Sex Trade.* London: Zed Press, 1997.

Shaheed, Farida. "Woman, State and Power: The Dynamics of Variation and Convergence Across East and West." In *Engendering the Nation-State: Volume I*, edited by N. Hussain, S. Mumtaz, and R. Saigol. Lahore, Pakistan: Simorgh Women's Resource and Publication Centre, 1997.

Silverman, Jay G., A. Raj, and J. E. Hathaway. "Dating Violence Against Adolescent Girls and Associated Substance Abuse, Unhealthy Weight Control, Sexual Risk Behavior, Pregnancy and Suicidality." *Journal of American Medical Association* 286, 3 (August 1, 2002).

Simon, Jonathon and Malcolm Feeley. "True Crime: The New Penology and Public Discourse on Crime." In *Punishment and Social Control: Essays in Honor of Sheldom Messinger*, edited by T. Blomberg and S. Cohen. New York: Aldine de Gruyter, 1995.

Simmons, Charlene Wear. *Children of Incarcerated Parents.* 7(2) California Research Bureau Note 2 (March 2000).

Sisters Inside. "Substance Abuse in Australian Communities, Submission to the House of Representatives Parliamentary Standing Committee on Family and Community Affairs, Queensland." Queensland: Sisters Inside, 2001.

Smart, Carol. "The New Female Criminal: Reality or Myth?" *British Journal of Criminology* 19, 1 (1979): 50–59.

____. *Feminism and the Power of Law.* London: Routledge, 1989.

Smith, Andrea. "Not an Indian Tradition: The Sexual Colonization of Native Peoples." *Hypatia* 18, 2 (2003): 70–86.

Snyder, Howard N. and Melissa Sickmard. "Juvenile Offenders and Victims: 1999 National Report" Office of Juvenile Justice and Delinquency Prevention 115 (1999).

Southern California Criminal Justice Consortium. *Los Angeles in Lockdown.* Los Angeles: Criminal Justice Consortium, 2001.

Speller, Adrian. *Private Sector Involvement in Prisons.* London: Church House Publishing, 1996.

Stastny, Charles and Gabrielle Tyrnauer. *Who Rules the Joint?* Lexington: Lexington Books, 1982.

Steffensmeier, Darrell and Robert Terry. "Institutional Sexism in the Underworld: A View from the Inside." *Sociological Inquiry* 56 (1986): 304–323.

Stein, Nan. *Bullying and Sexual Harassment in Elementary Schools: It's Not Just Kids Kissing Kids.* Wellesley, MA: Wellesley College, Center for Research on Women, 1997.

Stephen, Lynn. "Democracy for Whom? Women's Grassroots Political Activism in the 1990s, Mexico City and Chiapas." In *Neoliberalism Revisited: Economic Restructuring and Mexico's Political Future,* edited by G. Otero. Boulder, CO: Westview Press, 1996.

Stern, Vivian. *A Sin Against the Future: Imprisonment in the World.* Boston: Northeastern University Press, 1998.

Sudbury, Julia. *Other Kinds of Dreams: Black Women's Organizations and the Politics of Transformation.* London: Routledge, 1998.

____. "Celling Black Bodies: Black Women in the Global Prison Industrial Complex." *Feminist Review* 70 (2002).

____. "Women of Color, Globalization and the Politics of Incarceration." In *The Criminal Justice System and Women,* edited by B. R. Price and N. Sokoloff. New York: McGraw Hill, 2003.

Sumar, Sabiha and Khalida Nadhvi. "Zina: The Hadood Ordinance and Its Implications for Women (Pakistan). *Women Living Under Muslim Laws Dossier #3.* International Solidarity Network, 34980 Combaillaux, Montpellier, 1987.

Thornton, A. "The Courtship Process and Adolescent Sexuality." *Journal of Family Issues* 11, 3 (1990):239–273.

Tjaden, Patricia and Nancy Thoennes. *National Violence Against Women Survey.* National Institute of Justice and The Centers for Disease Control and Prevention, November 1988.

Tonry, Michael. *Malign Neglect: Race, Crime and Punishment in America.* New York: Oxford University Press, 1995.

____. *Sentencing Matters.* New York: Oxford University, 1996.

Toor, Sadia. "The State, Fundamentalism and Civil Society." In *Engendering the Nation-State: Volume I,* edited by N. Hussain, S. Mumtaz, and R. Saigol. Lahore, Pakistan: Simorgh Women's Resource and Publication Centre, 1997.

Torres, Anália and Maria do Carmo Gomes. *Drogas e Prisões em Portugal.* Lisbon: CIES/ISCTE, 2002: 34–36.

Totten, Mark. *The Special Needs of Females in Canada's Youth Justice System: An Account of Some Young Women's Experiences and Views.* Ottawa: Department of Justice, 2000.

Transactional Records Access Clearinghouse. *National Profile and Enforcement Trends over Time* [online database]. Syracuse, NY: Syracuse University, 2002. Available online: http://trac.syr.edu/tracins/findings/national/index.html.

Traugott, Mark (ed). *Repertoires and Cycles of Collective Action.* Durham, NC: Duke, 1995.

Trepanier, Monique. "Trafficking in Women for Purposes of Sexual Exploitation: A Matter of Consent?" *Canadian Woman Studies* 22, 3–4 (2003): 48–54.

Truong, Thanh Dam. *Sex, Money and Morality: The Political Economy of Prostitution and Tourism in South East Asia.* London: Zed Books, 1990.

UN, Committee on Economic, Social and Cultural Rights. *Concluding Observations on Nepal.* Geneva: UN, 2001. UN Doc. E/C. 12/1/Add.66.

UN, Committee on the Elimination of Discrimination Against Women. *Concluding Observations on Nepal.* New York: UN, 1999. UN Doc. CEDAW/A/54/38.

UN Department of Public Information. *Body of Principles for the Protection of All Persons Under Any Form of Detention or Imprisonment.* New York: UN, 1989.

____. *UN Convention Against the Illicit Traffic of Narcotics.* New York: UN 1991.

____. *Platform for Action and Beijing Declaration: Fourth World Conference on Women, Beijing, China, 4–15 September 1995.* New York: UN, 1995.

UN, Human Rights Committee. *Concluding Observations on Nepal.* Geneva: UN, 1994. UN Doc. CCPR/C/79/Add.42.

U.S. Census Bureau, Department of Commerce. *The Hispanic Population.* Washington, DC: Department of Commerce, May 2001.

U.S. Congress, House Committee on Armed Services. *The Andean Drug Strategy and the Role of the U.S. Military,* 101st Congress, 1st Session. Washington, DC, January 1990.

U.S. Department of Justice. *FY 2002 Budget Summary.* Washington, DC: U.S. Department of Justice, 2001.

U.S. Department of Justice. *Sourcebook of Criminal Justice Statistics.* Washington, DC: Bureau of Justice Statistics, 2001.

____. *Budget Trend Data from 1975 Through the President's 2003 Request to the Congress.* Washington, DC: Justice Management Division, 2002. Available online: http://www.usdoj.gov/jmd/budgetsummary/btd/1975_2002/2002/pdf/BudgetTrend.pdf.

____. Federal Bureau of Investigations. *Uniform Crime Reports: Crime in the U.S.* Washington, DC, 1961–2002.

____. *Sourcebook of Criminal Justice Statistics 2001.* Washington, DC: Bureau of Justice Statistics, 2002.

U.S. General Accounting Office. *Immigration and Naturalization Service: Overview of Recurring Management Challenges.* Washington, DC: Government Printing Office, October 2001.

——. *Southwest Border Strategy: Resource and Impact Issues Remain after Seven Years. Report to the Congress.* Washington, DC: Government Printing Office, August 2001.

U.S Government Accounting Office. *Illegal Aliens: Significant Obstacles to Reducing Unauthorized Alien Employment Exist. Report to the Congress.* Washington, DC: Government Printing Office, 1999.

U.S. House of Representatives, Committee on the Judiciary. *Police Misconduct,* Hearings Before the Subcommittee on Criminal Justice, Serial No. 50, parts 1 and 2. 98th Congress, 1st Session. Washington, 1984.

U.S. Office of Immigration Statistics, Department of Homeland Security. *2002 Yearbook of Immigration Statistics.* Washington, DC: Department of Justice. Available online: http://uscis.gov/graphics/shared/aboutus/statistics/ENF2002list.htm.

U.S. Office of Management and Budget. *Budget of the United States Government, Fiscal Year 2004.* Washington, DC: Government Printing Office, 2003.

U.S. Refugee Committee. "Country Report: Italy" 2001. http://www.refugees.org/world/countryrypt/europe/italy.html.

U.S. Sentencing Commission. *Special Report to the Congress: Mandatory Minimum Penalties in the Federal Criminal Justice System.* Washington, DC, 1991.

van de Veen, Marjolein. "Rethinking Commodification and Prostitution: An Effort at Peacemaking in the Battles over Prostitution." *Rethinking Marxism* 13 (2001): 30–51.

Vermont Department of Health. *Youth Statistics: The 2003 Vermont Department of Health/ Education Youth Risk Behavior Survey.* http://www.outrightvt.org/resources/stats.html

Vetten, Lisa. "Paper Promises, Protests and Petitions: South African State and Civil Society Responses to Violence Against Women." In *Reclaiming Women's Spaces: New Perspectives on Violence Against Women and Sheltering in South Africa,* edited by Y. Park, J. Fedler, and Z. Dangor. Johannesburg: Nisaa Institute for Women's Development, 2000.

Vetten, Lisa and Zohra Khan. *"We're Doing Their Work for Them": An Investigation Into Government Support to Non-profit Organisations Providing Services to Women Experiencing Gender Violence.* Johannesburg: Centre for the Study of Violence and Reconciliation, 2003.

Vetten, Lisa and Collet Ngwane. *"I Love You to Destruction": An Analysis of Convictions and Sentences in Cases of Spousal Homicide.* Johannesburg: Centre for the Study of Violence and Reconciliation, forthcoming.

Wacquant, Loïc. *Les Prisons de la Misère.* Paris: Raisons d'Agir Editions, 1990.

_____. "The Comparative Structure and Experience of Urban Exclusion: Race, Class and Space in Paris and Chicago." In *Poverty, Inequality, and the Future of Social Policy: Western States in the New World Order,* edited by K. McFate, W. J. Wilson, and R. Lawson (eds.). New York: Russell Sage Foundation, 1995.

_____. "'Suitable Enemies': Foreigners and Immigrants in the Prisons of Europe." *Punishment and Society, The International Journal of Penology* 1, 2 (1999): 215–222.

_____. "Deadly Symbiosis: When Ghetto and Prison Meet and Merge." *Punishment & Society* 3, 1 (2001): 95–134.

_____. "Deadly Symbiosis." *Boston Review* 27, 2 (2002): 23–31.

Waldner-Haugrud, Lisa and Linda Vaden Gratch. "Sexual Coercion in Gay/Lesbian Relationships: Descriptives and Gender Differences." *Violence and Victims* 12, 1 (1997).

Walker, Samuel, Cassia Spohn, and Miriam DeLone. *The Color of Justice: Race, Ethnicity, and Crime in America.* Belmont, CA: Wadsworth, 2000.

Walkowitz, Judith R. *Prostitution and Victorian Society: Women, Class and the State.* Cambridge: Cambridge University Press, 1980.

Walmsley, Roy. *World Prison Population List.* London: Research, Development and Statistics Director, 2003.

Warner, Kate. *Walkin' the Talk: A History of Sisters Inside.* Queensland: Sisters Inside, 2001.

Watterson, Katherine. *Women in Prison.* Boston: Northeastern University, 1996.

Welch, Michael. "The Role of the Immigration and Naturalization Service in the Prison-Industrial Complex." *Social Justice* 27, 3 (2000).

Wertheimer, Richard, T. Croan, and J. Jager. "Qualitative Estimates of Vulnerable Youth in Transition to Adulthood: Final Report Submitted to the Annie E. Casey Foundation." *Child Trends.* Washington, DC, February 2002.

White, Deborah Gray. *Ar'n't I a Woman? Female Slaves in the Plantation South.* New York: Norton, 1985.

White, Luise. *The Comforts of Home: Prostitution in Colonial Nairobi.* Chicago: University of Chicago Press, 1990.

Wial, Howard. "The Emerging Organizational Structure of Unionism in Low-Wage Services." *Rutgers Law Review* 45 (1993): 671–738.

Wijers, Marjan and Lin Lap-Chew. *Trafficking in Women, Forced Labor and Slavery-like Practices in Marriage, Domestic Labor and Prostitution.* Utrecht: STV, 1997.

Willis, Paul. *Learning to Labor: How Working Class Kids Get Working Class Jobs.* New York: Columbia, 1977.

Wilsey, Mary. "Doing Time Behind Foreign Bars." *Wanted in Rome* 12, 15 (1996): 3–5.

Wilson, James Q. and Richard Herrnstein. *Crime and Human Nature.* New York: Simon and Schuster, 1985.

Wilson, Nancy, "Stealing and Dealing: The Drug War and Gendered Criminal Opportunity." In *Female Criminality: The State of the Art,* edited by C. Culliver. New York: Garland Publishing, 1993.

Wolch, Jennifer. *The Shadow State: Government and Voluntary Sector in Transition.* New York: The Foundation Center, 1989.

Women's Prison Association and Home, Inc. *Family to Family: Partnerships between Corrections and Child Welfare.* New York: Women's Prison Association and Home, 1998.

Woods, Clyde. *Development Arrested.* New York: Verso, 1996.

Young, Elise. *Keepers of the History: Women and the Israeli-Palestinian Conflict.* New York: Teachers College Press, 1992.

Young, Jock. *The Exclusive Society. Social Exclusion, Crime and Difference in Late Modernity.* London: Sage, 1999.

Zaffaroni, Raúl. "La Mujer y el Poder Punitivo." In *Sobre Patriarcas, Jerarcas, Patrones y Otros Varones,* edited by Alda Facio and Rosal a Camacho (eds.). Costa Rica: Llanud, 1993.

Index